In this book, Phyllis Martin, a well-known Africanist scholar, opens up a whole new field of African research: the leisure activities of urban Africans. Her comprehensive study, set in colonial Brazzaville and based on a wide variety of written sources and interviews, investigates recreational activities from football and fashion to music, dance and night-life. In it, she brings out the way in which these activities built social networks, humanized daily life and forged new identities, and explains how they ultimately helped to remake older traditions and values with new cultural forms.

Leisure and society in colonial Brazzaville

African studies series 87

Editorial board

Published in collaboration with
THE AFRICAN STUDIES CENTRE, CAMBRIDGE

A list of books in this series will be found at the end of the volume.

Leisure and society in colonial Brazzaville

Phyllis M. Martin

Indiana University

CAMBRIDGE
UNIVERSITY PRESS

Published by the Press Syndicate of the University of Cambridge
The Pitt Building, Trumpington Street, Cambridge CB2 1RP
40 West 20th Street, New York, NY 10011-4211, USA
10 Stamford Road, Oakleigh, Melbourne 3166, Australia

First published 1995

Printed in Great Britain at the University Press, Cambridge

A catalogue record for this book is available from the British Library

Library of Congress cataloguing in publication data
Martin, Phyllis.
Leisure and society in colonial Brazzaville / Phyllis M. Martin.
       p.   cm. – (African studies series)
Includes bibliographical references (p.).
ISBN 0 521 49551 2
1. Leisure – Congo (Brazzaville) – History.
2. Congo (Brazzaville) – Social life and customs.
I. Title.   II. Series.
GV143.C66M37   1995
790′.01′35′096724–dc20   94–48636   CIP

ISBN 0 521 495512 hardback

CE

For Jennifer and Philip

Contents

Plates

Maps

Tables

Acknowledgements

It is sometimes only in retrospect that one can distinguish the influences and events that shape one's life. Raised in a secure family environment by supportive parents, who both passed away recently at a good old age, I always assumed that my mother was the dominant presence in my early years, for her guidance and encouragement supported many of my youthful endeavours. But as colleagues and friends asked the question 'how did you become interested in writing about leisure?', I realized that my father had a great deal to do with it. As a girl, I did not think it odd that, in answer to my pleas, he took me along to matches between Hearts of Midlothian and Hibernians, the two Edinburgh professional football teams. The volatile and largely male crowds made such occasions a quite different cultural event from the traditional American family outing 'to the ballpark'. Although a modest man, my father would occasionally reminisce about his glorious career as a goalkeeper on a small-town YMCA team at a time when the 'Y' was very much a Christian youth organization and every player had to be a 'tea-totaller'. There are other childhood memories such as the music hall ditties, which my parents might break into as we were driving along in the car; the cinema club I attended; and the museums, historic monuments and parks of the Scottish capital. Such early experiences surely had something to do with my readings on leisure. I should also acknowledge the example of my older brother and sister who pioneered a trail that diverged from our somewhat parochial roots. They introduced me to jazz, foxtrots and bossanova long before I came across Highlife in Accra and 'Congo music' in Brazzaville.

Much more recently, a reading of Hugh Cunningham's *Leisure in the Industrial Revolution* excited my intellectual curiosity and made me wonder whether a similar study might be possible and pertinent in an African city. In the early 1980s, when this project was little more than a glimmer in the eye, the exciting new history of southern Africa was beginning to enlarge the boundaries of social and cultural history continent-wide. I was encouraged to pursue this research although the small colonial capital of French Equatorial Africa seemed a far cry from the industrial towns of South Africa. Early feedback came from members of the African history seminar at the School of Oriental and African Studies where I presented a paper entitled 'Towards a history of leisure in Brazzaville'. The response was most encouraging, although the problems of applying the concept in an Africa context were raised. I later heard that one seminar member, while cutting the grass on a following Saturday afternoon, had stopped to wonder: 'Is this work or leisure?' -a question to which I will return.

I would like to acknowledge the help I received from organizations and individuals whose support allowed me to complete this project. For funding, I acknowledge with gratitude fellowships I received from the National Endowment for the Humanities, the American Philosophical Society and Indiana University.

Numerous individuals helped me to conceptualize this work and suggested sources. I thank them collectively. Sometimes conversations in a library cafeteria, a conference hotel lobby or the hallways of a university provide timely insights. For taking on the task of reading all or part of the manuscript and giving me valuable comments, I would like to thank George Brooks, Bill Cohen, Paula Girschick, Chris Gray, John Hanson, Joe Miller, Helen Nader, Andrew Roberts and the readers of Cambridge University Press. Special mention must also be made of Roger Frey for his help with maps and photographs as well as his interest in my work.

Without friends on three continents who gave me hospitality and personal support, the research would have been more arduous and less fun. I owe special thanks to Elizabeth and David Birmingham, Claire Blanche-Benveniste, Jean-Michel Delobeau, Ursula Den Tex, Jane Droutman, Tamara Goeglein, Janet and Peter Hammond, Miep Lieftinck, Sidone and Jean-Pierre Ngole, Dennis, Don and Elinor Simmons, the Sisters of Saint Joseph of Cluny, Karin and Bertil Söderberg, Bengt Sundkler, and Alice Ngole Walimeya.

The book could not have been completed without the encouragement of my Bloomington friends. I acknowledge their help collectively, but especially that of Joan Bird and Patrick O'Meara, who have shown many times that there are no friends like old friends.

Most of all, many thanks to my very dear friends, Jenny and Philip, who have shared in my work and leisure and, in so doing, have taught me a great deal over the years.

Abbreviations

AA	*Annales Apostoliques*
AEF	Afrique Equatoriale Française (French Equatorial Africa)
AEH	*African Economic History*
AGPSE	Archives Générales des Pères du Saint-Esprit, Chevilly
AHR	*American Historical Review*
ANB	Archives Nationales du Congo, Brazzaville
AOM	Archives Nationales, Centre des Archives d'Outre-Mer, Aix-en-Provence
APSE	*Annales des Pères du Saint-Esprit*
ASA	Archives of the Salvation Army, London
ASMF	Arkivet, Svenska Missionsförbundet, Riksarkivet, Stockholm
ASOM	Archives de l'Académie des Sciences d'Outre-Mer, Paris
ASSJC	*Annales des Soeurs de Saint-Joseph de Cluny*
BCAF	*Bulletin de la Comité de l'Afrique Française*
BCPSE	*Bulletin Général de la Congregation des Pères du Saint-Esprit*
BCSSJC	*Bulletin de la Congregation des Soeurs de Saint-Joseph de Cluny*
BDAEF	*Bulletin de Documentation d'AEF*
BICA	*Bulletin d'Institut d'Etudes Centrafricaines*
BRSC	*Bulletin de la Société des Recherches Congolaises*
CAB	Club Athlètique Brazzavillois
CCAH	*Cahiers Congolais d'Anthropologie et d'Histoire*
CEA	*Cahiers d'Etudes Africaines*
CFCO	Chemin de Fer Congo-Océan
EHESS	Ecole des Hautes Etudes en Sciences Sociales, Paris
FAC	Fédération Athlètique Congolaise
IECA	Institut d'Etudes Centrafricaines, Brazzaville
JAH	*Journal of African History*
JO	*Journal Officiel*, AEF
MC	*Les Missions Catholiques*
MF	*Missionsförbundet*
MCI	*Le Monde Colonial Illustré*

ORSTOM Office de la Recherche Scientifique et Technique Outre-Mer, Paris

SDAM   Service de la Documentation et des Archives Municipales, Brazzaville

SMF   Svenska Missionsförbundet

Introduction

In 1936, a controversy erupted over Brazzaville football. The subject of debate was whether players should wear shoes in matches or play barefooted. The European administrators of the Native Sports Federation decreed that wearing shoes encouraged violence on the field, that Africans were unsportsmanlike, and that they must, therefore, play barefooted. Some team captains, who were also part of the urban elite and wore shoes on a daily basis, were so outraged that they wrote to the Governor-General of French Equatorial Africa (AEF) asking him to reverse the ruling, which, on the advice of sports administrators, he did not. This shoes controversy brought to a head the already contentious relationship of European sports organizers with players in Bacongo and Poto-Poto, Brazzaville's two African districts. When the team leaders organized a boycott, the official football league collapsed. The Catholic mission, old adversaries of the administration for the hearts and minds of African youth, quietly built up their teams from disaffected players. Some older players simply retired from league play but continued to participate in informal matches in their spare time, as they had done since they were youngsters in the city streets. Young players and those too poor to own shoes had little interest in the conflict and went on playing barefooted, as they had always done.[1]

This incident, preserved in a file in the Congolese National Archives under the rubric of 'Petitions to the Governor-General',[2] captures the essence of this book which reconstructs the daily-life history of an African colonial town through exploring how the inhabitants created, contested and occupied their leisure time. The mediation of social relations through cultural symbols, forms and events has been a powerful theme in recent studies of life under colonial rule. Simple dichotomies of tradition and modernity, domination and resistance have faded away, as scholars have rather sought to understand colonialism as an arena of negotiation in which all kinds of political, cultural and social transformations were worked out. In the changing and sometimes volatile conditions of new colonial towns, where social relations and cultural forms were characterized by a greater degree of choice and experimentation than was possible in the more deeply rooted patterns of village life, the 'debate' was particularly intense.[3] The stakes, which had a great deal to do with control, security and identity, were also high. Beyond that, however, choice was to do with 'communities of taste', which from an individual perspective did not always coincide with the preferences of others in a social group, such as generation, ethnicity, class or gender.[4] Leisure activities and interests might include sport, fashion, music and dance, sociability in particular bars and cafes, and association membership. These topics are at the heart of this book whose overall theme is summed up in what Frederick Cooper has called 'the struggle for the city', which he describes as 'cultural as much as political, and it goes on every day, as well as bursting forth when basic structures are at issue'.[5]

The city in question is Brazzaville, once the capital of AEF and now the capital of the Republic of Congo. Situated on the north banks of Malebo Pool where the Congo river forms a great lake before it hurtles through its rapids to the ocean, the modern town officially dates its establishment to 1880 when the Tio ruler, Iloo, ceded the site to the French representative, Savorgnan de Brazza.[6] Sprawling for some 15 kilometres along the Congo river, the modern city's population is well over half a million. In many respects, it typifies the overblown capitals of developing countries, as inhabitable living space is ever more crowded, people swarm daily around the law courts contesting property claims and the tentacles of the city continue to absorb the countryside, spreading out beyond the Djoué river to the west and along the foothills of the Tio plateau to the east. Today, Congo is one of the most highly urbanized countries in Africa and about a third of the population lives in Brazzaville. A recent special issue of the journal *Politique Africaine*, devoted to Congo, took as its title 'Congo, a suburb of Brazzaville', a theme explored in articles dealing with the capital's economic, social and cultural attractions.[7] While this rapid urbanization dates only from the Second World War, a small but influential nucleus of townsfolk have lived in Brazzaville since the early twentieth century, and it was they who were often pioneers in developing the new activities and tastes that went with being 'people of the city'.[8]

In modern-day Brazzaville, Sunday is the big day for leisure, as it was in the colonial period. Taking a taxi to visit friends on the other side of the city, the passenger finds the driver delighted to talk about the latest bands and pop singers whose music blasts forth from the speaker at the back of his cab. Friends meet at popular cafes and bars to eat local food such as fish, brochettes, manioc leaves, rice, baguettes and manioc bread;

drink local varieties of Kronenberg beer or soft drinks; and dance to the music of home-grown stars such as Youlou Mabiala and his 'Kamikaze' band, or the ever-popular Zairois maestros such as Franco. Others follow the crowd moving towards the *Stade de la Révolution* where the top Bacongo team *Diables Noirs* ('Black Devils') plays the Poto-Poto champions, *L'Etoile du Congo* ('Star of Congo'). Boys around the market and on the platform of the railway station hawk sports and film magazines from France and Zaire. In the streets and on open patches of ground, youths are playing *mwanafoot* (Lingala, 'children's football'), women gather in recreational dance associations which are also mutual-aid societies, men play dominoes and cards, and people stroll about in their 'Sunday clothes'. As darkness falls on Saturday and Sunday evenings, the life of the town throbs on, especially in Poto-Poto, where an animated street-life continues long after people have gone to bed in the quieter suburb of Bacongo.

Time, work and leisure

This book explores two aspects of leisure in the colonial town. One was the struggle to create a new order of time and space, which grew out of European attempts to impose colonialist and capitalist structures and African efforts to create a congenial environment to suit their needs beyond the harassment of colonial control. While urban boundaries of time and space were often initiated through laws and limits imposed by town administrators, employers and missionaries, they were also initiated and adjusted by African responses, which might be confrontational or non-confrontational, depending on the advantages. Since neither the African nor European population was monolithic, a variety of positions might be adopted. Thus, leisure time and place were arenas of contest and mediation within European and African sub-communities as well as between them.

Evans-Pritchard, in his work on the Nuer, pioneered the study of African rural time as a social construction embedded in the activities of daily life. Time, he found, was task oriented. The 'daily time-piece is the cattle-clock' and, 'the round of pastoral tasks' marked the passage of the day. Economic and social activities caused people to 'pay attention to the movements of the heavenly bodies and to the ecological variations that they cause', but there was no abstract measurement of time.[9] Studies of rural time in Central Africa have come to similar conclusions. Villagers have a well-structured sense of time that is honed to their economic, religious and social life, and time is valued according to tasks and activities, so that work to produce goods or services, socially significant time, and recreational time are all valued differently.[10] There is a clear sense of different activities being associated with time, for example, 'time for amusement', as opposed to the more significant 'time for work', 'time for weighty conversation', or 'time for mourning'.[11] But time is constructed around the event rather than the contrary, as in industrialized societies. Village or task-oriented time is, therefore, 'elastic' and based on the activity. Abraham Ndinga-Mbo, the Congolese historian, has suggested that whereas European time 'enslaves', villagers rather think of 'creating' time.[12] A seminar at the University of Marien Ngouabi came to the similar conclusion that, 'among rural people, time does not carry the weight and importance that we attribute to it in our modern way of life. Time floats in its imprecision and inexactitude. It is made in the image of the society which conceived it.'[13]

The transformation of European time, its measurement, and the emergence of concepts of work and leisure is a story that is well documented and is broadly paralleled in twentieth-century Congo, as the forces of capitalism, colonialism and Christianity expanded their spheres of influence. Jacques Le Goff associated the regulation and segmentation of time with the needs of the medieval church and early forms of capitalism. Bells and clocks were 'instruments of economic, social and political domination', wielded by merchants who ran a commune and for whom 'time cost money'. A 'new harshness' crept into the measurement of the working day for both employers and workers.[14] Schedules and calendars became tools of temporal regularity, replacing the seasons and natural control with social control.[15] However, workers also benefited from these temporal developments, for clocks introduced a precision of measurement which could be used to their benefit.[16] In nineteenth-century industrializing societies, too, the exactness of telling time became not only a means for employers to enforce work-discipline, but a focal point for workers struggling to improve their conditions of employment.[17] It was in this context that divisions of work time and leisure time sharpened, with certain days such as Sunday and weekends taking on their distinguishing characteristic as holidays, or time without work.[18] Rybczynski, in his book *Waiting for the weekend* makes the claim that 'there has never been a human society that did not recognize the need for regular days off'.[19] However, articulating different notions of time that have evolved in different societies is a tricky business. Indeed, they can be the basis for conflict, as Keletso Atkins has shown in her work on Zulu workers in South Africa, where rural perceptions of a month based on a lunar calendar collided with European employers' efforts to impose work duration and pay based on the variable month of the Gregorian calendar.[20] In Brazzaville, pre-existing notions of the week and the demands of Ramadan also entered into negotiations over schedules and work-discipline.[21]

The towns and mining complexes of colonial Africa were the principal arena for imposing, contesting and negotiating a new consciousness of time. As Le Goff noted for medieval Europe, time was a 'net in which urban life was caught'.[22] In towns, a combination of pressures, not only workrelated, but also urban regulations, the scheduling of events both religious and secular, and peer pressures, contributed to a temporal awareness that carried more weight than in the countryside. Even those without clocks and watches developed 'a consciousness of time, learned and shared among the population, that is different from non-urban settlements'.[23] In Brazzaville, as people engaged in town life, they accommodated temporal schedules which were among the 'anchors of normalcy' in town life.[24] This was part of the very process of being a townsperson. Even those who came and went from rural areas and were less identified with town life or with wage-labour might choose to adopt schedules that, for example, involved Sunday as a holiday, since most people relaxed then and recreational activities were organized on that day.

However, the process of taking over new concepts of urban time was long, uneven and incomplete, especially in a town such as Brazzaville where, for the first fifty years of its history, the nucleus of permanent townsfolk was small in comparison to temporary migrant workers. It is not the intention to suggest here that a new temporal consciousness happened all at once, in a linear manner, or attached to some process of 'modernization'. On the contrary, it is rather suggested, as Halbwachs pointed out in his work on collective memory, that several notions of time coexist in any society. While dominant institutions such as the town hall or the church may contribute disproportionately to the emergence of an urban sense of time, the overall experience of time is built up from social relations between institutions and individuals.[25] Le Goff found that in the Renaissance period, people lived with an 'uncertain' and 'un-unified' time in which national, regional and rural time varied, while Thompson noted that in pre-industrial towns, where many worked outside the orbit of wage-labour, task-oriented time coexisted with 'harsher' schedules.[26] In spite of the pressures of the urban situation, Atkins found that Zulu workers in nineteenth-century South African towns 'did not completely discard their temporal identity'. This she attributes to their position as migrant labourers and the deep-rooted nature of their traditional understanding of time. Attitudes also varied from period to period and from one group to another.[27]

Although leisure is primarily a concept of time, it also involves use of space. Cooper, writing about British attempts to colonize time in Kenya through inducing Mombasa dockers to adapt their work to capitalist rhythms, describes efforts to control workers through a 'narrowing of the spatial arena', separating those in the 'capitalist domain' from the undisciplined work culture outside.[28] In the highly contested ground of South African towns and work areas, issues of legal and illegal space, of segregation and squatters, were at the heart of the political struggle, as people engaged in 'holding their ground'.[29] In Brazzaville, there was no shortage of space, at least before the last decade of colonial rule. Indeed, there is barely a description before 1940 that does not refer to the sprawling nature of the settlement and the problems of cross-town communications. However, Europeans had an agenda that was related more to where and how people lived than to the amount of space at their disposal. Through urban planning and through what they called the 'beautification' of the areas where they worked and played, Europeans used space to protect their interests, not least of which was segregated leisure, where physical space was an instrument of social and psychological distancing.[30] The planned division of the town into two African districts and a European centre, which had been carried out by the eve of the First World War, not only aided a divide-and-rule strategy but had an important impact on the creation of urban identity.

Thus, although the small and struggling French colonial settlement at Brazzaville, undercapitalized and near the bottom of French colonial priorities until the Second World War, may seem very different from the emerging industrial complexes of the Central African copperbelt or South Africa, many of the same issues were played out, albeit on a smaller scale. The records of Europeans who tried to run the town and the memories of Africans who lived in the colonial period suggest that the struggle was none the less intense in daily life experience.

Leisure, though an abstract concept, is about concrete activities, and these take up a large part of this book. While Africans came to terms with townlife by creatively integrating new and old activities, Europeans also engaged in constructing their vision of a colonial society. As Eugen Weber has succinctly put it, it was not enough to be free from work, the question was 'free for what?'.[31] The dominant colonial class had a clear agenda derived from their dealings with subordinate groups in contemporary Europe, whether youth, women or the underclasses; from the need to impose colonial and capitalist order; and from prevailing generalized perceptions of indigenous societies and the European *mission civilatrice*. In many ways, colonialism was an effort to enforce 'a cultural project of control'[32] which sought to reach out beyond wage-earners to those whom administrators were fond of calling the 'floating' population, who might contaminate the 'stable' elements in the town. Yet on a more specific level, the nature and depth of that control depended very much on popular initiatives, on the role of local elites as auxiliaries and on the instruments of domination available to colonial rulers. Even individual relations might influence the shape that a particular 'project' might take, whether it got off the ground or became a source of dissension and opposition. As the 'shoes controversy' and other incidents in the history of African football show, an activity that might at one moment seem a triumph of cultural hegemony could become a vehicle for resistance. Thus football, fashion and pop bands had different meanings for different individuals and groups within the town's population. Even participation varied. While some workers, like their counterparts in early twentieth-century Europe, might be too 'drained, numb, sluggish and stupefied' by long hours of work to 'play', and were more likely to be 'besotted by drink',[33] others grasped opportunities to incorporate familiar and imported institutions into their urban environment and create autonomous spheres of cultural activity.[34] As Terence Ranger noted: 'Colonialism *can* be seen as a single system', but it was also 'a giddy variety of existentialist experience'.[35]

The meaning of leisure has been inferred in the above discussion, and it is certainly easier to talk about through describing concrete activities than to define it, because that is the way it is experienced in daily life. As an abstract issue, leisure is most powerful in the minds of those who seek to impose certain activities or to structure time and space. The ambiguity of the term must be admitted, for it is open to personal interpretations even within a single culture. However, this does not preclude serious study of an important aspect of human experience. Rather, we need to understand its meaning and significance at different points in time and space. As Anthony Giddens notes, the study of leisure has 'suffered' because it has been perceived as a relatively minor sector of social life compared to other activities which are viewed as more crucial in social behaviour, and because of the ambiguity of the term 'leisure' as opposed to play.[36] Huizinga, in his famous study of *Homo ludens*, noted the universality of play and claimed to have found a word for play in every language.[37] And certainly, such a word exists in all the major languages spoken in Brazzaville. However, as Giddens points out, leisure is more than play, for it is juxtaposed with work and it can involve both non-obligated activities, what in Central African terms would be 'time for amusement' or non-productive time,[38] and activities that involve fulfilling social obligations, such as membership of an association or visiting relatives. The activities discussed in this study are those that informants mentioned when they were asked what they did in 'time for amusements'.

Where informants knew French, the word *loisirs* was used and understood. The answers included playing or watching sport, performing in dance groups, dressing well and going to bars, meeting in recreational clubs or gathering informally with friends and family. In the context of the colonial town such activities were full of significance for, as we said at the outset, they were to do with choice, control, identity and security as people mediated and contested social relations.

Writing Congo's colonial history

The colonial experience through much of AEF (Moyen-Congo, Gabon, Ubangi-Shari and Chad) is chiefly a tale of neglect, exploitation and brutality, especially in the early days of colonialism.[39] Compared to France's other colonies, from Indochina to the Antilles and Algeria to Madagascar, Central Africa ranked at the bottom of French colonial priorities. Once the area was conquered and kept out of the hands of European rivals, it was handed over to concessionary companies who operated an 'economy of pillage' for some thirty years.[40] The situation improved somewhat after the First World War, when the publication of such exposés as Gide's *Voyage au Congo* (1927) and Maran's *Batouala* (1921) fuelled the fire of reform. Metropolitan subsidies and a measure of economic investment, cut short by the Depression, made possible the construction of the Congo-Océan railway (1921–34), which was begun twenty-three years after the Belgians had completed a comparable rail link between Léopoldville and the port of Matadi. Opposition in France also brought an end to concessionary-company rule by 1930. It was only during the Second World War, however, when General de Gaulle fortuitously claimed Brazzaville as the capital of Free France, that the capital and the colony emerged into the limelight of French colonial policy. After the war, Congo was the recipient of French investment and the capital experienced a short economic boom which was the catalyst for a large increase in the urban population.[41]

Once Congolese historiography had emerged from its colonial phase, much given to glorifying the activities of 'great men' such as Brazza, Marchand and Eboué, scholars focused attention on the early French presence and the experience of concessionary-company rule. The late Henri Brunschwig pioneered the publication of edited collections of documents on the conquest period.[42] The tragic period of concessionary-company rule was researched by Catherine Coquery-Vidrovitch, and her huge study remains the definitive account.[43] In the 1970s and early 1980s, structuralist studies using core-periphery and modes of production analyses documented Congo's position in the world economy and the roots of dependency.[44] Other studies which have investigated the African penal code (the *indigénat*), the colonial health service, the spread of sleeping sickness, forced labour, taxation demands and the construction of the Congo-Océan railway have shown the extent of colonial abuses and African initiatives.[45]

Until recently, the study of town life in Equatorial Africa had largely been left to sociologists, urban geographers and development specialists. The seminal work of Georges Balandier and other scholars from ORSTOM (Paris) and its Brazzaville counterpart, the Institut d'Etudes Centrafricaines, during the last decade or so of colonial rule laid the groundwork for other studies since independence.[46] More recently, urbanization has been the focus of a 'team' of researchers at the University of Paris and several volumes, including contributions relating to Congo, have been published in a L'Harmattan series.[47] In recent years, scholars in Congo have also turned their attention to social history and popular culture, although most work has been focused on the period since 1960, and too little has been published, given the logistical problems African scholars have getting their work into print.[48]

This history of Brazzaville, therefore, is set in the context of a colony whose story of neglect and abuse goes far beyond the clichéed euphemism of 'Cinderella' which often appears in cursory references to Congo in anglophone textbooks. At times Brazzaville was a haven from persecution and harassment in rural areas, but it was also a dangerous place for those whose understanding of the world was based on village society. Furthermore, those who sought refuge or work in the town often found themselves the victims of inadequate food supplies and unemployment. As for European colonial administrators, a chronic lack of funding found them struggling to make do and many were eternally engaged in conversations about where their next posting might be and how soon they could leave.

A note on this book

The book consists of seven chapters and a conclusion. The first two chapters discuss the economic, demographic and spatial development of the town which was the essential background for the development of leisure time and space. Particular reference is made to the foreign elites who were the indispensable auxiliaries of colonial rule and the purveyors of new ideas on urban culture, especially in the town's early history. The segregation of space grew out of interactions between Brazzaville's European and African populations, each struggling to protect perceived interests. The shaping of space contributed to the social distancing of people, not only Africans and Europeans, but also the populations of Poto-Poto and Bacongo which in turn contributed to the making of urban communities and identities. The third chapter, entitled 'The emergence of leisure', takes up the question of time and suggests how people may have gradually been caught in a 'net' of urban time. The policies followed by the dominant institutions to mould and discipline the leisure time of the population are discussed, as well as elite and popular responses.

Four chapters disaggregate the idea of leisure and look at specific activities. Each chapter tries to ascertain how townspeople drew on village life for inspiration, as they also appropriated foreign ideas. Although living in the town had a great deal to do with discontinuities, most people, especially those who came from adjacent districts of lower Congo, kept in touch with their rural roots. It seems important not to impose artificially the division between 'pre-colonial' and 'colonial' Africa that pervades scholarship, far less 'traditional' and 'modern', as it exaggerates lived experience. As we have already noted, the activities discussed are those that were most mentioned by informants and those that appear in the written accounts. A chapter is devoted to football, which was the favourite sport of the young men who constituted the majority of Bacongo and Poto-Poto's population for most of the colonial period. Efforts by teachers and administrators to channel enthusiasms into other sports because of pressures on equipment and facilities met with little success, for football corresponded to the needs and tastes of urban youth far beyond the actual physical exercise. Another chapter considers entertainment to be found in the streets, public spaces, bars, beer-gardens, cinemas and cafes. The streets remained the largest recreational space but, as entertainment became commercialized, it also moved indoors. Fashion and clothes are discussed, for they were symbolically important in mediating social relations, accessible to everyone but the very poor and a significant means of display. Finally, a chapter is devoted to European leisure, not only because many ideas were seized on and refashioned in African terms, but because the colonial discourse provides additional insights into the social and cultural dynamics of town life.

The nature of the sources means that the discussion may privilege some activities over others. Public leisure is favoured over private, group activities over individual, boisterous moments over quieter ones. These are not necessarily the activities that come to mind when one thinks of leisure in an African city. Leisure is also remembered as sitting around in a compound, chatting while the evening meal is being prepared; women tying their hair and exchanging news; playing cards; strolling with friends in the evening and buying doughnuts from fast-food sellers who sit with lanterns at the roadside; or, in Brazzaville, watching the thundering rapids of the Congo river. Such moments seldom make it into the historical record and, therefore, do not feature large in this book. But they are no less important in the cultural life of the town than the activities that are described.

1 An African crossroads, a frontier post and a colonial town, *c.* 1880–1915

As it was the impoverished capital of an imperial backwater, Brazzaville's initial development was slow and uneven. The great majority of its inhabitants lived in rough huts near their workplaces, and suffered from chronic food shortages and erratic employment. These circumstances had a great deal to do with colonial policy, the disruption of indigenous economies by concessionary companies and river steamers, and local responses to foreign occupation.

Many of the labourers on the waterfront or on construction sites were young migrant workers sent by their family heads to earn cash. Some had come on their own account to earn money for material goods and marriage payments. Also significant as an urban elite were foreigners, recruited by Europeans or drawn to the Central African capital by stories of opportunity. Arriving at the Pool, the French on the north side and the Belgians across the river at Léopoldville were in a region with no previous direct contact with Europe and with none of the trained auxiliaries indispensable to the functioning of capitalist enterprise and colonial rule. In the French case, lack of investment in education further retarded the training of local elites for several decades, so that West Africans as well as workers from coastal regions of Central Africa and from the French West Indies dominated skilled and semi-skilled jobs. These foreigners were also purveyors of new ideas on leisure. Some who stayed for extended periods or permanently, married local women or brought wives from their regions of origin.

For Europeans, the main priorities were survival, creating order from perceived chaos and shaping a more familiar and benign environment, goals not much different from those of African workers. For almost three decades, Europeans lived in close proximity to their workers since they lacked the resources to do otherwise. It was only when Brazzaville superseded Libreville as the capital of French Congo in 1904 and, five years later, became the capital of AEF, that the colonial ministry granted subsidies to start planning and constructing a segregated town. A long report by the first Mayor, written in 1915, shows that by that date the physical layout of the town had taken on its modern contours and the European community had begun to distance itself from the African population. At the same time, other significant developments had transpired. The indigenous Tio had been replaced by other African workers; European commerce had arrived in the form of concessionary companies; and a small nucleus of permanent townsfolk was established. This chapter traces these developments which were essential in Brazzaville's growth from a frontier post to a small colonial town.

At a crossroads

In 1882, Léon Guiral neared the Congo river after a fifteen-month journey through the rainforests of Gabon and the sandy plateaux to the south. He describes how he saw in the distance 'a cloud of vapour' and heard 'a continuous roar'. His guides informed him that it was the noise of the rapids. As he wrote:

The march came alive and the pace increased. We climbed another hill and at last I saw the valley of the Congo. The spectacle before my eyes I will never forget. At this point, the river widened out into a huge lake. The surface of the water glittered in the sunlight and the horizon seemed to blend into the sky. The constant roar of the endless Ntamo rapids gave this panorama an inexpressible grandeur.[1]

Guiral had arrived at the Pool, the point where the Congo river comes out of a narrow corridor and widens into a lakelike expanse about 30 kilometres long and some 20 kilometres across at its widest point.[2] Dotted with many islands, the largest of which, Mbamu, divides the river into two main branches, the Pool is navigable at all seasons. The crossing from Brazzaville to Kinshasa takes half an hour by ferry; by canoe double that time or longer, depending on the season of the year and the strength of current (see map 1). The Pool is the great terminus of inland navigation on the Congo, for on exiting the relative calm of its lake the river takes a tumultuous path through a series of cataracts and rapids, cutting through the western rim of its basin and plunging down some 300 metres before it reaches the ocean 500 kilometres away. The obstacle bars all river traffic so that for centuries transportation of goods to and from Atlantic markets was dependent on porterage along overland trails, which fanned out from both sides of the Pool to reach the coast north and south of the Congo estuary.

Through the remarkable configurations of the river, the region had huge economic significance (see map 2). Upstream was the gateway to hundreds of kilometres of waterways; 1,300 kilometres of navigable

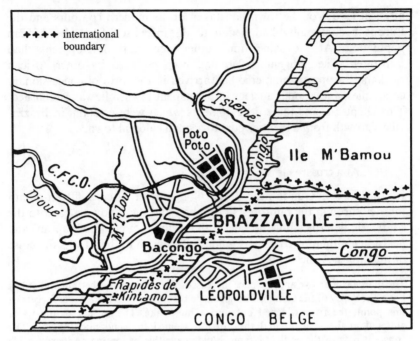

1   The Pool region (based on a map in Roger Frey, 'Brazzaville, capitale de l'Afrique Equatoriale Française', 1954. (Since all the maps used as illustrations are taken from French texts, the spelling of place names follows the French convention)

water separated Brazzaville from Bangui on the Ubangi river, or a boat could travel 1,700 kilometres to Stanley Falls (Kisangani) on the great Congo bend.[3] Tributaries on the right bank such as the Sanga, Alima and Likuala-Mossaka, which lay in future French territory, were all major arteries of African trade. The Frenchmen who arrived in the late nineteenth century were quick to realize the potential for a river port. Charles de Chavannes, appointed by Brazza to administer the fledgling French post in 1884, reported that Brazzaville was the key to exploiting Equatorial Africa. The best outlet to Atlantic shipping, he argued, would be from the Pool along the old caravan route to the Loango coast, rather than the tortuous and costly Ogowe route through Gabon to Libreville. His prediction was to prove correct, even if it took the French another fifty years to complete the railway link from Brazzaville to Pointe-Noire.[4]

The Pool was a Central African crossroads centuries before the arrival of French and Belgian forces; sixteenth-century Europeans knew by repute of the great inland slave and ivory market. Several important

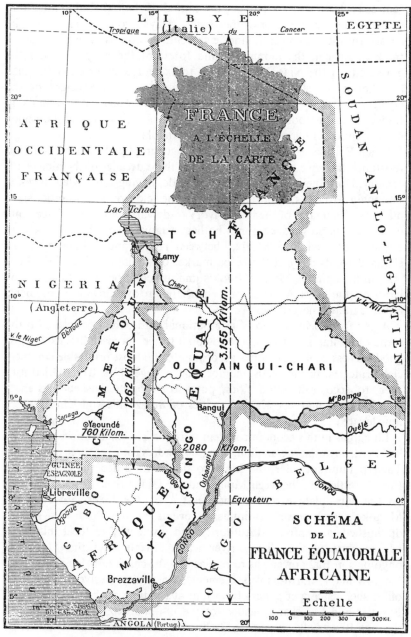

2 French Equatorial Africa (reproduced from Georges Bruel, *La France Equatoriale Africaine*, Paris: Larose, 1935)

centres such as Mbanza Kongo, the capital of the old Kongo kingdom, or Manyanga, at the foot of the rapids, relayed goods to and from the coast. In the seventeenth and eighteenth centuries, Loango traders trekked through the mountains and forest of the Mayombe and the grasslands of the Niari-Kwilu region to exchange imported cloth, guns and liquor for slaves and ivory at the Pool. At the height of the eighteenth-century slave trade, as many as 6,000-7,000 slaves were likely traded from the Pool to Loango coast markets each year, and thousands more arrived at international markets in Angola.[5]

When Europeans broke the barriers of geography, disease and African resistance to arrive at the Pool in the last three decades of the nineteenth century, ivory fuelled the great Congo trade, having superseded slaves as the main overseas export, following the closure of Atlantic slave markets.[6] Estimates of the inland ivory trade vary, but from all accounts it was an impressive amount. Father Augouard of the Holy Ghost Fathers reported in 1881 that between eighty and a hundred tusks changed hands daily at the Mfoa market on the north side of the Pool and, in his opinion, 'Stanley Pool is undoubtedly the largest market for ivory on the West African coast', perhaps an overglowing assessment, but remarkable nevertheless.[7]

Apart from being a hub of international trade, the Pool was also the scene of an important local and regional traffic, as specialists exchanged goods across ecological zones according to the most profitable commercial strategies. In the 1880s, manioc, maize, vegetables, fruits, dried fish, beer, tobacco, salt, raffia cloth, pots, iron objects, baskets and mats overflowed at markets where the cities of Brazzaville and Kinshasa are now located.[8]

Linchpins in this economic system were the Tio chiefs whose ancestors had controlled the region along the Pool shores for over three centuries.[9] Their paramount ruler, the Makoko Iloo, who ceded the land for the French settlement 'between Mpila and the Djoué river' to Brazza, lived on the Mbe plateau to the north-east.[10] By the 1880s, however, the Makoko's real power to influence events at the Pool was greatly diminished, as centralized authority had given way to local 'big men' who supervised the Congo river trade directly. Yet the Makoko's ongoing spiritual power was recognized by the chiefs of Mfoa and Mpila, the two major north-bank settlements, since they received symbols of office such as copper collars from him at the time of their investiture.[11] Baratier and Marchand, leaders of the ill-fated expedition that passed through Brazzaville *en route* to Fashoda, both thought that the power of the Makoko at the Pool had probably been exaggerated by Brazza to strengthen his position; a necessary 'myth', wrote Marchand, to bolster

French claims in the face of their rivalry with Leopold II's International Association.[12]

The settlements of Mfoa and Mpila were sizeable in a region of low population density.[13] They were composed of trading houses headed by big men who presided over family members, clients and slaves. Although Mfoa and Mpila had population concentrations that in this region merited the word 'town', neither had a unified structure. The clusters of trading houses acted as a corporate group on important matters of trade, but were only loosely joined in unstable alliances for other matters.[14] Leaders of overland caravans or canoe flotillas might spend weeks negotiating prices with local chiefs as 'autonomous equals' while enjoying their hospitality.[15] Such negotiations were carried out in a temporal framework, for the ebb and flow of trade was tempered by seasonal constraints. While the river traffic bringing goods to the Pool moved with the winds and currents of the rainy season, the overland traffic took place in the dry season when conditions were more favourable. Around the Pool, the Tio middlemen had to orchestrate these activities and keep stores of goods for their upstream and downstream trading partners.[16]

As Guiral approached Mfoa in 1882, he was met by a band of 400-500 men armed with guns.[17] At the market he described an *animation extraordinaire* and noted that 'all the people of the upper river are represented'.[18] The chief's power extended westwards across a ravine to high ground overlooking the river, where he gave land for the French post in an area later known as the Plateau, the administrative district of the European town. Four kilometres east of Mfoa on the edge of the Pool was the settlement of Mpila, with about three thousand people. In the rainy season when river conditions favoured the arrival of canoe traffic the population was swollen by traders and boatmen from upstream. The Catholic mission reckoned that about half of Mpila's population were the Bobangi or 'peoples of the river' who dominated the middle Congo trade.[19]

The Pool Tio were enormously successful as specialized traders, growing only enough for their subsistence and acquiring other necessities and luxuries through trade. The English missionary Bentley noted the stores of cloth that powerful individuals possessed; big men were 'so rich' that their wives did not need to do agricultural labour, and there was 'scarcely any ground cultivated'.[20] Guiral also reported that 'industry no more than agriculture absorbs the Batekes...the trade of the upper river is concentrated in their hands'. Furthermore, he described them as 'fussy' and with so much surplus cloth that they 'are difficult to please with presents'.[21]

As the French arrived, north-bank Tio power was also being contested by farmers and traders from the lower Congo in a process of gradual encroachment that had been going on since the sixteenth century. Moving into lands between the Pool and the coast, Bakongo-related groups known as Lari, Sundi and Kongo had established themselves as essential middlemen in the long-distance trade with Europeans. By the late nineteenth century, they had pushed back the Tio whose power had previously extended west of the Djoué river. Although rivals for land, these lower Congo peoples were trading partners of the Tio, since they controlled the overland caravans that passed through their region.[22] They were also principal suppliers of manioc to Mfoa and Mpila, as they were to become for the colonial workforce. Vulnerable Brazzaville administrators treated the villagers west of the Djoué river with caution, fully aware that they had both the power to close the caravan route and to stop food supplies, which they did on occasion, whether to control prices or to protest against European actions.

Thus the Pool had been an African crossroads for centuries. The settlements on the north bank were famous, for they were a place where fortunes could made quite beyond the dreams of ordinary villagers. In Kilari, the region of Mfoa and Mpila was known as *mavula*, or 'the place to grow rich', with opportunities for wealth far beyond those available through the lineage structures that controlled village society.[23] The arrival of Europeans seemed to put all this in jeopardy. The traders of Mfoa were the first to lose out as the French made it their principal landing on the river; and by the turn of the century, concessionary companies had expelled others from prime spots along the river. Finally, the Tio were left with their settlement at Mpila on the edge of the colonial town, but many withdrew upriver or to their heartland on the Mbe plateau.

Yet the word *mavula* continued in use and is still used today when Kilari-speakers talk of Brazzaville. Although old avenues to wealth were all but gone, new opportunities to profit from the white man's economy took their place. While many Tio refused to participate directly in the colonial economy, others took their place in the settlements around the Pool. Although colonial rule in the heart of Africa presented a plethora of dilemmas, it also opened a whole range of new options.

Locals and foreigners

In order to understand the emergence of an urban time and new forms of leisure, it is useful to consider the composition of the workforce. As might be expected in a town in the making, most jobs involved clearing the bush, construction and labouring on the waterfront. At the same time, the administration and trading companies needed skilled artisans, mechanics and clerical workers, while individual Europeans employed a number of servants. Others worked on their own account farming patches of land, trading food, cloth and other essential and luxury goods, catching and smoking fish, or transporting people and goods in canoes and rickshaws or 'pousses-pousses'. Individuals were thus integrated into the town's economy in many different ways and had various experiences of working hours and conditions.

The position of Brazzaville in the French scheme of things affected the types of jobs available. For the first twenty years, it was little more than a transit point to service huge expeditions that passed through the Pool area on their way to imperial campaigns in Ubangi-Shari and Chad. Faced with horrendous logistical problems, leaders simply took matters into their own hands, ignored local administrators, and requisitioned materials, boats and labour at will.[24] Urban development was minimal, as funds were siphoned off to subsidize expeditions which languished at the colonial outpost while awaiting the arrival of river transport. The availability of jobs fluctuated erratically according to the ebb and flow of expeditions. In 1892, the colonial administration employed over five hundred workers and soldiers who were paid on a daily or monthly basis and given daily rations.[25]

Once the backdoor to its important West and North African possessions had been secured through the occupation of Chad and Ubangi-Shari, Equatorial Africa lapsed into obscurity in the official mind. A map of AEF published in the *Bulletin du Comité de l'Afrique Française* in 1910 is chiefly remarkable for the small areas marked 'really occupied' as opposed to much larger areas denoted 'nominally administered'. French lack of interest resulted in most of Congo, although not Brazzaville, being turned over to rule by concessionary companies. By 1900, some twenty companies dealing in ivory and rubber had established their headquarters along the Pool, displacing the last Tio traders but contributing to an upsurge in Brazzaville's population through the creation of jobs.[26] After 1898, the completion of the railway from Kinshasa to Matadi at the mouth of the Congo cut out the costly caravan route to the coast and helped to make Equatorial Africa more attractive for commercial interests. On the river, neither the Tio nor Bobangi could compete in freighting bulk produce. By 1902, over a hundred steamers, most of them working for companies on the Free State side of the river, plied the Congo basin.[27]

The composition of the Brazzaville workforce was influenced not only by job opportunities but by African responses. Particularly striking was the virtual 'disappearance' of the Tio. In a strategy that might be characterized as 'avoidance protest' many Tio withdrew from the Pool area rather than be absorbed into the colonial economy.[28] On the Mbe plateau and along the river banks upstream from Brazzaville, they continued fishing, hunting, trading and farming, while resisting demands from the colonial authorities for forced labour and food for the urban market. They grew enough for their subsistence but did not produce much of a surplus. According to Jan Vansina, the reasons were cultural as well as economic. While realizing the economic importance of farming, the Tio did not value it highly and were not inclined to change their production strategies on the dry, sandy expanses of their plateau heartland. Nor would they engage in wage-labour, which they perceived as akin to slavery. For the same reason, few sent their children to school, since it involved manual labour in the mission gardens.[29]

The Tio, however, continued to trade with their African neighbours and used their knowledge of the river to bypass colonial demands. They became smugglers on the Pool, buying cheap absinthe on the French side of the river and selling it at high prices in the Free State where it was a popular but illegal drink among Léopoldville workers. Against government regulations, they carried ivory to the south side of the Pool where prices were higher. Administrators also complained that the Tio deprived Brazzaville of urgent food supplies by loading their canoes with manioc, dried meat and fish for Kinshasa markets where there was a greater variety of products and often better prices. Mayor Girard accused them of an 'underhand malice' which deprived the town of essential provisions.[30]

Some Tio continued to live at Mpila on the outskirts of Brazzaville, catching and smoking fish which they sold to African buyers on both sides of the Pool. They were joined by refugees from the Belgian side of the river, who escaped the systematic and oppressive labour demands of the Free State, sometimes to fall victim to similar problems in French Congo.[31] The Mpila chief also defied the administration's demands for workers. In 1898, having consistently resisted forced labour quotas to clear public lands, he was seized and imprisoned to 'set an example'.[32] Overall, the disengagement of the Tio from the Pool region, which they had dominated for so long, was remarkable. In 1905, only one Tio, the state ferryman, worked for the administration. By 1914, a missionary reported that among 6,000–7,000 Africans in Brazzaville, 'coming from all countries', the number of Tio was very small. In 1948, they were only 6 per cent of the town's population and took little part in the economic and political developments of the post-war era. However, they retained some status in the town as the original owners of the land. They were also known for their magic and their prowess as fishermen and hunters.[33]

As the Tio withdrew, workers from the lower Congo took their place.

The opening of the Free State railway effectively brought the overland caravan business to an end, while the end of railway construction forced young men accustomed to wage-labour and a cash economy to come to the town just at the point when the establishment of concessionary companies created a boom in jobs. Workers from nearby regions showed up in gangs and stayed for the duration of a project for which they received a daily wage and rations. For the construction of the first administration buildings on the Plateau, Chavannes hired sixty-two Lari workers, who were then replaced with workers from the same area after they went back to their villages.[34] In 1901, of ninety-three workers hired by the Public Works department, eighty-two were labourers and of these fifty-four were 'Bacongo' and twenty-eight 'Loangos' who had lost their jobs as porters.[35] Young men from the Pool area established a pattern of migrant labour, living in Brazzaville for much of their working lives but maintaining close contact with their villages and returning to be married.[36] Their wives gradually moved to the town, but on a semi-permanent basis since they retained their land in rural areas and went back to the villages with their children at the beginning of the planting season.[37]

Women from the lower Congo, who had been major suppliers of manioc bread to slave caravans and to Mfoa and Mpila, continued to be the main providers of food for the colonial town. Initially, the administration sent parties of soldiers and porters across the Djoué river to buy food for which they negotiated through local chiefs. Women also carried manioc to the town themselves, arriving in small groups and selling their produce directly to the administration or supplying individual workers through a market established in 1891.[38] It was not a question of the Lari and lower Congo people rushing into the urban economy, however. Living in a well-populated area with thriving local markets, food producers would only sell their surplus in the town if it was profitable to do so. Furthermore, like Tio and Bobangi fishermen and smugglers, they played off the Pool settlements against each other, shipping manioc, chickens, goats and eggs to the Belgian side of the river when prices were higher. They also used food as a weapon to protest against overpowering European demands. After villages had been terrorized and raided for food and women taken hostage by members of the Marchand expedition, the Brazzaville population had to pay the price, as manioc bread became 'invisible' and the 'natives took their revenge'.[39] Faced with a food crisis after the arrival of the concessionary-company workers, the administration issued an edict in 1904 prohibiting the export of manioc out of Brazzaville 'for whatever reason', and 'until the inhabitants of the villages in the region have the time to raise their production to meet these new needs'. Transgressors were punished with up to five days in prison and a 1- to 5-franc fine.[40] However, the colonial administration with few resources had little success in enforcing such an edict.

In the early history of Brazzaville, the peoples around the Pool were not only significant as labourers and food suppliers, they were also important as the first Congolese elite. Lari children enrolled in mission schools, first at Linzolo 28 kilometres from the Pool where the Holy Ghost Fathers had established a mission station in 1883, and then at Brazzaville. After a couple of years, they tended to drop out and take jobs with concessionary companies and the administration, leaving before they had finished their 'Christian training' and becoming prey to 'bad company' as far as their teachers were concerned.[41] Children from the Pool area and the lower Congo also attended schools of the Swedish Evangelical Mission which had established seven stations throughout the lower Congo by the 1920s. Their small Brazzaville mission, begun in 1911, had a school and workshop for training carpenters, masons and other artisans.[42]

The growing reputation of the settlement also pulled in migrant labour from other areas of Equatorial Africa and the abusive treatment of villagers in rural areas by concessionary companies operating their 'economy of pillage' also caused people to flee to the town. Workers from Chad and Ubangi-Shari found passage on the vessels that plied the Congo river. Concessionary-company employees also arrived from out-lying areas to work at Brazzaville factories.[43] There was a constant flow of people coming and going from the Belgian side of the river, as well as refugees fleeing from Free State reprisals against their villages. Workers from Kasai were remarked on in accounts by several Europeans. Some were railway construction workers who crossed the river after the Matadi-Kinshasa line was completed. Kasai women were engaged in trade and also had a reputation among workers for their excellent beer.[44] The replacement of the Tio by peoples from upriver is also shown by the missionary decision to use Lingala in their work. A 1914 report by the Holy Ghost Fathers noted that a priest had started to work in the new lingua franca, 'Bangala', which was being substituted for Kiteke since that was no longer an important language in Brazzaville.[45]

Lack of skilled labour and competition from the Free State forced employers to recruit skilled workers from further afield. An official report to the Governor-General emphasized the importance of foreign labour, naming in particular 'mechanics, smiths and carpenters from Senegal, woodworkers from Sierra Leone and Accra, smiths and laun-drymen from Cabinda, and plantation overseers from São Tomé'.[46] In the second half of 1901, the Brazzaville administration listed 195 foreign workers who had officially applied for 'embarkation permits'. Their destinations were named as Cabinda, Loango, Sierra Leone, Accra, Dakar, Lagos and Libreville.[47]

As the report to the Governor-General indicated, the jobs filled by workers were affected by the nature of their previous contact with whites and by perceptions that Europeans had of their skills. In their reports and conversations, whites passed on their biases, which in turn were exploited by African workers to their advantage. Young men from Loango who took jobs as domestic servants are a good example. With the closure of the caravan route, hundreds found themselves without jobs and arrived in Brazzaville to 'retool' and find wage employment. While some found work as labourers and porters, many took advantage of European perceptions that 'Loangos' made excellent servants. For Veistroffer, 'they can do quite well in work such as sewing, washing, ironing, and cooking'.[48] For Brunache, 'the Loangos are very skilled tailors and they like to use a sewing machine and an iron'.[49] Challaye also noted that 'many Loangos work for Europeans as boys'.[50] Leaving their families as young as twelve years old, aspiring wage-earners usually joined other family members in the town. Starting as an odd-job boy under the cook an individual could move up through the ranks to command the kitchen and do gourmet cuisine.[51] After a few years, young men usually returned home to find wives, but then returned to Brazzaville to continue in domestic employment. Some became permanent towns-folk, others retired to their regions of origin.[52]

Demand was high, as a single household would employ as many as five servants: a cook, his helper, a server at table, one or two for housework and laundry, and a gardener. However, this state of affairs was not necessarily what employers wanted, but rather a system that they were forced to accept by the young men who exchanged information as they worked in neighbouring houses on the Plateau or along the Plaine. Three European accounts confirm that they found their servants 'over-specia-lized' as valets, cooks, laundrymen or gardeners, each refusing to do another type of work, even when they had 'little to do'.[53] Gaston Bouteillier, who worked as a factory agent between 1902 and 1903, estimated that five-sixths of the servants were from Loango. Against his will, he found himself hiring four servants. 'Whites are obliged to have several servants', he wrote, 'because each will only do a specialized task; for example, a laundryman will not clean shoes'.[54] Deschamps in 1911, shared the same opinion that 'all servants have their specialization' and refused to carry out another task, rather suggesting to their employer that another 'specialist' be hired.[55] This system clearly worked as an informal labour union, preserving and creating jobs for the greatest number of workers. Based on the number of Europeans in Brazzaville in 1913, domestic servants probably made up about a quarter of the African workforce. Since they were more tied to the urban labour market than casual labourers, they were a more permanent part of the labour force and an influential segment of the working population.

Others from Gabon and Loango were employed as carpenters, bricklayers, factory overseers and guards, or worked for the customs service on the docks and river boats.[56] In 1892, all the twenty-five bricklayers used by Monseigneur Augouard in the construction of the cathedral were from Loango.[57] Missionary-trained tailors were also noted for their fine work, and were sought out by the fashionable.[58] Men from Loango were also excellent ivory carvers who from the mid-nineteenth century had engaged in a thriving tourist industry with European and American factory agents and ships' crews. With the end of the caravan trade which closed many coastal factories, these craftsmen moved to Brazzaville where they set up stalls or hawked their wares door to door. They also promoted their craft at the annual Fourteenth of July Fair, which was added to the official program in 1912 to show-case the 'industry' and 'progress' of Africans under French rule.[59]

Gabonese who had received training at factories on the coast and along the Ogowe were actively recruited for work in Brazzaville by the French. By the time the post at the Pool was established, a generation of Gabonese had graduated from mission schools. After the capital of French Congo had been moved from Libreville, some clerical workers were transferred to Brazzaville.[60] Educated Gabonese occupied an important place in the capital's African elite throughout the colonial period. They are especially remembered as stylish dressers who influenced fashion trends, and they were among early football stars.[61]

Gabonese women had also arrived at the Pool by the turn of the century. They lived with European and African men in a variety of arrangements, although they were generally lumped together under the rubric of 'prostitutes' in European reports, when they were not married under civil law or in the church. Gabonese women particularly sought out white men who could give them more support and status than African workers. Having been in touch with Europeans at Libreville and coastal factories, some had adopted European dress, had learned French cuisine and could organize the household of a white man. A European man might set up house with an African woman at a fixed fee per month, or they contracted a temporary marriage through paying a bride-price to the woman's relatives, or they engaged in casual sex. Relationships were often quite stable, lasting for the duration of a man's stay in the town, with such women being refered to as 'housekeepers' (ménagères) by European men.[62]

Administrators and missionaries blamed women from upper Congo as a source of 'immorality' in the town. For the Swedish missionary Samuel Hede, Brazzaville was 'a hard mission field like all such commercial centres' and 'hundreds of women from upper Congo are professional prostitutes'.[63] In 1909, probably influenced by recent legislation in France, Administrator Cureau asked the Lieutenant-Governor to regulate prostitution, arguing that the administration should do all that it could to 'deter debauchery' but if 'women cannot be deterred they should be subject to formalities' such as registration with the police and regular medical examinations for venereal disease.[64] Once the Brazzaville hospital was built it was given the task of examining the few women who chose to be registered publicly. Not surprisingly, rather few did. According to a report of 1912, about fifty 'turned up every Saturday to be examined at the dispensary'.[65]

Without foreign workers from West Africa, especially Senegal, but also the Gold Coast, Sierra Leone and Dahomey, the French administration and companies might not have survived. West Africans were recruited to perform specific tasks, from clerks to factory agents, and soldiers to carpenters. Many Senegalese originally arrived in Central Africa as *tirailleurs*, hired by Europeans who stopped at Dakar *en route* to Equatorial Africa. The pattern was established by Brazza in his first expedition, and others did likewise. The hope was to find soldiers with some previous experience in the conquest army, but the policy was also useful as a divide-and-rule device. When experienced soldiers were unavailable, Europeans would take raw recruits, and give them a crash course on being a *tirailleur* on board ship or at Libreville or Loango, before setting out for the interior.[66] Finding recruits was often difficult since service in Central Africa was not popular among volunteers, given the long voyage, the overland journey and conditions that were more uncertain than in West Africa.[67] Describing his arrival in Dakar to review the 'troops' recruited by an advance party, Paul Brunache wrote that 'there were about forty in rags: porters, dockers, shoe-shine boys, about 16 to 22 years old with little military bearing. Only one had served as a *tirailleur senegalais*. As for the others, they had perhaps seen rifles in the distance in the hands of soldiers on parade.'[68] More systematic recruitment was necessary for a larger expedition such as Marchand's, when Mangin went into the Kayes region and recruited 480 men, many of them experienced soldiers who had worked under his command previously.[69]

Senegalese generally had two-year contracts, with their passage home guaranteed.[70] Many stayed after their contracts had expired, since it was easy to pick up employment, after having been a *tirailleur*. Their army training, the respect and fear in which they were held by local populations and their familiarity with European notions of time and discipline made veterans highly sought after for positions of authority. Army veterans monopolized the police force or militia, positions which former *tirailleurs* welcomed, since they paid more than most other jobs and included the possibility of rewards through abuse of position.[71] Senegalese were also hired as overseers of work gangs. Six former *tirailleurs* hired by Bouteillier had come to Central Africa to fight in Ubangi-Shari campaigns. After leaving military service, they worked for the Compagnie de Sangha before going down-river to Brazzaville. When they appeared for work, they were still wearing their red fezzes and military jackets. Bouteillier issued them with work orders and appointed them over Lari and Loango labourers to sort rubber and cut grass.[72] Former soldiers were also favoured for employment by the Post and Telegraphs Department, by the customs and as mechanics on river boats. In 1913, the Public Works Department employed fourteen Senegalese masons and seven carpenters.[73] Given the high demand for their labour on both sides of the river, these workers were able to take advantage of their situation. The French suspected the Belgians of encouraging Senegalese workers to break contracts by offering them high wages as earthworkers on the railway. According to Baratier, the Senegalese 'return to the French side and show more arrogance than ever, accepting the sixteen franc fine for breaking their contract'.[74] Some former *tirailleurs* were traders, using their status with local and European populations and knowledge of the area to good effect. Guiral noted ex-soldiers who were making 'a fortune, buying products cheaply on the upper Ogowe and Nguni rivers and selling them to factories'. He added: 'They follow European styles as closely as possible and aspire to be *grande monde*.'[75] Some obtained plots of land in Brazzaville and opened stores in the Plateau and Plaine districts, dealing primarily in cloth. In his 1915 report on the state of Brazzaville, the Mayor referred to 'numerous Senegalese traders'.[76] As they settled in the town, Muslim West Africans including the Senegalese tended to be subsumed in local speech by the generic name of 'Houssas', a reference to the northerners who used the river routes through AEF to arrive at the capital.

Initially, the colonial administration paid for the transportation and support of wives of foreign workers whom they recruited, but in 1905 this was cancelled because of the expense.[77] Even before this decree, however, individual Senegalese had sent for their wives, or young men had gone home to be married and returned with their families. Others married local women who converted to Islam. The growing number of Brazzaville Muslim families, which included workers from Chad and

Ubangi-Shari as well as West Africans, was shown in the establishment of a Koranic school in 1902.[78]

Other foreigners were English-speaking West Africans from the Gold Coast and Sierra Leone, known locally as 'Coastmen', and black colonial administrators from the French Antilles. West Africans were chiefly recruited by concessionary companies in their regions of origin. A family might let a young man go to gain experience in business and, once it became known that good jobs were available, others followed. Some took 'temporary wives' for the duration of their stay in Congo as Europeans did, or married local women. Most, but not all, returned home after a few years, perhaps to invest their earnings in trade and build large houses.[79] When Swedish missionaries arrived in Brazzaville, they were approached by over fifty West African Protestants who asked them to organize services in English.[80] Also influential in the cosmopolitan community were black colonial administrators from the French Antilles.[81] Europeans sometimes treated them as honorary whites, as when good football players were allowed to play for the white *Club Athlètique Brazzavillois*. Some low-level West Indian civil servants lived in the African section of town and were particularly influential in introducing new ideas on popular music, as were accordion-playing workers from the Gold Coast and Sierra Leone.[82]

Thus, in the space of three decades or so, the workforce on the north shores of the Pool had undergone a dramatic transformation. The precolonial Pool economy had been disrupted through the imposition of European commercial capitalism and a stratified society based on new technical skills and work in the colonial economy was taking shape. At the same time, there were many workers who were still attached to lineage-based, rural economies and participated in the urban economy erratically while continuing to be firmly attached to village societies. This was true, for example, of the women from the Pool, Boko and Mindouli regions who sold surplus food to the Brazzaville market, or Tio and Bobangi boatmen and fishermen who profited from smuggling on the Pool. Within the colonial economy, a class of African elites had emerged, many of them West Africans but also those from Gabon and Loango, as well as local populations who were missionary educated. Those with technical skills, such as river-boat mechanics, stone-masons and carpenters, also took leadership roles in urban society, for they had a cash income and specialized knowledge that others did not have.

A mission of inspection sent from France in 1913 to investigate the potential workforce of Moyen-Congo carried out a study of the situation in Brazzaville. Their report gives some insights into the various levels at which workers were integrated into the economy. Mostly the report

Table 1   *Brazzaville African population estimates 1900–1961*

Date	Total	Men/Women/Children	Source
1900*	5,000		a
1902**	2,000		b
1909*	4,000		c
1911(1)**	5,000		d
1911(2)*	6,362	3,400/1,450/1,512	e
1912*	3,800		f
1913(1)**	6,000–7,000		g
1913(2)*	10,199	5,274/3,116/1,809	h
1925*	20,000		i
1931**	15,000		j
1932*	15,928	7,840/4,364/3,724	k
1933(1)*	14,796	7,274/3,944/3,578	l
1933(2)*	19,100	8,800/5,400/4900	m
1936(1)*	18,694	5,360/5,693/7,641	n
1936(2)*	19,972		o
1937*	23,436	12,891/6,341/4,204	p
1938**	30,000		q
1945*	41,080	17,680/10,000/13,400	r
1948*	60,000		s
1950*	78,300	31,100/21,300/25,900	t
1952*	77,400	32,100/20,700/24,600	u
1955*	87,300	34,000/24,900/28,400	v
1961*	127,964	37,443/32,965/57,556	w

* official estimates, or censuses
** missionary estimates
a Bonchamps, 'Rapport sur la région de Brazzaville'
b 'Brazzaville', *BCPSE*, 21 (1901–1902), 668
c AOM, 4(2)D3, General report, Brazzaville, 1909
d ASMF, E.11, Brev från Kongo, H. J. Lindgren to SMF Directors, 18 October 1911
e AOM, 4(2)D7, Annual report, Moyen-Congo, 1911
f Speech by Governor-General Merlin, *JO*, 15 October 1912 (This estimate is difficult to correlate with others; although he said, 'no fewer than 3,800', this seems to be a substantial underestimate.)
g "Brazzaville", *BCPSE*, 27 (1913–1914), 55
h Girard, 'Brazzaville', 35
i Speech by Governor-General Merlin, 1925, quoted in Frey, 'Brazzaville, capitale de l'Afrique Equatoriale', 48
j AGPSE, 278AIII, 'Bulletin historique: vicariat de Brazzaville (1931–53)'
k AOM, 4(2)D57, Annual report, Subdivision of Brazzaville, 1933
l AOM, 4(2)D57, Annual report, Subdivision of Brazzaville, 1933
m *Recensement et démographie des principales agglomerations d'AEF*, vol. III (Brazzaville: Haut Commissariat de l'Afrique Equatoriale Française, Service de la Statistique Générale, 1955), 4 (The variation of these figures for the period c.1930–6 is difficult to explain, but there were considerable population movements among the unemployed due to the world

depression. A further factor making estimates uncertain was the opposition of the followers of André Matswa to any kind of collaboration with the colonial government.)

n AOM, 4(2)D68, First trimester report, Subdivision of Brazzaville, 1936

o AOM, 4(2)D68, Second trimester report, Subdivision of Brazzaville, 1936

p Governor-General Reste, *Action économique et sociale*, 205

q Charles le Comte, 'La mission devant les yeux d'un jeune', *APSE* (May 1938), 146

r ANB, GG456, Service de Statistique, 31 December 1945

s AOM, AP2302(1), Report of M. Zoccolat for Ruffel Mission, 2 June 1948

t 'Population autochtone estimation au 1/1/50', *Annuaire statistique de l'Afrique Équatoriale Française*, vol. 1, 1936-50 (Brazzaville: Haut Commissariat de l'Afrique Equatoriale Française, 1950), 36

u Census estimate, September 1952, *Recensement et démographie*, 4

v Census estimate, December 1955, *Recensement et démographie*, 4

w *Rencensement de Brazzaville, 1961*, République du Congo, Service de Statistique (Paris: Ministère de la Coopération, 1965), 11

concentrated on the erratic nature of the workforce and resistance to 'work discipline'. Three categories of workers were distinguished. The most 'lazy' and 'despicable' were those recruited in distant villages, who had deserted or had high levels of absenteeism. Of almost one hundred workers recruited on a three-month contract by the Public Works department in the Niari valley, fourteen 'fled' before they arrived at Brazzaville, and sixteen fell sick from beriberi. The remaining fifty-eight averaged eighteen-and-a-half days per month, and some did not appear in the workplace for three to five days at a time. A second group of workers, recruited by the Mayor in villages close to Brazzaville for construction work in the town, received a monthly wage and daily rations. However, once these men had earned a certain income, they left once they were paid. This meant that each month there was a turnover of about a third of the labour force, with new workers having to be recruited. A third group, those who lived in Bacongo and Poto-Poto, were referred to by the inspector as 'quite a stable workforce'. In particular, reference was made to workers at the administration's brick-making plant, 'some of whom have worked there for four to five years'. However, even the Senegalese 'often miss work the day after they are paid'.[83]

Thus, by the eve of the First World War, a nucleus of workers such as artisans, semi-skilled labourers, domestic servants and office workers was staying for extended periods in Brazzaville; and population figures suggest the number of women and children was also increasing (see table 1). Incipient class divisions were also evident. The Mayor's report in 1915 referred to the 'growing number of Africans with European manners and tastes who buy European goods whenever possible'.[84] These workers were pioneers in adopting and appropriating new ideas on time and recreational activities, for their status was as much based on their knowledge of urban culture as on their economic position.

Segregating space

For the first twenty-five years of Brazzaville's existence, only a few scattered buildings indicated the European presence. Yet they symbolized the primary institutions of colonialism (see map 3). A cluster of mud-brick thatched houses marked the administrative post where a handful of colonial officials lived on the Plateau. Nearby was the military post, appropriately enough called Chad. For a Belgian visitor in 1898, the marines and *tirailleurs* carrying out manoeuvres on a large parade ground were 'the principal vital element' in the French settlement.[85] In 1908, the military post took on greater significance when the AEF forces were separated from those in French West Africa and a separate command was established in Brazzaville, thus increasing the importance of officers and soldiers in both European and African communities.[86] Several kilometres distant by the Pool, three trading companies, the French house of Dumas and Béraud, a Belgian company and the Dutch Nieuwe Afrikaansche Handelsvereeniging, had established factories. Individual traders included two Portuguese, a Spaniard and three Senegalese who had stores by the river.[87]

The most visible symbol of European power and authority, however, was the mission station of the Holy Ghost Fathers which occupied prime land on a hillside overlooking Mfoa. Under the direction of the energetic and ambitious Monseigneur Augouard, Bishop of Upper Congo, 1890–1921, a gothic-style cathedral that could hold over a thousand people was dedicated in 1894. Built in stone, brick and wood, with a bell-tower topped by a cross that rose twenty metres into the air, it was surrounded by a two-storeyed bishop's 'palace', schoolrooms, dormitories, workshops and gardens where children and workers laboured to grow essential food supplies. The whole complex, contrasting sharply with the simple houses of colonial officials, was a constant reminder of the power of the church and the weakness of the state, a bitter pill to swallow for many turn-of-the century Frenchmen, engaged at home in a fierce debate to reduce the power of the church. Augouard's domineering manner did nothing to endear him to colonial administrators, but it made him a powerful figure among his congregation, as did his longevity at a time when most Europeans stayed less than two years or succumbed to tropical fevers. The bishop's stamina was only rivalled by that of Mother Marie, who spent almost fifty years in Africa, most of them (1892–1929) as head of the Sisters of Saint Joseph of Cluny convent at the foot of the

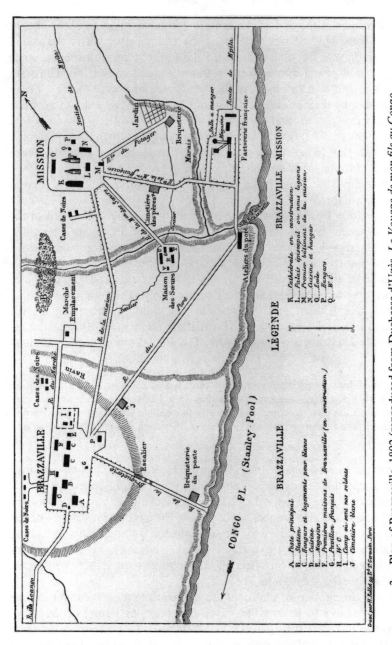

3. Plan of Brazzaville, 1892 (reproduced from Duchesse d'Uzès, *Le Voyage de mon fils au Congo*, Paris: Librairie Plon, 1894)

mission hill. By the end of the century 150 boys, many of them bought out of some kind of servitude along the Ubangi river where the inland slave-trade was still active, attended the Catholic mission school, while 95 girls and young women were in training at the convent for Christian marriage and motherhood. As they graduated and were married off to each other by their missionary sponsors, the couples settled in one of five Christian villages around the mission station.[88]

By 1900, the Brazzaville Administrator could report to his superiors in Libreville that 'where there was a small French post, a town has been born'.[89] Monseigneur Augouard was more grudging but wrote in 1902: 'Brazzaville is far from being what one might call a town, but it is no longer a village.'[90]

Population fluctuated with the economy, increasing at the turn of the century when the concessionary companies arrived and again after 1909, when Brazzaville became the capital of AEF and labourers were needed for the construction of official buildings. Reliable censuses of the town's population are only available for the 1950s onwards and any estimates before then are just that, and vary considerably. The coming and going of migrant labour, and of women and children according to the agricultural cycle, made for a fluctuating population. Official counts generally fell below the actual figure. The annual report of the Administrator of Moyen-Congo in 1912 summed up the problem:

This must be very approximate, for a census is in the eyes of the population above all a financial measure, which they seek to avoid as long as they can. Administrators have to count as discreetly as possible for villagers get annoyed and see it as an infringement of their person: they send women and children into the bush.[91]

Estimates by missionaries who knew the local populations well as they went about their parishes can also be used to obtain approximate town population figures when other sources are lacking, although missionary calculations are also suspect, since they might have had a vested interest in exaggerating or diminishing populations for their superiors and home congregations. These are used in table 1, however, in preference to passing comments by travellers and other short-term visitors to Brazzaville, when official estimates are lacking.

It was the haphazard nature of urban growth that most caught the eye of early visitors to Brazzaville. Given the sprawling nature of the town, people lived beside their places of work. Living near those from the same region was a secondary consideration, although these two factors might coincide, as it did for domestic servants from Loango who established a 'village' near their employers on the Plateau. 'Brazzaville seems to have developed spontaneously without method, order or preconceived plan', reported Félicien Challaye in 1905. It is a 'scene of picturesque disorder'.[92] Along the Pool, workers' quarters and makeshift camps were interspersed with factories, warehouses, boat-yards, stores and bars. Africans and Europeans clustered around the workplace on the Plateau, at the military post, along the Plaine, or around the mission station. Former *tirailleurs*, who worked for the administration, like those from the Loango coast, had their own village on the edge of the Plateau. Challaye was surprised to find an African market adjacent to the European club and a Dutch store nearby.[93]

Nor were the European houses much better constructed than those of African workers, especially those of administrators who, lacking the means to do otherwise, had to accommodate their life-style to local conditions. Administrator Bonchamps in a long report to his superiors in Libreville reluctantly agreed with Monseigneur Augouard, who had reported that Brazzaville administrators lived in 'hovels'. He furthermore warned his superiors that something must be done or European colonial officials would leave to work for the concessionary companies which offered better conditions. Challaye summed up the situation: 'They live in Brazzaville like troops on manoeuvres in a poor Alpine village.'[94] For Charles Castellani, only the Dutch and Belgian factories had a 'European allure',[95] while the Catholic mission remained the model of colonial achievement. Between buildings the bush ran wild, with expanses of tall grasses, ravines, streams that flowed into the Congo, and woods, making cross-town communication difficult.

The removal of the capital of French Congo from Libreville to Brazzaville, and its establishment as the capital of AEF, brought the matter of town planning to a head. In 1909, the colonial ministry finally granted a subsidy for town 'improvements'. Two years later, Brazzaville was given independent status as a 'Commune' with a mayor and a four-member town council appointed by the Lieutenant-Governor of Moyen-Congo from 'leading Frenchmen over twenty-five years old'.[96] The first measure to segregate urban space was introduced in 1909 when land on the west side of the Plateau was designated as the African district of Bacongo. Two years later, several kilometres away on the other side of town just north of factories on the Plaine, a second African area of Poto-Poto (Lingala, 'mud', for the marshy ground on which it was located) was surveyed and plots allocated for house construction.

The colonial discourse on town planning revolved around several considerations, some growing out of prevailing European thought on colonial cities, and some based on local circumstances. Primary considerations may be summed up as prestige, health policies, the cultural

incompatibility of Europeans and Africans, and law and order. Under-
lying all the arguments was the slow but sustained growth of the town's
population and the administration's search for a better means of
control in the face of rioting over food shortages and poor living
conditions.

For Mayor Girard, writing after segregation measures had been
introduced, African houses built next to those of Europeans had
'constituted a serious obstacle to the growth of the town', and moving
out workers had 'left land free for the construction of important
buildings'.[97] Planning a capital worthy of the name was in part necessitated by Brazzaville's new pre-eminence within AEF, but it also helped
alleviate the humiliation of many French as they looked across the river
to the impressive Belgian colonial settlement. Descriptions of visitors on
both sides of the river are replete with invidious comparisons. From the
earliest years of the Brazzaville post, Europeans on the French side
crossed the Pool frequently for supplies, leisure amenities and the social
crowd in Léopoldville. In 1898, the Chief Administrator of Brazzaville,
newly arrived at Léopoldville via the Matadi railway, had the unfortunate choice of crossing the Pool in Monseigneur Augouard's steamer or
the boat of the Free State Governor, since the Brazzaville administration
did not own one.[98] For Veistroffer, 'Léopoldville is an important centre,
truly a small town when one compares it with Brazzaville's poor straw
huts', and Baratier found in 1897 that 'it is impossible to go ashore at
Léopoldville without making a painful contrast'.[99]

Although Brazzaville was never to catch up with Léopoldville–Kinshasa, the principal jewel in the Belgian colonial crown, and situated as it
was at the centre of a much wealthier colony, it had begun to look more
like a capital city on the eve of the First World War. By 1912, the
European town boasted a new Governor-General's residence, the offices
of the Lieutenant-Governor of Moyen-Congo, a treasury, law courts, a
post and telegraphs building, the Pasteur Institute, a military hospital
and a town hall. A single dirt road linked the Plateau to the Plaine,
ravine crossings were improved and a wooden bridge spanned the Mfoa
river.[100] The *mentalité* of the colonial rulers was shown in the termi-
nology for the white district, referred to as the 'town', while Bacongo and
Poto-Poto were referred to as the 'villages', a nomenclature also common
in other French colonial towns. Since all the major public buildings were
in the European town, architectural distinctions reinforced racial and
legal ones.[101] New roads, although not much more than tracks at the
time, were named to 'immortalize the heroes of Congo expeditions'.[102]
The annual Fourteenth of July procession stamped the mark of France
firmly on the white town, starting in the Place de Brazza and wending its

way along the Rue de Lamothe, Rue Crampel, Avenue du Commerce and Rue Ballay.[103]

While the need to provide 'space' for the development of the white town was a fundamental justification for the forced removal of Africans, prevailing views on the control of disease also justified segregated residential areas as far as Europeans were concerned. Administrator Bonchamps, observing the flood of concessionary-company workers at the turn of the century, drew attention to the 'health hazards of thatched huts being put up everywhere'.[104] The battle cry of safeguarding European health through population segregation was also sounded by the Mayor, who claimed that the removal of Africans from the town centre made 'the European areas considerably more healthy',[105] and by Governor-General Merlin who, in his speech to the opening session of the Executive Council of AEF in 1910, noted 'hygienic measures have been ordered for all towns' and 'these have been happily implemented for Brazzaville'.[106] Gabrielle Vassal, the wife of the Director of Health Services in the 1920s, also noted that Governor-General Merlin had emphasized the 'distancing of African areas' in a 'systematic' manner for 'reasons of hygiene'. She went on to reiterate the commonly held view that 'Europeans have every interest in living far from the natives, to "separate" themselves, and to "segregate" themselves in order to avoid tropical illnesses'.[107] Pressure on officials to introduce health regulations including residential segregation also came from the Pasteur Institute which had set up its Central African headquarters in Brazzaville in 1909.[108] The major concern guiding town planning apart from European notions of hygiene was malaria control. The prevailing theory at the turn of the century was that prevention was helped by distancing Europeans from malarial parasites carried by Africans and transmitted by mosquitoes, primarily during the night. Such issues took on greater urgency for officials with the arrival of more European families (see table 2).

Distance and natural barriers had, therefore, to be placed between white and indigenous populations. For the British, experience in India was the principal model, while the French drew their inspiration from North Africa where a segregated settlement existed in Algiers even before the conquest of 1830.[109] All over the tropical world, local populations were moved or new locations were developed for Europeans, preferably on high ground such as 'hill stations'. In towns such as Freetown and Lagos where an influential class of African property-owners was already entrenched, Europeans opened up new areas of town rather than alienate strong indigenous elites. In Brazzaville, where a well-established and self-conscious African elite was still in the making and where even the Senegalese lived in rudimentary housing, whites had no compunctions

Table 2   *European population of Brazzaville 1900–1962*

Date of Census	Men	Women	Children(a)	Total
January 1900	241	7	0	248
31 December 1913	485	67	21	573
July 1926	305	87	44	436
1 July 1927	428	126	76	630
31 December 1931	748	230	115	1,093
1 January 1936	541	214	154	909
31 December 1936	575	270	193	1,038
31 December 1938	609	331	244	1,184
1 April 1940	717	350	294	1,361
23 December 1940	663	313	219	1,195
1 January 1942	848	364	354	1,566
1 July 1944	802	383	338	1,523
1 July 1945	822	405	401	1,628
8 April 1946	1,033	593	672	2,298
1 July 1946	1,215	649	613	2,477
31 January 1947	1,367	847	777	2,991
1 July 1947	1,517	928	848	3,293
31 December 1947	1,526	940	865	3,331
30 June 1948	1,821	981	903	3,705
15 January 1949	1,893	1,064	1,009	3,966
30 June 1949	2,205	1,173	975	4,353
1 January 1950	2,649	1,350	1,091	5,090
1 March 1955	2,180	1,408	1,632	5,220
1 January 1962				6,135

(a) under 15; in 8 April 1946, under 20; in January, 1950, under 15; in 1955, under 20

Sources: 'Population européene de la Commune Mixte de Brazzaville de 1900 à 1950', *Annuaire statistique de l'Afrique Equatoriale Française*, vol. 1, 41; 'Recensement de la population non-autochtone de Brazzaville, March 1955', *Annuaire statistique de l'Afrique Equatoriale Française*, vol. 2, 1951–1955 (Brazzaville: Service de la Statistique, 1955), B1–16; Frey, 'Brazzaville, capitale de l'Afrique Equatoriale', 152; *Recensement de Brazzaville, 1961*, 11

about removing workers in accordance with their urban plan. Anyway, the upper crust of white society, the administrators and military officers, already occupied the prime spot on the Plateau with a magnificent view over the rapids.[110]

Explanations of the origins of segregation in Brazzaville have also focused on cultural issues based on Administrator Bonchamps' report which claimed that 'there is good reason to remove the two villages of Loango and Senegalese workers' since they 'are turbulent neighbours for the Residence'.[111] In his comprehensive and frequently quoted description of colonial Brazzaville from the European perspective, Roger Frey has taken this to refer to drumming and dancing which enraged whites, keeping them awake at nights and causing them to press for the removal of Africans from their vicinity. Gilles Sautter also notes that the 'influx of population had decided the public authorities to separate the European and African population' and that 'Europeans wanted to sleep and drummers kept them awake'.[112] There is certainly good evidence for this interpretation, for four years after Bonchamps' report, the administration did issue a draconian decree which imposed restrictions on drumming, affecting not only recreational dancing but also funeral rites and the celebrations for the end of mourning known as *matanga*. Not only was 'drumming and noisy dancing' limited in time and space, that is to hours prescribed by the administration and on the outskirts of the town, but Africans had to give advance notice and pay a fee, which was particularly resented, since it was set at a rate that was difficult for workers to meet.[113] The actual decree read:

Tams-tams and other noisy dances are formally forbidden within the urban perimeter of Brazzaville except in an area from the Felix Faure bridge to the Dutch House and from the so-called Glacière River to the Djoué river on the other side, where the tams-tams and other noisy dances will be authorized in exceptional cases on advance demand, and all natives who want to obtain such permission must pay a fee of five francs ... these dances can only be authorized once a week from 6 p.m. on Saturday until Sunday morning and any contravening of this decree will be punished by a fine and 1-5 days in prison or either of these.[114]

These spatial restrictions roughly corresponded to the areas that were later to be designated as Bacongo and Poto-Poto.

The whole question of 'turbulent' neighbourhoods needs to be explored at different levels, however, and beyond the cultural realm to the harsh realities of daily life. Riots by workers also forced drastic action by the authorities, and designing the locations of Bacongo and Poto-Poto was as much an effort to diffuse an explosive situation through reorganizing space as it was to satisfy European demands for a more prestigious, healthy and culturally pleasing colonial town.

The most serious problem facing African workers on a daily basis was hunger. Although those employed by the administration had rations as part of their pay, many had to spend a great deal of time finding food. Reports of undernourished and starving people are common in early accounts, and they continued as late as the 1920s. It was a problem created by colonialism. Having disrupted the pre-colonial exchange system which delivered food to the Pool markets, the administration was unable to ensure a supply itself. The difficulties that had dogged the town since its early days, when the nearest Tio villagers refused to supply the foodstuffs, continued. In 1900, Administrator Bonchamps reported: 'I have tried to get them to take up food cultivation but have hardly succeeded.' Faced with desperate pleas by concessionary companies, whose workers were deserting when faced with inadequate food supplies, Bonchamps reported to his Libreville superiors that 'to solve the problem, it is necessary to force villages at several days journey to bring manioc to sell at Brazzaville ... coercion and violence have been necessary'.[115] Militia parties were sent out into the Tio hinterland to forcibly requisition food, yet this was counterproductive. If the administration accused villagers of being 'apathetic' and 'uncooperative', the problem was all too often of their own making. One report noted that, 'the native's heart was no longer in the fields as it had been before. He could not forget the terrible years of rubber collection and famine. Even when he planted food for himself he was always afraid of seeing his sorghum and manioc requisitioned.'[116] At the same time, smugglers across the Pool defied the 1904 decree forbidding the export of manioc. The administration also found it hard to attract food supplies from producers to the south and west of the town, although it was in plentiful supply in local markets. After caravans with food were stopped and pillaged on the road to Brazzaville by desperate workers, women refused to bring their produce to town. As a counter-measure, the government introduced a decree making it illegal to stop porters carrying food destined for sale in the town 'on the roads or in the urban area', but this appears to have remained a dead letter.[117] Feeding children and workers was an ongoing problem even for the Catholic mission, which had the best-organized operation in the town. To some extent they 'solved' the problem through the labour of school children in the mission gardens and by sending their steamers upriver beyond the Pool to load up with fish, meat and manioc. But in 1901, 1903 and 1912, the missionaries had to send some children home because of lack of food and high prices.[118] The Mayor's report gives a glimpse of workers' conditions and the conflict brought by hunger and despair. Reviewing his term of office, he noted:

A large workforce was indispensable to ensure the good order of public services and the success of the many private enterprises in the capital. Now, in order to recruit workers easily and to avoid desertions which create havoc on the work sites, we had to feed our workers well. This workforce existed in Brazzaville, but its food supply was extremely difficult to ensure and was notoriously insufficient. The arrival of manioc was rare and there were very few caravans. *Chikouangue* or manioc bread, the basic food, currently sells for fifty centimes, and still we could not get what we needed. The market often seemed a scene of unimaginable disorder; barriers were broken down and convoys pillaged by the starving. The police often had to intervene and themselves undertake the allocation of food arriving in the market.[119]

Food riots reached their peak in 1911, yet the problem was by no means solved. Attempts to supplement government workers' diets through importing rice from Belgian Congo and Indochina had little success, since workers refused to accept rice in place of manioc bread, and some of them fell sick with beriberi. Faced with chronic desertion rates, the administrators sent police to requisition food from the main markets to feed Public Works employees, but to little effect.[120]

Having created the conditions for chaos and faced with the failure of their policies, the town administration turned to law-and-order measures. It was in this context, therefore, that the policy of spatial segregation was introduced. Bacongo and Poto-Poto were divided up into *quartiers* with appointed 'chiefs' responsible for upkeep, security, tax-collection, health control, policing 'vagabonds' and 'perpetrators of disorder', and providing *corvée* labour on demand. Every Sunday the chiefs met at the Mayor's office to discuss problems and receive further instructions.[121] Thus, the town government attempted to impose a more systematic surveillance of the town's population, while shifting the burden of responsibility to their African auxiliaries. The 'perfectly aligned streets' of the Christian villages as well as the discipline and inspection carried out by missionaries in the name of hygiene and order was a model for Bacongo and Poto-Poto. Furthermore, the kind of systematic police operation that could be mounted against a consolidated village had been shown in 1908, when fighting broke out in the Christian village of Notre Dame de la Merci. In a pre-dawn raid whip-wielding policemen had moved in, and suspects were rounded up, imprisoned and fined.[122]

Responses to removals varied greatly. While some workers were glad to exchange the squalid conditions of workers' camps for the chance to acquire plots of land and build more substantial houses, others resisted regimentation in their new 'villages' and efforts to mobilize them in activities such as street cleaning. 'Putting into practice these ideas met with numerous difficulties', the Mayor noted, and 'many police have been mobilized with little result.' The 'solution' to these problems, that is handing over the supervision of day-to-day matters to *quartiers* chiefs 'brought imperfect results' but was, nevertheless, 'a considerable improvement over the state of anarchy that had existed previously and allowed the administration's orders to be carried out more easily'.[123]

In the long run, the most significant result of spatial segregation was not the division of Brazzaville into European and African areas, although that was highly significant as long as colonial rule was in place. It was rather the division of the African population between Bacongo and Poto-Poto which corresponded in the official mind to pre-existing population divisions based on 'race'. Given the European mind-set, 'turbulence' in the town's population was perceived in 'tribal' terms and the 'solution' had to be fitted into a similar framework by giving different 'tribes' separate areas of the town in which to live. In so doing, Europeans fostered a new urban ethnicity whereby, as elsewhere in Africa, 'invented' labels could be appropriated by Africans and filled out through their own initiatives and imagination.[124]

Although it is indeed likely that food shortages might have caused migrant workers to gravitate for support towards those from the same region, and that casual labourers from the same area might be hired in gangs for specific projects, it was also the case that workers had previously lived in heterogeneous settlements around their places of work. Nor were populations clearly defined by language as much as administrators thought, for Kituba, which originated as a lingua franca among the traders and railway workers of lower Congo, was the dominant language on the north side of the Pool, spoken all over the town.[125] Swedish missionaries who arrived in 1911, knowing Kituba from their previous mission stations in the lower Congo, found that they could use that language in their work all over Brazzaville, in Poto-Poto as well as Bacongo.[126]

However, by creating Poto-Poto and Bacongo based on their perceptions of pre-existing 'tribes' and languages, Europeans channelled migrant workers to specific parts of the town where others from the same region lived (see map 4). The very name Bacongo, as well as its location on the south side of the town, indicated that it was to be for people from the Pool and the lower Congo region, while Poto-Poto, located to the north of the town was reserved for 'people from the upper river' and foreigners such as those from West Africa and Gabon. The tidy nature of these arrangements, in the European mind, was summed up by Governor-General Merlin, who told his Executive Council: 'The natives now have their own *quartiers* according to their race.'[127] Each household head received an identity card from the Mayor's office stating his 'race' and the number of people in the household. All men in wage employment, or who paid taxes, also had to produce their cards, which the Mayor noted was 'a means of efficiently controlling the coming and going of individuals'.[128] Even the process of choosing a 'race' must have been filled with ambiguities for early migrants, for a label such as 'Bondjo' was a figment of the European imagination and the term 'Bangala' was also of recent origin, taken on by people between the Congo and Ubangi to distinguish

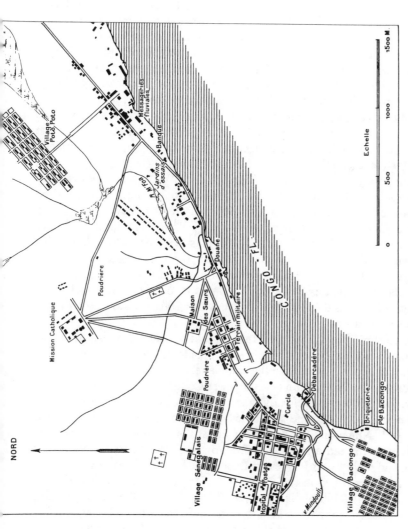

4   Plan of Brazzaville, 1911 (reproduced from Roger Frey, 'Brazzaville, capitale de l'Afrique Equatoriale Française', 1954)

themselves from their neighbours in the eyes of whites, and broadened in its use at the Pool to denote all workers coming from the north.[129]

In the long term, language also played a significant role in shaping the distinct identities of Poto-Poto and Bacongo. In Brazzaville, as elsewhere in Africa, missionaries made some crucial decisions which privileged certain languages over others and helped familiarize people with a new lingua franca. Since their arrival in the upper Congo, the Holy Ghost Fathers had worked in stations along the Ubangi river and had started to use Lingala in their work. With the establishment of Poto-Poto for the 'people from the upper river', Monseigneur Augouard decided to split the Brazzaville work in two with Kikongo- and Kituba-speaking priests given responsibility for Bacongo and others told to start learning Lingala for the work in Poto-Poto.[130] The language policy was hardly plucked out of thin air, but as already noticed, it simplified a complex situation as many languages, including Kituba, were spoken in Poto-Poto at the time. The effect of missionaries in contributing to perceptions of ethnicity and language should not be minimized, especially when coupled with official policy. By the eve of the First World War, missionaries claimed that about a third to a half of the town's population were baptized Catholics, while the mission youth club was drawing hundreds of young people after mass on Sunday and after work.[131] In 1914, the missionaries reported 3,000 in attendance at Sunday masses at the cathedral, and this is consistent with other accounts both in the mission records and by observers. Masses were said in French, Lingala and Kituba. In 1913, the Catholic missionaries reported the success of their work with the 'Bangalas' (that is those in Poto-Poto), with 1,200 baptized Catholics and 1,700 catechumens.[132]

Finally, in their division of the population, the administration was guided by its perceptions of how the 'people of the lower Congo' and those from upriver fitted into the colonial economy. The identification of those from the Pool region and the lower Congo as the main local source of skilled workers had already taken place. Noting that 'the Balalis and Basundis quickly became auxiliaries of our occupation', Mayor Girard went on: 'Numerous Bakongos are agents of European factories; they know how to read and write sufficiently to keep inventories and order stock and have a keen interest in their work.'[133] This emerging elite were now to be separated in their own part of the town, and furthermore, in an effort to 'stabilize' this part of the workforce, the administration encouraged 'Bakongo' workers to bring their wives to their new housing in Bacongo.[134] On the other hand, Poto-Poto, had a much more heterogeneous population. It included foreigners such as the West Africans, other Central Africans and a growing crowd of casual labourers coming off the boats from upriver, who often ended up in such administrative categories as 'vagrants' and 'prostitutes', or the 'floating population' of the town. These people were perceived as potentially dangerous, not only because they were difficult to control as they came and went from the town, but because their socialization and acculturation to colonial order was weaker than that of populations who lived on the Bacongo side of town.

By the eve of the First World War, the modern contours of Brazzaville were in place. Space had been divided up on an administrator's drawing board. In tracing lines on the town plan, however, colonial officials had created an urban space whose long-term social impact they may not have fully realized, for Africans took over space and made it meaningful. As Cooper has argued, 'society not only shapes space, space shapes society'.[135]

Conclusion

In just over three decades of French rule, a small town had come into existence on the north banks of the Pool. The pre-colonial economy of the Pool had been overtaken by the arrival of concessionary companies. The Tio who had orchestrated trade for over three centuries had been marginalized, although they continued their independent economy on the Mbe plateau and profiting from smuggling in the waters that they had once controlled. A small but influential group of foreign and local elites had established themselves as auxiliaries to a growing number of European administrators, businessmen, missionaries and soldiers. Some workers were well integrated into town life, although they and their families maintained strong ties with the rural areas.

While Europeans designed the colonial town for their own ends, which were in part to do with pressures from African workers, they aided the creation of identities shaped by new boundaries of space, language and class. The distinction of Poto-Poto and Bacongo was consolidated by the tendency of most people to spend leisure hours on the side of town where they lived. Severe logistical problems had been created through the long distances that separated different parts of the town. Instead of living close to the workplace, many had to spend a great deal of time and energy just getting to and from work. Inhabitants of Poto-Poto who worked for the administration or as domestic servants had to allow at least forty minutes to walk to offices and residences on the Plateau, while those in Bacongo who worked for the concessionary companies on the Plaine had the same problem. And many had to repeat the return journey twice, since they went home during a two-hour lunchbreak and returned in the afternoon. As the town expanded, women also had to walk further and further to their gardens. Five kilometres separated Bacongo from Poto-Poto - thus, when an individual arrived home from work, he or she hardly bothered to walk back to the other side of the town in search of sociability or recreation, and at times such coming and going was controlled by curfews, since it involved walking through the European part of town after dark. Occasionally, on Sundays or for special events, people might make the cross-town trek. While not suggesting that where one lives is a definitive factor in the creation of identity, there is no question that in colonial Brazzaville, the distinction between living in Poto-Poto or Bacongo was significant, especially in the later colonial period when a politicized ethnicity emerged.

2 TAKING HOLD OF THE TOWN, 1915–1960

Brazzaville's development as a thriving colonial capital was long delayed. Equatorial Africa remained near the bottom of France's colonial priorities until 1940 when General de Gaulle, casting about for a piece of French soil to legitimize the existence of Free France, found it on the banks of the Congo river. Communications with the global economy were improved with the opening of the Congo-Océan railway linking Brazzaville to Pointe-Noire in 1934. The actual construction was a severe drain on AEF's thin population and economic resources. In the years after the Second World War, when Brazzaville received capital for several large construction projects, the town became a magnet for workers and young people from rural areas seeking schooling and employment.

Between the world wars, a permanent town population with a keen awareness of their needs and aspirations came into being. Over the first four decades of the century, the number of immigrants who arrived and stayed increased, although they also maintained strong links with rural areas, particularly those who came from the Pool, Boko and Mindouli regions. Swedish missionary schoolteachers in the late 1930s continued to find that school-children, especially girls, from the Pool and lower Congo districts tended to disappear in the wet season, when they returned to their family land with their mothers to work in farming. Furthermore, the allegiance of the Lari who lived in Brazzaville to André Matswa, a nationalist agitator in the eyes of the French, was sustained in the face of persecution through support from rural chiefs.[1]

After the Second World War, immigration reached a fever pitch, with women and children joining male family members in the town. Between 1948 and 1960, as Brazzaville's population tripled, sub-communities based on recreational activities were significant in building social networks and developing a consciousness of place in the urban milieu (see table 1).[2] The number of Europeans also increased, associated with railway construction in the 1920s and the surge of public and private investment immediately after the Second World War. With improved housing, health care and schooling in the European town, more women and children arrived (see table 2).[3] While Governor-Generals Antonetti (1924–34) and Reste (1935–9) launched urbanization plans which aimed at better cross-town communications and the 'beautification' of the white town, Africans living in Poto-Poto and Bacongo shaped their surroundings to suit their needs, which at times meant contesting European encroachments and definitions of legal and illegal space.

Economy and population

Forty years after its establishment as a colonial post, Brazzaville was still a small commercial, military and administrative centre. In 1921, it was the headquarters of four large companies and thirteen smaller trading houses which had survived the First World War. African workers were employed in much the same kind of work as they had been earlier in the century. Much of the interior was still in the grip of the 'pillage economy' imposed by the remaining concessionary companies which, in the face of increasing outrage in France, were finally phased out by 1930.[4]

Mayor Girard's report had been both premature and self-serving in its optimistic tone concerning urban development. Furthermore, the weak economy was made worse by the First World War, whose impact was similar to that of the huge expeditionary forces of the late nineteenth century. Just as these had drained resources from Brazzaville's struggling economy and harassed local people, so did military operations during the war. As the AEF capital was the command centre for the defence of the 3,000 kilometre frontier between the French colony and German Kamerun, Brazzaville's residents again experienced the ebb and flow of men and supplies. The provisioning of soldiers at the military camp accentuated the long-standing problem of food supplies in the capital.[5] In 1916, 3,000 African and 200 European soldiers were repatriated from the campaign, which by then was essentially won. Nothing had been done to prepare for their arrival, and in the face of a potential mutiny, starving troops were let loose on Bacongo and Poto-Poto to fend for themselves. Gardens were pillaged, women with provisions attacked, houses looted, and traders too scared to go to the market. The economy was further weakened by transportation problems. Fewer ships arrived in the Atlantic and the army requisitioned available river transport to carry men and supplies to the front.[6]

Many workers left town to escape recruitment and taxes, which were increased to compensate for a decline in other sources of revenue. Anti-German propaganda and preparation, which included a line of cannons along the Pool, were almost too successful as they seemed to confirm rumours of an imminent German invasion. The fearful fled and others only stopped long enough to pick up uniforms and advance pay before disappearing into the bush. The colonial authorities set up surveillance posts along the frontiers with Belgian Congo but they could not stem desertions and flight. In 1918, misery was compounded by the Spanish influenza epidemic which killed several hundred Africans and seventeen Europeans.[7] Altogether, 1,775 recruits from Moyen-Congo went to war. On their return, veterans with experience of European town life introduced new tastes in fashion, music and dance, and demanded more leisure amenities.[8]

After the war, as concessionary companies petered out or were forced out by economic and political pressures in France, AEF experienced a 'belated spurt' of public investment.[9] The newly appointed Minister of Colonies, Albert Sarraut, argued that colonial investment would benefit France as well as subject populations. Concerning Central Africa, he also noted: 'The history of AEF is short and melancholy ... the hour has come when, for the sake of our national prestige, we need to show to our English neighbours in Nigeria and our Belgian neighbours in Congo that we are capable of developing this vast territory and justifying our occupation and rule of it.' In particular, Sarraut argued that public capital must be granted for the railway on which Equatorial Africa's future depended.[10] In 1921, the work was begun. For AEF administrations it became an all-consuming passion for which thousands of African lives and other economic projects were sacrificed.[11]

Once the Brazzaville section of the railway was complete, the main function of the town was as a 'sorting point' for workers transported on river boats from Chad and Ubangi-Shari or marched overland from other regions of Moyen-Congo. At the height of railway building through the Mayombe forests and mountains, camps for workers in transit were set up near Mpila and Poto-Poto. Men stayed for three weeks for health checks, vaccinations and 'acclimatization' before being sent to the main work site. The whole operation was run by the military to counter high desertion rates among workers who ran away and hid with sympathizers in Poto-Poto. Supervisors tried to cut down on this seepage of labour by imposing a 7 p.m. curfew and prohibiting workers from going into the nearby European business district on the Plaine. In the years 1930–2, the average number of workers in the two camps was about 1,100, with the men, already weakened by months of travel, crowded together in poor conditions.[12] At the same time, refugees from labour recruiters in lower Congo fled to Brazzaville to hide in Poto-Poto and Bacongo, as news of the horrific conditions on the Mayombe construction sites and the high death-rates among workers filtered through.

Conditions in Brazzaville's African areas were already tense at a time when the Depression had thrown many out of work. A report from the last part of 1932 noted that there were 2,117 out of work in Bacongo and Poto-Poto. These numbers were probably low given the notorious problems of census counts.[13] A further problem for the population was increased taxation between 1929 and 1933, imposed to compensate for a decline in customs receipts but affecting the population when many were unemployed and could least afford it.[14] In 1934, according to official estimates, 70 per cent of those unemployed were young, single men who had come to town on their own and were without family.[15] As people met to discuss their problems and develop strategies for survival, articles about 'communist agitators' and 'vagrants' appeared in the newly established European newspaper, *L'Etoile de l'AEF.* They urged the government to extend its surveillance of the population, and the administration responded with a census, identity cards to register those with the right to live in the town and new barracks for the militia in Poto-Poto and Bacongo.[16] Among the autonomous activities that fell under suspicion as a cover for popular agitators were local football teams.[17]

As the AEF economy was beginning a mild upswing following the completion of the CFCO and the end of the Depression, the Second World War broke out. Developments in Brazzaville are well documented, but mostly through a narrow political lens.[18] Rather less has been written about the experience of ordinary people. What seems to persist in the popular memory is a dual tale of de Gaulle's heroics overlaid upon popular suffering. As in the case of the First World War, rumour informed people, since the government censors suppressed news from Europe. According to one man: 'The French talked about it at table and the "boy" would listen. Even if they could not understand everything, they heard something and reported this. Cooks, waiters and clerks were the main sources of information until France capitulated and it was announced on the radio.'[19] After that, Europeans started to talk with African elites about German atrocities. Propaganda to encourage enlistment portrayed the Germans as about to appear on the Congo river. 'People fled into the bush because they were afraid of the war. They said that Hitler was coming.'[20]

In Brazzaville, where de Gaulle appeared on several occasions to make key speeches, he became a living legend as the great deliverer from the threat of Nazi conquest. 'His name was on everyone's lips,' said one informant.[21] 'He delivered Brazzaville from Hitler,' agreed two women, remembering the war.[22] De Gaulle was *mokondzi ya etumba*, or a 'powerful warrior' (Lingala, 'chief of battles'). He appeared with arms upraised in victory on the most expensive wax prints. His image was sculpted in dance masks. After his visit to Poto-Poto and Bacongo in 1942, young men performing kyébé-kyébé puppet-dances produced a uniformed de Gaulle as a puppet. Stories that imagined the power of the French leader through local idioms were legion: de Gaulle could turn himself into a beautiful woman and seduce the opposing generals; Hitler sent planes to destroy the capital but de Gaulle caused the town to disappear; when de Gaulle spoke to the troops each man could hear the words in his native tongue.[23] Some intellectuals and nationalists had a different view, however; one writer suggested that de Gaulle had become a 'capitalist fetish'.[24]

As in the case of the First World War, there was an underside to popular experience, remembered by those who lived through it. 'During the War, Brazzaville was completely dominated by fear,' said one informant who was seventeen when the war broke out. 'There was forced enlistment of soldiers.'[25] In the villages around Brazzaville, 'the sight of a red fez sent people scurrying into the bush'. During the war harassment by the militia reached new peaks and they earned the name *mbulu-mbulu* (Lingala, 'jackal'). Men sought medicines that might protect them against recruitment.[26]

Concerning the experience of workers, there are parallel stories. One version emphasizes job opportunities on war-related projects. The population of Poto-Poto increased by 3,000 as workers arrived for construction projects such as improvements at the river port, an officers' training school, temporary housing for troops *en route* to North Africa and communications improvements. Several hundred jobs were also created at a government factory to produce military uniforms. Other memories relate to the burdens of war, and especially those carried by women. With plantation rubber supplies from Latin America and the Far East cut off, the government reintroduced forced wild rubber gathering, notorious in popular memory through the tyranny of concessionary companies earlier in the century. The wild rubber campaign reached its peak around 1943. Porters arrived in Brazzaville each day, delivering loads of vines to the prison yard where processing took place.[27] 'African women suffered terribly during the war,' said one Catholic nun who lived in Brazzaville at the time. 'They were rounded up in Poto-Poto and Bacongo and taken with their mortars and pestles to process the rubber. They had to pound and boil it. I cried to see them.'[28] Other women spoke of the rubber processing, too: 'Women suffered a lot here.' One added: 'There were shameful things that happened. I can't speak about it.'[29] Imported goods such as salt, cloth, matches and soap were scarce.[30] 'Life was very expensive and there was a great shortage of goods.' 'You had to be a French citizen or be an *évolué* to have a ration card. I did not understand and I never applied.' 'We didn't have a ration card for bread.'[31]

After the Second World War, Brazzaville received grants from the colonial government which allowed it to take on the appearance of a modern city. French policy linked development of the franc zone as a self-sufficient economic system with national recovery, and the government put into operation an overseas development programme through FIDES (*Fonds d'investissement et de développement économique et social des territoires d'outre-mer*).[32] A ten-year social and economic development plan allowed Brazzaville 'to modernize before one's very eyes', according to Roger Frey, assistant to the Mayor at the time.[33] Large public works projects such as an airport, new port facilities at Mpila, a hydro-electric scheme on the Djoué river, a new hospital and other public buildings created jobs and drew workers from the countryside. At Mpila, there were a few small factories for manufacturing tobacco, shoes, soap and drinks. Some of the wartime installations remained, such as a uniform factory which was converted into making civilian clothes such as uniforms for football teams and Scouts. A powerful transmitter, received from the United States in 1943 as a means of beaming the voice of Free France to all parts of Africa and Europe, now carried a variety of programmes. By the 1950s, Latin American music, jazz and Congo guitar band music were being broadcast locally and heard on short-wave radios in West Africa.[34]

If a rapid and visible transformation took place over a few years, it did not have much substance in generating solid and permanent jobs. The problem was stated in a five-yearly report by Monseigneur Biéchy of the Catholic mission in 1955. The post-war 'prosperity' of the town had been hollow since it was based not on local industry but on administrative and commercial construction needs, he noted. Once these projects were completed, high unemployment set in.[35] In 1953, almost half the adult male workers were unemployed.[36] Yet rural-to-urban migration, especially by young people, did not stop. Data from interviews suggest some reasons for continued rapid urban population growth in spite of high unemployment. According to Georges Balandier, expectations of a better life brought people to the town in spite of the reality. In Bacongo and Poto-Poto, informants gave as their principal reasons for leaving villages: the attraction of the wage-labour market and the hope of accumulating goods with which to enhance social position; lack of wage employment in rural areas; joining family already in the town; education; and the perception of the town as a 'place of refuge', free from family constraints or problems relating to crimes and witchcraft accusations.[37] Marcel Soret, who carried out an investigation associated with the first reliable census in 1951 in the midst of a 'fever of immigration', had similar findings. Among young men, the great majority came to find work (56 per cent) or to join family members with a view to finding work; others emphasized schooling (7 per cent). But there was also the pervasive perception among young people that the town was a place of independence from the authoritarian structures of rural family life, and a place where life would be easier and more fun on account of the great variety of entertainment. Whereas men tended to emphasize work, young women came primarily to join their husbands or to be married to men who had preceded them. In Bacongo, 85 per cent of the women interviewed gave these reasons, while 14 per cent came to join other family members, and 1 per cent came for education.[38]

Thus, in the last fifteen years of colonial rule, the Brazzaville population tripled, from around 41,000 in 1945 to around 134,000 at the time of independence in 1960. The population was youthful, with an average age in Bacongo in 1951 of nineteen for women and twenty-three for men. In 1961, it was eighteen for women and nineteen for men. In the last decade of colonial rule, more women than men arrived, so that by independence their numbers in the population were almost equal. For Bacongo the ratios of women to men were 885:1,000 in 1951, and 911:1,000 in 1961; and for Poto-Poto, 685:1,000 in 1951, and 938:1,000 in 1961.[39]

If the late colonial period was a time of unemployment for many in the population, it was a period of prosperity for some. Several factors contributed to the development of a much more highly stratified society than had previously existed.

Due to lack of French investment in Equatorial Africa schooling had been rudimentary throughout the colonial period. The prominent role of the Catholic church in Brazzaville can partly be explained through its virtual monopoly of education and youth organizations well into the 1920s. West Africans, Gabonese and workers from Belgian Congo continued to be significant in the workforce as late as 1938, since employers continued to hire them in positions that needed literacy and certain technical skills. There were still no qualified African teachers, only monitors in the Brazzaville schools.[40] The demand for literate workers was so great that a young man with one or two years of education could drop out of the church school and promptly find work with the administration or trading companies.[41] In 1939, only 300 Africans in the whole of AEF had primary education certificates. The only government school in the colony that offered post-primary education, the Ecole Edouard Renard, was opened in 1935. In that year it had ten pupils, compared to 930 pupils in eight similar schools in French West Africa. In other words the system in Equatorial Africa was about twenty-five years behind that of West Africa.[42]

A stated goal of the development plan was 'to separate out an African elite whom AEF needs in order to raise itself to the level of a modern country'.[43] This was to be the catalyst for the rapid post-war political and social transformation of Brazzaville's elites and explains part of its attraction for young people. After the war, several secondary schools for boys were opened in order to provide future civil servants. By the 1940s, also, the Sisters of Saint Joseph of Cluny could report that hundreds of girls were receiving primary education 'in response to the demand by young men for educated wives' and, in the last few years before independence, the nuns opened a secondary school for girls with funds from the colonial government.[44] Some elites owed their social positions to new roles as political, trade union and local government leaders.[45] These promotions, especially in the civil servants' ranks, where African functionaries were integrated with Europeans by the 1950s, led to 'a spectacular development of a *petite bourgeoisie*', a social group 'with good salaries and money to spend'.[46]

Although delving into such matters as Brazzaville's development or underdevelopment, its population size and related issues of class, age and gender, may seem to be an overlong detour from the main themes of this book, such data actually provide the essential context for the study of leisure. Issues of economy, society and culture are inextricably intertwined. Leisure, as we have noted, is about what one can afford, about personal taste and about creating new cultural forms to suit personal and community needs. Thus, the amenities and institutions that developed in the town were deeply affected by the nature of its population. Leisure is also about the shaping and negotiation of urban space, and this is the subject to which we now return.

Shaping space

Against the dramatic backdrop of the Congo-Océan construction, the Depression, the world wars and erratic employment, ordinary people incrementally came to terms with town life. A great deal of power was clearly in the hands of those who ran the town and imposed regulations. However, such measures were often responses to the initiatives of Bacongo and Poto-Poto dwellers, who transformed their surroundings into their own social and cultural space.

For the first three decades or so of Brazzaville's existence, a great deal of energy had to be given over to the material side of life. Workers were too transient or too hungry or too concerned with the logistics of survival to do much in the way of adapting their environment. As noted in the previous chapter, Christians and their mentors at the Catholic mission were most successful in clearing the land and constructing buildings that marked their presence and power. On the eve of the First World War, other buildings, symbolizing the major institutions of colonial power had appeared on the Plateau and along the waterfront. As Raymond Betts has noted in his study of French colonial architecture, such structures conveyed a 'sense of permanency'. Individual Europeans might come and go, but multi-storeyed buildings of brick, wood, iron and stone, and later of reinforced concrete, showed that the colonial rulers intended to stay.[47]

The process of designing a colonial capital had not proceeded much beyond segregation, however, when the First World War imposed its demands. Descriptions from the early 1920s describe shoddy houses and modest colonial buildings scattered around an untamed landscape. In European accounts, the best that could be said was that 'Brazzaville is like a large park, with scattered trees and flowers', or that it had 'magnificent natural surroundings' which were 'not diminished' by the poor and unpretentious state of the buildings. Although segregation had been instituted a couple of decades earlier, the various parts of the town had not been joined in an integrated plan, and negotiating streams, ravines, marshes and snakes was still a major undertaking for those who had to cross the town to work. The single main road laid out in 1910 to join the Plateau to the Plaine was a sea of mud in the rainy season.[48]

Although mostly immersed in the challenge of railway building, Antonetti decided to take this situation in hand. As the terminus of the Congo-Océan line, Brazzaville had a large role to play in his future vision of AEF. Colonial officials who had served in towns such as Saigon, Tunis or Fez were wont to make comparisons with the poor conditions that they found in the Congo capital, and Antonetti was no exception. In explaining his plans for the capital, the Governor-General acknowledged his debt to General Lyautey of Morocco, whose urban planning was a model for French officials in other African towns.

As Lyautey had created a 'zone of separation' between the European and 'native' towns for health and security reasons, so Antonetti proposed to complete the segregation of the town's population started by his predecessors. In a speech to the Governing Council of AEF, he declared the need to 'resolutely distance the native villages from the white town'. His vision of Poto-Poto and Bacongo was the mirror image of that of Governor-General Merlin almost twenty years earlier. Social order was equated with physical order. The two African districts 'are perfect in their conception and realization', he explained to a visitor, 'vast rectangular spaces separated by broad streets that lead to a central avenue. The enclosures are of uniform size and are lined along the street symmetrically.' The poor quality of African building materials and the pouring of resources into the European town rather than into improvements in Bacongo and Poto-Poto was raised to an aesthetic principle in the official discourse. In Poto-Poto and Bacongo, 'the houses are built of traditional African materials, square and spacious and lead on to a yard managed by the family', said Antonetti. Finally, 'each race has its own area to avoid collision or conflict. The population is clean, well-clothed, hard-working and visibly disciplined.'[49] In the 1920s, administration workers destroyed two remaining blackspots, the 'Bangala' Christian village of Mariage near the Plaine, and Dakar, a village of Senegalese workers on the Plateau. Their inhabitants were sent to live in Poto-Poto in the sections reserved for their respective 'races'.

The significance of race in the official mind was demonstrated as much by the exception as by the rule, since the only village allowed to remain self-contained was the Christian village of Saint Firmin, created for Euro-Africans by Monseigneur Guichard, Augouard's successor at the Catholic mission. A joint social engineering project of the missionaries who supervised the village and French administrators who granted land, the goal was 'to protect the households of young *métis* from the vices of Poto-Poto and Bacongo'.[50] After the First World War, the Catholic Sisters and Fathers had opened special schools for children of European fathers and African mothers, many of them fathered by soldiers at the military base. While feeling a special responsibility to these children, European missionaries also believed their moral fibre to be suspect given the circumstances of their conception. The plan was, therefore, to keep these children separate from the potentially contaminating influence of the Poto-Poto and Bacongo inhabitants in their formative years, to marry them off to each other and to settle the couples at Saint Firmin. Andrée Blouin, the child of a French father and a mother from the Ubangi-Shari region, who was left at the convent by her parents when she was three years old, had a biting explanation of the project in her autobiography, namely:

Uniting these two like aberrations of the species, however, did not provide all the necessary safeguards against their potential for disrupting things. Their presence as a couple in this black and white society tended to present questions without comfortable answers. Obviously, the best thing would be to keep all of this third species together and removed, for the most part from the rest of the system.

In her opinion, the village was part of 'a diabolical plan to keep the couples of mixed blood under the surveillance of the Catholic missions forever'. Taken to visit Saint Firmin by the Sisters when she was ten years old, she found it 'repellent', and rejected such 'a made-to-order marriage' at the hands of her missionary sponsors in favour of leaving the convent school and making her own way in Poto-Poto.[51]

With segregation now complete, those in power launched a plan to fine-tune the shaping of space. With a subsidy from the Minister of Colonies, the town administration proceeded to implement town plans developed first by Antonetti and then by Governor-General Reste, who also set up an Urbanization Commission and a municipal Architecture Service to oversee 'improvements'. By 1928, so much road and building construction had been initiated that a visitor noted: "The capital, so long neglected, today gives the impression of a vast construction site.'[52] Writing enthusiastically in the widely read periodical, *Le Monde Colonial Illustré*, and comparing the Brazzaville of the past and present, one eyewitness noted that the 'town on paper' had become the 'town of action'.[53] Marshes were drained and roads were upgraded with a stone base to facilitate the passage of the few motor cars that had made their appearance. New buildings included a railway station at the terminus of the Congo-Océan line, an African hospital, a technical school, and primary schools in Poto-Poto and Bacongo (see map 5).

Segregation was now carried a stage further with plans to 'beautify' the European part of the town. The arrival of white women with a great deal of leisure time to fill, and children who needed to be entertained with such standard French activities as outings in the park, gave some impetus to town planning. European visitors from Léopoldville also continued to motivate efforts to clean up and make elegant the Equatorial African capital. In 1931, the town budget included funds to employ two African foremen and twenty workers to plant trees and bushes and to lay out and maintain gardens, parks and squares. A 1933 report noted that in four months 1,500 flowering bushes and mango trees had been planted, many of them along main roads so as to create tree-lined boulevards. Gutters had also been installed for better drainage.[54] The difference between the European town and Poto-Poto and Bacongo became increasingly marked. As the Congolese historian Scholastique Dianzinga has noted, 'European space was privileged space' which benefited from the investment of scarce resources. The contrast with Bacongo and Poto-Poto which were 'almost forgotten in terms of material improvements' was 'flagrant'.[55]

Further leisure amenities included a large park with a bandstand and tennis courts overlooking the Pool by the Place Savorgnan de Brazza. Statues of colonial worthies were long discussed but slow to appear due to lack of funds. Once again, the Catholic mission was the pace-setter. A statue of Monseigneur Augouard was unveiled before large crowds, who were entertained with bands and a fireworks display. Finally, in 1944, an

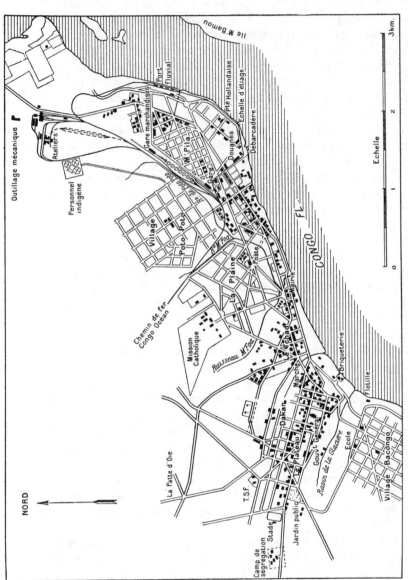

5 Plan of Brazzaville, 1933 (reproduced from Roger Frey. 'Brazzaville, capitale de l'Afrique Equatoriale Française', 1954)

ornamental lighthouse in honour of Brazza was inaugurated by his daughter on a promontory above the Pool. Plaques to commemorate the famous explorer and other colonial heroes were also installed on official buildings as they were received from a Paris association, *Le Souvenir Colonial Français*, which raised money for suitably engraved plaques to be dispatched to the colonies for installation at appropriate points.[56]

Faced with the embarrassment of entertaining Léopoldville athletic teams without a proper stadium, something the Belgian colonial capital had had for several years, the exclusive white social club, the Club Athlètique Brazzavillois (CAB), received funds from the administration to build the town's first sports ground. A football match between a CAB team and the '*Coqs*', a European team from Léopoldville, inaugurated the Marchand Stadium in 1927 with the Governor-General in attendance.[57] In the 1930s, another exclusive European social club, the 'Caïmans', opened a private swimming pool, while a small airfield put Brazzaville on the map for the aeroplanes that hopped across Africa from Paris. For their evening activities, Europeans had a selection of hotels and restaurants to choose from in the Plateau and Plaine districts.[58]

The crowning achievement in the development of leisure amenities for the white population, however, was the construction of a scenic road, nostalgically called La Corniche (after seaside highways in towns such as Nice). Winding its way for 8 kilometres along the river banks, at 50 to 80 metres above the thundering Kintamo rapids, the road gave access to views of magnificent grandeur in the heart of Africa. Here, in the cool of the evening, Europeans in their rickshaws or motor cars could look across to Léopoldville-Kinshasa and Mbamu Island or, turning inland, could see the sweep of the capital from Bacongo in the south-west to Poto-Poto in the north-east, with the Tio plateau on the distant horizon.[59]

As Europeans were imagining and making a reality of their colonial capital, the inhabitants of Poto-Poto and Bacongo were coming to terms with these arrangements and envisioning their own urban improvements in spite of their limited means. In the crisis of the Depression, the necessities of African life collided with the demands of European leisure, for among those most affected by the spreading tentacles of the white town were the women, who saw prime farmland gobbled up for new roads, parks and sports facilities.

After the havoc of the First World War, Brazzaville's food supply was more stable but not always adequate, and workers still went hungry. Jean de Puytorac, who arrived as a company agent in 1920, noted that passengers who disembarked from the steamer from Bangui looked much healthier and better fed than his thin employees.[60] The African community was 'never sufficiently provisioned' in the opinion of Gabrielle Vassal, who noted that fighting frequently broke out in the marketplace over food supplies.[61] Continued Tio resistance to incorporation into the colonial economy also perpetuated food problems. An administrator reported to the Governor-General in 1926 that 'the Makoko has not provided us with a single worker nor has he collaborated in any way in the provisioning of Brazzaville; he has not undertaken any agriculture'.[62]

The food situation had, however, gradually improved due to two factors. One was the response of farmers in the nearby Pool, Mindouli and Boko regions to market opportunities. Profits from the sale of manioc in the town had been used to buy knives and aluminium basins which facilitated farming and increased production. Administrators in the Pool district reported 'immense plantations' for provisioning the town. Furthermore, as the colonial administration became entrenched, it was able to cut down on highway robbers and provide more secure access for porters carrying food to the town. The construction of the railway also improved the transportation of food from rural areas south of the capital.[63]

These supplies, in themselves, could not feed the Brazzaville workforce, however. Furthermore, with prices rising due to the arrival of more Europeans and rising demand created by workers in CFCO camps, many could not afford to buy food. The situation had also been improved by women who lived permanently in the town opening up gardens on patches of land in order to feed their families. Given the fragile balance of supply and demand, the administration had positively encouraged these activities and turned a blind eye when farmers strayed onto unused land in the European town. In a memorandum to the Mayor of Brazzaville, Antonetti discussed the problem of obtaining sufficient manioc for the daily rations of administration workers and soldiers. 'In no case must bread be given to women,' he wrote. 'The cultivation of gardens by women must be encouraged to compensate for poor supplies.'[64] All over the town, in the many empty spaces, marshlands and nooks and crannies along the river banks, urban agriculture flourished. Women also cut firewood for household use and sale.

Having applauded these efforts in the 1920s, the administration changed its mind a few years later as they set about more stringently enforcing the boundaries of European and African space, in pursuit of their 'beautification' policy. With the building of roads and parks, many women found their gardens jeopardized, yet they were reluctant to open up new areas on the urban perimeter, for that involved walking greater distances with their loads. In order to clarify the position, at least in the minds of whites, the Mayor passed several new ordinances to define 'legal' and 'illegal' space more clearly. For example, "the planting of gardens and the cutting of trees for a hundred metres on either side of a municipal road is forbidden'.

For African families, the crackdown came just when the Depression was taking its toll on wage-earners. Workers were forced into all kinds of strategies in order to survive. Some left town for the rural areas or went to look for work in Pointe-Noire, where the new port was under construction. Robberies in the European sections of the town increased; others 'lived off their friends and hoped for one day of work'.[65] Some of the unemployed, who were accustomed to buying food, now became producers, collecting palm-oil, or catching and smoking fish. Women increased illicit beer-brewing and young women engaged in prostitution to help support their families. Men also joined female family members in market gardening in order to pay their taxes.[66]

The European authorities approved farming by the unemployed in principle, but in practice they opposed some of the places where African farmers chose to open up new land. Farming beyond Poto-Poto and Bacongo was prohibited because it was an area not patrolled by the militia.[67] On the other hand, areas close to the roads were 'unsightly' in European eyes, and choice areas along the river which were farmed by Bacongo women had been made 'illegal' with the building of the Corniche. This tussle over uses of space went on for several months. Finally, the administration decided to make some examples by prosecuting offenders. In one incident in 1932, twenty-one individuals appeared in court charged with 'having made plantations along the Corniche, in spite of having been forbidden to do so by the Chief Administrator of the Autonomous Subdivision of Brazzaville'. Two others were charged with resisting arrest and 'causing a scandal on the public road'.[68] In spite of being prosecuted and fined, farmers seem to have continued to defy the administration where possible. A short time later the Lieutenant-Governor of Moyen-Congo again complained to the Mayor about local farmers and demanded that he take further action, writing: 'It seems to me that those who live in Bacongo, especially the women, have poorly understood the ordinances concerning the protection of trees along the roads, as well as those in the forest reserves.'[69] The Mayor agreed that the 'destruction' of wooded areas around the capital had taken place in defiance of town regulations and that some places, that were favourite locations for European outings (*promenades*) were in danger of losing their 'tourist attraction'. He assured his superiors that 'the strictest surveillance' would be imposed and that African chiefs in

Bacongo and Poto-Poto would be told to 'strictly control farming in order to protect trees and land along the roads'.[70]

African priorities also clashed with those of the municipal authorities over rubbish disposal. Since the early days of Poto-Poto and Bacongo, the administration had tried to impose its version of cleanliness and neatness on the African population. Here was an issue *par excellence*, through which prevailing European notions of Africans as dirty and undisciplined could be worked out. While householders kept their yards swept clean, they resisted demands for *corvée* labour to clean the streets of Poto-Poto and Bacongo in their free time.[71] Again, the Mayor's frustration is revealed in his report that 'refusal by workers to help clean the roads and squares in their villages' was 'solely due to laziness'. Due to lack of co-operation, 'rubbish accumulates in an unsightly manner'. The issue had remained unresolved, for in spite of 'numerous recriminations' and 'a large number of police mobilized' there had been little improvement. With the failure of the stick approach, the Mayor had offered a few carrots, organizing competitions for 'the best kept houses', going on tours of inspection with the Governor-General on Sunday mornings and handing out 'rewards'. Not surprisingly, this approach, more akin to wage than forced labour, met with better success.[72]

The struggle over a 'tidy' environment, as opposed to a clean one, did not go away, especially as the population of Brazzaville grew, as notions of urban hygiene occupied planners, and as the European 'leisured class' gave more attention to its surroundings. In 1922, the administration introduced the first decree for rubbish collection, and in 1931 the service was further regulated. 'Throwing rubbish on public streets or private property' was forbidden. Pick-ups in the European town were scheduled on a regular basis but no such service was introduced in Bacongo and Poto-Poto, where the inhabitants 'must carry their rubbish to special designated areas', where it was to be buried. Although most of this organization was given over to *quartier* chiefs and the militia to supervise, mayors continued to show up from time to time on tours of inspection.[73] During the Depression, the unemployed were allowed to work off tax debts through street cleaning.[74] In the case of Mpila, which was outside the city limits but which was a 'scenic attraction' for those who came off the Léopoldville ferry and for 'walkers and people in cars passing by', the need to ensure that the houses and streets were kept tidy and in good repair was particularly important for officials, since they did not want visitors to have 'a bad impression of the administration of the colony'.[75]

Within their limited means and within the constraints imposed by the colonial administration, people in Poto-Poto and Bacongo also took initiatives to organize space. The Congolese scholar Jean-Pierre Banzouzi has suggested that village public space (Kikongo or Lingala, *zando*, or market-place) and communal space (*mbongi*, Kikongo, the house for meetings of unmarried men) was replaced in the town by the streets, bars, 'bars-dancing' and cafes, that is 'the public place where one meets, where one talks, drinks and eats; these have become the place of discourse'.[76] Such social institutions developed slowly in the colonial town.

According to the account of a European commercial agent in 1902, people lived, worked and played in the area around the factory. After work and on Sundays, they relaxed by strolling in the streets, chatting with friends, smoking, gambling, playing cards, or dancing and singing to the sound of the accordion. Liquor could be bought at factory stores or from local brewers for Saturday-night binges.[77]

Following the establishment of Poto-Poto and Bacongo, workers had to become accustomed to the new spatial arrangements, but these were soon appropriated for local needs just as the Europeans were changing the face of the Plateau. In 1920, Jean de Puytorac described a walk he took one evening, when he asked one of his factory workers to show him Poto-Poto. On leaving the Plaine, he wrote:

We went along a path with high grass on either side, curving to avoid obstacles, crossing the zone that separated Brazzaville proper from the native village. Trunks of trees, laid end to end, helped us to cross the marsh. At last the ground became firm. We arrived at a large square surrounded by houses. It was the *zandu na mbwa* [Lingala, 'the dog's market']. Opposite, in the direction of the Bateke plateau was a broad street from which other narrower roads led off at right angles. My guide took one of these roads, which like the others was bordered by bamboo or branch fences...the people were little pressed for time, others walked under the palms, the mangoes and avocado trees. Between the houses, in empty spaces, there were bananas, manioc and Angola peas ... from time to time a man passed playing his *sanza* [thumb piano] similar to that of the guard at the factory.

The market-place was a centre of public activities. Drawn back to the *zando na mbwa* by the sound of drumming, Puytorac and his companion found that preparations for a funeral were under way.[78]

As popular culture developed in Bacongo and Poto-Poto, it demanded more specialized uses of space. A good example of this was the construction of the first regulation football field, which was undertaken through the initiative of players who wanted to upgrade their playing facilities and their skills. The origins of football will be discussed more fully in a later chapter but, in brief, it truly was a sport of the streets, popularized by barefooted players in rough-and-tumble games. 'CARA had its birth in the dust of Poto-Poto', states a history of one of the great present-day city teams.[79] The geometrically laid out streets might be monotonous to the eye, but they made an excellent playground for young footballers.

The houses were set back within enclosures, and only an occasional bicycle interrupted play. By the 1920s, football was a passion among young workers, and games marked by crowds of spectators were a common sight.[80] In a few years patches of open ground were no longer adequate for big matches, yet asking for permission to use mission or school yards impinged on the footballers' autonomy. At a meeting of the leaders of the newly organized Native Sports Federation (*Fédération Sportive Indigène*), it was decided to request permission from the Mayor to clear a piece of ground for a football field. Flavien M'Bongo, a bicycle-repair man in Poto-Poto, who was the founder and president of the federation, was designated to go to the Town Hall, where he was successful in obtaining permission. Emmanuel Dadet, a monitor at the Urban School and a keen player, remembered what followed: 'Every Sunday and holiday for six months, sometimes in the rain, office workers and labourers armed with hoes, spades, shovels, rakes and machetes, worked to clear the bush, dig out roots and stumps, level the ground and mark the playing field.'[81] A few Europeans heard of the enterprise and turned out to watch. To inaugurate their ground the leading football team of Poto-Poto, *L'Etoile* organized a match against *Mutuelle* of Kinshasa, a team of players who had attended Brazzaville schools but who were working on the other side of the Pool. The players invited the Governor-General to attend the game, which was played in front of a large crowd as part of the Bastille Day celebrations in 1930. The home team lost 0–1 but those who were present remembered the occasion as a triumph for African football.[82]

As populations settled in Poto-Poto and Bacongo and demanded entertainment, amenities such as shops, bars, cafes, cinemas and dance-halls sprouted up. In theory, a decree of 1930 to encourage African entrepreneurship prohibited ownership by Europeans of such establishments but, in practice, many Portuguese opened up cafes and bars, and the administration turned a blind eye. In 1933, there were forty-six places selling drinks in Bacongo and Poto-Poto, forty of them owned by Europeans.[83] Soldiers from the military base were a steady clientele. The public life of the streets still remained at the heart of African recreation. On Sunday afternoons and on public holidays such as New Year's Day and the Fourteenth of July, dance groups took over the main squares and streets. At the same time, however, recreational life had also moved inside, especially for activities appropriated from Europeans such as the new pop music, watching films, partnered dancing and sociability in bars.

After the Second World War, the expansion of the city's population was reflected in overcrowding in Bacongo and Poto-Poto and the occupation of lands on the town's perimeter (see map 6). Property

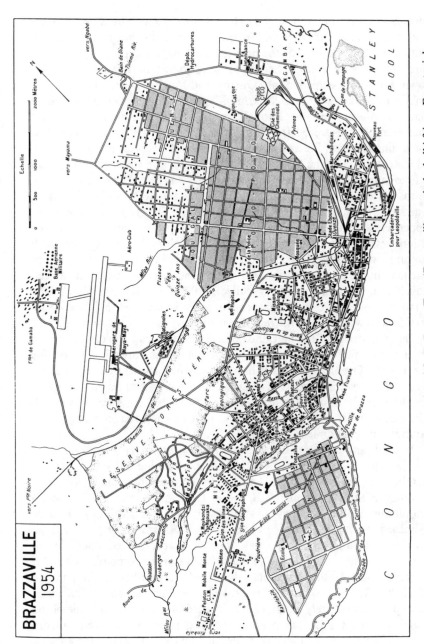

6 Plan of Brazzaville, 1954 (reproduced from Roger Frey, 'Brazzaville, capitale de l'Afrique Equatoriale Française', 1954)

owners in Poto-Poto and Bacongo had divided up their holdings into lots and put up new additions within their compounds, but as families ran out of accommodation for the next generation, young people moved out into surrounding areas, where they were joined by newcomers to the town. Poto-Poto extended into Ouenze and Mungali, while Bacongo was linked to Makélékélé and Mukondji-Nguaka. In Ouenze, a new street was added every month although, by the 1950s, unemployment meant that many houses were left in a half-finished state. The new areas lacked the animated street life and leisure amenities of Bacongo and Poto-Poto, which remained at the heart of town life.[84] When *quartier* six was added on the outskirts of Bacongo after the war, it was given the Kilari name of 'Bousana' meaning 'isolation' or 'sadness relating to solitude', because it was so quiet and people went to bed so early.[85] The growth of an African upper class who could afford better housing and amenities and the willingness of the administration to provide upscale housing with running water and electricity for the new political elite, their junior partners in the administration, resulted in the construction of subsidized housing in districts popularly called 'Tahiti' or 'Bacongo-Chic'. The 'Plateau des Quinze Ans' (named for army veterans with fifteen years service who were among the first householders) was also established.[86]

The persistence of the ingrained official attitude that Africans could be shunted around in the name of urban planning was shown in a report for the French Overseas Ministry in 1948 on the urbanization of Brazzaville.[87] The resulting events also show, however, that times had changed, for the mobilization of townspeople against such threats was successful. The struggle for city space was now part of the broader struggle for political and economic advancement.

A significant problem addressed in the Inspector's report was not only the growth of the town's African population, but also the growing number of Europeans who had taken up positions made available through FIDES investment. Between 1945 and 1960, the European population tripled. Any new town plan, the report argued, must include increased residential space for white families. The Inspector proposed the draconian solution of 'a partial or total evacuation of Bacongo' to undeveloped areas along the Djoué river, several kilometres away. M. Zoccolat's justification for a plan that would have involved the removal of 20,000 Africans was one dredged up from the annals of European town planning, namely placing the privileged on the windward side of the poor, or in his words: 'The prevailing winds, on an average coming from the south-west, necessitate a residential quarter on the west side of Brazzaville.'

Once the plan became known in Bacongo, a cross-section of the

population, from householders to newcomers and from young people to
the educated elite, were joined in opposition. All had something to lose.
Established families were long-standing property owners; travel to and
from the workplace would be increased; the new areas had none of the
ambiance or leisure facilities of Bacongo; and, for many, Bacongo was
simply home. After two years of increasingly heated debate and no
resolution in sight, and with the population of Bacongo already alienated
through the persecution of Matswa supporters, the Governor-General
decided to intervene by calling representatives of all the parties to a
meeting at his office. The compromise solution declared that 'Bacongo
should remain where it always has been'; that 'a new building program
for cultural, sports, medical and administrative facilities' should be
undertaken; and that 'the limits of Bacongo should be extended northwards'. The controversy had by no means been taken care of, for in
return for these concessions, African leaders had to agree that 'the
Corniche of Bacongo will be converted into a *quartier residentiel de
luxe*'.[88] While compensation was offered for property owners, the aliena-
tion of this prime location to Europeans was no more acceptable to its
inhabitants than it had previously been, as was demonstrated in an
upsurge of popular demonstrations.[89] The Bacongo residents also
weighed in concerning the Corniche with letters to the Grand Council of
AEF and articles in the press. In one such letter, Ange Goma wrote in
the Catholic newspaper, *La Semaine de l'AEF*:

Approving the removal of the people who live along the Corniche quite simply
shows that the African must always pay the cost of bad public policy. But, we
who inhabit the *quartier*, we have grouped ourselves together and are vigorously
resisting all attempts to give us compensation for removal. Furthermore, from
the legal point of view, the abandoning of this district cannot be justified without
the government in return deciding to construct houses in any new zone. This
quartier is among the very oldest in Brazzaville. Its official existence goes back to
1890. Several generations of Congolese have been born here, and it has been
developed by them in the real sense of individual property. Can one then, and
without grave remorse, unilaterally decide that about 2,000 people should from
one day to the next leave their environment [*habitat*] and rebuild a house in an
unknown zone, and all this in a period of unemployment and crisis?[90]

Jean-Felix Tchicaya, who had been elected as a Congolese Deputy in
1946, also took up the Bacongo question in an open letter to the High
Commissioner of AEF, which also appeared in *AEF Nouvelle*, a publication of the African elite. For Tchicaya, 'parking people according to
race' must be abandoned. Open spaces and parks were simply 'green
curtains' designed as barriers between different population groups.
Better models for future urban development, he suggested, were the few

Europeans who had moved into Poto-Poto.[91] Resistance to the loss of the Corniche was ultimately successful as the administration faced with 'political incidents', abandoned the plan. Segregation in Brazzaville had run its course, and Europeans no longer could dictate the shaping of space.[92]

While there were obviously many issues involved in popular resistance to forced removal, being close to sources of entertainment was certainly one. No one wanted to be sent to a distant location several kilometres removed from the heart of town life. The sprawling nature of Brazzaville remained a logistical problem, for travel to both work and play. Rickshaws and bicycles were used by Europeans until after the Second World War when cars and taxis became common, but such transport was beyond the means of ordinary people and only used for special occasions. One informant said: 'We hired "pousses-pousses" for weddings and paraded in them. When people saw that you rented three or four, they said "this man is rich".'[93] '"Pousses-pousses" were just for whites. They cost one or two francs,' said another.[94] Office workers aspired to buy bicycles, especially Raleigh bikes since English products had great status among the Brazzaville elite in the 1930s. In 1946, in an effort to cut back on erratic work attendance, the town administration also bought eight trucks to transport employees to and from work twice a day, since there was a long lunch-break according to French tradition. Two years later, the administration also reported that it had bought 2,000 bicycles to be sold on credit to their office employees, which 'caused great satisfaction'.[95]

Emerging identities

At the end of colonial period, therefore, the major spatial division of Brazzaville's African population remained that between Bacongo and Poto-Poto. The physical space created by the administration in the early part of the century had been appropriated by workers and their families, and had come to be associated with different population groups. Bacongo was home for those whose modern identity of Balari, Bacongo and Bassoundi linked them to the larger group of Bakongo-related peoples. In 1950, Soret's survey found that 93 per cent of those living in Bacongo were born there or were from four neighbouring districts.[96] Poto-Poto was characterized by its heterogeneous and cosmopolitan nature, with populations from all over AEF as well as West Africa, the Antilles and Belgian Congo. Before the Second World War, migrant male workers greatly outnumbered women, whereas in Bacongo the closeness of villages of origin allowed women to maintain homes both in the town and the country. The colonial policy that helped to 'create' an urban ethnicity cannot be described merely in terms of 'divide and rule'. As suggested in chapter 1, the allocation of urban space was closely linked to the European perception of 'tribes' in the interior of the colony. The notion of latent hostility between them, even if peoples had had little or no historical contact before the colonial period, pervades colonial discourse, as the administration sought to impose law and order on the urban population.[97] One administrator claimed success in overcoming African 'laziness' through dividing workers in teams according to 'race' and playing on their natural rivalries. An article about organizing football suggested that 'among young people teams should be formed from those of the same race', since 'diverse origins constitute one of the best means of forming competitive groups'.[98] On the other hand, Reste advocated marriage between townspeople of the same 'race' as a means of injecting stability into the urban population.[99]

The emerging class distinctions of Poto-Poto and Bacongo noted by Mayor Girard in 1915 continued in later decades. The people of the Pool and lower Congo, having chosen to profit from opportunities in the colonial economy, now constituted a large part of the African upper class. In the Pool region and in lower Congo, the urban economy touched villages at some distance. For example, in the Kinkala district, 80 kilometres from the capital, prosperity associated with the town was demonstrated in material possessions. A missionary wrote in 1931:

The inhabitants of the Boko region are, in general, better dressed than their brothers in other regions, sometimes with a certain richness and a visible taste, especially in the case of those who have spent time in the town. One is surprised to find numerous houses made of cut bricks and tombs of chiefs also built in brick and decorated with various souvenirs of their life: a pousse-pousse, some oil lamps, gramophones, crystal glasses, etc.[100]

The emergence of those who lived in Bacongo as an African upper class was further amplified through their schooling and employment as office workers and in other semi-skilled jobs. A report on the Poto-Poto and Bacongo government primary schools in 1934 found that 36 per cent of the students were 'Balali' and another 14 per cent were their close neighbours, the 'Bacongos' and 'Bassoundis'. At the Urban Technical School, 69 out of 128 students were 'Balalis'. Summing up his findings, the writer concluded that: 'The Balalis find themselves ahead of others in their education and this has given them pretensions. It has resulted in their almost exclusive success in finding jobs in the government, public services, commercial enterprises and domestic employment. Their sense of superiority will only grow.' The Administrator went on to note that the Lari were a 'labour aristocracy' and urged the Governor-General's

office to recruit 'Bateke and other races' for the Brazzaville schools so as
to diversify the workforce. At the moment, he noted, 'the Balali of
Bacongo are to all intents and purposes the only stable part of the
population'.[101] Another report, about the same time, expressed the
similar view that 'there is a radical difference between Poto-Poto and
Bacongo. Poto-Poto is the village of foreigners, people from the upper
river, the Hausa and Senegalese. Certainly, some of these are *évolués* and
African functionaries, but they stand out in the population because they
read the newspapers ... and they lead somewhat isolated lives.'[102]

These distinctions were symbolized in the street signs the administration chose for Poto-Poto and Bacongo in its town plan of 1933. While
streets in Bacongo were named after such worthies as Voltaire, Victor
Hugo and Marshal Joffre and chosen to 'allow our African subjects who
are curious and want to know and live the past of the Motherland to be
instructed through searching in their books for the significance of the
names cited', Poto-Poto streets were given names such as Rue Mongo,
Rue Hausa and Rue Mbochi, which seemed to correlate better with a
population less grounded in town life and closer to its rural roots.[103]

To these multiple strands in the growth of urban identity must be
added the question of religion, for the principal supporters of André
Matswa were the Lari of Bacongo, and they were supported through
contacts in rural networks. According to Balandier, about 90 per cent of
those who lived in Kinkala district were Matswa sympathizers. The
report cited above which recorded the numbers of Lari in school or
working for the administration was found in a file marked 'confidential',
for the inquiry grew out of the nervousness of the colonial administration
that their best local auxiliaries were drawn from the very people who had
been most alienated by the persecution of Matswa. André Matswa was
by no stretch of the imagination a nationalist agitator. He was, in fact,
the organizer of a mutual-aid association formed in 1926 in Paris by
young men who wanted greater participation within the existing colonial
structures. However, other circumstances such as the unrest that followed
the imprisonment of Simon Kimbangu in the lower Congo region of
Belgian Congo, and the numbers of unemployed due to the Depression,
brought a crackdown by the French authorities, the trial and exile of
Matswa and his principal supporters, his death in prison, and his
renaissance as a messianic figure in the religious beliefs of the Lari.[104]
After 1930, when an angry crowd of 1,500 Matswa supporters, many of
them clerks working for the administration, demonstrated at the Town
Hall to protest at the sentencing of their leader, and were fired on by
troops, leaving several dead and many wounded, 'things were never
again the same between the Lari and the administration'.[105] The Mayor

noted that 'all our native auxiliaries who work with whites have thrown themselves into politics and become insolent, even menacing'.[106] These events together with continued resistance by Matswa's supporters to paying taxes and the 'iron fist' response of colonial officials, contributed to the urban identity of the Lari in Brazzaville and the distinctiveness of Bacongo where most of them lived. On the other hand, by the 1930s, Poto-Poto was firmly associated with the 'northerners' from 'upriver', people such as the Bobangi of the middle Congo and the Mbochi of the Alima who as a result of the Depression and the ruin of the rural economy came in greater numbers to settle in the town.[107]

Conclusion

What appears to have happened in colonial Brazzaville, therefore, is the 'creation' of an urban ethnicity, brought about through a combination of the colonial organization of space, emerging class interests, and religious and political allegiances. As a final note on this subject, the origins and definition of the terms 'Lali' or 'Lari' have been the subject of several discussions.[108] Although the term 'Balali' appears in the earliest colonial documents, the people labelled thus seem, in pre-colonial times, to have been linked more closely to the broad Kiteke-speaking group than to Kikongo-speakers of the lower Congo. West of the Pool, they contested land with the Tio who retreated onto the Mbe plateau. In the town, however, the Lari seem to have shed their associations with the Teke and taken on a close association with the Bakongo-related populations south-west of the Pool. This appears to have been influenced in part by class interests, for to call a Lari in Brazzaville a Teke was seen as a term of abuse. In one instance a man who had taken a job as a cook's assistant was mocked by his cousin that it was a job fit for a Teke.[109]

The question of emerging ethnicity, especially in Brazzaville where it became heavily politicized with the advent to power of President Fulbert Youlou, and the locus of fighting in 1959 on the eve of independence, is one that needs to be approached with care. There is a danger in overstating the case through examining the problem retrospectively. It must be noted that throughout the colonial period, workers from lower Congo and the Pool also lived in Poto-Poto where one of the seven *quartiers* created in 1912 was reserved for the 'Bakongos'.[110] In 1932, 25 per cent of Poto-Poto were 'Balalis', 'Bacongos' or 'Bassoundis', and in 1951, they were about 16 per cent of Poto-Poto's population.[111] Furthermore, as the town grew, the reality of daily life was often different from the neat reports of colonial administrators. As early as 1918, the 'Mongo' area of Poto-Poto was 'saturated' and the population spilled over into other areas. And in newer areas such as the eastern extension of Poto-Poto, Ouenze, which was full of the unemployed in the 1950s, people from all over AEF lived side by side, and the area was distinguished more by the poverty of the people who lived there than by their regions of origin.[112] On the other hand, the association of Bacongo with an African elite who came from the Pool district and from the lower Congo was firmly based. Within Poto-Poto, there was also an influential elite, especially of foreigners such as Gabonese administrators who worked for the colonial service, but their number remained small in relation to the rest of the migrant population.

While the African population engaged in taking hold of the town and making it their own, the European population was increasingly marginalized in its own small world. A guidebook to Brazzaville published in 1953 conveys this insularity.[113] The population of the town for 1937 is given as 1,184, and for 1953, there is the comment that 'it has now passed 5,000'. In this account, 'Brazzaville' is the colonial town minus its African 'villages', now legally elevated to 'Communes'. The descriptions are almost entirely of the European town, except for references to the Cathedral of Saint-Anne and the Eboué Stadium, which had been constructed as a joint venture of church and state on the edge of Poto-Poto in the 1940s. The streets listed are all in the European part of the town, and the maps are excellent, but only for distinguishing roads in the Plateau, Chad and Plaine districts. Poto-Poto is an empty space save for the single main road that bisects it from west to east, the 'Rue de Paris', and Bacongo has equal treatment with the main thoroughfare, the 'Rue de Brazza', marked. Nothing could more clearly symbolize European perceptions of space in the colonial city and their isolation from the tens of thousands of African townspeople, some of whom came to the European 'town' to work but all of whom lived and played in the streets of Poto-Poto and Bacongo.

3   The emergence of leisure

The sounds and sights of time were evident in the colonial town in the form of bugles, gunshots, bells, drums, watches and clocks. People responded to them according to the level of their contact with urban institutions. The most affected were wage-labourers and Christians. There is evidence that an 'uneven' experience of time persisted and that the articulation of temporal patterns was central in the negotiation of relationships. Those most oppressed by time through their conditions of employment developed a keen awareness of their right to 'free time' and resisted attempts by employers, administrators or teachers to encroach on it.

Europeans had a large stake in the time of their workers, subjects and converts. Missionaries everywhere were engaged in the grand task, 'to remake Africans through their everyday activities'[1] and Congo was no exception. In their quest to develop a Christian elite, missionaries prescribed disciplined notions of time, work and leisure, as the panacea for the prevailing sickness of 'laziness'. Administrators and employers shared similar notions that time-discipline was a basic step in 'accustoming the native to regular work' and 'creating a disciplined workforce to open up the country'.[2] Europeans intervened in African leisure time when the health and efficiency of the workforce seemed to be at stake, or when African activities impinged on the insulated life of the white community. The self-employed or unemployed were not outside the range of European interest, as they were part of the environment in which labour was reproduced. Laws against vagrancy and fines levelled against unpunctual employees show a continuing struggle over definitions of time and order. While European hardliners advocated punitive measures, liberals passed on technical knowledge of leisure activities such as sport and new forms of music. All this was part of the process through which the concept and content of leisure emerged.

Negotiating time

As was noted in the Introduction, rural time was reckoned, not through mathematical abstractions, but through the interaction of ecological, economic and social events. Kimbochi, Kikongo and Lingala speakers use the same word for rain and year, since rainfall is the defining factor in the economy of farmers, fishermen and hunters. In a broad sense, it was the rhythm of the seasons that marked the passage of time.[3]

People also reckoned time in smaller units. The Kongo marked two main seasons and three intermediate ones, which correlated with rainfall and the cultivation of essential crops such as manioc, corn, bananas and peanuts. The Mbochi distinguished six seasons according to rainfall, fishing and farming strategies. Lunar months were recognized and influenced planting among the Kongo. They were also important to women keeping track of their pregnancies. A four- or five-day week, often associated with markets at specific geographical locations, was the norm. Within the day, there were many ways of referring to points in time, although not in a mathematical manner. The Mbochi distinguished fourteen points in the day and night, all related to natural events such as the height of the sun or moon in the sky, the sound of cocks, birds and toads, and the appearance of bats.[4] Among the Kongo in the early part of the twentieth century, people kept track of the passage of days and weeks through 'knots tied in a string, notched sticks, and similar mnemonic aids'.[5] In other words, Central Africans had an appreciation of a time that related to village economies and social life.

The week was a key element in the Congolese organization of time. Most of those who arrived as workers in Brazzaville were accustomed to observing a day, in some places two days, within their week when no agricultural work in the fields or heavy work in the forest was permitted.[6] It was a day when these areas were given over to spirits and ancestors; to break the prohibition could result in dire consequences for an individual or their family. In practice, this was not unobligated time free for recreation, as the production system would not allow it, especially for women. The pace of daily life was slower and more relaxed and the work-load might be lighter, but it was not a day with 'work suspended', as Weber has described the weekend.[7] Women had to undertake domestic chores around the compound, fetching water, soaking manioc, processing palm-nuts, and preparing other food.[8] Men also did lighter work close to home or took care of social and political obligations. Two Zairean writers have also argued that if this weekly day was a rest from the hard labour in the fields and forests, the notion of a day free for recreation was not part of local culture; neither was an extended holiday period. On the contrary, according to the prevailing work ethic, those who were too sick or too old to work were to be pitied.[9] Events that fulfilled social obligations, such as *matanga*, often took place during the dry season when the work-load was less. Times of recreation when people could gather for entertainment such as wrestling, dancing, music and clowning also coincided with slack work periods or evening relaxation, rather than with a particular day of the week. Thus, in considering any correlation between the schedules that a worker would encounter in the town and the pattern of rural time, it can be said that the village week was marked by a 'rest day' with activities that were different from those of other days, a day when the workload was lighter and the pace of daily life more relaxed, but that country people were unfamiliar with a specific day associated with recreation rather than work.

The culture of work also varied with social roles. In his study of Tio society in the late nineteenth century, Vansina noted that all women were overburdened with work and that girls had little leisure, since they started helping their mothers from an early age. Married men's work was commensurate with that of women, but the labour of young men, who were responsible for the defence of the community, was under-utilized. They were generally able to choose when they wanted to work, and 'were the only group to follow completely their inclinations with regard to their use of time'. The imbalance in work responsibilities made women bitter towards young men who 'cared only for their toilet'.[10] These gender distinctions also prevailed in the town. Young men in the workforce were the main consumers of leisure activities such as sport or going to cafes and bars. Women, on the other hand, carried to the town their expected productive and reproductive roles. To have too much leisure was to be an irresponsible wife and mother, or a prostitute.[11]

The sounds of European time coexisted with natural time in the colonial town, and doubtless people heard what was most relevant for their daily life. Buglers played the reveille at the military post. The church bell called Christians to mass or marked the beginning of the work day for the mission community. A school bell punctuated children's work and play. The clock in the cathedral tower displayed precise, mathematical time. Along the Plaine and on the Plateau, work bells sounded the intervals of the day. At 6 a.m. on the Fourteenth of July, guns at the military post announced the start of the national holiday. European men displayed the importance of time with their pocket-watches on chains, as did African elites in their Sunday outfits. Wrist-watches became popular by the 1930s, and were ordered through catalogues.[12] At the same time, many townsfolk continued to adjust their day to the sounds of birds or cocks crowing, the position of the sun, the level of rainfall, and the seasonal flow of the river.

If the sounds of time announced the beginning and end of work hours, they also introduced the wage-earner to leisure. It was the very conditions of employment that brought workers face to face with the value of time. At the turn of the century, 'free time' was in short supply since workers for the administration and factories put in ten-hour days from 6 a.m. to 11 a.m., and from 1 p.m. to nightfall, six days a week.[13] Such harsh conditions were part of the exploitation of French workers at the turn of the century. If the *fin de siècle* was a *belle époque* for the middle class, it was hardly experienced thus by ordinary workers. Shop employees worked fifteen- to seventeen- hour days and waiters from 8 a.m. to midnight.[14]

Among workers arriving in Brazzaville, some already had experience in capitalist and Christian time. At the turn of the century the European week was gradually displacing the local week among Christians and traders in the lower Congo. They were 'using European calendars and learning the names of the months and using them in their transactions with white men and in writing letters, agreements, etc.'.[15] Brazza advised his agents to appoint Senegalese, Kru and Loango workers to positions of responsibility, so that newly recruited local workers could learn from them. It was their familiarity with the European system of work discipline, often learnt in the army, that made the Senegalese so valuable as overseers. 'Mix workers from different areas in different tasks', Brazza instructed one of his agents, so that 'knowledge of work can spread as quickly and as far as possible'.[16] At the turn of the century, Brazzaville factories commonly established work 'teams' led by a few Senegalese who were former sergeants and corporals in the colonial army; strict disciplinarians, they were respected and feared by local workers.[17]

Within the new time patterns, workers became attuned to Sunday as a rest day, a day with 'time to spare'. Even at remote postings, a lone European and his employees would observe Sunday as a day free from work.[18] In 1883, Albert Veistroffer, a member of Brazza's expedition, was left to organize a post on the Ogowe where he noted: 'We observed Sunday as a day of rest for all the workers.' Later, at Modzaka in 'Bondjo' country, he wrote: 'Every Sunday, I had a big meeting where I entertained everyone with magic lantern shows and music.'[19] From the earliest days of the French post at the Pool, all factory and administrative employees had a free day on Sunday, which was patterned differently from others – whether sleeping in late to recover from a Saturday night hangover, going to church, wearing 'Sunday best', watching or playing sport, attending a *matanga*, taking part in dance groups or passing time with friends. Those who worked for the administration on a monthly basis, such as labourers engaged for a specific project, were paid on the first Sunday of every month, a practice which by 1913 workers were resisting when Sundays fell several days into the month.[20]

The prominence of the Catholic mission and the large number of Christians, whether practising, nominal or lapsed, was a key factor in spreading the notion that Sunday was a rest day. Those with some European schooling had usually learned their sense of time in the tough environment of a mission boarding-school. Missionaries pioneered the use of time to impose a new order. Clocks and bells symbolized the importance of punctuality in the life of the church. The use of a bell was the beginning of the new system, not least for its symbolism when it replaced African drums at the mission stations. In 1885, Augouard wrote from Linzolo near Brazzaville that the mission had received a donation of a large bell from France, 'which will beneficially replace the drums which we were obliged to use for the daily exercises'.[21] In 1902, the original bell for the cathedral tower in Brazzaville was replaced with one donated and dedicated in Poitiers, Monseigneur Augouard's home parish. When Father Zimmermann arrived at Loango in 1896, he carried in his baggage four clocks for missionary churches in the Congo. The priests and brothers of the Holy Ghost Fathers were trained in all sorts of practical skills such as clock- and watch-repair, which they passed on to African workers.[22]

The battle for control of time went on relentlessly in Christian schools and mission stations. One priest reported in a missionary magazine: 'In the Christian villages we wage war on our poor blacks.'[23] The philosophy of Father Libermann, founder of the Holy Ghost Fathers, shaped the attitudes of missionaries who set out for Central Africa. In an essay on the 'General State of the Black Population', he wrote about their 'feebleness of character, a temperament given to laziness as is usual in hot countries, and an inclination to vanity'.[24] Father Carrie, the founder of the Congo mission, shared Father Libermann's views on schedules as a means of routinizing daily life. In 1888, he wrote to Brazza that the mission was concerned with 'inspiring the African with the love of work', and 'we seek a man useful to society'.[25] In a lengthy treatise on 'The work with children in the Vicariate of French Congo', Carrie issued precise instructions for daily life on the Mission Station. Children in primary school started the day with 'rising and prayers' at 5.30 a.m., followed by manual labour at 5.45 a.m., breakfast at 8 a.m., washing at 9.30 a.m., and classes at 10 a.m. For the rest of the day they followed a similar tight schedule, with a brief time for recreation after lunch and, again before prayers, and bed at 8 p.m. Mission children also learned the significance of Thursday afternoon, the traditional 'half-day' for French school children, through their relief from labour on the mission farm or in the classroom. On Thursdays, they finished work at 10 a.m., and then went to catechism class. After lunch, at 2 p.m., came time for 'washing clothes', followed by 'practical training' which might include fishing by the river. Similar rules were laid out for workers and seminarians.[26]

Most of all, those at the mission stations must have anticipated Sunday as a day of rest, and a break from the weekly schedule. After attending mass at 8 a.m., the rest of the day until chapel at 6 p.m. was given over to periods of time variously named on Carrie's schedule as 'supervised recreation', 'free recreation' and 'walk and swimming lessons'. As Josef Pieper noted in his famous book on the nature of leisure, the festive quality of a holiday depends on it being exceptional.[27] Sundays and the great festivals of the church were also distinguished through dress and food. Normally, the priests were charged by Carrie 'to wage a war on luxury' but 'on the great festivals and on Sunday', their charges could have 'special cloths'. When children arrived at the station, they were issued with three cloths: one for everyday use, one for Sundays, and one to be worn only on important festivals such as Easter and returned the next day to the priests. As for food, Carrie wrote, 'it is to be plainly cooked but on great festivals one can add a sauce or a little lard or fat' and 'on the great festivals of the year, such as Christmas, Easter, Pentecost, the Sacred Heart of Mary, and Saint Joseph's day, one can give the child something better to eat if possible'. He suggested slaughtering an animal or buying antelope or pork.[28] In the period when there was little to distract workers on Sunday in terms of public leisure, the excitement of a Catholic holy day drew large crowds of curious spectators. The spectacle of the bishop's procession on Easter Sunday and Corpus Christi was watched by thousands of people, with the police called out to manage the crowds. On such occasions the cathedral, which could hold 2,500 people, after it was expanded in 1911, was filled to capacity, with people pressing at the windows.[29] The mission youth club attracted hundreds of young workers for games, sports and recreation and helped to establish the 'festive quality' of Sunday among many of the young men who arrived in Brazzaville in the early part of the century. By the 1920s, Sunday was firmly established as the day for football matches, recreational dancing, crossing the Pool to visit friends and relaxing at home or in neighbourhoods.

Having underlined the significance of Sunday in the work week which they had imposed, Europeans then found that workers insisted on their day off. In 1902, paddlers refused to transfer a European across the Pool on a Sunday morning. One company director explained that 'one cannot get them to work, especially on Sunday'. His assistant had to go door to door to persuade men who had Saturday night hangovers to turn out for work. It was only when threatened with a whip by the European factory manager that the men appeared and pushed their boat into the river.[30] Absenteeism and lateness to work by administration employees was especially marked on Monday mornings. Employers blamed heavy drinking on Sundays for the problem. In 1933–4, several clerks were punished with two to four days without pay for offences such as 'arriving at the office drunk', 'being late for work without reason' and 'repeated negligence in service'.[31]

The struggle to find labour for Sunday street cleaning, referred to in the previous chapter, can be interpreted as simply a struggle over forced labour, but there is also evidence that it involved worker resistance to a loss of their 'spare time'. According to the Mayor, workers told him that they had 'no time'. The administration saw this as confirmation of 'laziness' for the men had plenty of time after work and 'especially on Sundays'. The problem was simply that they preferred to 'waste their leisure in singing, dancing and games'.[32] In matters of Sunday work, Europeans were divided, and workers lobbied missionaries to approach the administration on their behalf concerning their rights to a day off. In a letter to the Governor-General, Monseigneur Biéchy, wrote that 'basing our position on Christian ideals, we would like to see Sunday work abolished'. His appeal to the Governor-General was not to end forced labour but to end it on Sundays, noting that *corvée* labour on that day should 'only exist for military emergencies'. He recommended that 'it is desirable that there be a day of complete rest, at least in the large centres'.[33] Evangelical Swedish missionaries who preached the Lord's Day observance also petitioned the government to end Sunday work. They were good allies for workers in their common goal, even if they differed from most on appropriate Sunday activities. Among Congo Protestants, breaking the peace on the Sabbath was not a mortal sin like paganism, adultery, drunkenness and dancing, but working on the Lord's Day could meet with disciplinary action such as temporary exclusion from the church and fines. African catechists and pastors were often tougher than missionaries in enforcing these measures, in order to separate Christians from 'pagans' and assert their leadership.[34] Even more liberal administrators such as Governor-General Reste advocated the need for Sunday work, although in his case it was to help urban families to be self-sufficient in food production.[35] It was not until the abolition of forced labour after the 1944 Brazzaville conference that the struggle between workers and administrators over forced labour on Sundays ended.

Workers also resisted the administration's attempts to eat into their after-work hours in the name of self-improvement. About 1904, a Frenchman had started adult literacy classes for workers in their 'spare time' and in 1911, with the establishment of the first Urban School, the administration asked the Principal to start evening adult literacy classes for orderlies, nurses and soldiers. Workers were directed to attend by their employers, but absenteeism was high, so much so that the Director of Political Affairs called on government departments to take action by fining or dismissing unwilling students. The students claimed that after working they were tired, and those who lived on the other side of the town did not want to make the journey to the school on the Plateau. Further implementation of the policy was interrupted by the emergencies of the First World War.[36]

While some workers had appropriated new ideas of time and defended their leisure, others remained outside regular wage-labour and retained older notions of time which affected their work habits. The main issue does not seem to have been misunderstandings caused by the lunar and Gregorian months, as it was for workers and employers in Natal, but the length of the work week.[37] It has been argued that the pre-existence of the four-day week with a day of rest, or at least of lighter work, may have aided the transition to the seven-day week. For Efraim Andersson, a Swedish missionary in the lower Congo for twenty years, the pre-existing practice of 'giving a certain sacred character' to days through their association with ancestors and spirits was 'a good preparation for the celebration of Sunday as the holy day of the church'.[38] On the other hand, the persistence of a rhythm of work associated with a four-day week was also responsible for absenteeism among workers at the Swedish mission. Teofil Ceder, who first established the mission and engaged labourers for building construction, noted the problem because his workers took 'one or two days off work each week'. His attempts to discipline them were apparently unsuccessful, for after he had 'yelled at them' and threatened to punish them, they left the work site. A report on the Brazzaville workforce in 1913 also noted that among Bacongo workers, 'they miss three to five days a month and the police have to go and fetch them', which may also be a reference to absenteeism associated with the rest day in the four-day week, but this is not certain.[39] From the earliest days of wage-labour employment at the French post, Chavannes wrote of chronic absenteeism, but again the sources do not usually give the reasons and, therefore, leave unresolved the extent of the correlation between erratic worker attendance and pre-existing notions of the week.

School records also show a correlation between rural seasonal time and absenteeism among children. It was exactly because of such pressures that missionaries preferred to have children in the tightly controlled confines of the boarding-school, rather than deal with day students, who were frequently absent. The records of the Urban Primary School are full of references to absenteeism related to seasonal occupation. Food shortages and the high price of foodstuffs in the town accentuated the role of girls in the household economy. The Sisters of Saint Joseph of Cluny and the Principal of the Urban School made frequent forays into Bacongo and Poto-Poto to search for students.[40] The absence of boys, who were helping with house repairs at the onset of the main rainy season, also appears in the school records.[41] The poorest attendance was after the long vacation, when students did not return for the new school year. Following the French tradition, these holidays fell in August and September, but in Congo, October is a busy agricultural month with the first rains. In this context, a Swedish missionary wrote to the Stockholm directors that 'the school is continuing but it is not certain that we will take a break since we fear that our boys will not return'.[42] In 1915, at the Urban School, only one girl in the eight to twelve age group, and none over thirteen returned for the start of the school year. In 1917 similar problems were reported. In July, 203 pupils had been in attendance but in October only 128 turned up for the beginning of the school year.[43] The continual struggle to fix a calendar that would accommodate village time was the subject of correspondence between the Governor-General's office and principals of public primary schools in 1921, 1922 and 1933. The demands of the farming, hunting and fishing seasons, the effects of torrential rain in the wet season which made travel difficult, and the practice of Ramadan when children fasted during the day and participated in celebration at night, were all highlighted as causing poor attendance and concentration at certain times of the year.[44] There were clearly other factors in erratic school attendance, but such reports confirm the persistence of a time necessitated by rural economies. It seems safe to assume, by extension, that similar constraints influenced those in the adult workforce who were not fully integrated into urban wage labour. Other reports on school absenteeism relate to simple truancy by children. Comments by teachers include: 'there are too many students playing truant, spending their days in the market or along the banks of the Pool';[45] and 'they come from the villages around Brazzaville and the long road gives them a chance to play truant and to arrive very late'.[46] Using the parish magazine as a platform, a monitor wrote to Catholic parents in 1934: 'Parents, if you want to make sure that your sons and daughters are coming to school regularly, follow them yourself. Some of them may "forget" to come back to school after the Christmas vacation. After your child takes his manioc bread in the morning, he may not come to school.'[47]

Thus the struggle over time and time-discipline continued. As was said at the outset, it is clear that urban workers experienced time in different ways and that those most committed to town life and to the urban labour force were most influenced by ideas of work and leisure. The large numbers of at least nominal Christians in Brazzaville also contributed to familiarity with European time schedules, even among those who were not in the wage-labour force. Among those who were self-employed, who worked in the informal sector of the economy and who were not Christian, older notions of time persisted. Even within the same family different notions of time coexisted. This was the case in the family of Bernard Mambeke-Boucher, as he recalled his boyhood home. His mother and father arrived in Brazzaville about 1914. His father, who was a Catholic, had attended primary school and worked in an office. His mother was not literate and had not converted to Christianity. When the family moved to Brazzaville, his father followed the work week of the administration; on Sunday he went to mass and then relaxed with his friends. On the other hand, his mother continued to follow the five-day week that she knew from village life, going to her farm at Mungali on Sunday unless it happened to fall on the fifth day of the week, when she stayed at home doing domestic chores and visiting friends. After the family had lived in Poto-Poto for several years, however, she gradually adapted her sense of time, through pressure from other women who were Christian or more adapted to town life. To remain tied to the older time was to be teased as being out of touch with town life. Furthermore, town regulations concerning drumming meant that the women's dance group, of which she was a member, met on Sunday afternoons. Gradually, Mambeke-Boucher recalled that his mother started to adopt town time and the seven-day week.[48] It seems likely that this kind of peer pressure to adapt to town ways must have been a powerful force touching many who stayed in the town, even if they were self-employed. In the rural areas, too, the coexistence of different temporal practices continued. In the 1950s, in villages in the Pool region, some markets followed the European pattern and were scheduled on certain weekdays, while others followed the traditional four-day market calendar.[49]

Consciousness of time as something that could be negotiated with employers is also shown in the relationships between domestic servants and their employers. In a 1934 census of male wage-labourers, the administration found that about a quarter of the workforce fell into this category.[50] Servants in Congo, as in France, worked long hours. In Brazzaville, servants were not allowed to live at their employers' residences but had to walk to and from work. Working hours were from about 6 a.m. to 3 p.m. and from about 6 p.m. to 11 p.m., at the employers' discretion. Servants who crossed from the Plateau to Poto-Poto or from the Plaine to Bacongo had to have notes from their employers to go through police lines after 9 p.m.[51] Gabrielle Vassal and her husband expected their servants to keep a prompt schedule, according to the rhythm of their employers' day. While her husband was at work, Vassal had her own activities which also punctuated her servants' working day. However, the fact that whites preferred to draw certain categories of worker from the same region allowed workers some limited possibilities of negotiating time. In the Brazzaville workforce where contracts were almost non-existent, regular holidays were unknown and at the discretion of employers. In a chapter in her book entitled 'Domestic worries', Vassal tells of her negotiations with servants over vacation time. Servants 'expected' ten to fourteen days, two or three times a year. Two months after her arrival in Brazzaville one of her servants asked for 'an advance on his pay and said that he wished to go off that evening' for two weeks. Vassal wanted to refuse since she thought the time he had spent in her employment was too short, but she decided to ask her more experienced neighbour, who informed her that 'it was the custom, as long as he gave me somebody to replace him'. Rather than lose her quite skilled employee, Vassal decided to agree to his demands and in due course a replacement showed up to take his place.[52]

Although workers in service jobs such as domestic servants and waiters and also casual labour remained particularly vulnerable to employer demands, others who were organized in unions or in workplace were able to win some concessions in hours of work after the Second World War. As in France, theory lagged behind practice. The protocols of the 1944 Brazzaville conference laid out the rights of workers to an eight-hour day with one day of rest per week. Yet, in 1954, those in prestigious jobs as port workers, drivers, river-boat employees and factory employees were often working well over fifty hours a week. A free afternoon on Saturday was becoming the norm for office and factory employees.[53] Demands for a forty-hour week and other improvements in work conditions such as annual vacations were the subject of strikes in 1950.[54] A major goal of workers was to change from a two-period day, broken by a long lunch-break in the French manner, to a single work period starting early in the morning and finishing by 2 p.m. The upsurge in the capital's population and the addition of new districts such as Ouenze and Makélékélé, together with minimal public transport, made it difficult for workers to go home and return in the allotted time. Government printing-plant employees were one of several unionized groups that demanded a single work period, claiming that they would be more efficient if they did not have to work on 'hot afternoons'. They also demanded transport to and from work.[55] A report commissioned by the Governor-General's office in response to increasing pressures noted that a single work period would satisfy demands for more leisure time and avoid the problem of office workers, who were 'too sleepy' in the afternoon to work effectively. The disadvantages, however, would be less efficiency in the proposed seven hour period from 6.30 a.m. to 1.30 p.m., and problems in the early morning for female employees who had to take care of children and get them to school.[56] It was only after independence that this single period work-day was introduced.

If workers appropriated Sunday as a day for recreation and taking care of social obligations, they also took advantage of the public holidays on the French calendar. In Brazzaville, New Year's Day and the Four-teenth of July were landmark public holidays. First celebrated on a large scale in 1891, Bastille Day was taken over by Africans as a popular holiday. The fact that mid-July coincided with the dry season when agricultural labour slackened off allowed many to participate in the events. Although over three decades have passed since the Fourteenth of July was last celebrated, those who lived in colonial times remember the carnival-like atmosphere, the long holiday from work, the visitors who poured into the capital from other parts of AEF, the fair where craftsmen had stalls, the football matches and march-pasts, the new cloths, the street dancing in Poto-Poto and Bacongo, and the free wine dispensed by the administration. Some have special memories such as the Scout or veteran who marched in parades, or the woman who wore an expensive cloth for the Government House reception which she attended with her civil-servant husband. Such holidays were transformed from a foreign import to a popular event in which people had the right to participate. In 1934, when a priest tried to stop Catholic women in Poto-Poto from participating in dance groups because he said they were 'immoral', the women took their complaints to the Mayor's office and won their case.[57] On the other hand, an occasion so full of meaning for the colonial rulers could be used against them, as when Matswa supporters boycotted the celebrations. In 1930 and 1933, chiefs refused to accept the usual presents from the administration and returned the free wine. Thousands stayed away from the celebrations. In 1931, the Mayor announced prizes for the best-kept houses and gardens, but Matswaiste leaders claimed these were spurious attempts to return money which had been confiscated from them in the first place. In the same year, the Inspector of Urban Schools decided to reward students for their work in preparing the fairground. However, when he appeared at a school assembly, he was booed by the students, who refused to accept anything from the colonial administration. Such treatment of a senior government official by young African schoolchildren was 'scandalous' from the European perspective.[58]

Laws, limits and leisure

The starting-point for this section is Hugh Cunningham's comment that leisure as an abstraction is most powerful in the minds of those seeking to impose the social order.[59] In the official discourse, the 'problem' of leisure in Brazzaville was much like that of the dominant class in early industrial Europe, where worker leisure time was seen as potentially threatening to the social order and where the 'dangerous' elements were those who defied integration into the regulated labour force. Catholic missionaries were by no means alone among nineteenth-century Frenchmen in thinking that Africans were in a childlike state and had to be disciplined accordingly.[60] In Congo, the precariousness and impermanence of the French and the climate of violence in which colonialism was born also affected European actions. Although the brutality of concessionary-company rule was primarily felt in the interior of the colony, prevailing attitudes spilled over among those who managed the factories along the Pool. On the Plateau, the administrators who constituted about one-third to a half of Brazzaville's white population throughout much of the colonial period dreamed of an 'ordered' population, a rallying call which was echoed even more loudly by army officers at the military post.[61] In search of a disciplined workforce and subject population, Europeans could not afford to hide behind the walls of segregated leisure. Active intervention in African lives through punitive measures, legal constraints or structured activities was necessary. By the 1930s, pressures from Africans, especially elites and young people, as well as competition from the Catholic mission, caused the administration to diversify their strategies. The official discourse was summed up in 1941 in Eboué's *La nouvelle politique indigène* (new native policy). Pointing out the different segments of the population and appropriate disciplinary measures, Eboué wrote:

This discipline will not only be ensured through the *indigénat*; not only by the courts that will punish incessantly and without mercy vagabonds and robbers; not only through a special prison where I plan to transfer delinquents; not only through policing health to control prostitution; not only through a repressive discipline carried out assiduously and vigorously. There will also be discipline aimed at improving society, for example, sports clubs, Scouts, paramilitary groups and recreational organizations. I am counting on all of these to offer the rootless native the structured life which is indispensable.[62]

In this statement, Eboué was essentially reiterating policies that had already been tried in Bacongo and Poto-Poto during the first six decades of colonial rule. Over time, a highly repressive system had given way to a more paternalistic one, especially towards the elite. But the statement also attests to sustained resistance by the town's population. While some embraced activities that suited their needs and fired their imaginations, others survived on the margins of society, unwilling or unable to be integrated into the new urban structures.

From the outset, prevailing European sentiment caused white men to treat an African male as a 'boy' regardless of age. The attitude was summed up by Inspector Frezouls in 1911. Writing of the way in which administrators 'severely punished any transgressions by the African population through the use of the *indigénat* and the Native Courts', he noted such punitive measures resulted from 'flagrant disobedience to their orders'. In other words, offences such as breaking a contract were primarily viewed as 'acts of insubordination' rather than breaking the law.[63] For Governor-General Antonetti the arbitrary and repressive nature of the *indigénat* was justified through the 'near barbaric state' of the people 'who have still not made reasonable progress in the disciplined life freely agreed to, which subordinates individual interest for the good of the community'.[64] As already noted, African auxiliaries such as *quartier* chiefs and the militia were agents in the imposition of 'discipline' and 'obedience'. The latter, who were often drawn from northern populations in Chad and Ubangi-Shari, frequently used their uniform and position to abuse the local population for their own gain. As late as 1953, an article by a member of the elite in the magazine, *Liaison*, entitled 'Bringing an end to the regime of the *mboulou-mboulou*', noted that militia in the capital 'do not hesitate to inflict shocking ill-treatment on the civilian populations'.[65]

A constant outpouring of decrees was the basis for the social order the French sought to impose. Brazzaville, as the capital of French Equatorial Africa, was the residence of a hierarchy of colonial functionaries who were AEF and Moyen-Congo administrators. These, together with individual Europeans, might at any time bring the attention of the Mayor to some 'problem' with the African population. Of all colonial laws, the most frequently invoked to control work and leisure discipline were the peculiar set of regulations known as the *indigénat*.

Implemented in West Africa in the late nineteenth century, this penal code was introduced in French Equatorial Africa in 1908 in order to regulate a cluster of decrees already in existence. Modified periodically, the *indigénat* was one of the most unpopular aspects of French colonial policy and a focus of resistance. Reporting on the significance of the 1908 decree, the Chief Administrator of Moyen-Congo noted that it 'determined the disciplinary powers of administrators in regard to the natives'.

Table 3   *Offences Prosecuted under the* Indigénat, *Brazzaville, April–December 1908*

Rowdiness, brawls, disputes and vagabondage	976 cases (54%)
Negligence in paying taxes	233 cases (13%)
Non-compliance with an administrator's summons	110 cases (6%)
Refusal to help when ordered to do so in cases of accident or public need	87 cases (5%)
Leaving a circumscription without telling the authorities	76 cases (4%)
Other offences	320 cases (18%)

Source: AOM, 4(2)D2, Annual report of Moyen-Congo, 1908

It would apply, he wrote 'to actions that are not wrong or contrary to our penal codes, but which necessitate repressive punishment in support of our influence and authority'.[66] The twenty-two offences listed in the initial document ranged from failure to pay taxes to lack of respect for a European. Infringements were punished by up to fifteen days in prison and a 100–franc fine. Such punitive measures could be applied by any official without going through the Native Courts. In practice any European could report an African under the broad mandate defined by the *indigénat* and have them punished. In the first nine months of its existence, April–December 1908, 1,802 cases were prosecuted in Moyen-Congo of which 65 per cent were in Brazzaville. According to the administrator, this was due to 'the presence in the capital of a relatively large number of individuals from different regions, turbulent elements who form the habitual clientele of the prison'. On an average, those punished spent seven days in prison and paid 13 francs for each infraction. Among the 'principal reasons for punishment', those relating to 'disorderly conduct' predominated (see table 3).

In the first eight months of 1909, 1,415 cases were prosecuted under the *indigénat* in Moyen-Congo; of these, 511 were in Brazzaville. The larger number prosecuted outside the capital was due to greater use of the penal code by rural administrators.[67] For the 1,374 offences punished in Moyen-Congo during the last four months of the year, the principal 'offences' again showed how the *indigénat* was used to control social behaviour (see table 4).

As the historian Antoine Aïssi has pointed out, the *indigénat* was part of a broader system of 'Native Justice', which was political and economic in its inspiration.[68] A steady flow of decrees published in the *Journal Officiel* shows continual efforts to control African life in Poto-Poto and Bacongo. These laws deal with 'problems' such as 'vagabondage', 'alcohol abuse' and 'prostitution', and their recurrence and modifications

Table 4   *Offences Prosecuted under the* Indigénat, *Moyen-Congo,
September–December 1909*

Rowdiness, drunkenness, scandals, brawls, disorderly conduct	360 cases (26%)
Refusal to pay taxes	215 cases (15%)
Abandoning loads by porters and paddlers	159 cases (12%)
Failure to answer an administrator' summons	95 cases (7%)
Vagabondage	90 cases (7%)
Leaving a circumscription without authorisation	69 cases (5%)
Continuing to complain after a situation has been regularised	30 cases (2%)
Outrageous behaviour to someone in authority	27 cases (2%)
Possession of illegal arms and munitions	7 cases (0.5%)
Practising sorcery	6 cases (0.5%)
Other offences	316 cases (23%)

Source: 4(2)D3, Report for the third trimester, Moyen-Congo, 1909

over the years bear witness to the inability of the administration to regulate effectively such autonomous aspects of popular culture.

The use of administrative *fiat* to limit African leisure took a different turn in the 1930s with its application to censorship. This doubtless applied to written materials which literate townspeople read in a random manner as books, pamphlets, magazines and catalogues, both secular and religious, fell into their hands.[69] However, the files on censored items that are extant in the Congo National Archives relate not to written materials but to films and to records, which may in fact have been a more serious issue, given the small number of literate people before the Second World War.

The earliest reference to silent films being shown in Brazzaville is from 1916 when a Portuguese entrepreneur had set up a projector 'in order to increase the sale of his coffee'.[70] In the early 1920s, Father Bonnefont, a priest responsible for Bacongo, brought second-hand equipment to Brazzaville and rented films from France to show in mission youth work.[71] By 1931, the Urban School had acquired a Pathé-Baby projector and 150 films which the teachers considered 'a precious tool to enrich learning through films on health and agriculture'.[72] While the precise contents of this particular collection are not known, some clues are contained in a report from a circumscription administrator in Ubangi-Shari who had received a similar, officially approved collection. Noting the good 'propaganda value' of the films, the administrator listed in his collection: twenty-four showing peasants engaged in cash-crop production, for example coffee in Brazil and silk in Cambodia; six on sleeping sickness; four on Paris and other towns in France; twelve on other parts of the world such as Yellowstone National Park and the Suez Canal; and five in the series 'Felix the Cat'.[73]

The advantages and potential pitfalls of the rapid development of photography and cinematography were recognized by the French Minister of Colonies who, in 1934, wrote to the governor-generals of francophone colonies that 'the cinema is becoming more and more an instrument of propaganda', and that 'the moment has come for colonial administrators to use the screen to their profit'.[74] A strict vigilance must be implemented over stray Europeans with photographic equipment who, wandering in remote corners of a colony, might photograph scenes that would raise questions about France's 'civilizing mission'.[75] The Minister also voiced his concern over subjects viewing the 'wrong' type of films, such as those that might explode the mystique of white superiority and encourage rebellious subjects, or those with scenes of 'immorality' which might have negative effects on impressionable audiences. With this in mind, he advised the Governor-General of AEF to follow the West African example and appoint a censorship board to review films and records.[76] The Governor-General and his advisers agreed that it would be relatively straightforward to review all major releases such as Hollywood films since there was only one cinema, owned by a Greek, where the new talking films could be shown. On the other hand, 'the impossibility of controlling gramophone records, since there are too many and they are sold in all the trading houses', was also noted.[77] In spite of this, the newly appointed censorship board was given full responsibility for licensing all films for public showing, issuing licences to all who wanted to show films, and authorizing the importation and circulation of gramophone records. In practice, it was already too late to stop the flow of records, and pressures from the French film industry meant that films that were passed for viewing in France also passed the Brazzaville censors. At its first meeting the Film Board viewed a film about the assassination of King Alexander of Yugoslavia in Marseilles, but decided that it could be passed since the actual scenes of the assassination were short and had already appeared in newspapers and magazines. In the late 1930s, several films were banned, all on the advice of the Ministry of Colonies. *Tempest over Asia* was judged unsuitable since it showed 'scenes of natives being tortured by whites'; an American film, *Hurricane*, was also denied a permit, the reason not given; and films by Warner Brothers were denied entry for two months in retaliation for their film, *Devil's Island*, about the French penal colony in Guiana, which the Minister's board of censors described as 'damaging to French prestige'.[78] In 1940, with the war in progress, the Director of the Intercolonial Information Service advised the Governor-General's office that a news report showing the German invasion of Belgium was suitable for Europeans, but 'for political reasons' should not be shown to African audiences.[79]

Following the Second World War, various government services such as the Education Department and the Department of Social Services continued to import documentary films and use them for educational purposes. In 1950, an AEF cinematographic service was established which received educational films through a department of the French Overseas Ministry.[80] Having promoted 'divide and rule' for decades, administrators now hoped that films might become a tool of national integration, through sending mobile vans around different regions with films of other parts of the colony.[81]

The main controversy, however, focused on the popular films from Hollywood and France shown nightly in Poto-Poto and Bacongo, and their impact on the young people who were the main clientele. Questions of violence and morality were at the heart of the discussion concerning what should be shown, and the age of general and restricted admission. Participating in this dialogue were representatives of the African Christian community. Publishing their opinions in the Catholic newspaper, *La Semaine*, they blamed adventure and gangster films for a rise in juvenile delinquency. For one writer, Pierre Eticault, these were the inspiration for 'the gangs of young people who specialize in robberies, murders and assault'. He also claimed that on-screen immorality was copied by impressionable girls and that the cinema and dance-halls kept young people out late without supervision.[82] To counter this insidious influence a *Centre Catholique d'Action Cinématographique* had been established in Léopoldville. In five years it had made thirty-seven feature films and fifty-five short documentaries which were distributed in Belgian Congo, AEF, Angola, Rhodesia and Mozambique.[83]

As was usual when issues of social control and morality were at stake, censorship engaged the church and state in dialogue. In a correspondence with the Governor-General, Monseigneur Biéchy touched not only on questions of delinquency and immorality, but also on the negative images of Europeans which, in his opinion, some films projected. Paradoxically, African stereotypes of whites were fuelled by the very medium that Europeans had introduced as an educational tool. 'Is it right', Monseigneur Biéchy wondered, 'that just when the role of the European is everywhere being questioned, whites should be shown in scenes of intrigue and frivolity, and half-naked?' Conveying his opinion of films being shown in Poto-Poto and Bacongo cinemas, he went on: 'Between two love scenes, we see Europeans in a fight. Isn't it better to show decent whites at work, those who must labour to make a living in workshops and workyards, and the peasant behind his plough?'[84] The Governor-General, while agreeing that 'it is desirable that films should be educational and show France in a good light', noted that too narrow an orientation in subject matter 'would pose a difficult commercial problem' since audiences might boycott cinemas if they were not given the films that they wanted.[85] There had already been trouble for cinema-managers when young audiences had jeered at the screen, rioted, and demanded their money back because a film lacked 'action'.[86] Thus, the limits on entertainment were set not only by a board of censors but by African consumers as well.

Leisure organized

The indigénat and the justice indigène came to an end following the 1944 Brazzaville conference.[87] However, even before the Second World War, some administrators had adopted a paternalistic mode towards African leisure which complemented but did not supersede the coercive approach of the earlier period. The recreational groups that Eboué referred to in his 1941 manifesto came into existence partly through pressures from young workers and partly from contemporary thinking in Europe, where church and secular authorities were endeavouring to develop 'rational recreation' among burgeoning town populations.

The Catholic priests drew their inspiration from work in French parishes. Since the mid-nineteenth century, the idea of patronages or youth clubs, where young people could find recreation and entertainment after work hours and receive training in religious, civic and social matters under the symbolic 'patronage' of a saint and the actual supervision of church workers, was a key element in Catholic social action.[88] In applying these ideas to youth organizations in Brazzaville, where there were so many single young men in the population, the mission had two goals: first, to provide entertainment and instruction for young Christians who were 'attracted by the smell of the town' and were subject to the 'bad example of pagan workers'; and second, to bring potential converts into the missionary net.[89] It was, therefore, not a coincidence that social work at the Catholic mission started just about the time that the Christian villages, which could be kept under close supervision, were being destroyed and their inhabitants sent to live with the general Bacongo and Poto-Poto population. While the impoverished administration had difficulty in organizing a functioning primary school, the Catholic mission embarked on an ambitious youth programme.

About 1907, the Brazzaville priests had started a recreational club, the Patronage Saint-Louis, where young workers met on Sunday afternoon

1   The youth club band at the Catholic mission, *c.* 1920 (Archives of
the Holy Ghost Fathers, Chevilly)

for organized activities such as games, music, drama and religious study.
As the club became popular, meetings were also held in the evenings.
Membership gave young people a chance to display their place in the
Christian community, for on Sundays and important church festivals
they marched in uniforms, carried flags, played in a trumpet-and-drum
band, formed an honour guard, and helped with crowd control.[90] In
1913, a large building for club activities was completed and inaugurated
before a crowd of Africans and Europeans. It was the first time that
anything had been done to provide leisure facilities for Brazzaville's
African population, so the missionaries had pulled off a major coup.[91] In
his speech, given first in French, and later translated for the African
audience, Father Remy explained the goals of the youth club:

We want our club to address the task of moral preservation; for you know, as I
do, that young people encounter dangers at every turn, if they are not kept within
the fold and guided ... first they have to diligently finish their work at their place
of employment...then, and only after their work is finished, can they come to the
club to play, amuse themselves, and exercise their youthful bodies, as is necessary.
That is why we have games of all kinds, and in this way we will distance them
from immoral dances and from dangerous company.[92]

The opening festivities were followed by a theatrical performance which was watched by 2,000–3,000 Africans and 150 Europeans from both sides of the Pool. By 1918, 700 young people were coming regularly to the club to play games and sport and to practise their instruments.[93] Seven years later, an administrator admitted that the colonial government had done little for the 'moral training' of Africans, and depended on missionaries for any kind of social work.[94]

Between the wars, however, colonial administrators, pressured by the expanding town population, by a perceived threat from opposition groups such as the followers of Matswa, by competition from the church, and by the needs of the colonial economy, modified their hardline attitudes and began to take a more active role in organizing young workers. Like the missionaries, they were in part influenced by developments in Europe, where adults had identified 'youth' as a problematic social category and had established a host of organizations to harness their energies and socialize them to middle-class values.[95] In France, by 1935, half a million young people were members of sports clubs, Scout troops, after-school study groups, and young workers' associations, both secular and religious.[96] In 1936, the Popular Front government appointed the first Under-Secretary for Leisure and Sport, dubbed by opponents the *Ministre de la Paresse* (the 'Minister for Laziness'). In 1936, also, as more liberal colonial officials were appointed, the Equatorial African government adopted a more paternalistic and less coercive posture. Although he did not abolish the *indigénat* and, like Eboué, advocated harsh disciplinary measures to control the town's unstable population, associated mostly with Poto-Poto, Governor-General Reste recognized the need for more investment in work and leisure training.[97] In this he was both acting on his own assessment of a historical situation where the system of concessionary-company rule 'had given the country nothing',[98] and was following the directions of his superiors in Paris. 'I want you to interest yourself in social work,' read a letter from the Minister of Colonies. 'It is indispensable from a human and political point of view in a country whose inhabitants are prey to intense misery.'[99]

The growth of a settled urban population was also cited as a pressing reason for investing in organized leisure. An article in the influential *Courrier d'Afrique* on 'Sport in Brazzaville' noted that 'African children are more and more distanced from the values and traditions of villages' and that 'something must be done to organize their leisure time especially on Sundays and Thursdays after school'. This could be done by private organizations, but it was time for the administration to commit funds to construct stadiums and velodromes. The writer concluded that 'sport cannot be restricted to the privileged few'. In particular, the means must be found for facilities in Brazzaville which had nothing to compare with those developed for the African population of Kinshasa.[100]

The *Stade Eboué* (Eboué Stadium), officially blessed by de Gaulle at the time he attended the Brazzaville conference, was a partial fulfilment of these new official directions. Together with Eboué, who had been a sportsman in his youth, and the other francophone-Africa governors attending the conference, de Gaulle watched segregated teams play football matches at the stadium which he inaugurated in 1944. It was also, for Brazzaville, a remarkable symbol of church–state co-operation. Built on the edge of Poto-Poto with a combination of mission and administration funds under the direction of the mission youth director, the stadium seated 32,000.[101]

Organizing these new initiatives was not only in the hands of mission-aries and administrators. Individual Europeans, who carried to Africa experience as youth organizers, also took a leading role in helping young people to acquire skills in the new recreational activities. A French dentist in the colonial service, Jean Mouly, was an amateur sportsman with previous experience in organizing football in Morocco and Mada-gascar. He was the first president of the 'native section' of the CAB and, in his spare time, coached promising athletes in football and gymnastics. His popularity with African players made him an essential intermediary in negotiations between town officials and Bacongo and Poto-Poto football teams in the early 1930s.[102] Likewise, the scoutmasters who established the first Brazzaville troop carried to Africa experience of Scouting in France.[103]

Efforts to organize African recreation at first targeted the elites. Scouting was seen as an excellent training-ground 'to form an elite who in turn will exercise a good influence over the masses' wrote a priest.[104] The emphasis on moral and physical training was symbolized in the partnership of the two men who founded the first troop in 1929. Adolphe Sicé was a military doctor and Director of the Pasteur Institute, and Father le Bail ran the youth work at the Bacongo Catholic mission. The Lieutenant-Governor of Moyen-Congo was appointed as honorary pre-sident, together with a committee of influential patrons in the white business community, who helped finance uniforms, equipment, travel and camping.[105] While they taught the usual Scouting virtues of physical fitness, selflessness and honesty, troop organizers emphasized the pa-triotic and paramilitary tradition of the organization. Scouts must be loyal and 'acquire the devotion that will make them good servants of the Colony', wrote le Bail.[106] In 1936, responsibility for organizing Scouts in Equatorial Africa was given to the chief military officer in the govern-ment. A memorandum prepared for the Governor-General's office noted that children in the Bacongo and Poto-Poto government schools were too young to participate, because of paramilitary training.[107] At the height of the Second World War in 1942 a patriotic rally at Pointe-Noire drew together over 1,400 Scouts from different parts of Equatorial Africa in a show of national preparedness. For the first time, Girl Guides, part of a newly organized group at the Catholic mission joined in. In a 1941 report, the bishop noted that 784 young people were registered in Brazzaville's Catholic youth organizations.[108]

Former Scouts tell of mixed reasons for joining the organization. Like those who marched in the youth club band at an earlier period they considered the symbols of success in the new society to be of great importance. These included wearing an attractive uniform and travelling outside Brazzaville for camping, or even to Europe, in the case of a few who went to jamborees overseas. One informant especially remembered the socks and shoes that he wore, and another that he wore a beret for the first time at Scout meetings.[109] The significance of such symbols was not lost on Europeans. At the time, a troop leader observed that 'young people in Scouts only see the uniforms' and that clothes were important in attracting boys to the organization. Once enrolled, a 'moral discipline' could be inculcated by leaders.[110] Yet, boys would not come without the uniforms. In 1952, a French Social Service worker reported that the number of Scouts had dwindled since funds had run out.[111] A similar comment appeared in a missionary report on youth work. 'Scouting is keeping up in the town,' it said, but 'in the bush it lasted as long as the uniforms, that is to say it was scarcely more than the clothing'.[112] Even in the town, interest fizzled out after a high point was reached during and immediately after the war. Missionaries blamed the attractions of the town for the fact that monitors were unwilling to stay after school and help as leaders. An article in *La Semaine* attacked the *évolués* for their lack of leadership in youth organizations, saying that 'speaking in long phrases and wearing sunglasses is not enough'; and that 'everyone will agree that leaning on a bar dressed up in a flashy suit [*un costume 'swing'*] does not forge a nation'.[113] It is remarkable that the failure of Scouting to catch on among young people occurred at the time when a new urban culture expressed by an interest in football, the cinema, fashion and music was booming. These activities all contributed to an emerging youth culture which to some extent cut across other divisions of class and ethnicity and were a much more powerful force than European-inspired organizations.

Other efforts of administrators to separate the urban elite in cultural organizations also met with mixed success. The need to start a club for school-leavers was first raised by the Mayor of Brazzaville in 1931 when he proposed action against the 'insidious political activity' of Matswa's followers among the Bacongo elite. To counter this influence he suggested that a club building with equipment, a library and a room for social events be constructed near the primary school. A few months later, little progress had been made, for the issue became yet another occasion for the Matswaistes to organize a boycott.[114] In 1935, the Catholics established an association for former students in their schools (*Associations des Anciens Elèves*), and in 1938 a similar organization was started by those who had attended Brazzaville's government schools (*Association Amicale des Anciens Elèves des Ecoles urbaines et professionelles*).[115]

Eboué also followed through on his goal of promoting a class of *notables évolués* among urban leaders to parallel the 'traditional' chiefs whom he had recognized in his *Nouvelle politique indigène*. In this endeavour, he depended heavily on three prominent Gabonese civil servants. Jean-Remy Ayouné, Jean-Hilaire Aubame and René-Paul Sousatte had all attended a Catholic seminary in Libreville or Brazzaville and were posted to the federal capital when civil service positions opened up for Africans in 1936–7. These young men, especially Ayouné, became close friends with Eboué and advised him on African matters. In 1942, and under the patronage of the Governor-General, they established *L'Union Educative et Mutuelle de la Jeunesse de Brazzaville* (Education Union and Youth Association of Brazzaville).[116] Their cultural activities and newsletter were subsidized by a grant from the Governor-General's office. In an early issue the President, Sousatte, as the voice of this small group of Catholic intellectuals, set forth the need for the organization. According to him, *évolués* felt isolated among the urban masses and needed to draw together for mutual help and self-improvement. Like so many other associations of the 1940s and 1950s, the organization was partly inspired by various types of mutual-aid association common in African village society. The organization was therefore not an 'innovation' wrote the President, but 'based on existing principles'. It also aimed at 'physical and intellectual education'. The members met first at each others' homes and then at the Catholic mission. There were sections for drama and music, sports and social events. The newsletter gives a sense of the leisure interests and aspirations of this particular group of Brazzaville's elite. Apart from regular meetings there were drama performances of plays written by members, such as *Sons of Empire*, a patriotic piece by Ayouné, which played to segregated audiences; dances; outings to Léopoldville; and a children's festival with a beautiful-baby contest under the patronage of Madame Eboué.[117] By 1944, however, the organization had only forty-four members and it never really gathered much support. According to one official report many events planned ended in a 'fiasco' because of the poor attendance and lack of interest. The organization had failed because the initiatives came too much from the administration and their chosen representatives.[118] As for the other community leaders, they were swept up in activities in Bacongo and Poto-Poto, often playing leadership roles in popular activities started through grassroots initiatives.[119]

After the war, in the more liberal atmosphere of the post-Brazzaville-conference period, the administration focused more on mass action and less on the elite. Initiatives involved the creation of a Department of Social Service, 'to research and improve the material and moral conditions of individuals', and a Service of Youth and Sports to oversee the organization of clubs in the workplace, in schools and in the townships. They also imported equipment and upgraded facilities.[120] Regional and national structures to institutionalize sport also came into existence. Participation by African representatives on executive committees paralleled their advancement in politics, local administration, the civil service and trade unions.

At the same time as trying to influence mass interests, the administration continued to attempt to form a cadre of community leaders through shaping their leisure. Post-war levels of public and private investment allowed the construction of 'cultural centres' in Bacongo and Poto-Poto which had meeting rooms for classes, lectures, conferences, and social events; and a reading room with books, newspapers such as *Courrier d'Afrique* and *France-Afrique*, and popular scientific, sports and news magazines from France.[121] The cultural centres also had radios and loudspeakers, film projectors and educational films, gramophones and records, and equipment for sports and Scouting. The administration also allocated funds for teachers and equipment for drama, art and musical activities. In Bacongo, for example, novice musicians could play saxophones, guitars, banjos, accordions and a piano.[122] In the early 1950s, the cultural centres ran programmes every night of the week. During the month of October 1950, for example, over a thousand people attended film shows with attractions such as *A tour of France, Around Paris, Goal!* and *Capturing and raising crocodiles*. Europeans such as military officers or engineers were invited to give lectures on their careers, and white women ran child-rearing and household management classes for the wives of the elite.[123] Organized by an African executive committee under the supervision of a European administrator from the Governor-General's office, membership was by application only, although friends and family could attend events. Individuals requesting membership had to sign a statement saying: 'I will follow regularly the different activities that are beneficial for my own improvement.'[124]

Flyers posted around Poto-Poto in November 1948 were quite specific on the targeted group, since they bore the heading: 'African elite of Brazzaville, your club has been born!' Proclaiming a 'Mass meeting at the commune centre', the announcement reported 'important subsidies from the federation budget under the High Commissioner's office, in order to give the indigenous elite a well-equipped meeting place'. At the first Poto-Poto meeting, 161 aspiring members showed up. The list of their names, ages and occupations is informative as it shows who were considered part of the 'elite' at this point in time: civil servants, monitors, artisans, clerks, orderlies, drivers, nurses, traders and mechanics. At a similar meeting in Bacongo, 183 members were enrolled whose occupations were much the same as their Poto-Poto counterparts, but with a noticeably greater number of domestic servants and tailors.[125]

Like other efforts by the administration to develop safe structures within which an African leadership might be formed in the European mould, the cultural centres met with only partial success.[126] The most lasting legacy of the experiment was the highly successful literary magazine, *Liaison*, published by African intellectuals with government subsidies during the 1950s. Today, it is an important record of their opinions, activities and talents. Among the activities of the centres, those that corresponded most with popular interests drew the largest crowds, so there was always good attendance for films, dances and sporting events. The football team at the Poto-Poto cultural centre was one of the top teams in the town; and several musicians who later played in popular bands started playing foreign musical instruments and learning Western harmonies and musical notation in classes at the cultural centres.[127] On the other hand, the centres were also a focus of resistance, expressed both overtly and through apathy. Posters advertising events were torn down and defaced with graffiti in Poto-Poto; attendance at lectures given by Europeans was markedly lower than for dances, films and other popular events;[128] and the football teams became a vehicle for breaking away from European control. The centres were probably most important for the elite, giving them experience in leadership roles and prominence among their peers, which could be turned to political advantage.

Conclusion

Attempts by the dominant colonial class to influence the leisure of those who lived in Bacongo and Poto-Poto were clearly part of the broader colonial strategy to regulate and reproduce an orderly urban society of productive workers and subject populations who would imbibe European values and coexist in a non-threatening manner with white society. All over francophone Africa, the authorities were seeking to develop such 'safe structures' to integrate African youth.[129] For a small section of the African elite such hegemonic strategies appear to have been successful. On reading the sources, however, one is left with the distinct impression that the French in Brazzaville had their backs to the wall a great deal of the time and were responding to the demands of the populations of Bacongo and Poto-Poto rather than setting the pace. Although attempts to develop youth organizations, for example, may seem to come from the top down, the sources rather suggest that the French, whether administrators or missionaries, were scrambling to develop initiatives demanded by Africans workers, most of them young men.

In the specific case of Brazzaville, the weakness of the colonial presence meant that resources of administrators were continually stretched and insufficient to accommodate popular demand. Before the 1930s, the lack of infrastructure and schooling meant that administrators tried to enforce colonial order primarily through coercive tactics. In the last thirty years or so of colonialism, pressure from the town's population forced European authorities to intervene in Bacongo and Poto-Poto life in a more paternalistic manner. Although influenced by a changing European climate towards the socialization of youth, the fact was that on the ground, Brazzaville administrators had little choice but to try new strategies as they were faced with an increasingly self-conscious urban population.

As has been repeated several times, it was the Catholic mission that pioneered the effort to organize the leisure of young workers. However, a close reading of mission reports to the mother house in Paris and to the Vatican also shows that pressure from the urban population had drawn the missionaries much further into social work than they had originally intended. During the 1920s, lack of resources had caused the work with young people to flag, but by the 1930s, the mission found that in order to retain their influence, they had to revive their *patronage* and involve themselves in sport and youth organizations far beyond the level they had originally anticipated. Once primary schools were established in Bacongo and Poto-Poto, competition from the secular authorities had to be reckoned with. In 1931, Monseigneur Guichard reported to his superiors that: 'The work is continuing despite difficulties. Ideas of independence and emancipation are spreading among the young people in Brazzaville and surrounding areas. The public schools are making a great effort to monopolize youth.' He went on to note that 'the Protestants are also very active' and that 'we are reorganizing our youth club which has been neglected for lack of personnel'.[130] A few years later, the Mission again reported 'the danger from the administration which is making a great effort to take over children and youth'.[131] A visitor to the Catholic mission in 1933 was impressed with the number of youth organizations in the town. He made the telling comment: 'We scarcely thought when we came to Africa that we would be arranging matches, sporting competitions and Scout troops...but once sports are established near us it becomes necessary for us to adopt them in order to main contact with African youth.'[132]

The conflict of church and state was recognized by the leadership of African communities who had mostly grown up under missionary tutelage, and it was exploited by them to improve the leisure facilities and equipment they needed, as will be seen in the next chapter. The new activities imported from Europe needed skills, equipment and facilities that townspeople did not have the resources to acquire. In this respect, if they wanted to appropriate European cultural forms, they had to find European sponsors to give financial and technical support, at least in the initial stages. The footballers who laid out their own football field in Poto-Poto could not upgrade their play without help from European sponsors, but they could negotiate with both the missionaries and the secular authorities to their advantage. Similarly, when the Brazzaville priests insisted that Scouts in their troop had to attend mass on Sundays, the members took their complaints to the administration, just as the Catholic women who wanted to dance in the Fourteenth of July festivities took their complaints to the Town Hall.

The struggle over leisure space, time and activities, which has been discussed in these first three chapters, was also played out in specific recreational activities in Bacongo and Poto-Poto. While the leadership continued to negotiate with Europeans, popular culture was taking on a life of its own quite outside the orbit of colonial relations. This will become evident as we pursue the study of these activities in the chapters that follow.

4 Football is king

The title of this chapter comes from a comment by Fulbert Kimina-Makumbu, Congo's premier sports journalist, who said in an interview: 'Football is everyone's sport, football is king.'[1] He was contrasting it with other sports such as basketball, athletics, cycling, volley-ball and boxing. All have their adherents but, since it was first played in Poto-Poto and Bacongo, football has retained its overwhelming popularity. The phrase 'King Football' is also used in the semi-autobiographical account of Jean-Claude Ganga, for many years Minister of Sport in the Republic of Congo.[2] For a former star of the Bacongo team, *Diables Noirs*, football is 'natural' for a Congolese boy.[3] It is fun, cheap, and easy to learn. It can be enjoyed at any level, for 'it involves no special talent'.[4] It is a game not just for players, but also for spectators, who can be fiercely partisan. A history of a top Poto-Poto club, *Renaissance*, recalls a heated controversy in the early 1950s which ended by splitting both the team and fans. As a result, 'many households and families were involved in real dramas in Poto-Poto. Children and nephews were chased from their father's house, spouses torn from their spouses, relations wouldn't speak to each other.'[5] While the hyperbole of a sports writer is probably present in the above statement, the intensity of emotions aroused by football is confirmed by other incidents described in this chapter. Football was also a socializing agency for young migrant workers, for through individual skills a boy or young man could achieve fame in the community and quickly pass from newcomer status to acceptance. Successful players were held in awe by the crowds, who gave them nicknames according to their styles, and they were followed in the streets by boys who idolized them. Recognition on the sports field could in some measure compensate for the ignominies of the colonial work-place and the tyranny of the *indigénat*. The history of sport in Brazzaville also turns out to be an unexpected window on the multi-faceted colonial experience, which demonstrates the interplay of culture and political life. Football involved not only co-operation and confrontation with church and state but also the working out of relationships and loyalties within the town's population. This chapter traces the history of football from its early days in the streets of Bacongo and Poto-Poto to its first 'golden age' when teams were organized through grassroots action, and to its glorious years after the Second World War, when top teams played before thousands at Eboué Stadium.

Football beginnings

The origins of football in Brazzaville are obscure, since neither written nor oral sources go back much before 1920. What seems clear is that the vast majority of Africans learned the game from watching others play, and then trying it out themselves in informal games. When the schools and mission introduced football in the late 1920s, it seems to have been more a response to popular demand than due to initiatives of teachers and youth organizers. Compared to anglophone Africa where, following the British tradition, 'muscular missionaries' and teachers established team games almost as soon as they arrived, the tradition of competitive sport was slower to arrive in francophone Africa.[6] In nineteenth-century France there was little physical education in the school curriculum and, when it was introduced in the early twentieth century, the German brand of mass gymnastics was favoured. The upper and middle classes took up team sports in private clubs, but funds for sports facilities in the state schools lagged behind.[7] In Brazzaville, the Urban School, which opened in 1912, had fifteen minutes of gymnastics in the daily curriculum.[8] At the mission stations, physical exercise was introduced for young people, but the Swedish Protestants favoured graceful exercises and gymnastics in the Scandanavian tradition.[9] At the Catholic mission, children also had gymnastics in their daily schedule, but their main physical exercise, growing their own food, was more utilitarian. The youth club, however, was the first European institution to sponsor team games. One that seems to have been a cross between golf and hockey, played with a stick and a makeshift ball, was popular with the priests and mission youth. There is no particular mention of football at the youth club before 1928, by which time it was 'the game in greatest demand'.[10]

The earliest organized matches that Africans watched were between European teams. As happened elsewhere, for example in Brazil and South Africa, foreigners organized games in their spare time and attracted the attention of local spectators.[11] The first white team remembered, called *Eléphants* by African crowds, was made up of French and Belgian players. A team at the military base, the *Equipe Sportive Militaire*, was nicknamed *Gobi*, after the French NCOs who played on it.[12] By 1913, Europeans had formed a *Union Sportive Brazzavilloise* which organized football and tennis matches, including international games against teams from Léopoldville. Crowds turned out for special matches, for example one staged in 1915 to raise money for the war disabled. Such occasions were sufficiently important in the small world of Brazzaville to rate a mention in both the Catholic mission and the Swedish mission journals. For a match between Belgian Congo and French Congo in 1914, the teams borrowed the playing field at the Catholic mission. African and European spectators watched a 'fierce struggle' and listened to a performance by the military band at half-time.[13] In Léopoldville, where the white population was two to three times that of Brazzaville, the Belgians, Flemish, French and British each fielded a separate team. African spectators admired and remembered individual players. An Englishman, who captained the *Nomades* of Kinshasa, was nicknamed *mabaya* (Lingala, 'planks' or 'beams') because of his shin-guards and powerful play, while the captain of the Belgian team, *Les Coqs*, a speedy player on the left wing, was called *tata ya bana* (Lingala, 'father of the children'). In 1926, European sports enthusiasts joined together to form an exclusive sports club, the *Club Athlètique Brazzavillois* (CAB). A year later, they moved from their makeshift ground to the newly constructed Marchand Stadium where a section was reserved for African spectators. Football was not just a game but a festive occasion, with bands, banners and multi-coloured team uniforms. Brazzaville crowds especially admired the CAB gear: their blue shirts emblazoned with a shield bearing the French cockerel, their white shorts and red socks.[14]

The comings and goings of workers, traders and family members across the Pool powerfully influenced the exchange of fresh ideas on popular culture between the colonial capitals. On the Belgian side of the river the Belgian missionaries and a local businessman were the first patrons of African football teams. In 1919, in Kinshasa, Father Raphael established the *Association Royale Sportive Congolaise* to formalize teams and organize competitions for African players.[15] According to the testimony of those involved, the desire to have teams that could give their cross-Pool rivals a good match was a primary consideration in the decision of African footballers in Poto-Poto and Bacongo to form their own clubs.[16]

Western sports were new in their structure, in their plethora of rules, and in their time-frame which reflected the industrial society in which they were born.[17] Sport as physical, organized and competitive exercise was not completely alien to the young workers who watched Europeans play football, however. Certain values such as courage, endurance and individual skill were also qualities admired in village recreational activities. Looking for analogues of modern sport in pre-colonial 'sportslike' activities is a bit problematic, nevertheless, especially moving from description to meaning. The problem is lack of research on village activities. John Blacking, in an essay on the subject, finds some continuities but also points out the very fragmented nature of the data. Social anthropologists of the mid-twentieth century wrote a great deal about kinship, marriage, religion, economies and political organization, but little about games, sport and dance. This did not reflect the interests of African societies, but rather those of field-workers for whom games and related topics were trivia. Thus 'a great opportunity was missed' not only to describe traditional sportslike activities, but to delve into their meaning.[18] Blacking does conclude, however, that European sport had some analogues in village activities and some Congolese examples seem to support this conclusion.

Eboué, a track and rugby star in France in his youth, spent two decades as an administrator in Ubangi-Shari before he was appointed chief administrator in Brazzaville. Writing of the physical challenges faced by young men in initiation societies, he found that they attempted to instil values in a similar manner to the training he had received in France. Eboué marvelled at skills in knife- and spear-throwing of young initiates; feats of physical endurance, including running over obstacle courses; and the energy and precision of dance, all attributes of Western sport. In a race along the Ubangi river, staged in honour of French visitors, three canoes, each with between thirty and sixty paddlers, covered 90 kilometres in six-and-a-half hours.[19]

Wrestling was another popular activity throughout the Congo-Ubangi region. On the middle Ubangi, men trained boys as wrestlers from the age of five and watched over their development until adolescence. Matches between village teams were publicized in advance and impatiently awaited. Hosts prepared food and beer for the visitors. Drums announced the beginning of the match and athletic dances were performed to warm up the crowd. Breaking rules met with disgrace and disqualification. The team with the most victories won. The victor and vanquished danced into the night, a practice less common in modern sport, however.[20] On the north side of the middle Congo, wrestling matches took place in a corridor formed by spectators. The contest lasted a few minutes and the winner went on to challenge another fighter.[21] In the lower Congo, wrestling was part of the physical training that men gave to young boys who would later be hunters and porters in long-distance caravans.[22]

Ball games were also known, for example among the Tio and in the Bakongo region. In one game similar to hockey, the players used a ball made from banana tree bark, or a carved piece of wood, or palm-nuts. Players cut their own curved sticks from forest trees.[23] Boys in the Kongo area played a kind of football, storing up a large supply of lemons in advance. The lemon, or 'ball', was placed on a line drawn on the boundary between two villages. The objective was to kick the lemon past the guard of the other team. If the opponents succeeded in stopping the 'ball', they would take turns kicking it towards the opposing team.[24]

Dancing for entertainment by young men and women was also a time to show off physical prowess, to display individual creativity, and to express corporate identity.[25] According to one Congolese writer: 'The best kyébé-kyébé dancers are given the same kind of adulation as the winners of a bicycle race. The crowds are critical and praise the stars who dance last. Dancers go to the religious specialist to obtain the power to do well.'[26] In the same way, Congo crowds gave adulation to star players, who also went to religious specialists to help their play.[27] In some respects, therefore, it can be said with some confidence that European sport must have resonated in the experience of the young men who watched football matches and, furthermore, must have contributed to the manner of their participation. It was not just a question of the conditions of town life drawing players and crowds to sport, continuities from village experience also influenced participation in the town.

Brazzaville football was a child of the streets, popularized by players in neighbourhood games. Football was a common sight around Poto-Poto and Bacongo by the 1920s. The straight dirt roads were playgrounds where boys could join together in scratch games.[28] Ganga describes the beginnings of his 'football odyssey' in the Aviation district of Bacongo.[29] He started at the age of five, playing barefooted with a rag ball. The games were timeless, for no one wanted to lose; the boys might stay out on the streets for up to ten hours, unless their mothers called them home. It was a world removed from adults. Only occasionally would an irate neighbour confiscate a ball kicked over a fence, or a mother call her son to run an errand or help in her farm. Schoolboys joined in after classes, on Sundays and during vacations. When the older boys played a *mwana-foot* team from another neighbourhood, the younger boys would cheer them on. A high point of Ganga's early years was when his brother-in-law, the caretaker of the Catholic mission field, allowed the boys to play there with a leather ball.

By 1925, young men set about organizing football in Poto-Poto and Bacongo more systematically. Foreign workers from West Africa, Gabon and the Belgian Congo, who already knew football, were important resources. In Poto-Poto, those who had attended the Urban School joined together in the *Club Scolaire Brazzavillois*, while another group started the team, *Napoléon I*. Members met to discuss club business; paid dues to buy balls, nets and uniforms; and volunteered to referee games. In 1929, they formed the Native Sports Federation to co-ordinate activities and arrange matches. The story of how the players received permission from the municipal authorities to clear ground and lay out a playing-field in Poto-Poto has already been told in chapter 2. By 1931, there were eleven independent teams, each with hundreds of supporters.[30]

The scramble for football

Given the numbers of workers who played or watched football, it is not surprising that sport became yet another field of combat for the Catholic church and the colonial administration. It was a three-cornered struggle, however, for at the centre of the conflict were the young men who had pioneered football teams in Poto-Poto and Bacongo. Their problem was how to take advantage of European expertise and funds without losing their autonomy. As they were approached by the administration with offers of equipment, coaches and well-maintained fields, they had little desire to see the tentacles of colonial authority reaching into their leisure. On the other hand, they could make only limited progress in raising the level of their game without better facilities, training and advice on how to improve their skills. In particular, they could not hope for success against their African rivals from Kinshasa, who had been organized for more than a decade in the *Association Royale Sportive Congolaise*; nor could they bring their level of play to that of the Europeans, whom they watched in Sunday-afternoon matches at the Marchand Stadium. According to some team captains at the time, 'love of sport' made them agree to a take-over of their Native Sports Federation by the colonial authorities in 1931.[31]

From the perspective of the colonial administration, even football was potentially subversive if it was allowed to flourish independent of European oversight. As we have noted, the Depression had thrown hundreds out of work and those who had lost their jobs in Belgian Congo returned to Brazzaville, swelling the numbers of unemployed. As far as the whites were concerned, the unemployed were the seeds of trouble. 'Red peril in black countries' ran a headline in *L'Etoile* in January 1931. 'A breeding ground for communism', wrote Monseigneur Biéchy to his superiors in Paris.[32] Also problematic for the French was the Matswa controversy and popular demonstrations in favour of the imprisoned leader. European nervousness was further increased by an incident on the Brazzaville–Kinshasa ferry, when a European who had beaten his African servant was stabbed to death.[33] Rumour was rampant among Europeans, who saw every servant, clerk and passer-by as a potential revolutionary and assassin.

In this atmosphere, then, any meetings of Africans fell under suspicion. In 1930, the editor of L'Etoile urged action:

What are these meetings that are going on continuously in Bacongo and Poto-Poto? The municipality, the Congo administration and the Catholic mission can no longer ignore them...why don't we act quickly, even a little harshly? There are too many vagrants living, we know not how, in Brazzaville. We need to purge the native townships and quickly.[34]

The best way to control African football seemed to be through Europeans overseeing the Native Sports Federation. The official position was explained by the Lieutenant-Governor in a letter to the Governor-General:

The Federation was created through a desire to develop sport. At the same time, however, requiring the native sports clubs to be affiliated with the official body will allow an additional means of surveillance, so that we can prevent undesirable elements who, under the cover of sport, get together for the purpose of political agitation and provoking disorder.[35]

The Governor-General agreed 'that it is normal and necessary that sports should be the object of special surveillance when you have reason to believe that public order is in danger'.[36]

The arrival of Frenchmen who had experience in sport and physical education also meant that there were more Europeans willing to help organize African teams. By 1930, team sports in France had become a mass phenomenon. Seen as a source of national rejuvenation and a training-ground for citizens after the First World War, schools received funds for physical education facilities and staff.[37] Similar developments took place in the colonies. A report on schools in AEF for 1931–2 noted that government funds had been allocated for gymnastics apparatus; students in Brazzaville had given gymnastic displays; and football teams had been organized in a number of schools throughout the region. 'The benefits of physical exercise for the development of the race and the acquistion of social and moral qualities (discipline, loyalty) are not in doubt', concluded the writer.[38] These developments meant that the colonial service by the 1930s included men with experience in sports organization.[39] In Brazzaville, the French were fortunate to have in their service Jean Mouly, an amateur sportsman popular with African football players since he helped to coach them in his spare time. For them, 'he was like our father'. He now became the mediator for negotiations between the administration and Poto-Poto and Bacongo team leaders. In a meeting, he laid out the advantages of a federation under European direction.[40] With help from Europeans and with government sponsorship, township teams would have access to equipment and uniforms and receive coaching from the best players in Brazzaville. They would also have help with expenses and permits when they wanted to travel to Kinshasa and other towns for away games. The argument was sufficiently attractive for team leaders to agree to the idea of a reconstituted Native Sports Federation under European direction to be set up with Mouly as its first president.[41]

Observing these events with some alarm was a third party, the Catholic missionaries. For almost two decades, their youth club had been invaluable in recruiting young people for the church. Now they saw members drifting away to join the autonomous township football teams and the administration's sports organization.[42] In 1933, therefore, the priests reinvigorated their youth work, setting up a new organization specifically for sport, the *Fédération Athlètique Congolaise* (FAC). A parish magazine, *Le Bon Message*, where literate Christians could follow mission events including sports reports, was started in the same year.[43]

The rivalry of church and state was to continue for the next five years, with African footballers able to play off one European faction against the other. The mission claimed that the secular authorities were trying to impose a monopoly on African sport through insisting that all African sports organizations had to join the federation, and that only teams affiliated with the federation could play on Brazzaville's municipal facilities.[44] For the missionaries, behind all this lurked an anti-clericalism exported from France and fomented by senior colonial officials who were also Freemasons. Administrators such as Mouly, on the other hand, argued that the priests were using sport for their own ends, that is to force young Africans who played on their teams to attend mass.[45] Africans were the real winners in this interchange, since they could choose to play for either church or state teams, depending on which offered them the best opportunities.

The initial days of football under the European-controlled Native Sports Federation and the FAC of the Catholic mission are remembered in Brazzaville as the first golden age of football.[46] Although there was loss of autonomy, some of the promised benefits materialized. With the help of government subsidies, nets, balls, shirts and socks became available to the top teams. Each club had a European president and coach who worked with the players to improve their skills. The municipal authorities cleared new sports grounds. African teams played before large crowds at the Marchand Stadium in warm-up matches before games between white teams. Old teams were reorganized and new ones were formed, for example *Racing*, named after the famous Paris club; *Coqs d'AEF*; *Nomades*, after the favourite British team in Léopoldville; *Union*; *Stade Africain* ('African Stadium'); *Lune Sportive* ('Sporting Moon'); and *Indépendant*. In the first Federation championship of 1931, twenty-seven teams competed. A cup was awarded to the winner, *Etoile* of Poto-Poto, while the players received sports equipment.[47] Spectators cheered their favourite players, whose nicknames became household words: Goye, called 'd'Artagnan' after the hero of *The Three Musketeers*; Bakaki, called 'Mikado', the name of the most powerful locomotive on the Congo-Océan line; Kinzonzi, 'Eleven'; Momengo, 'Show-off'; and Makosso, 'Hammer'.[48]

The Federation co-operated with the *Association Royale Sportive Congolaise* of Kinshasa to organize matches. In 1931, a game was played at Bacongo between the Brazzaville champions *Etoile* of Poto-Poto and *Union* of Kinshasa. A large crowd from both sides of the Pool turned up to watch. The Brazzaville team won 5–1 and received a large silver trophy. After the game, boisterous crowds danced in the streets and celebrated throughout the night. In March 1936, the sports authorities of Kinshasa and Brazzaville organized the first inter-club tournament in which twenty-five teams and their reserves, 350 players in all, participated.[49] As football developed, so did fan loyalties. Supporters followed their teams, crossing the Pool for Sunday matches or trekking across town to see matches between Poto-Poto and Bacongo teams, or between government school teams and Christian teams.

Within three years of the take-over by European administrators, the Native Sports Federation had fallen on hard times, however, and African players and fans, disillusioned with white management, staged boycotts and strikes. Team captains who had negotiated with European organizers had been promised a stadium; plans were drawn up, but they did not materialize since the finances were not forthcoming. African clubs, as long as they played on open pieces of ground, could not collect gate-money from spectators to cover expenses. The equipment provided by the federation was never adequate, even for major teams.[50] Dadet, who played at the time, remembered that players often showed up for matches 'in a pitiful state, with old shorts, torn shirts and socks and broken-down shoes'.[51] Africans felt cheated and claimed the available funds were being given to white athletes, pointing out that the CAB had remodelled its Marchand Stadium with new changing-rooms, tennis courts and athletics facilities. After Mouly returned to France, he had been succeeded by Captain Daudet as director of the Sports Federation. 'What the *Fédération Sportive Indigène* did not recognize', he told the Governor-General, 'was the level of enthusiasm among African players.' There were never enough facilities, European personnel or funds for equipment to match popular demand. As players became disillusioned with the football organization, they were erratic in attending training session and matches.[52] Others took up the option of playing for the Catholic mission where sports continued to be well organized. They played for FAC teams that had become bywords for excellence in Brazzaville football, such as *Olympique* of Bacongo. Reporting on a victory in the magazine *Le Bon Message*, the writer noted that the mission teams were 'as good as the best in Kinshasa'.[53] Representing a mission team, whether in gymnastics, or football or athletics, meant being well turned out, for the shirts and shorts were sewn by the Sisters and schoolgirls at the Javouhey convent. Uniforms were given out for important occasions and turned in afterwards to be laundered and repaired. While the Christian gymnasts and football players at the 1933 Bastille Day march-past could show off their smart gear, the Federation teams were shoddily clad.[54]

A further rift between African footballers and European administrators developed from their conflicting views on the purpose of sport. Africans, although serious about improving their skills, were in it for fun and unwilling to be regimented by whites in training sessions. Europeans, on the other hand, were interested in the inculcation of values such as 'team-spirit', 'perseverance' and 'fair play'. When Captain Daudet took over as president of the Native Sports Federation, he was much more heavy-handed than Mouly had been. He and other organizers had little understanding that players who worked long hours and daily walked several kilometres across the sprawling city might be late or miss a practice. Daudet recommended a military solution for erratic attendances at practices. The civilians, who were the presidents of African teams, did not have enough time to devote to their responsibilities, he claimed, and were constantly changing due to home leaves and other postings. To provide more continuity, the supervision of the football should be turned over to military officers and training put in the hands of the militia.[55] Such a measure was in line with the belief of several administrators that sport, like Scouting, was 'a preparation for military service' since it 'prepared robust, strong men for service to the country'.[56]

Disillusioned with an organization that they had only reluctantly entered in the first place, African footballers left the Native Sports Federation in droves, bringing about its final demise by 1937. The final break came over the question of football shoes, the incident that was the starting-point for this book. In 1936, François Makosso had died in hospital from complications following an injury. The rudimentary state of medical care available to Africans in the Congo meant that sports injuries were potentially a life-threatening matter.[57] The correspondence between four team captains and the colonial administration is worth quoting at some length. It conveys the position of African elites and it gives a good sense of the colonial discourse. Although wearing shoes on or off the field was intrinsically important for a variety of reasons, they clearly had become symbolic of the issues of control and autonomy that had plagued the history of the Native Sports Federation.

Following the death of Makosso, Monsieur Benilan, who was Director of the Native Sports Federation at the time, called a meeting of his all-white executive committee. He reminded his colleagues that on several occasions he had raised the matter of violent play on the football field. Benilan believed that a possible 'solution' was to ban the wearing of shoes, which he said contributed to accidents. Since Africans first learned the game barefooted in the streets of Poto-Poto and Bacongo, the President suggested it would be no great sacrifice for players to give up shoes. He also pointed out that FAC and Belgian Congo teams played barefooted. After some discussion, the committee agreed to the measure although the secretary, Monsieur Dupon, who refereed Sunday matches, warned of possible repercussions:

There will be problems. Many Federation players are accustomed to playing in shoes and, in everyday life, they are being worn more and more frequently. It is the same in the Belgian Congo. It will be difficult to apply this decision and, without doubt, some will leave the Federation. This will compromise the results of our next tournament which will be reduced to school teams and youth teams, only.[58]

Not surprisingly, the leaders of African football were outraged. It was not only a matter of gross European intervention in the football teams they had pioneered; it was also an assault on their status as an educated elite, who wore shoes to work.[59] Furthermore, since they were accustomed to wearing football shoes, reverting to playing in bare feet, which involved a different technique of controlling the ball, might affect the quality of their game. Many decided that this was the last straw and simply left the federation. However, four captains of the leading teams of *L'Etoile, Renaissance, Coqs d'AEF* and *Nomades* decided to petition the Governor-General to reverse the decision.[60]

In defence of their position, the four captains reviewed the history of Brazzaville football, pointing out that Africans, themselves, led by Flavien M'Bongo, had first organized the game which they loved as a *'sport passionant'*. Since the inception of the European-led federation, there had been three leagues: 'A' teams which wore shoes; 'B' teams which played barefooted; and 'C' teams for youth twelve to sixteen years old. The captains noted that the 'A'-team players were those who had first started playing football in Poto-Poto and Bacongo in 1919. 'Most of them are clerks and skilled workers', and 'they have always played in shoes'. The letter went on:

For the first time (it was in February 1936), a player had the misfortune to break a leg during a match. This incident resulted in the death of our sadly missed comrade after about two months in hospital. Because of this, and with the agreement of Mr Dupon, the President has asked that all players play bare footed, and, beyond this, has excluded teams that wear shoes. Since he has not achieved the hoped-for results, the President has disqualified and excluded for life all players using shoes.

We ask ourselves, Mr Governor-General, why Mr Benilan has not proposed that these players show up at the office or workshops in bare feet? We do not wear shoes out of vanity or ostentation, but quite simply, as we wear trousers or shirts. So, why are these articles imported into our country? And, since whites first began to play football, has there never been a single occasion when they had an accidental injury?

Mr Benilan is only imitating what has happened in the Congo Sports Federation in Kinshasa. But what takes place there should not to be imitated here, for Mr Benilan seems to be ignorant of the reasons for Kinshasa action.

The Native Sports Federation has only once spent money on football shoes. It was in 1934 when twenty-two pairs of shoes were distributed to two teams, and that is all. Yes, we do not pay our dues, but we have arranged, ourselves, to buy shoes. So what are the President and Secretary complaining about?

We love association football, Mr Governor-General, and that has always been why we have played. Since Mr Benilan no longer wants us in that federation which, nevertheless, belongs to us, allow us, Mr Governor-General, to request permission to establish an autonomous native association for association football. In that way, we will be able to continue playing as we have done for a long time, and will no longer be dependent on the Sports Federation of Mr Benilan.

The letter concluded by noting that the sports ground at Poto-Poto did not belong to the Federation since it had been cleared by African players, with authorization from the Mayor of Brazzaville in 1929. The captains, therefore, asked that the ground be given to African football teams.[61]

Govenor-General Reste, having just arrived in Brazzaville, based his response on a memorandum sent to his office by Mr Benilan, entitled 'Elements of a reply by President Benilan of the Native Sports Federation'. In this lengthy rebuttal of the team-captains' petition, Benilan sought to refute their points. He noted that, contrary to their claim, there were often players with and without shoes on the same team. Since Africans were accustomed to playing barefooted when younger, it could be argued that they played worse when wearing shoes, which 'are clearly uncomfortable for them'. He went on:

Shoes encourage players to substitute brutality for skill. The incident that resulted in the death of François Makosso is an example. We must point out that it is the unanimous opinion of the Europeans who have been involved with association football that it has not been possible since 1919 to create in our natives a sporting spirit in the true and noble sense of the word.

The Léopoldville Federation plays barefooted and, like us, they implemented the policy after having played in shoes. Have Africans in Belgian Congo more goodwill or a more sincere liking for sport than those in Brazzaville, since they prefer to play all the same? It is worth asking the question. It is certain that the blacks of Belgian Congo, kept in hand by an energetic and powerful federation, have no choice but to obey their directors. We can imitate our neighbours without shame in matters which they manage well. The Catholic mission of Brazzaville, which is not Belgian and which has excellent players, also insists that all team members are barefooted.

It is a pity that the native players themselves admit that they have no money to pay their dues, but use it to buy shoes which are much more expensive. There is in this admission unconscious proof of the near-impossibility of our blacks to organize themselves seriously without the continual help of Europeans.

Monsieur Benilan went on to suggest that African leaders were taking advantage of the arrival of the Governor-General, hoping to obtain concessions from the new administration. He advised:

In conclusion, it would be politically inadvisable, in my opinion, to reverse the decision taken by the committee of the Native Sports Federation in its meeting of 21 March 1936. To allow the players to form a dissident federation, alone or with the aid of friendly Europeans, would obviously be full of danger for future developments. The players involved are already, for the most part, quite old; in one, two, three or four years, they will no longer be able to play, whereas the youth teams now forming in the Urban School and in the government schools and which are constantly increasing in number will be in two or three years great teams, playing barefooted. A little patience and tenacity is all that is required.[62]

Ruling in favour of the directors of the federation, Governor-General Reste called on the African players to accept the decision, adding that 'by agreeing to abide by the wise decision of the Committee, players will give an example of the rigorous discipline which is in keeping with the most sincere and passionate spirit of sport'. He also denied the players' claim to the Poto-Poto ground which, he said, belonged to the Brazzaville municipality.[63]

The 1936 shoes controversy was the death-warrant of the Native Sports Federation. Two years later, it was disbanded through lack of support and the remnants merged with the Native Branch of the CAB.[64] Domination by Europeans was simply unacceptable to African players. For all but a small minority, wearing shoes to play football was not the main issue. Most still played barefooted since they could not afford shoes, and many preferred to do so. In this, Mr Benilan was correct. Some players find that they have a better 'feel' for the ball and can kick it with more power when they are barefooted.[65] In 1936, the main points at issue were the overbearing nature of white power and the failure of European administrators to provide the promised equipment and facilities for African football. Following the controversy, players who left the federation organized their own matches or joined the Catholic mission teams. As Benilan had predicted, the older players who had dominated township football for twenty years retired from competitive games rather than play shoeless, but they were in a small minority. On the eve of the Second World War, the Catholic mission was again the focus of organized football in Brazzaville. In 1937, in a march-past in honour of the newly appointed Monseigneur Biéchy, 1,000 uniformed schoolchildren and youth-club members marched by, including thirty-four football teams with members of all ages.[66] Father le Comte, trained as a specialist in youth work in French parishes, arrived to run the youth club.[67]

Football's second golden age

The influx of migrant labour into the town after the Second World War, especially the boys and young men who continued to predominate in the population before the mid-1950s, brought about another upsurge in popular support for Brazzaville football. The game was played at all levels. Small boys learned in the streets as their fathers had done; mutual-aid associations organized their activities around football; *mwanafoot* flourished and became more highly structured than it had previously been; public and mission schools each ran several football teams; and the big Poto-Poto and Bacongo clubs continued to draw thousands of spectators to Sunday games at various venues of which the most important was Eboué Stadium. With funds from the Overseas Ministry in Paris, the Education Department and the newly established Social Services of AEF supplied more equipment, although they could never keep up with demand. Football remained 'king'.

While colonial initiatives led to the setting up of national organizations such as the *Fédération des Sports de l'Afrique Equatoriale Française* (FSAEF) to administer sport, football fully retained its popular roots. In

Brazzaville, players and supporters identified with teams through place, age, class, ethnicity and religion. Sport also became caught up in political rivalries in the decade before independence. Intense rivalries often erupted into violence on and off the field, and magic was used to try and ensure success. While such dramas were being played out at the grass roots, sport remained an arena for contesting control by church or state, and 'independence' movements by football teams paralleled political resistance to colonialism.

In the late 1940s, the Mayor of Brazzaville asked for a report on African football. Prepared by Dr Lieutenant-Colonel Bellocq, the President of the Football Committee of the FSAEF, the document reveals the great popularity of the game. Interestingly enough, shoes still defined the senior and junior teams. The players had finally won the war, for with football boots now in daily use among a wider segment of the population, administrators could no longer deny them to the top teams. The report noted that 'the price of boots was prohibitive for junior players', but that interest was so great that the writer 'intended to ask the FSAEF to establish an annual competition for these teams without boots for which the prize would be fifteen pairs of boots'. The wearing of shoes in a top club was, therefore, a significant moment in the life of a young player, marking the transition from apprentice to master player.[68] In the report, nineteen teams were listed as 'senior teams, wearing boots': of these, seven played for the Catholic mission's FAC, two were sponsored by the CAB, four were attached to military or technical schools, four were sponsored by companies or government departments such as the police, and two had broken away from FAC and formed an independent *Union Sportive Brazzavilloise* under European patrons. Eleven other teams wearing shoes were in the process of being established. The mission's FAC also ran twenty-six 'junior' teams which played barefooted. Thus, about thirty teams with about seven hundred and fifty players were engaged in organized football in Brazzaville, stretching resources to the limits. Because of this problem, the report concluded that organizers must direct young people into other sports such as athletics and basketball.[69] The report also shows that the Catholic mission had maintained its 'massive presence' in Brazzaville sport.[70] In 1946, in reponse to a request for more help, the Holy Ghost Fathers had dispatched to Brazzaville nineteen priests and lay brothers trained in youth work, and the work of FAC in Poto-Poto (*Jeunesco*) and Bacongo (*Association Sportive de la Mission* or ASM) had been divided to cope with growing demands.[71]

2   Brazzaville Select Football Team, *c.* 1945 (courtesy of Fulbert Kimina-Makumbu)

As African leaders began to contest European dominance in political life and in the workplace, so they began to question colonial authority in sport, especially the long-standing power of the Catholic mission. The politics of football led not only to breakaway movements from European control but also to conflicts between African leaders, who were jockeying for position in their communities through sport, as they were doing in local and national politics.

On several occasions between 1945 and 1951, African leaders led 'independence' movements from mission sponsorship in order to form their own teams which received recognition from the governing body of sport. The use of Eboué Stadium, which was managed by the Catholic mission, was a means of leverage which the priests used when teams protested any grievance. In the case of two teams playing under the name *Lorraine*, disputes with the FAC organization had ended with them breaking away and finding an independent European sponsor, who had sufficient resources, interest in African football and status in the white community to mediate with the church and sports administrators, so that the teams could exist independently as the *Union Sportive Brazzavilloise*. The tensions between the Catholic mission and the colonial authorities, now mitigated to some extent through the setting up of FSAEF, could still be exploited by players and their European patron in such negotiations.

The most famous breakaways from the FAC were those that gave birth to two leading contemporary teams, *L'Etoile du Congo* of Poto-Poto (previously *Renaissance*) and *Diables Noirs* of Bacongo. In both instances, African players were dissatisfied with their treatment by the mission organization and sought autonomy to run their own affairs.

The case of *Renaissance* was avidly discussed by fans and sports organizers, since the team was the terror of Brazzaville football, winning the city championship five years in a row, 1945–50. In the controversy, there were two major problems, one concerning player relations with the Catholic mission and the other a power struggle between two African leaders. For players who were not well off financially and had many family obligations the situation was increasingly unfair. While football brought recognition and status in the community, it brought few material rewards. According to Mambeke-Boucher, a member of the *Renaissance* team, players went unrewarded while the mission pocketed the gate money at Eboué Stadium.[72] The stadiums were packed with spectators for their matches, for 'we were first class players'. Yet the FAC kept the lion's share of the proceeds, providing no compensation for medical insurance, transport for away games in Bacongo, Léopoldville or Pointe-Noire, or sufficient equipment. 'At the end of the matches, we did not even have lemonade money, nothing.'[73] At a *Renaissance* club meeting, the executive committee decided to send a letter to the Director of Social Services, asking that the club be allowed to leave the mission organization and, instead, represent the Poto-Poto Cultural Centre. The only serious problem, once recognition had been received, would be equipment and use of the stadium which the players wanted the administration to negotiate with the mission.[74] Embedded in the controversy, also, was the personal animosity of two prominent African leaders. The captain of *Renaissance*, Dominique Sombo, was a rival of Jacques Dingha, the powerful African director of *Jeunesco*. While Sombo's supporters thought Dingha arrogant and in the pocket of the missionaries and European sports administrators, Dingha blamed Sombo for posting notices around Poto-Poto attacking him. When it looked as if *Renaissance* would boycott matches in protest, administrators became involved. What most concerned them was fan reaction, for if the dispute led to a 'disruption of the season', it would incense thousands of spectators who had already expressed their frustration through demonstrations and 'disorderly conduct'. Outbreaks of popular discontent must be avoided and the rift patched up until the end of the season.[75] The latter was apparently achieved, for *Renaissance* went on to win the city championship again, and their existence as an independent club in the Brazzaville league was recognized by FAC. In celebration of their independence and to disassociate themselves from their mission connections, the *Renaissance* leaders changed the name of their club to *L'Etoile*, evoking the memory of the leading Poto-Poto team in the first golden age of Brazzaville football.[76] The name *Renaissance* passed to a reserve team of younger players who had broken with the senior team due to lack of playing time.[77]

A second dispute between FAC and players also took place on the other side of town in Bacongo. The starting-point was the fierce rivalry with Poto-Poto teams and the inability of any Bacongo team to win the town championship. In Bacongo, several teams played under the sponsorship of the *Association Sportive de la Mission* but none of them was a match for the powerhouse Poto-Poto teams, especially *Renaissance* (now *L'Etoile*), with its dominance of the city championship. With this in mind, the leaders approached the missionaries, suggesting that a new team be formed from the top players of all the other Bacongo teams. When the missionaries refused, the Bacongo footballers took the matter into their own hands. Clement Massengo, one of the players involved, marvelled in retrospect at the intensity of Bacongo loyalty which caused teams to give up their best players willingly in order to establish the new team. He remembered the episode:

We decided that the time had come to make up a team to take on the best of Poto-Poto, who were always beating us at the Eboué Stadium. We had to choose a name. We first thought of *Diables Rouges* ['Red Devils'] after the national champions of Belgium; then we thought that *Diables Noirs* ['Black Devils'] would strike fear into the hearts of our enemy. But how could a team of the *Association Sportive de la Mission* take on the name *Diables Noirs*? The priests were furious. They would not accept this. Young people, in general, decided to boycott mass. There were very few people there. Boys threatened the girls so they stayed away, also. Then Monseigneur Biéchy heard of the controversy and agreed to the name.[78]

Again it was the intensity of fan support and the fear of violence that caused the sports authorities to intervene and mediate between African footballers and the mission. Following their recognition as a team, the *Diables Noirs* were also allowed a percentage of the gate money at big games to help finance expenses. Team fortunes were again helped by a sympathetic European, in this case a Frenchman, Aimé Brun, who volunteered his services as an adviser and trainer, although at a time when sport was still segregated, other Europeans criticized him for being too close to African players. With his coaching, *Diables Noirs* became famous for their style of play. They abandoned dependence on sweeps down the wing and aerial crosses on the British model, which had dominated Brazzaville play up to that point, and introduced a short passing game with close marking on defence. When the Bacongo team entered the town championship in 1950, a reporter noted that 'the players were convinced that they had a sacred mission to fulfill', that is to beat Poto-Poto teams.[79] In 1952–4, *Diables Noirs* accomplished their goal, remaining undefeated not only in Brazzaville but on both sides of the Pool.[80]

With the formation of *L'Etoile, Diables Noirs* and the reconstituted *Renaissance*, all members of a city league founded in 1953, Brazzaville football entered a second golden age.[81] Below the level of the top teams, there was a proliferation of school teams, driven by an upsurge in primary education. As important were the neighbourhood *mwanafoot* games. Boys began to organize their own championships according to their *quartier*, with help from fathers and uncles who were football enthusiasts. The influence of primary education and middle-school education as well as the aspirations of the young were seen in team names: *Robin* (after Robin Hood); *Indians* (from cowboy and Indian films); *Nice* and *Lille* (top French teams); and *Phantom* and *Hope*. The championship games were written up in the press, and scouts for the top teams watched for promising young players. Parents had mixed feelings, for boys often used the excuse of practising football when they wanted to roam around the town with their friends.[82]

Football players remained amateur and received little or no compensation for their efforts. In 1960, writing in *La Semaine* on the 'scandal' of Brazzaville football, Sylvain Bemba, a respected commmentator, accused the Brazzaville league of treating its players 'like machines' with little rewards for their willingness to 'risk their bones in every match'.[83] In the years before national independence, a few players were able to exploit professional opportunities through recruitment by Paris and Marseilles clubs, thus moving football from the realm of recreation to the world of work.[84]

Supporters transformed sport into a mass phenomenon. If it had not been for its massive popular following, football surely would not have received the amount of attention it did from white administrators. Crowd control appears in official reports as a significant problem, almost as much as organizing youth. 'Those who are interested in sport are at the point where it seems to be a permanent preoccupation with them,' reported Captain Daudet in 1934.[85] And twenty years later, a representative of the French Overseas Ministry toured Africa and told the AEF Federal Committee on Sport: 'Since my arrival in Africa, I have been struck with the infatuation of African crowds with sport.'[86] Having written about the 'chauvinism' among players and club directors, in his long report on Brazzaville football, Lieutenant-Colonel Bellocq wrote that for 'the public, it is certainly a circus; lacking an education in sporting behaviour, their excessive chauvinism becomes degenerate; in certain ways, the public corrupts the players, causing them to "play to the gallery", encouraging reprehensible gestures and sapping the authority of the referees and organizers'.[87]

No other form of popular culture could rival the excitement generated by football matches. To be part of the crowd was to be at the heart of a city experience. Nowhere else could one encounter drama on such a large scale and share it with old and new friends. Where else could fans stand shoulder to shoulder with thousands of others, as they could at the Eboué Stadium in Poto-Poto, at the Marchand Stadium on the Bacongo side of town, or at the Queen Astrid Stadium in Léopoldville? For big games, 'waves of supporters' made the trek across town to see their team play Bacongo or Poto-Poto rivals. Bands, dancing and hand-made flags displaying team colours gave the stadium 'an air of festivity'.[88] In the 1930s, players were preceded onto the field by bugle-and-drum bands. Musical instruments were written into the budget of the Native Sports Federation.[89] At half-time, the municipal brass band or the Native Police band entertained the crowds. For the Amnesty Day celebrations on 11 November 1935, teams marched onto the field to the music of the Native Sports Federation and the Catholic mission youth club bands.[90] Team colours were sported by the crowd as well as the players: for example, the yellow and black of *Diables Noirs*; the blue and yellow of *L'Etoile*; and the red and black of *Renaissance*, which, at its reorganization in 1951, chose the colours of the top French team, *Nice*.[91]

From its earliest days, football generated intense loyalties, creating and reinforcing bonds among townspeople. Although the leaders tended to be those with some Western education who could negotiate with white authorities, clubs were essentially democratic. Some of the most influential supporters were those who had never been to school but who as traders or property owners had resources and stature in the community. Football meant playing, supporting, discussing team fortunes and the play of individual stars, gambling, and seeking to influence the outcome of games through magical practices. When Ganga was transferred from Brazzaville to a teaching job at Loukouo in 1950, he gathered with friends at a cafe on Sunday afternoons to drink beer and wine, listen to music, and engage in long, heated conversations about Brazzaville football. A reporter for *La Semaine* visited at the weekends and kept the young men posted on the latest developments.[92]

Crowds continued to revel in individual artistry by players who could dazzle opponents with their footwork or their commanding presence. In 1951, Monsieur Bertrand, the principal European administrator in charge of sport, lectured students at the Urban School that 'spectacular demonstrations' lacked 'team discipline' and the 'sporting spirit', but his remonstrances fell on deaf ears.[93] Fans showed their appreciation for team-work such as passing and solid defence, but their affection for individual stars was marked. Star players continued to be referred to by graphic nicknames that described their style. In the second golden age of football, these included: 'Elastic', Etienne Massengo, a great goalkeeper; 'Dr Fu-Mancho', Clement Massengo, after the Chinese mastermind famous through film; 'Dancer', Camille Sangou; 'Phantom', Ange Baboutela; 'Technician', Etienne Mayinguidi; 'Steamboat', Oscar Seppenith; 'Magician', Jean-Michel Mbono; 'Double', Gaston Dissi; 'The Law', Joseph Mobenga; and, 'Eight', Dennis Ouamba.[94]

In some cases, visibility through sport aided advancement in national affairs. Emmanuel Dadet and Bernard Mambeke-Boucher were two such men who gained prominence through sport and popular music.[95] Mambeke was a household word through his dominance on the football field. Born in Brazzaville in 1919, he was one of the first students to enroll at the Ecole Edouard Renard and became a teacher and civil servant. He was described in a newspaper article: 'As for Mambeke, he was the greatest player of the earlier generation. He was called *Roi de la Plaine* ['King of the Playing Field'] and no name was borne so well. His prodigious ease reduced adversaries to the position of humble slaves submitting to the royal will. Mambeke was the perfect all round player.'[96] Dadet was in the first class to enroll at the Poto-Poto primary school in 1925 and then became a monitor and an administrator in the town government. He was in the group of footballers that established the Native Sports Federation, but was better known as a referee. He was also a musician who organized the town band in the 1930s and pioneered the new popular music. Living in Poto-Poto, these two men blended in their lives popular roots, French education and experience of working within the colonial system. Their prominence in the community allowed them to emerge as political leaders in the pre-independence period. Mambeke joined the *Mouvement Socialiste Africain* and received an appointment as Minister of Education and Youth in 1957. Two years later he was elected a member of the Territorial Assembly which led the country to independence. Dadet was elected to the French Union Assembly after the Second World War, held several ministerial posts between 1958 and 1960, and was appointed the Republic of Congo's Ambassador to the United States and the United Nations in 1961.[97]

Football teams reflected and shaped emerging identities in the city, where class, occupational, ethnic and religious loyalties coexisted, just as clubs world-wide have expressed the variety of social distinctions that exist among urban populations.[98] Some examples of Brazzaville teams illustrate this point: *Olympique* and *Diables Noirs* (Bacongo) and *Renaissance, L'Etoile* and *Lorraine* (Poto-Poto), (city neighbourhoods); ASM and *Patronage* (religious affiliation); *Diables Noirs*, the Lari team (ethnicity); *Cheminots* (railway workers), *Gendarmerie*, and *Police* (occupations); CAB (race and class); *Ecole de Cadets* and *Ecole Generale de Clercs* (future administrative and military elites). Some clubs were very diverse in the origins of their players, while others were more oriented to urban ethnicity. All major clubs were required to register with the administration and some extant records give the names, occupations, ethnic groups and places of residence of team members. For example, one team sponsored by the *Compagnie Générale de Transports en Afrique* in 1944, included six clerks, one electrician, three fishermen, two labourers, one apprentice carpenter, one tailor, and one clerk working at the Courts of Justice. The same fifteen players are listed with ten ethnic labels. All lived in Poto-Poto or its extension, Ouenze, except for one who gave 'fishing village' as his place of residence. The reserve team was as diverse in its composition. In the case of two teams that played for a department of the administration, on the other hand, all registered as Lari and all but two lived in Bacongo. Among the reserves, too, the Lari predominated.[99]

The fans of *Diables Noirs*, which drew the vast majority of its players and supporters from Bacongo and was identified as the Lari team, expressed their loyalties in familial terms. One modern-day supporter said: 'I support *Diables Noirs*. That is our team. That is the team that our ancestors founded. It is our team from Boko in the Pool region.'[100] Families were drawn together by team loyalties, especially older and younger men. Clement Massengo came to admire his wife's father, who was an influential organizer of *Diables Noirs*. Massengo was well educated, while his father-in-law had not attended school, but through football they came to respect each other a great deal.[101] The sports journalist Fulbert Kimina-Makumbu said that he would be unhappy if his sons chose to play for another team.[102] Older club members tried to help young players, especially finding them jobs. When Etienne Massengo the goalkeeper died following a knee injury in 1954, team members returned to his village with the body, and built a tomb for the burial.[103] To the Lari, the team was affectionately known as *yaka dia mama* (Kilari, 'manioc of mother'), meaning that *Diables Noirs* sustained its fans who would stay with their team whether it won or lost, just as children accept the manioc bread prepared by their mother, whether it is good or bad.[104]

As football developed a longevity and history, supporters thought of those who had established the game as founding fathers or 'elders', sources of guidance and wisdom. In 1951, when the Poto-Poto players broke away from the FAC and rejected the name *Renaissance* because of its association with missionary domination, they decided to revive the name *L'Etoile*, which evoked memories of the first autonomous teams. The team leaders decided to seek the blessing of Joseph Ebilard, a grand old man of Brazzaville football, who had captained the first Urban School team and the legendary *Etoile* team almost twenty years before. In telling of the event in which he participated, Mambeke-Boucher remembered:

One Sunday, we went and said to Joseph Ebilard, 'You were the captain of *L'Etoile du Congo*. Now you are no longer playing, and *L'Etoile* no longer exists, will you give us permission to take up the name?' We offered up a demijohn of palm wine and a bottle of rum. Then he said to us: 'My children, you have done well. I will give you my blessing, if that is what you want.' He poured some palm wine on our heads. Then he said, 'Now you can take up the name of *L'Etoile du Congo*.'[105]

The official history of *Renaissance/CARA* also recounts the importance of family ties in the history of their team. This made all the more traumatic the breakaway of *L'Etoile*, when households and families 'would not speak to each other'.[106]

The Africanization of football from its earliest days was also shown in the use of magic to influence results. As kyébé-kyébé dancers and Ubangi-Shari wrestlers went to religious specialists to receive power to perform well, so did football players.[107] But beyond that, supporters and players used magic not only to prepare themselves for a match but to try and ensure victory.

The employment of team magicians and the use of special medicines in individual and team preparation is part of sport all over Africa. In colonial Zimbabwe, boxers wore medicines in armbands or rubbed them into small incisions in their skin to ensure success.[108] Zulu religious specialists prepare teams for football matches.[109] In Cameroon, Sierra Leone, and in Liberia, supporters and team members perform rituals to influence results in their favour.[110] In Nairobi, teams budget for religious specialists.[111] On the middle Congo, where resources were seen as finite, a match started with a preordained number of goals. The role of team magicians in this zero-sum game was to steal points from their opponents while protecting their own goals.[112] African sport is 'bathed in the occult', wrote a Zairois referee.[113]

The use of supernatural forces to influence the results of football is explained by modern sportsmen in various ways. One explained that in all the pressing problems of life, whether concern for a sick child, marital problems, lack of material resources or winning an important match, the ancestors must be consulted. In this context the 'ancestors' are any great footballer who has died and whom young men may want to consult in preparing for a game. Medicines prepared by a religious specialist will allow this communication to take place.[114] Another noted that superior talent is not natural, and excessive skill by an individual player can only be explained through the intervention of supernatural forces, which have given him this 'force' or dexterity.[115] The success of a team must involve the 'taming' of occult forces in their favour. Team directors set aside sums of money to employ the best religious specialists, who were considered as important for the psychological and emotional preparation of players as a trainer was for their physical conditioning.[116]

In the early days of Brazzaville football, the potency of rituals and medicines controlled by West African marabouts were particularly sought after by the leading clubs. Apart from the power of Islamic magic, the very success of the Senegalese in colonial society showed that they had access to powerful charms. One religious specialist was popular with several teams, who competed for his services, thus pushing up his fees and earning him the name of 'Merci beaucoup'. The day before a big match, players would hand over chickens, kola nuts, and dirt taken from the training-ground of the other team, so that he could produce the medicine to ensure success.[117] If a magician was unsuccessful in ensuring a winning season, he would be dismissed and another employed. Religious preparations for matches took different forms, although all were designed in some manner to strengthen a team and to stop the supernatural forces allied to the opponent from doing their work. Captains and team members were given talismans and amulets to wear, or special preparations to rub on their skin. A goalkeeper might be given a charm to improve his leaping ability, or a forward an attachment for his shoe to guide the ball between the goal posts. A skilled magician could turn the opponent's ball into stone or make the ball invisible until it was in the back of the other team's net. A favourite tactic was to bury a talisman in the centre of the playing field the night before a big match, while watching out for spies from the other team.[118] Swedish missionaries were slow to encourage Protestants to participate in town football since Sunday games contravened their belief in the Lord's Day observance. However, they began to form teams in the 1930s when they saw a need to keep young Christians attached to their mission, and away from the 'heathen' practices of township teams.[119]

Enterprising businesses in France exploited the business of 'good-luck' charms by marketing in Africa through a mail-order catalogue service.

The High Commissioner of AEF authorized an inquiry into such practices in 1953 and the correspondence of the French and AEF security police are preserved in the colonial archives. In her newsletter, one Nice entrepreneur suggested the efficacy of a 'sporting medallion' carrying an image of a football match. She offered similar medallions for boxing and cycling, and advised that the medals would have 'more value' if personalized with the initials or date of birth of the owner on the back. Other businesses as widely scattered as Paris, Damascus and New Delhi offered similar charms for success in love, exams, material wealth and sport. The High Commissioner, supported by the three African representatives to the French Assembly, inserted a warning against such 'charlatans' in the newspaper *France-Equateur-L'Avenir*.[120]

The failure of European organizers to mould sport in their own image is particularly shown in the behaviour of the African crowd. Disputes were frequent both on and off the field. While players might dispute calls, engage in dangerous play and fist fights, spectators were known to invade the field during and after the game, attack linesmen and referees even after a game, throw missiles onto the field in shows of displeasure and vandalize the stadium.[121] Such crowd violence and 'hooliganism' is as old as spectator sport itself, whether in Britain, Brazil or Congo, but the local causes and manifestations vary in time and place.[122] In Brazzaville, they are easy to describe but difficult to explain, and they cannot be reduced to a single cause. While administrators and African elites might emphasize the lack of 'sportsmanlike' conduct on the part of players and spectators, the reasons for intense emotions among fans could be as diverse as social identity, political animosity, unemployment and economic deprivation, high stakes in gambling, drunkenness, the 'rebellion' of youth and the unemployed, inexperienced referees and 'lack of leadership' on the part of sports organizers.[123]

Conflicts tended to coalesce, however, around two broad sets of opponents: the rivalry between Christians and 'lay' teams, and the hostility of Bacongo and Poto-Poto supporters. In the early years of football, a meeting between a team from the Catholic mission and one representing the Native Sports Federation often ended in scuffles in the crowd and fighting on the field. The very organization of sport, with the mission youth club and the Native Sports Federation as the two organizing bodies, encouraged the rivalry. At big games such as those organized for Fourteenth of July celebrations, the top Catholic team was usually matched against the best team from the Native Sports Federation. When *Olympique*, the FAC team from Bacongo, played *L'Etoile*, the Native Sports Federation champions from Poto-Poto, disputes on and off the field were compounded by cross-town rivalry.[124] Benilan,

President of the Sports Federation in the mid-1930s, blamed the priests for encouraging antagonisms by conveying their hostility to the secular authorities to their congregations. The situation in football had become so bad that the Catholic mission 'hesitates when it is asked to field teams against the lay Sports Federation for fear of an incident, injury to players, legs broken, etc.'[125] The Mayor's report on football in the late 1940s also blamed player and fan animosities on the hostility of the mission FAC and the 'lay' CAB and USB teams.[126]

The most persistent rivalry, however, was that between Poto-Poto and Bacongo teams. From the earliest years of Brazzaville football, such matches frequently ended in disputes.[127] In 1934, Captain Daudet appealed to the administration for funds to build a neutral sports ground, which would help with crowd control when the fiercely partisan supporters watched their teams play.[128] In 1942, Monseigneur Biéchy agreed that it was time for the Catholic mission to set up separate organizations for Bacongo and Poto-Poto, given the numbers involved in sport. But he warned that having two committees would 'encourage the natural opposition between the two villages, leading to a permanent cleavage'.[129] In the late 1940s, Bellocq also referred to the 'intense sports rivalry between Bacongo and Poto-Poto' as a root problem for the 'unsportsmanlike' conduct of spectators and players.[130] In 1955, the much respected Emmanuel Dadet in an article on 'The role of a sports spectator', noted that games between Bacongo and Poto-Poto clubs at the Eboué Stadium were like wars between 'two enemy camps'. Spectators had forgotten that they were only rivals in sport.[131]

Football could not dissociate itself from politics. In the 1930s, chiefs and political leaders in the Pool area who supported Matswa told their people to boycott all official events, including football matches, and to refuse to accept 'presents' of sports equipment, which might have been bought by the authorities with confiscated funds.[132] And in the tense climate that preceded independence in 1960, a politicized ethnicity spilled over into sport. The ascendancy of the Matswaistes under Fulbert Youlou, who became Mayor in 1956 and whose party won the elections of 1958, helped to polarize the town between the 'people of the north' in Poto-Poto and the 'people of the lower river' in Bacongo. Reports from the mid-1950s describe increasing violence among spectators, with referees and players having to be given police protection after games.[133] Reviewing the problem in 1959, the football correspondent for *La Semaine* wrote that 'the time is not far off when, in Brazzaville, meetings between Bacongo and Poto-Poto will take on the appearance of a military campaign'. While 'supporters of Poto-Poto come to the stadium with machetes ... at Bacongo women and children arm themselves with huge pestles'. The report concluded that 'incidents of this nature have been taking place for a long time'.[134] In fact, football matches between major teams were curtailed in the months before independence when there was political violence in Brazzaville streets.[135]

On the other hand, the peculiar ability of sport to unite as well as divide allowed fans to forget their differences and to forge a broader sense of identity when regional or international matches were staged. When a Brazzaville select team played against a Léopoldville–Kinshasa team, Bacongo and Poto-Poto fans buried their differences and became Brazzavillois. When the first match was staged between a white team and an African team and the game was drawn, there was dancing in the streets of both Poto-Poto and Bacongo. And as independence approached, Brazzaville players joined their national team to play matches against other colonies in AEF. Thus sport contributed to a growing sense of nationalism, as it has done all over the world.

Conclusion

Football arrived in Brazzaville as a foreign import, a game played by white men in their leisure time as an African crowd looked on. For many who watched, the game must have resonated with the village experience of sportslike activities that challenged young men and entertained their community. If football was introduced by Europeans, it was quickly appropriated by African players. Missionaries and colonial administrators saw in the structures and values of Western sport a useful means of providing disciplined and healthy leisure for urban youth, but they were only partially successful in achieving these goals. Some elites, who wrote in the sports pages of the Catholic press in the 1950s, decried the 'unsportsmanlike conduct' of the crowd as much as Europeans did, but they also used sport to assert their independence against church and state and claim leadership roles within Bacongo and Poto-Poto. Football could express class interests, but it could also reinforce and shape urban ethnicity and, in the experience of the African crowd, football took on its own meaning and local colour.

The history of Brazzaville sport highlights the problem of trying to designate a cultural activity shared by so many as 'popular', 'elite', 'colonial' or 'indigenous', or as an agent of control or a means of resistance. Football in Brazzaville defies such categorization, for any such analysis becomes a mirage as one delves deeper into the historical record. At different points in time and place, specific groups did work and play out their interests through sport, and it seems that one can, indeed, speak of a 'popular', 'elite', 'youth' or 'ethnic' consciousness expressed through football. But, overall, when one is faced with drawing conclusions, the historical experience defies attempts to label it neatly.

5   About the town

At the heart of town life was the entertainment of the streets, open squares, bars, beer-gardens, dance-halls and cinemas. Public amusement was often to be found out of doors, especially in the early days. By the 1920s, some entertainment took place in enclosed spaces, where the owners charged admission and served food and drinks. These establishments were usually associated with new forms of amusement such as films or partnered dancing. Pervading such recreational activities was an urban music which, like other aspects of leisure such as football and fashion, drew its inspiration from local and foreign sources in Bacongo and Poto-Poto. While rhythms, instruments and lyrics were brought from all over Central Africa, the civil servants from Guadeloupe and Martinique, the domestic servants and craftsmen from the coast, and the *tirailleurs*, artisans and clerks from West Africa all contributed to the evolution of new forms of entertainment. In this cosmopolitan environment, the celebrated 'Congo music' of the 1950s was born.[1]

Such attractions helped 'pull' young migrants to the town, especially after the Second World War. As people came together to share common interests, they did so not only informally but also in more structured mutual-aid associations with strong recreational orientations. Although such groups existed early in the century, for they were institutions transported from rural areas and adapted to town life, they became significant in the later colonial period, when a larger number of people lived in the town for longer periods. Such networks, crucial in dealing with extraordinary expenses associated with sickness and mourning, were almost as important to personal well-being and social maintenance as work itself. They were particularly important to women, fulfilling a double need for support and recreation.

Early entertainment

At the turn of the century, workers had few options for amusement. They might gather with groups of friends to smoke (both tobacco and hemp), play cards, gamble and drink or, especially after they were paid, go to one of the bars set up in factories, which were little more than a few tables and chairs.[2] Brawls over women were common even in the 1930s, as they were simply in short supply.[3] Levels of alcoholism were high and the effects probably worsened by meagre intakes of food. Such consumption patterns had been set from the earliest years of European expansion when workers at factories on the coast and along the lower Congo and Ogowe rivers were paid in tokens to be spent in factory stores, which were well stocked with drinks. In some instances, Europeans made partial payment of wages in liquor.[4] In 1897, Baratier found that 'Africans will not agree to work without some alcohol as payment'.[5] In 1897 and 1898, among imports for personal consumption in French Congo, alcoholic beverages constituted 23 per cent and 15.2 per cent of the total. At the Pool factories, it was common for workers to stop at the store and buy drinks which provided an antidote to boredom, separation from family and tough living conditions, as well as being a focus for social gatherings.[6] Although such a high demand for liquor was beneficial to trade, the administration eventually realized the short-sightedness of its policy as it struggled to find a healthy and adequate supply of workers. Furthermore, it saw control of drinking as a necessary step in imposing order on the town's population, especially in Poto-Poto. Official policy was erratic, however, boxed in by competing pressures. If prohibitions were placed on imports, customs duties fell, wine producers complained and the sale of African-brewed drinks increased. In any case, many workers preferred palm-wine, or local beer or alcohol brewed or distilled from maize, manioc or a mixture of both.[7] In 1906, Gentil tried to ban the sale of alcoholic drinks, noting 'a rapid and sure decline in the excellent workers who voluntarily engage for several years', but howls of protest from European producers caused Merlin to relax the restriction a few years later, so that it only applied to drinks with an alcoholic content over 60 proof. After the First World War, Governor-General Augagneur again took up the fight, prohibiting alcohol consumption both imported and local. The effect was to increase the sale of cheap wine which was not part of the ban.[8] As for the liquor brewed by women locally, its manufacture continued unabated, in spite of sporadic police raids and arrests of women, and their daughters who helped in the business. Official reports from the 1930s claimed that the worst offenders were the wives of the police and *tirailleurs* who, instead of enforcing the law, turned a blind eye to what was going on in their back yards.[9]

Sunday afternoon crowds generally meant one of two things: either they were going to a football match or they were making for the well-known spots such as the Rue de Paris or the Grande Place in Poto-Poto, where regional dance groups performed. The latter was an invented urban tradition well established by the 1920s and another means of creating new sub-communities around the notion of ethnicity. Poto-Poto with its great mix of peoples was the side of the town most famous for its dance associations, which performed dances 'inherited from the ancestors', to quote one informant. It was a 'tradition' that grew out of the physical division of the the town into *quartiers* for specific 'races' and identities taken over and made real by the dance groups. Each *quartier* had its recognized drummers and dance group, and there was fierce competition between them. The *quartier* chiefs were involved in the events, each making sure that his area of the town was well represented in the Sunday afternoon festivities and on special occasions.[10]

Andrée Blouin, in her autobiographical account, recalled 'the dazzling spectacle in the Grande Place of Poto-Poto' on Sunday afternoons in 1938. Groups from different regions occupied different sides of the square. The dancers were

marvellously bedecked in blue, red, and white paint, *perles* and fantastic costumes. The *tam-tam* drums were irresistible, their intricate, insistent rhythms drawing participants from the farthest corners of the town. Anyone who wished to join in the dances could, and many ordinary people did. Dressed in their brilliant Sunday *pagnes*, the excited crowds shouted and clapped as the dancers competed among themselves to see who could leap the highest, dance the strongest, win the most applause.

Like other spectators, Blouin was particularly captivated by the kyébé-kyébé dancers in their 'voluminous costume, a skirt and a cape of straw, looking like giant birds'. They whirled around and around like a top at an ever-increasing tempo, 'the straw flying out in great wheeling circles'. Around the square were 'shaky little wooden tables' where petty traders were selling peanuts, piles of charcoal, cigarettes, matches, sardines, condensed milk and salt. The whole occasion had a festive quality.[11]

Some groups were quite informal while others planned and practised their dances regularly. Following village tradition, they created new dances for special occasions. Starting with the first big celebration of Bastille Day in Brazzaville in 1891, the Fourteenth of July became the 'traditional' time for the *quartier* dance associations to show off their latest steps, songs and costumes for the gathered crowds.[12] Each year, the kyébé-kyébé puppeteers, for example, prepared the raffia costumes that covered the dancers from head to foot, carved and painted new puppets which usually represented beautiful women or important individuals as in the case of General de Gaulle, and composed new dances. Each year new songs which complemented the character of the chosen puppets were practised and performed, a love-song for a beautiful

3 'Kyébé-Kyébé' dancers, Brazzaville, *c.* 1950 (courtesy of Roger Frey)

woman, a more martial air for a famous man. The young men who were the centre-piece of the performance went into training like football stars and received special medicines to give them skill and stamina. The less skillful dancers 'warmed up' the crowd, which excitedly anticipated the arrival of the best performers and tried to guess the figures that the new puppets might represent. Associated with the Mbochi and Kuyu of the middle Alima region, the kyébé-kyébé association retained its predominant characteristics in the town as an all-male club, with women and non-members barred from even seeing the puppets before the performance.[13]

Early in the century, dances associated with new musical instruments and rhythms also made their appearance in Brazzaville. They were probably introduced by Cabindans and West Africans or those who had been in work-camps during the construction of the Léopoldville–Matadi line when thousands of workers had mingled together and exchanged musical ideas in their leisure time.[14] By the late nineteenth century, Cabindan bands were playing tunes borrowed and adapted from the Portuguese and Euro-Africans in Luanda on whistles, concertinas and harmonicas.[15] The Sierra Leoneans and the Kru of Liberia who worked along the Atlantic coast also found their way to Brazzaville and seem to have introduced their distinctive way of playing the guitar, associated with palm-wine music. The accordion which could replicate the flowing rhythms of the local *likembe* (Lingala, 'thumb piano') could be heard in the streets near the Pool factories by 1902.[16]

Between the wars, a new wave of music and dancing swept through the lower Congo and the Pool district, alarming missionaries since it was so 'infectious'.[17] Emerging from the work-camps, and perhaps associated with the return home of railway construction workers, came dances known as *agbaya* and *maringa*. *Agbaya*, performed in a circle without partners, was probably the older of the two; it was later replaced by the partnered *maringa*, especially in towns such as Matadi, Boma, Brazzaville and Kinshasa. According to one observer of *agbaya* dancers in Brazzaville in 1929, the dance had 'the allure of a rhythmic game. A musician played a kind of guitar that sounded quite muffled.' The dancers, both men and women, were in a circle, 'changing their weight from side to side in time to the music, while staying in the same spot, swinging their arms and clapping their hands'. A dancer would break out of the circle to dance in front of another, the women before the men and vice versa, returning to join the circle, and another taking his or her place in the middle. It was also observed that 'the women danced with downcast eyes'.[18]

Increasingly popular, and superseding the *agbaya*, however, was the *maringa*. Bands were at first made up of a *likembe* which provided the melody; a bottle struck with a metal rod, which took the place of the older gong and supplied the basic rhythm; and a small, skin-covered frame drum, a *patenge*, held between the legs, which supplied a counter rhythm. The musicians played local tunes reworked through foreign influences. By the 1920s, accordions and acoustic guitars were taking over the melody line from the *likembe* in *maringa* bands.[19]

The characteristic movement of *maringa* dancers was a hip motion that shifted the body weight alternately from one leg to the other, in a manner similar to the rumba which was later to sweep the older dances away, but which in Congo was heavily influenced by the older *maringa* dance and musical forms. Popularity of the partnered dancing spread like wildfire throughout the Congo region, touching even remote villages by 1935.[20]

Entrepreneurs in the towns and rural areas opened up dance-halls which charged an entrance fee. Whereas traditional dancing took place in open spaces, partnered *maringa* was danced 'in the interior of huts made from palm branches, to the sound of the accordion'.[21] The 'explosion' of dancing in the lower Congo in the 1920s and 1930s worried missionaries not only because they saw them as sensual but because they were accompanied by a good deal of drinking. As the speaker at the inauguration of the Catholic youth club indicated, they were exactly the kind of 'dishonest dances' that the missionaries feared would seduce their converts in the town. Describing *maringa* dancing at a village in the lower Congo where an enterprising nurse had constructed a dance-hall and charged admission, one missionary account reported that 'the couples are entwined in each other's arms and undulate their bodies in such a dissolute fashion that there is no longer anything that could be called aesthetic in it. Everything is becoming shameless and obscene. This is the brutal fact. It is sad to say, but it is a fact; our people have lost the sense of honest dancing.'[22] Similar dance-halls existed in Brazzaville in the 1920s, and perhaps before. A report on the impact of the Depression reported that 'the dancehalls are less frequented because people lack money'.[23]

While *maringa* dances were widespread among ordinary people in town and country, the tastes and emerging sense of class identity among the urban elite were turning them more in the direction of European and Latin American music. The period of the First World War when so many foreign soldiers were billeted in Brazzaville, as well as the return of veterans from France, acted as a catalyst for introducing the latest in European music and dance.

Trans-Pool contacts also facilitated the spread of both *maringa* and European dances on both sides of the river. With a boom in the wartime and post-war economy of the Belgian Congo, Léopoldville experienced an upsurge in population which was around 30,000 when the impact of the world Depression caused a temporary exodus in the workforce.[24] During the colonial period, the Pool served as a channel of communication rather than as a barrier between the two capitals.[25] Informants were universally adamant that it was easy to cross the Pool in spite of the international frontier and that people did so frequently, to work, for football matches, to visit friends, and to attend dances and cinemas. In the early 1920s, six to eight ferries crossed the Pool daily in both directions on a regular basis. Since the last one left about 5 p.m., before darkness fell, people often stayed overnight and caught the first boat back in the morning.[26]

Descriptions of a top Kinshasa dance-hall in 1923 confirm the linkages between the two sides of the river, not least because a Brazzaville band was playing. In the absence of accounts from the north side of the Pool, the descriptions show the kind of dances that the Brazzaville elite might be enjoying at the time. At the 'Apollo-Palace' the most popular dance time was from 4 p.m. to 7 p.m. on a Sunday afternoon. A curfew may have precluded dances later in the evening. Men paid an entrance fee of 3 francs, women entered free and those who came to watch were charged 1 franc. The dance-hall had white walls and a cement floor. On one side of the room were African men dressed in a wild assortment of clothing, both new and second-hand, on the other side were women, some expensively dressed and others in dresses that must have arrived in town through the second-hand market.[27] When the band started to play, the men crossed the room to the women and requested a dance. The favourites were one-steps, foxtrots, waltzes and the 'highly fashionable Cakewalk'. The lead musician played the melody on an accordion, others provided harmonies and rhythm on bamboo flutes, a drum, and a bottle struck with a metal rod.[28] Also, in a street near a European hotel, a group of visiting musicians from Brazzaville was entertaining passers-by with some 'French tunes'.[29] Clearly, if the small town on the north side of the Pool could not support its musicians, it was easy enough for them to find opportunities in the larger Belgian Congo capital, and this trend continued into the period of rumba music in the 1950s. The interchange between the musical worlds of the two capitals, which was crucial in the outpouring of Congo music in the last decade of colonial rule, had already been established thirty years previously.

For the Brazzaville crowd, there was also entertainment to be had from the sights and sounds of a brass band or a marching group with bugles and drums. In the 1930s, there were at least six such bands which played on religious and public holidays, at sports competitions, for dances and at Sunday afternoon concerts. They were important not only for the spectacle they provided but also for the training in techniques and theory that they gave to musicians, some of whom used their skills to play in rumba bands after the Second World War.

European religious music was familiar to many through the hymns and ritual of mission churches. As early as 1884, Monseigneur Augouard had imported a harmonium to accompany singing at the mass. It was a great drawing card among his congregation, 'an instrument of propaganda' according to Chavannes, head of the French post.[30] Other instruments at the Catholic mission were a piano, and a violin and cornet played by Catholic brothers at mass.[31] Once the mission youth club was established, the boys learned to play trumpets, bugles and drums in a band that played for processions and in church. When mission sports teams competed, the Catholic youth club band led them onto the field and played at half-time.[32] Swedish missionaries also introduced European melodies, but complained that their congregations tended to transpose them into an African mode of singing which involved different intervals and rhythms. Instruments also underwent changes in the hands of African congregations. In 1941 the Protestant Council banned the use in churches of a new drum called *kibandi*, which appeared in 1934, and mimicked a European band drum, with its diameter greater than its length, unlike indigenous cylindrical drums. The missionaries disapproved of *bandi* music because it over-excited their congregations who were 'tempted to use it for playing old heathen dance tunes'.[33] Musically, however, the most exciting religious group for townspeople was the Salvation Army, which arrived in Kinshasa in 1935 and crossed to open a mission in Brazzaville two years later. The uniforms and flags created a huge stir, but it was the band music that, according to an officer, 'played a great part in helping to attract the crowds right from the beginning of our activities'. At their first open-air meetings in Kinshasa, Army musicians led the crowd in singing with a portable organ, a violin, a concertina and a trumpet. Local musicians seized the chance to learn the European instruments and songs. Two years later, a Léopoldville brass band led the Christian soldiers into Brazzaville.[34]

The military bands that played in parades and march-pasts whenever visiting dignitaries visited the AEF capital were also crowd-pleasers, playing mostly French military tunes and traditional songs. Band musicians were well trained, since as early as 1892, specialized musicians had been sent by the French army to train regimental bands in Equatorial Africa.[35] West Indian soldiers posted in Brazzaville, especially those from Martinique, were among the first to introduce Caribbean music in Poto-Poto and Bacongo.[36] Finally, by the 1920s there was a Town Band and the band sponsored by the Native Sports Federation. In 1927, Emmanuel Dadet, who had been influenced by Antillean groups singing and playing informally around Poto-Poto, received permission from the Mayor to form a municipal brass band. A grant was provided for the instruments that band members could not otherwise afford.[37] The Native Sports Federation also formed a band to play at sporting events and for performances by massed gymnasts. In 1934, it was granted a subsidy to replenish its instruments which included bugles, trumpets, cornets, cymbals, drums, saxophones and trombones.[38] Thus, brass-band music was another well-established form of popular entertainment in the town before the Second World War.

Walking in the streets of Bacongo and Poto-Poto in the 1920s, a passer-by might also hear gramophone-music floating out of a window.

Africans who worked for Europeans were familiar with such musical devices from the early part of the century, but it was only after the First World War that they were sufficiently common and affordable to be bought by the elites.[39] By 1938, they were so widespread that in Poto-Poto, 'every sector of the town had a sign saying "phonographs repaired"'.[40] They could also be bought at the Portuguese shops in Kinshasa where there was always a larger selection of goods, or through catalogue order. The craze for things English made 'His Master's Voice'(HMV), sold at the store of the British-owned *Société de Kwilu-Niari*, the most popular brand.[41] The appearance of gramophones among the grave-goods of Lari 'big men' by 1930 shows the status that such possessions signalled to local society.[42]

Records also flooded the African market, so much so that the newly appointed censorship board recognized the impossibility of applying screening procedures to records as well as to films.[43] To try and stop the flow would be like putting a finger in a broken dike. Records from South and West Africa, Europe and the West Indies were widely available. The French-owned Pathé recording company and the British-owned Zono-phone company had started selling records in South Africa in 1907, and HMV made its first recordings in South Africa in the mid-1920s.[44] These records found their way into the stores around the Pool. In West Africa, Zonophone started recording highlife music in 1927 and sold their records in Brazzaville and Léopoldville.[45] Trans-Atlantic music also became better known through the record industry. For example, First World War veterans played Charleston music with French words. But the most influential recordings were played by low-level Antillean civil servants who stayed in Poto-Poto and invited local elites to hear recordings by Cuban groups such as 'Septeto Habanero', released on the HMV label.[46]

As the new music and dance became established, the social leaders integrated it in their celebrations where village music had once reigned supreme a decade of so before. Signs of a society in transformation appear in the journal of a Swede who described a wedding reception in Bacongo in 1932, 'like a summer wedding in Sweden', with guests sitting under a temporary awning, eating and drinking, and music supplied by a gramophone.[47] The pronounced class differences and preferences of Bacongo and Poto-Poto were marked by music and dance preferences. While labourers in Poto-Poto danced to traditional orchestras of drums, scrappers and bamboo flutes in open spaces, the clerks of Bacongo had moved indoors to dance-halls decorated with palm branches and flags, where they danced foxtrots and tangos to the sound of an accordion.[48]

By the late 1930s, the arrival of the Latin American rumba was a momentous event in the development of modern dance and music, for to a large extent it swept away the class preferences of the elite and the masses and simply became the basis for popular urban music by the end of the colonial period. Around the Pool, people responded to a music and dance form that they found both familiar and novel. The antecedents of rumba originated in Central Africa; crossed the Atlantic with slaves, many of whom were taken to Santo Domingo and Cuba in the late eighteenth and nineteenth centuries; and returned with West Indians and West Africans to colonial towns where rhythms and melodies were reworked and transformed in the Congolese rumba that emerged with the help of electric guitars and the recording industry. While the music was familiar, the similar movement of *maringa* and rumba dancers may also explain why Congolese so quickly embraced the new dance forms.[49] White society also developed a craze for Latin American dance music, especially the rumba after it had been featured and made respectable at the Chicago World Fair in 1932, but they and the African elite also took over the upper-class tango, the *biguine*, a dance akin to the Brazilian samba but deriving from Martinique, and other dances from the other side of the Atlantic.[50] The first Brazzaville band to play Latin American music was started by Jean Réal, a Frenchman from Martinique, who worked as the artistic and entertainment director at the Congo-Océan Hotel and was well known in Poto-Poto and Bacongo. About 1934, players from Poto-Poto joined his 'Congo-Rumba' band which specialized in Latin American dance music.[51]

Taking his cue from Réal and other Antilleans, Emmanuel Dadet formed a dance band from among the members of the Town Band and started to inject an African element into Latin American rumbas. His 'Melo-Congo', which is remembered as Brazzaville's first African-led modern dance band, was greatly in demand for social gatherings of the elite, playing a great variety of music, from older waltzes and foxtrots to the new rumbas, *biguines*, and tangos. 'Melo-Congo fills a gap that has existed for too long,' wrote one enthusiastic reporter in 1942.[52]

Bars and associations

The years after the Second World War saw a proliferation of bars and 'bars-dancing', where live bands and gramophone records amplified over loudspeakers helped popularize 'Congo music'. Following the Brazzaville conference and the liberalization of official policy on many aspects of African life, the laws that banned selling alcohol in public places to African customers were partially lifted. Entrepreneurs responded to demand by greatly expanding the number of dance-halls and bars in

Poto-Poto and Bacongo. The Catholic newspaper *La Semaine* noted that wine-producers had flooded the African market with their 'unhealthy' products. Consumption in French Equatorial Africa had increased seven-fold between 1938 and 1953. It was advisable not to reintroduce limits, however, the writer argued, for it had been proven in the past that to do so only led to increased production and consumption of illegal locally brewed drinks.[53]

Ten of the top 'bars-dancing' advertised in the African section of *France-Equateur* in January 1955. Opening hours were still limited by municipal regulations from about 4 p.m. to 10.30 p.m. on weekdays, and from about 4 p.m. to midnight on weekends and holidays. All these establishments advertised music on gramophone records, with the appearance of live bands as a special feature.[54] Brazzavillois usually frequented bars on their own side of the town where they liked the ambience, the type of music played and the clientele. Among popular places to meet friends and dance were 'Chez Faignond', 'Gaité-Brazza', 'Folies-Brazza', 'Congo-Zoba', 'Mon Pays', and 'Boudzoum Bar' in Poto-Poto; and 'Lumi-Congo', 'Beauté-Brazza', 'Chez Hughes', 'Nouany Bar' and 'Mouendo-Koko' in Bacongo.[55] But people would also cross town, if a popular band was playing. Jean-Claude Ganga remembered that when he was a young man the best dancing in Bacongo was at the famous 'Lumi-Congo' where young people from the Dahomey and Aviation neighbourhoods gathered. Yet when a popular group was featured, such as 'Jazz-Bohème' led by Bernard Massamba 'Lebel', 'even people from Poto-Poto would arrive'. Mambeke-Boucher also remembered that 'there was so much to do in Poto-Poto, why would we go to Bacongo?' but that he and his friends might do so if there was a big football match, or a famous band was playing, or a friend was giving a party.[56] Different night-spots were known for different kinds of music. 'Lumi-Congo' offered Latin American recordings and suggested to readers of *France-Equateur*: 'Pass your evening in a lively ambience.' The top night-spot, 'Chez Faignond', with its mixed clientele of Europeans and upper-class Africans, advertised European records on weekdays, African and West Indian music on Saturday evenings, and jazz on Sundays.[57]

Such places of entertainment were essential gathering points for making acquaintances, catching up on news and listening to the new music. One writer credited bars with creating a 'fraternal consciousness',[58] and this was true to some extent. Yet bars also showed the social distinctions that characterized relationships. One popular meeting-place, 'Gaiété-Brazza' was owned by a Dahomean and was mostly frequented by people from that part of West Africa, especially after a dispute over a

woman caused the owner to close the bar to Congolese for a time.[59] The
top bars were class oriented and had doormen who turned away
customers who might lower the tone of the establishment. The most
celebrated 'bars-dancing' in Poto-Poto and Bacongo vied with each other
in their elegance and reputation. 'Chez Faignond', for example, at the
heart of the entertainment district on Rue M'Bakas in Poto-Poto, was
opened by a member of a well-known Euro-African family in 1948. The
manager had once been a choirboy at the Catholic mission. He was
credited with a good knowledge of his customers' tastes, and contributed
to the bar's success by judiciously mixing old favourites with recent
releases. The largest crowds arrived when famous groups such as
Kinshasa's 'OK Jazz' and 'African Jazz', or Brazzaville's own 'Bantous
de la Capitale' were featured live.[60] 'Chez Faignond' was also popular
with Europeans from Léopoldville who crossed the river for Poto-Poto
night-life when social segregation was maintained by law in the Belgian
Congo capital and curfews still operated in the African sections of the
town.[61]

Not least among the attractions of 'Chez Faignond' and other top
'bars-dancing' were groups of stylishly and richly dressed young women,
who ostentatiously showed off the latest fashions in *pagnes* and short
dresses, hairstyles, make-up, jewellery and head-scarves. They also
composed and performed songs and dances to entertain the clientele.
Organized in groups with names such as 'The Rose', 'Shining Star',
'Violette', 'Lolita', 'Dollar', 'Elegance', 'Durban' and 'Diamond', each
was headed by a male president who represented them in business
transactions, writing letters, doing publicity and negotiating with bar
owners. These were mutual-aid associations and, like many other such
groups, they were drawn together by common interests, in this case,
dancing, music and fashion. Like other associations, also, they paid dues
which members could draw on for extraordinary expenses, especially
those relating to sickness, burials and *matanga*. If a member died the
others would go into mourning for an agreed amount of time and then
stage a big 'coming-out' celebration akin to the traditional *matanga*,
which would involve new dances, music and cloths.[62]

Balandier has suggested that, apart from being mutual-aid associations, these were associations of 'high-class prostitutes', and indeed,
grouping together in this manner was excellent strategy for young
women who wanted to go to the top bars and draw the attention of the
male clientele through their dress and dancing.[63] Nevertheless, informants, thought that prostitution in Brazzaville had never been highly
organized and that these groups served many functions, of which the
primary one was mutual aid. At the same time, composing and

performing songs and dances and dressing in the latest fashions both fulfilled genuine interests and allowed the young women to entertain wealthy men who might also solicit them for sex and pay them well.[64] Such associations of stylish women also existed in Kinshasa, where they started about 1943. Indeed, some of the Brazzaville groups which bore the same name as those on the other side of the Pool were initially 'sponsored' from Kinshasa, as the Brazzaville groups also sponsored new groups in Poto-Poto and Bacongo.[65]

In contrast with such 'casual' prostitution, based as it was in mutual-aid societies, the main attempt to organize prostitution in Brazzaville was carried out by the colonial power. The contradictions and irony of such efforts are obvious, when one considers the frequent colonial discourse which lumped the 'prostitutes' of Poto-Poto with 'vagrants' and other undesirables created by migrants to the town. The setting up of official brothels was associated with the Second World War when numbers of Allied troops were stationed in the town, many of them *en route* to North Africa and the Middle East. In the decree of 1909, prostitution had been legalized, as it was in France, and women who agreed to medical inspections once a week had the advantage of not being troubled by the police.[66] However, this decree had limited impact, since few women wanted to go through such inspections, and the great majority who engaged in prostitution did so privately. At times they were an important source of income for their relatives, as during the Depression when families were desperate for cash to pay their taxes, and levels of prostitution in the town increased.[67] In 1939, however, the French, wanting to control the spread of venereal disease in France, had introduced tougher measures whereby a prostitute could be sentenced to three months in prison for refusing a medical examination. A year later in Brazzaville, a similar decree was introduced which made it mandatory for every prostitute to carry an official permit which was issued after a woman had submitted to a medical exam, finger-printing and being photographed. Refusal carried a prison sentence, as in France.[68] Most controversial, however, was the decision to open official brothels. The project went ahead in spite of opposition from some administrators, who noted that it was contrary to all the work being done in France to promote family life, that it was bad for the administration's 'prestige' and contrary to government policy which had consistently criticized prostitution.[69] The Bacongo brothel, which was built on the side of the town where there was an airfield and a school for training parachutists *en route* to Chad, was notorious with the local population. Called 'La Visite', it was run by a Euro-African woman from Cabinda remembered as 'Madame Rose'. It is not clear who received the remuneration.

According to informants, people in Bacongo were so afraid that their daughters would be coerced into going to the brothel that some families sent their unmarried daughters back to the villages, some arranged marriages, and brothers pretended that they were the husbands of their unmarried sisters.[70] This episode was remembered as among the 'terrible things that happened' to women during the war, together with forced rubber-processing.[71] In 1946, when the wartime crisis had passed, the brothels were made illegal and the official discourse returned to condemnation of prostitution with such statements as: 'Too many young people are coming to the town, the girls are living off prostitution and the boys are vagabonds.'[72]

That the fashionable young women who performed at Brazzaville's bars had formed themselves into mutual-aid associations is not surprising, given that these were an essential feature of town life. Their focus was very diverse, from *quartier* dance associations to music groups at the cultural centres, and unemployed young men who played sport. Like football teams, some of which were also mutual-aid associations, they represented many types of social groups within the town, organized around class, religion, age, gender, occupation, regions of origin, or simply recreational interests.

Like so many other cultural activities in the town, membership of such an association was being part of a 'community of choice'.[73] In this case, their origins were firmly rooted in rural traditions, that is, revolving savings societies called *kitemo* in Kilari or *itemo* in Kiteke. In such groups, men and women would contribute on a regular basis, in kind before the monetization of the economy, and they would have the right to all the contributions of others on a regular basis, depending on the number of members in their group. The concept was carried to the town and existed among workers from an early period. In 1919, it was reported that 'in Brazzaville, there is scarcely a group of boys, police or workers who are not part of a small *kitemo* where dues, sometimes minimal, are paid at the end of month after they are paid by employers'.[74] This report, and also one in 1915, emphasized the importance of the institution for the societies around the Pool and the sizeable amounts of money to which an individual could have access if he was part of an association of big men selling agricultural produce to the town.[75] A 1933 report, noting that both savings associations and burial societies were common in the town, credited them with helping families deal with the Depression years.[76]

Although such revolving savings associations, *tontines*, continued in the town, the need for support in a crisis led to the transformation of the institution into what were known as *muziki* (Kilari, Lingala and

4 Meeting of the women's association 'Kela-bala' (Kilari, 'caring for children'), Poto-Poto, June 1989. The women are singing and dancing accompanied by a band of male musicians (Phyllis Martin)

Kikongo, 'friendship'), and it was such arrangements that were the focus of the recreational groups that have been described here. They became particularly important for women with expenses relating to their children but without access to adequate incomes.[77] In Balandier's survey in Poto-Poto, 4 per cent of women were living independently or with other women, but the actual numbers were much higher as many were not recognized in the census on which the survey was based, since they were living in a men's households, but on a temporary basis.[78] Unlike the *kitemo*, *muziki* members only received support from the central fund to which they had contributed when they were faced with a crisis, usually illness, death or costs relating to a *matanga*. In the town, the latter were more and more costly as they became an increasingly lavish means of honouring the dead and the family. In the early 1930s, they were still quite small-scale even for elite families, that is, usually parties at home or in the street where the family might put up a palm-branch shelter for guests.[79] Twenty years later, however, the *matanga* for an elite family meant announcements in a newspaper, printed invitations, and great expense on new cloths and clothes. The celebrations were usually held at bars where food and drink was served to the guests. But even for ordinary people, sickness and death involved expenses which personal as well as monetary support from other *muziki* members helped to cover. The recreational element in *muziki* was also important since even evening meetings to practise dances or discuss business matters created social networks and enriched individual lives.[80]

Music in the mix

After the Second World War, Congo music grew out of social gatherings and the recording industry in Léopoldville, through which it was popularized. Borrowing a phrase from a study of popular music in South Africa, it was 'music in the mix'.[81] Groups of youthful musicians found opportunities to play at *matanga*, parties and wedding receptions and other gatherings of *muziki* or families who had substituted the new music and dance for more traditional styles. In return, band members were given food, drink and a collection taken from the guests. If they were good, word spread and they received other invitations, thus building up their reputations.[82] When large associations scheduled their annual dances at famous bars, they usually invited a live band, which led to further recognition. For example, in 1954, the Association of Waiters and Domestic Servants announced its annual celebration in the "Soirées de Poto-Poto" section of *France-Equateur*. It was to be held at the 'Folies-Brazza' and featured the 'Mysterious Band' from Léopoldville and a group of dancers from an association called 'Chef de Toilette', also from Léopoldville.[83]

Informal music groups which started off in Poto-Poto and Bacongo might evolve into mutual-aid associations that performed for social gatherings. These were the training ground for several famous Congo musicians. According to official policy which required associations to be registered with the authorities, eight Poto-Poto groups with 168 members were listed with the Department of Political Affairs in 1948.[84] There were doubtless many other groups whose structures were not formalized. Among the best-known bands were 'Les Mélomanes Congolais' ('Congolese Music Lovers'), established in 1945 under Félix Malekat; Paul Kamba's 'Victoria-Brazza' established in 1943; and 'Congo-Jazz'. Bacongo groups included the popular 'Jazz-Bohème' of Bernard Massamba 'Lebel'; the 'Cercul Jazz', which was the band of the Bacongo cultural centre; and 'Jazz Dahoméen'. In the early days, many musicians who had no formal musical training took advantage of lessons on band instruments and sol-fa offered by Elaine Pepper, a French musicologist, at the newly opened Bacongo and Poto-Poto cultural centres. Musical evenings on Thursdays and Saturdays included listening to different types of music on records and the radio. Bands approved by the cultural centres were helped with the purchase of instruments, a great attraction for young musicians who could not afford their own.[85]

These small groups led the way in the evolution of the Congolese rumba in the fifteen years before independence, as the previous generation had popularized *maringa* music. Singers and composers such as Paul Kamba, Bernard Massamba 'Lebel' and Antoine Moundanda sang in Lingala, Kituba and Kilari. European-sounding brass-band instruments gave way to singers with guitars which, better replicating the flowing notes of the *likembe*, were more familiar to the African ear and to some extent replaced the accordion. Experimentation with combinations of instruments continued, limited only by group creativity, versatility and access to European instruments. In some groups, drums and balaphones from village orchestras were adapted for rumba, *biguine*, *son*, and cha-cha rhythms; in others, such as the group led by Antoine Moundanda, who won the Osborne prize for the best African recording in 1955, the *likembe* was played together with European instruments.[86] Although band names frequently included the word 'Jazz', the essential musical inspiration came from African and Latin American roots. In naming their groups after the North American genre, young men were rather reflecting their fascination with the American soldiers, especially African-Americans, who were based at a military camp in Léopoldville during the Second World War. Although 'swing' and 'bebop' had its adherents at elite bars such as 'Chez Faignond', where American records were played on Sundays, it did not challenge rumba among ordinary people. Only in the 1960s did American jazz and soul music have a prominent place in the evolution of the Congo rumba, for example in the music of the great Kinshasa musician, Tabu-Ley.[87]

Three band leaders in the post-war period introduced new singing styles and instrumental combinations in Brazzaville. Of these the singer, band leader and composer Paul Kamba was the most prominent. His career is worth recounting briefly for, like many of the early leaders of urban culture, he combined his personal talents with training received from Europeans. He also provided a model for those less familiar with negotiating and exploiting the opportunities in the colonial town.

Born in 1912, Kamba spent his boyhood around the Brazzaville mission where his father was Monseigneur Guichard's cook. He attended the mission's Jeanne d'Arc Primary School and was a choirboy in the cathedral. He was a good football player, known by his nickname *libaya* (Lingala, 'plank' or 'beam') because of his toughness, and then became a well-respected referee for FAC, not an easy task given the contentious nature of Bacongo and Poto-Poto football. Like many seeking a good job, Kamba worked for a time in Kinshasa, for the Post and Telegraph Services, and then returned to Brazzaville to take up a position as a clerk for the Congo-Océan railway. Later he worked for the Services of Mines. At the time of his death he was Secretary-General of the government employees' union (*Syndicat des Contractuels et Auxiliaires du Gouverne-ment-Général de l'AEF*).

At the same time as he was making his mark on the football field, Kamba was drawing other young people in Poto-Poto around him to make music after work and on Sundays. In the late 1930s, they formed a mutual-aid association called 'Bonne Esperance' ('Good Hope'), whose principal activity was to sing, play and experiment with the new rumba sounds, reworking them in an African idiom. Kamba's position as a civil servant made him known in European circles and, during the Second World War, he and his musical group were asked by Jean Réal to help entertain the Allied forces. Appearing in shows at the Congo-Océan Hotel, Kamba and his friends enhanced their experience of performing in public and learnt more about Latin American music. In 1948, he was appointed by the colonial authorities as head of the music section at the new Poto-Poto cultural centre. He became a lobbyist for young men who wanted access to instruments and lessons to improve their skills.

At the same time as he was working with one foot in a music world sponsored by Europeans, Kamba's fame and popularity in Poto-Poto and Bacongo were growing. His principal talent was as a singer, and in 1943 he formed his famous 'Victoria-Brazza' band which provided vocal backing and accompanied him on guitars, drums and accordion. When his group rehearsed after work, people would gather around in the yard or street in Poto-Poto where he lived. He sang in Lingala, and the lyrics and music reverberated in the minds and experience of his listeners. He was a gregarious and friendly individual and, like the top football players, he was followed by young boys when he walked through the streets of Poto-Poto. Kamba's 'Victoria-Brazza' were much sought after to play at *matanga* celebrations, wedding receptions and parties, and the band also received engagements from 'bars-dancing' to play. As its fame spread, it was also invited to play in Kinshasa where a group member handled engagements and publicity. Kamba was the first from Brazzaville to record his music at the Ngoma studios in Kinshasa and his records further established the popularity of 'Victoria-Brazza'.[88]

Kamba was the first great singer of Lingala popular songs on the Brazzaville side of the Pool. The eyes of the generation who heard him sing light up when they talk of him. He became something of a star. 'Women were crazy about him. He had so many girl friends,' said a member of his group.[89] In one of his famous songs, 'Marie Thérèse', written in Lingala about 1949 and recorded by the Ngoma company, Kamba teased his listeners with the seductive power of 'Victoria-Brazza', which caused trouble when men and women went off to bars to listen to the magical music, leaving their spouses and family responsibilities behind:

> Mbonda ya Victoria eboma mabala e,
> Miziki ya Victoria eboma mabala e,
> Marie-Thérèse Epanzola, eboma mabala e,
> Mingongo ya Victoria eboma mabala e,
> Marie-Thérèse Epanzola, eboma mabala e,
> Miziki ya Victoria, chaud!

> Victoria's sound brings trouble in households,
> Victoria's music brings trouble in households,
> Marie-Thérèse Epanzola, it brings trouble in households,
> Victoria's voice brings trouble in households,
> Marie-Thérèse Epanzola, it brings trouble in households,
> Victoria's music is hot![90]

Like other musicians of his time, Kamba never made enough money to give up his job as a civil servant. Even the top musicians had to settle for recognition rather than financial gain. At celebrations such as *matanga* parties, they were rewarded with food and drink and a collection taken from among the guests. When they played in bars, they might receive a small percentage of the income from drinks sold. There was little monetary reward even for those who made recordings. In a 1985 interview, the famous Zairois guitarist, Kasanda wa Mikalay, 'Doctor Nico', who started playing with 'Africa Jazz' when he was about fourteen years old, noted: 'The musicians were paid little or nothing for their work.'[91] 'We did not know about royalties then,' reported a saxophonist from the 1950s in an interview.[92] The owners of recording studios paid a flat fee which was split up among members of the group.

Paul Kamba's career was cut short when the government posted him away from Brazzaville to Mossaka, the capital of the Likouala region. Shortly afterwards, in 1950, he died, probably from tuberculosis.

Two other figures are remembered as pioneers in the early days of Congo music in Brazzaville. On the Bacongo side of town the best remembered is Bernard Massemba 'Lebel', whose 'Jazz-Bohème' drew crowds to the 'Lumi-Congo' bar.[93] Like Kamba, Massamba 'Lebel' worked in a government office and served as an organizer and inspiration for-up-and-coming young musicians through his role as Vice-President of the Bacongo cultural centre. He performed songs with a South

American–African inspiration, supported by guitars and small drums. He never recorded his music, however, and in 1954, his career was cut short by his death in a car accident, removing another talented player from the Brazzaville music scene.[94]

A third pioneer of popular music in Brazzaville was a talented guitarist, Zacharie Elenga, known as 'Jhimmy', who introduced the Hawaian style of playing to the two Congo capitals. Jhimmy 'did not hesitate to set society on fire' and dancers went 'hysterical' when he played. He drew devoted followers during 1950–2 when he was a dominant figure, playing in bars on both sides of the Pool and recording his music at Kinshasa studios.[95] Those who remember Jhimmy speak of his guitar-playing in almost hushed tones, searching for words to describe his magic. Famous guitarists such as Doctor Nico acknowledge his influence on their musical development. Jhimmy, like Kamba, sang of his power to transform the moods of those who listened, as in the rumba 'Beware of Jhimmy', which he recorded with the Opika company in Kinshasa:

> Baninga, baninga, baninga, baninga,
> Botika tembe,
> Oyo ya lelo, oyo e bokomi kokanisa,
> Bokomi kolela.
> Baninga baninga, baninga, baninga,
> Botika tembe,
> Oyo ya Jhimmy, e okomi koseka,
> Okomi kodenda.
> Banga Jhimmy, banga Jhimmy,
> Muana yango jeune, muana yango e,
> Okomi koseka, okomi kodenda.

> Friends, friends, friends, friends,
> Don't doubt,
> For now you are wondering,
> You're crying.
> Friends, friends, friends, friends,
> Don't doubt,
> With Jhimmy's music, now you are laughing,
> Now you are showing off.
> Beware of Jhimmy, beware of Jhimmy,
> This boy is young, this boy,
> Now you're laughing, now you're showing off.[96]

In 1952, at the height of his career, Jhimmy left Brazzaville and went to live in the Central African Republic, his mother's country of origin.

Shortly afterwards he stopped performing in public, shocking his many admirers.[97]

The rapid loss of these three musicians was a blow to Brazzaville music fans and to the young men who aspired to enter the big bands. Since they made only a few records and died before the rise of the modern Congo music entertainment business, they are little remembered and often go unnoticed in surveys of modern popular music. The initiative passed to the south side of the Pool and musicians from Brazzaville crossed to Kinshasa to help form new bands that experimented with the evolution of the Congo rumba. The disinctive 'Congo music' style with several guitars playing interlocking melodies complemented by different combinations of instruments, such as saxophones and clarinets, came into existence by 1960. Around 1957 the electric guitar arrived at the Pool and was quickly integrated into the Congolese rumba. Among the top bands followed by fans on both sides of the Pool were Kallé Kabasele's 'African Jazz', which started in 1953, and the 'OK Jazz' of Luambo Makiadi 'Franco', named after a bar where he played in 1956. Co-founders with Franco of one of Africa's most famous bands were several Congolese including the clarinet and saxophone player Jean-Serge Essous, the guitarist Daniel Loubelo 'de la Lune' and the composer and singer Edouard Nganga 'Edo'. Like those who dominated the rise of European and American rock groups in the 1950s and 1960s, these musicians were representative of the burgeoning population of young people in the two capitals as independence approached. Franco was seventeen when OK Jazz was formed, Loubelo was twenty-one and Edo was twenty-three. Like their European and American counterparts, they were heroes for the young people of the city. Top entertainers, both individuals and their bands, received recognition on both sides of the Pool, so a great deal of coming and going of stars and audiences continued. On the eve of independence some of the Congolese players returned to Brazzaville to establish a band that would rival the best in Kinshasa. The 'Bantous de la Capitale' was launched at 'Chez Faignond' in August 1959.[98]

People also gained familiarity with the new popular music through listening to records and the radio, which spread the fame of the stars and bands not only around the Pool but throughout Africa. Gramophones were still too expensive for all but the elites, but the sounds of music drifting out of bars, cafes and cinemas was part of city life, especially on Saturday evening and Sunday.

The recording of local singers and bands developed as a cottage industry in Kinshasa after the Second World War. The pioneers were a group of Greek entrepreneurs who had arrived in Belgian Congo as refugees during the war. In 1948, Jéronimidis launched his Ngoma company. A keen musician, with some knowledge of local languages, he travelled all over the region in a small truck, stopping in villages to search out promising young musicians who might be given an opportunity in Kinshasa. Paul Kamba was the first singer from the Brazzaville side of the river to record with this company. In the course of the 1950s, three other small companies, Loningisa, Opika and Esengo, were also established by Greek entrepreneurs. The studios were small and the technology simple, with musicians playing into a microphone which was hooked into a tape recorder. Studios bought instruments and encouraged young musicians to gather, discuss ideas on composition and technique, and improvise and practise on instruments they could not afford to buy for themselves. Tapes were sent to Paris, London or Brussels to be pressed into 78rpm or 45rpm records and returned to Congo for sale.[99]

By 1955, Ngoma listed almost a thousand titles in its catalogue.[100] In 1957, Sylvain Bemba noted that studios were 'producing records at an ever increasing pace' to keep up with demand. The popularity and, therefore, the life of a record was about three months.[101] Small stores and stands around market-places and at the roadside undercut European stores in the sale of records. A lively black market developed across the Pool. Records bought in Kinshasa were smuggled across the river at night in canoes and motorboats disguised as fishing craft in order to avoid customs duties. Women crossing the Pool by ferry hid records in their cloths. Smugglers brought samples to Brazzaville sellers who put in orders for future consignments. Before a public holiday such as New Year or the Fourteenth of July, or when a *matanga* was being organized, suppliers received especially large orders from their Brazzaville customers. Buying records and cloths was now an intrinsic part of public holidays and major social gatherings.[102]

After the Second World War, music broadcast over the radio was a common sound in Bacongo and Poto-Poto, in people's homes, in cafes and bars or at public listening points set up by the government. In the 1930s, a small transmitter had been erected by the European radio club and a few in the African upper class paid subscriptions to have their sets hooked up to broadcasts from 'Radio-Colonial Paris'. The programmes that ran for a few hours in the early evening were mostly classical and light music, opera, reviews of films and news reports.[103] The construction of the most powerful transmitter on the African continent during the Second World War changed the situation; in 1946, the radio station became Radio Brazzaville under the administration of Radiodiffusion Français. Broadcasting for about six hours per day, the programmes were primarily oriented to the European population but, in

1950, a second programme, Radio AEF, was introduced for African listeners.[104]

The cost of having a radio at home involved a double expenditure for Poto-Poto and Bacongo consumers. One was the subscription of 100 francs per month to be hooked up to distribution points that were installed around Poto-Poto and Bacongo. This system allowed broadcasts to reach the homes of those who did not have electricity. The other was the cost of the radio itself. Sets were widely available in stores and advertised in several attractive models in newspapers such as *France-Equateur*. While the subscription was within the range of many who were self-employed or wage-earners, the actual receiver was an expensive outlay. Many were willing to save up or borrow in order to buy one, however, for the status, novelty and entertainment. A set was the central focus of a room much as had been the case in the early days of the radio in America and Europe. Friends were invited to come to visit at certain times of the day specifically to listen to programmes, which were more than the background noise that they have become for so many today.[105] In 1951, the demand to be hooked up to the broadcasting system was so great that it could not be satisfied. One new listener who had invited his friends to gather around his set was ecstatic. 'If I could I would spend all day listening,' he was reported as saying.[106] Radio Kinshasa, Radio Belgian Congo and Radio Angola could also be heard. Those who could not afford a radio for their homes could listen to programmes over loudspeakers which the administration placed in public offices around Poto-Poto and Bacongo, in much the same way Americans had gathered at newspaper offices to hear news reports and baseball scores in the early days of broadcasting in the United States.[107]

Programmes were a mixture of what the French administration wanted African audiences to hear and what listeners requested. Broadcasts ran from about 6 p.m. to 9.30 p.m. each day, with some time given to news and readings from 'folklore' tales in five African languages (Kituba, Lingala, Oubangui, Sango and Chadian Arabic); a short segment on what the programme terms *musique folklorique* (that is 'traditional music' now juxtaposed with the new pop music); sports reports; readings from *Liaison*; and a variety of talks on topics such as the activities of the cultural centres, Scouting, life in France and in the French Union (including West Africa, Madagascar, Indochina and the Antilles), nutrition and medical problems, farming and herding, and education. Every day, listeners could hear a variety of music, both on Radio Brazzaville and Radio AEF, with a half-hour scheduled on Radio AEF for 'records requested by African listeners' on weekdays, and one hour on Sundays.[108] Programme listings included classical and light music from Europe; Latin American music played, for example, by the bands of Edmundo Ross, Armando Orefiche, Ibéria, Sebastian Solari and Feijo; the big-band music of Glenn Miller; French singers of romantic ballads such as Edith Piaf and Tino Rossi; the jazz greats, Benny Goodman, Duke Ellington and Count Basie; and Poppa John Gordy and his piano ragtime.[109] By 1960, Africa was 'awash' with Congo amplified music played over the radio by 'OK Jazz', 'African Jazz' and 'Bantous de la Capitale'.[110]

Popular songs became a vehicle for expressing the frustrations of daily life and dreams of the future.[111] Although the pioneers such as Kamba and Massamba had a primary education and jobs as civil servants, most of the young musicians had little schooling and led marginal lives.[112] This first generation, which received few of the monetary rewards of later band members, chronicled the economic deprivation that they saw and experienced, thus continuing a tradition of social commentary through song found in village society. One of those who adapted the *likembe* as an instrument that could be played in combination with Western-style instruments was André Nkouka 'Courant' ('Running'), who joined with Antoine Moundanda to form a rumba band. He composed a cha-cha entitled 'Come to Brazzaville and see' (Kilari, *yiza mavula yiza tala*), warning his girl friend of the problems of life in the city:

> Brazzaville ya mbote kua
> Ka bisalu pele bue tu sa.
>
> Refrain:
> Yiza mavula yiza tala Congo eh.
>
> Thérèse mu nge ni kuendela
> Me ngombele, me ngombele.
>
> Ku zandu bidia bitsamuni
> Ka mua bongela pele.
>
> Bu ma koko mu posi
> Ni mua sila tailleur fils.
>
> Ntsala za muntu ni m'pata
> Muatu ka bue tu sa.
>
>
> Brazzaville is so beautiful
> But there is no job, what can we do?
>
> Refrain:
> Come to Brazzaville and see the Congo.

Thérèse, I will die for you
I'm lost, I'm lost.

There's plenty of food in the market
But there's no money to buy it.

When I put my hand in my pocket
I only feel the tailor's thread.

Money is one's cushion [feather] dear,
Money solves everything.
So what shall we do?[113]

Most songs were about relationships between men and women. Written and sung by young men, mainly for other young men and women, their main audience, the lyrics expressed the search for new forms of relationships and were a creative response to the lyrics of Western and Latin American pop songs heard on the radio, and to the images viewed on cinema screens. The French singer and film star Tino Rossi was a great favourite with Brazzavillois for his fashion-sense and style, as well as for the romantic ballads he sang. At the five cinemas of Poto-Poto and Bacongo in the 1950s, audiences were enthralled by romantic epics such as *The Adventures of Don Juan* and *The Robbers of Baghdad*. Action films about Tarzan or Zorro or cowboy heroes of the American West, which had a strong romantic story line, were also crowd-pleasers.[114] A new vision of romantic love was expressed as *bolingo ya sentiment* (Lingala, 'sentimental love'), which, according to Sylvain Bemba, appeared in the language around this time.[115] A popular song by Paul Kamba called 'Catherine' talked of family opposition and individual sacrifice in the name of true love.[116]

Conclusion

Thus, in the 1950s, the new popular music coexisted with older music and dance forms in the town. Wandering along the Avenue de Paris or the Rue de la Paix on Sunday afternoons, one could watch dance groups representing different areas of AEF performing, accompanied by traditional orchestras and drums.[117] From there, it was only a step across the road to enter a 'bar-dancing' where rumba and swing were being performed in the 'best manner of Saint-Germain-des-Près'.[118] Nor was there any hard-and-fast line between those who danced to the village drums and those who danced to the rumba beat or, indeed, those who preferred to go to football matches on Sunday afternoons. Certainly, the elite tended to dance to the European and American music and older people might prefer the older dance forms, but there were many who liked both. Two men who danced with their regional associations on Sunday afternoon said that they went on to 'bars-dancing' in the evenings.[119]

There was no question of the rumba displacing the older dance associations in the colonial period, but the latter were fading in popularity, especially among young people as well as the elites. The influx of development funds after the Second World War had resulted in a remarkable expansion of education in AEF after years of neglect. By 1960, Congo and Gabon were near the top of literacy rates for Africa, with a school enrollment rate of 70 per cent in Congo, and the figures in Brazzaville even higher.[120] For young people in the town with even a couple of years of education, the new dance and pop music was part of their 'brave new world' and, in this perception, they may have appropriated some ideas on 'modernization' from their teachers. Phrases such as *danses folkloriques* and *danses modernes* designated the old and the new, with many young people firmly committed to the latter. In a 'Grand Celebration of Folklore' sponsored by the administration at the Poto-Poto cultural centre in 1953 to raise money for the centre's activities, few showed up for the *danses folkloriques* in the afternoon, whereas a large crowd appeared for an evening of dancing to a popular band.[121]

The discussion of both football and public entertainment draws attention to the fact that a great many leisure activities were male-oriented, especially before the Second World War. There has been some discussion of prostitution, although it must be said that no systematic study has been carried out and, as Luise White has shown, prostitution from the women's point of view is very much to do with work, not recreation.[122] One explanation for the male focus on leisure is that there were simply many more men in the colonial town than women and it was not until the very end of the period, between about 1955 and 1960, that the population achieved some balance. It was also at this time that girls were going to school and some young women delaying the age of marriage.

Explanations have to go well beyond numbers, however. Women simply had less time than men. In the town, as in the countryside, they had both productive and reproductive responsibilities to take care of. Collecting firewood and farming often meant walking several kilometres each day. Looking after children also took a great deal of time in the town with fewer family members around to take care of them. Many women preferred to stay close to home. When female informants were asked to talk about their 'time for entertainment' or leisure, they usually laughed and said that they did not have any, although they might go on to talk about mutual-aid associations or going on Sunday afternoons to dance or watch others perform in Poto-Poto. Whereas men sought out public entertainment, women tended to gather with their friends or fulfil family obligations.

Socializing was usually with members of one's own sex. In 1962, the French researcher Jeanne-Françoise Vincent found in her study of Bacongo women that 'married men and women live in separate worlds', that husbands went out on their own, and 'in the area of entertainment, the separate existence of husband and wife is marked'. This comment applied to most adult women, since the vast majority of women were married or at least engaged by the age of seventeen. Once they were married, women usually stayed at home, and their husbands would go out without telling them where they were going. The main exceptions were men of the elite some of whom aspired to companionate marriages in the Western sense or wanted to appear at functions with their spouses.[123]

'Separate' leisure was not just to do with lack of time, therefore, but also the cultural perception that any good wife and mother would not have leisure time, and that public leisure was not a female category. A woman with time for entertainment or one who went out on her own was almost by definition an idle woman or a prostitute. Joining with others in associations was socially acceptable, as well as providing a means of support and recreation. It seems that these perceptions have a great deal to do with continuities from village societies, where the amount of time free of work was less than that available to men, especially young men. Even on 'rest' days when they were not engaged in hard work in the fields, women's time was taken up with household chores. Also, village sociability is often along gender lines. It seems that these deeply rooted patterns continued in the colonial town. It must also be said that with less access to cash than male wage-earners, women not only did not have much 'time to spend' on entertainment but also little money. Although attitudes in the town have begun to change, some of these perceptions persist. As for the rural areas, a social worker in 1987 noted that village women have to be taught that it is legitimate for them to have time for recreation.[124]

6   Dressing well

At the turn of the century, servants and labourers at the factories along the Pool marked New Year's Day by dressing in their finest clothes. Strolling along the Avenue Félix Faure which bordered the river, women wore 'their most colourful cloths'. Men were dressed in waist-cloths or trousers and jackets. Some wore imported second-hand clothes such as frock coats and velvet opera hats. Particularly eye-catching were five 'Loangos' in white shirts, trousers and English army red coats. On Sundays, workers also cast aside their work clothes and donned their 'Sunday best'.[1]

Clothing is an important marker of time. As one writer has argued concerning Saturday night in America, dress 'makes concrete ordinary time and extraordinary time'.[2] During the week in Brazzaville, most people wore few or old clothes as they laboured in the hot climate on construction sites, at the factories, in the market, on the river or at their farms. Some who worked for Europeans wore special uniforms and, indeed, that was not least among the attractions of such jobs.[3] Yet employers often issued or insisted on clothes that satisfied their dress conventions, communicated the subordinate role of workers, and accentuated their place in the colonial hierarchy. As was clear in the controversy over football boots, monitors, clerks and those with Western education had to wear regular European clothes to work. Indeed, clerks were fined 'for lack of proper dress at the office'.[4] Servants, on the other hand, had to wear shorts and neither they nor waiters were allowed to wear shoes. The *tirailleurs*, including those who were school graduates but who were doing military service, went barefooted, while the police who patrolled Bacongo and Poto-Poto wore red fezzes, shirts, shorts and leggings, but no shoes.[5]

It was on Saturday evenings, Sundays and public holidays that individuals had choice in the matter of dress and donned their best outfits. On these occasions clothing and ornamentation not only conveyed the moment in time but also personal taste, resources and status. Material possessions are a 'live information system', noted Mary

Douglas. Dress is also what Balandier referred to as part of 'the social façade', whether to convey social realities or disguise personal predicament.[6] The presentation of self in outward display was an important aspect of pre-colonial society and it was a tradition transferred and transformed in the urban area. To discuss leisure and society in Brazzaville without taking account of the importance of dress would be to miss a central part of the story.

The convergence of clothing traditions

Many Brazzaville workers came from Central African societies where dress was little associated with utilitarian needs, for neither climate nor work conditions made this necessary. Rather, clothing and personal ornamentation conveyed identity, status, values and the significance of the occasion. This Brazza found out as he approached Mbe for his momentous meeting with the Tio ruler, Iloo, in 1880. In his record of the day, Brazza relates how his guides suggested that he and his men change their clothes, 'for the Makoko is a very great chief': to be taken seriously as the representative of an equally powerful ruler, the visitors must dress appropriately. Brazza quickly donned the dress coat of his naval uniform while his men 'took off their rags and put on their sailors' uniform'.[7] At the royal court, the Makoko Iloo appeared in royal regalia:

He wore a large copper collar, as did his principal wife. Four pages carried a folded red cloth on their shoulders. A young man, chief of the pages, wore a uniform acquired through trade which he wore with the buttons at the back. The ruler wore a large cloth [*pagne*], rings on his ankles and arms, and an intricately embroidered hat, fastened to his head by an iron pin with two very long feathers attached.[8]

While such momentous meetings were hardly the stuff of daily life, the importance of dress on special occasions was paralleled in the experience of ordinary people in pre-colonial Central Africa. Although there were local variations in styles of cloth and ornamentation, personal display through dress was essential in the wielding of power, in statements of identity, and in displays of well-being. It also expressed societal values of vanity, modesty and dignity. In the northern equatorial forest zones, where few clothes were worn apart from skirts of raffia, skins or bark cloth, jewellery, bodily decoration and elaborate coiffures conveyed social distinction.[9] In the more highly stratified societies of Loango and the lower Congo, clothing was a visible reminder of a person's place in society. Foreign visitors in the sixteenth and seventeenth centuries marvelled at the quality of prestige raffia cloth which they likened to 'velvet, brocades, satins, tafettas, and damasks'.[10] Specialized weavers produced cloths which might only be worn with royal permission, while commoners wore lesser-quality cloths. Dress was not only a status symbol but a display of power, since the cultivation of trees, the processing of threads and the weaving of cloths represented a considerable investment of labour which only important men could control. Elders could manipulate power through the circulation of raffia cloth which they judiciously distributed to juniors and dependants who lacked cloth or the means to acquire it.[11] For the Tio, also, Vansina has written that 'the greatest differences in the standards of living between people were seen in their personal appearance, in clothing and jewellery, thus the wealthy and the chiefs could show whom they were'. Furthermore, fine dress not only marked occasions such as the meeting of powerful men, but also holidays when 'men paraded with beautiful raffia wrappers with fringes at the edge'.[12]

Some Central Africans also had long experience of importing foreign cloth, clothes and accessories, and of integrating them into their dress. From the mid-seventeenth century, foreign textiles from Europe and the East Indies were replacing locally produced raffia cloth in the dress of the powerful. Old and new clothing traditions coexisted, symbolizing the changing bases of power. Important individuals wore animal furs, leopards' claws, copper jewellery and other traditional marks of status, together with the finest European trade cloth. Trading families became powerful through distributing imported cloth to relatives and other dependants.[13] By the 1880s, cheap cottons from Manchester were driving local raffia cloth off the market at Mfoa and Mpila, along the Congo river, and on the Tio plateau.[14]

As imported trade cloth became more widely dispersed among common people, the powerful appropriated exotic clothing and accessories to underline their distinction. Social differentiation was thus maintained through the rarity of goods.[15] Writing from the struggling French post at Brazzaville in 1885, Brazza noted that, in dealings with powerful individuals, 'it is necessary to give them something that no one else has ... old clothes, especially bright colours, lace or braided coats, hats and helmets'.[16] In Loango, vivid evidence of the integration of foreign and local dress exists on carved ivory tusks sold in an early tourist trade. In scenes of daily life which spiral around the tusks, porters, traders, hunters, farmers and artisans go about their business dressed in imported trade cloth, hats, shirts and jackets.[17] Photographs, sketches and descriptions by Europeans show that military caps or top hats were especially popular among chiefs, interpreters and successful traders. However, hats are a good example of the convergence of clothing traditions, for they were power symbols in Central Africa long before the European pith helmet made its appearance. In the Kongo region, appointment to an office was accompanied by the presentation of a cap sewn from pineapple fibres. A chief in the hierarchy had the title *mfumu a mpu*, or 'chief of the cap'.[18] Among both the Tio and the Kongo, the word for hat, *mpu*, was also the term for political power.[19]

What is being suggested, therefore, is that migrants to the town already had a well-informed knowledge of the symbolic importance of dress and the association of style, finery and status. Furthermore, particular cloths or ornamentation were used to mark special occasions. Those who had access to goods from the Atlantic trade had been mixing indigenous and imported cloth, clothes and accessories for centuries. Clearly there was a strong sense of what has aptly been called the 'politics of costume'.[20] As new ideas on clothing were introduced by workers from other parts of Africa, by West Indians and by Europeans, they were being grafted onto an existing praxis, rather than introducing new means of social distinctions. On the other hand, experience in colonial Brazzaville brought change as well as continuity, for new opportunities and inspiration in the matter of dress presented themselves. Many who had previously lacked access to cloth and clothes now had the chance to wear them every day and to experiment with different fashions outside work time and place. In the pre-colonial era, initiative had been in the hands of the traditional elites who had seen this power diffused among trading families with access to imported goods. In the colonial town, however, anyone with access to cash could buy cloth or second-hand clothing. Dressing well meant trying out new items and combining them in different styles. Fashion was both a matter of individual taste and of resources. As such, it was important in distinguishing social groups and a source of competition and sometimes conflict between them. It became an agent of change as well as confirming existing divisions.

The foreigners who filled so many of the positions as artisans, clerks and servants in Brazzaville's early labour force were pioneers of fashion. Since they had often been educated by Europeans and came from regions that had much longer-established contact with Europe than did the Pool area, they were particularly influential in introducing western styles in men's dress. Describing his impressions of Dakar in 1892 while *en route* to Congo, the Duc d'Uzès in a letter to his mother, noted that 'some Senegalese are dressed in the latest Paris fashions, with hats, jackets, shirts, ties, trousers, belts, shoes, and canes'.[21] At Libreville, stylish men in suits and women in long dresses promenaded in the streets in their leisure time.[22] In 1901, a priest visiting the sick in Brazzaville encountered 'Christians from Senegal and from all the West Coast'. Most of them, in his opinion, 'imitated whites in everything detestable; in the streets, we meet the crudest sort of dandies'. Describing these lapsed Christians, the priest noted that they were wearing 'real trousers, jackets, soft-brimmed hats, carried canes and had a cigarette hanging from their lips'. The most 'resourceful' were wearing 'down-at-the-heel shoes left behind by some explorer'.[23]

As African urban elites became identified with colonial society and its structures and symbols, the ornate military uniforms of the early period gave way to more conventional attire modelled on the dress of European administrators and factory agents. In the years before the First World War, white and khaki starched suits were high fashion on Sundays. However, there were also styles that were self-consciously locally inspired. For example, servants from Loango wore their shirts outside their trousers. One European wrote: 'I tried several times to get my boys to dress like you and me with the shirt tucked inside the trousers, but they said that is for whites and continued to do it their own way.'[24]

In the 1920s, men from Gabon and Loango continued to be fashion leaders. This seems to have been inspired not only by status but also by a deep appreciation of clothes. They socialized in clubs that were oriented to their interest in dress. They wore suits sometimes with waistcoats, and used accessories such as canes, monocles, gloves and pocket-watches on chains. Evening and Sunday parties consisted of drinking aperitifs and listening and dancing to European and Latin American music on the gramophone. Polished leather shoes were too expensive for most men, but canvas shoes were increasingly worn. Shirts with detachable collars were fashionable among older men, but young people who wore them were considered dressing beyond their station.[25] Foreign women also influenced fashion among women in Brazzaville. Whereas West Africans introduced new styles of wearing African cloth, women from Cameroon, Gabon and Loango introduced European clothing. At the turn of the century, some women from the coast wore corsets under satin and silk dresses. Some fashions were a modification of the cloth wrapper - for example, cloth was made into a long dress belted at the waist with a strip of cloth. In another style, a long piece of cloth like a scarf was attached to the bodice and hung loosely on either side of the outfit. In the 1920s, some Gabonese and Loango women wore short dresses, high-heeled shoes and silk stockings, and powdered their faces with rice flour. There were a variety of hairstyles: some tied their hair with black cotton thread and arranged it in bunches on either side of the head; others straightened their hair and had a parting in the middle. Head-scarves were tied in a variety of fashions, one shaped like a European pillbox hat.[26]

Interaction with Europeans also influenced tastes in clothes. According to informants, their fathers and grandfather wanted to dress as much like Europeans as possible, for this was the mark of an *évolué*. Although the term is now completely discredited, it was a label once carried consciously and proudly, for it demonstrated achievement in the new society, Western education, knowledge of European manners and sophistication as a townsman. Furthermore, those who worked in offices or as monitors had to conform to the European dress code, so they became accustomed to wearing Western dress.[27]

Most Africans observed whites from a distance, but servants who looked after their employers' clothes were conduits of information. They noticed styles and the quantity of clothes Europeans possessed, thus confirming the association of power, clothing and display. Servants who helped their employers unpack quickly discovered the number of clothes that a European brought to Africa.[28] An offical guide published by the office of the Governor-General for colonial officers preparing for an eighteen-month tour of duty in AEF in 1913 gave a detailed clothing list which included a helmet and a lightweight hat, six white uniforms, six khaki outfits, several lightweight shirts, a flannel belt and a rubber raincoat. The list also recommended high-top lacing, leather boots to guard against insect- and snake-bites, a pair of leggings, and light leather or rubber shoes for evening wear.[29] Helmets which were thought essential to avoid death by sunstroke came in many varieties. A well-known tropical outfitting store near the embarkation quays in Bordeaux claimed to have the biggest selection of helmets, with 600 'always in stock'. Each style had a name such as 'Cairo', 'Kitchener', 'Indo' and 'Damas' for men; 'Kid' and 'John' for children; and 'Mode' for women. It also advertised uniforms in shantung silk with removable buttons for all ranks of agents, officers and doctors, and interchangeable custom-made attachments for collars, to signify every rank in the colonial service.[30] Officers of the French colonial army were renowned for being fastidious in the extreme and helped to accentuate the formality of European dress in Brazzaville.[31] Africans did not merely view such clothes from a distance. Since Europeans often discarded old clothes when they left Africa, second-hand items fell into the hands of their servants or were sold in the African market.

European women, too, also confirmed the association of clothing and status. They had large wardrobes, especially those who were married to upper-level administrators or army officers, for they had to attend many social functions and further their husbands' careers as 'incorporated wives'.[32] The popular journal *Le Monde Colonial Illustré* featured a fashion column with clothing tips for French women in the tropics. According to Gabrielle Vassal, her daily routine normally involved four changes of clothes: her gardening outfit, her about-the-house clothes, her tennis dress and her social-event outfits.[33] Magazines and catalogues from leading French order companies such as *Saint-Etienne* were received in the post by Europeans. Once discarded, these found their way into African hands, becoming a topic of conversation among the fashion conscious who took them to tailors and seamstresses to have styles copied. They sometimes ended up as wall decorations in houses.[34]

Familiarity with European-style clothing came not only from observing Europeans but also from a mission-school education. Most of those who arrived at the Brazzaville Catholic mission in its early days were marginal members of African society, often children whom Monseigneur Augouard had bought out of conditions of servitude along the Ubangi river and who arrived at the mission with nothing.[35] For those who lacked the means to acquire European goods, missionaries were potentially an excellent source of clothing. Indeed, this was a prime attraction of a mission station where the distribution of clothes must have echoed the patron-client relationships of big men and dependants in pre-colonial times. In 1890, Monseigneur Carrie warned the directors of Catholic schools against giving cloth 'too soon' to children who came to the mission, 'for they will take it and leave'.[36] Andersson's account of Protestant mission stations in Brazzaville and the lower Congo confirmed the attraction of material possessions: 'The young lads who invaded the schools had very varied motives such as good clothes and literacy.'[37] The demand for uniforms by those who joined Scouts and were involved in gymnastics and football has already been noted.[38] As in so many other aspects of urban culture, Africans played off church and state in the matter of clothing. In 1914, noting the poor attendance at the newly established Urban School, the Mayor sent messengers around Bacongo and Poto-Poto to ask why parents were sending their children to the Catholic mission rather than the government school. The answer came back that the missionaries gave children uniforms and a meal in the middle of the day. The Principal suggested to the Mayor that a local tailor be given a contract to sew uniforms and that special caps be ordered from France as a means of competing with the Catholics for students.[39] Africans continued to see the church as a useful source of clothing well into the colonial period. In 1949, the Governor of Moyen-Congo reported to the Governor-General that 'part of the success of the Salvation Army seems due to the fact that they distribute quantities of cloth for the uniforms of their members'.[40]

Missionaries consciously taught gender roles in Christian marriage through clothing. In the multiple weddings that they sponsored at the cathedral in the 1920s, couples vividly showed their economic and social position in the household and in colonial society through their dress. Men wore suits, shirts, ties, shoes and hats, in keeping with their position as wage-earners and their jobs as clerks or trading-company agents. The 'domestication' of women and their future roles as wives and mothers was also demonstrated. They wore blouses, cloths, headscarves, beads around their ankles and went barefooted.[41] As Monseigneur Augouard wrote in one report about the training of convent girls, 'we do not have need of *grandes dames*'.[42] Lack of access to wage-labour also meant that few women could buy the clothes that men wore. When asked why women did not wear shoes, informants simply stated that they could not afford to.[43]

The association of clothing with status and class was also very much part of the message of the church. Boarding-schools promoted class distinctions among children, since the few whose parents could afford to provide them with clothes had permission to wear them on Sundays, while poorer children wore their school uniforms. Prefects appointed to keep order in the dormitories and school yard wore grey caps and carried whistles. Others in the Christian hierarchy, whether seminarians, choir-boys or members of the youth club band were issued with special uniforms. The ultimate display of power was the magnificence of the cathedral clergy in their vestments and regalia at Sunday mass.[44] Through observation of Europeans, therefore, Africans added to their repertoire of ideas on appropriate dress. As Terence Ranger has suggested, 'the successful manipulation and control of symbols' was at the 'core' of the 'colonial experience'.[45]

Clothing and consumers

These various clothing traditions, whether homespun or foreign, were woven through the styles worn in Brazzaville in the early colonial period. By the 1920s, one of the first things noticed by a visitor from a rural area, especially one coming from upriver, was the marked difference between the dress of townspeople and that of villagers.[46] Daily-life interaction in Bacongo and Poto-Poto brought the development of clothing styles that confirmed and contested issues of gender, class and age. Fashion was to some extent influenced and constrained by the availability of cloth and of clothing, especially on the second-hand market. Entrepreneurs, both African and European, responded to the growing number of consumers and stocked larger selections of cloth, ready-made clothes and acces-sories. The coming and going of workers and friends across the Pool also influenced dress, as it did music, sport and other aspects of urban culture.

Among young workers clothes had great appeal. They were fun, highly visible and easily movable, all advantageous to the migrants who constituted a large part of the population. They were also more accessible and affordable than other desirable goods such as oil lamps, furniture, bicycles and gramophones which were beyond the reach of most workers, at least before the Second World War. Missionaries continued to talk disapprovingly of young men who were engaged in a 'clothing frenzy' and landed in debt because of expensive tastes in clothes.[47] In the 1920s, Gabrielle and Joseph Vassal also wrote that Brazzaville servants could be 'half dying of hunger' but would go and buy new clothes 'as soon as they are paid'.[48]

While such comments may reveal as much about the Europeans who wrote them as they do about the actual situation, other evidence, both written and oral, does confirm considerable expenditure on clothes. In the 1932 census of the male workforce, the administration registered about one tailor for every hundred inhabitants of Poto-Poto and Bacongo. Of these tailors, twenty-nine lived in Poto-Poto and a hundred and twenty-one in Bacongo, reflecting the greater number of relatively prosperous elite men and women who lived in Bacongo and their great interest in fashion.[49] Not included in these figures were seamstresses who worked for both African and European women. The most sought after were those trained at the convent where French nuns passed on their considerable sewing and embroidery skills to girls and young women. Although the training was oriented to producing wives and mothers, convent graduates found these skills extraordinarily useful as a means of supporting themselves, especially when their marriages failed or they hit hard times.[50]

Only after the Second World War is it possible to have more precise data on the place of clothes in consumer budgets. In general, they confirm patterns of expenditure hinted at in descriptive accounts earlier in the century. According to surveys in Poto-Poto and Bacongo, everyone was involved in dressing well. Reviewing a wide range of social situations, from a worker who rented a room with a mat and a few knick-knacks to a successful trader or civil servant, Balandier wrote that 'vanity in clothing is important: and it is universal; it presses heavily on budgets. "Sunday clothes" are in contrast to the old clothes of week days.'[51] A survey of 1,000 budgets by Soret in 1951 found that clothes made up, on an average, 21 per cent of expenditures, compared to 53 per cent for food, 7 per cent for drink, 5 per cent for rent and taxes, 4 per cent for savings and 10 per cent for diverse expenses (entertainment, presents, etc.).[52] About the same time, in Poto-Poto, there was one tailor for every two hundred inhabitants; in Bacongo, one for every ninety-five inhabitants.[53] Even the unemployed made 'desperate efforts' to keep their threadbare clothes in good order. They depended on family members or friends for second-hand items or bought used clothing with small change that they earned through odd jobs.[54]

Although employers and church organizations continued to hand out uniforms for members of their organizations, they were no longer a significant source of clothing for the general population by the 1920s. The clothes that individuals wore on Saturday nights or on Sundays were very much a matter of personal taste, availability and price. With more workers entering the wage-labour market and the development of a stable town population, especially in Bacongo, manufacturers and retailers responded to African demand by increasing the range and variety of consumer goods.

The association of wages with consumerism was established very early in the process of European expansion in Central Africa. As noted in the previous chapter, Brazza advised his men to pay workers with tokens that could be exchanged in factory stores. This was later changed to a cash wage in answer to worker demands.[55] In 1888, six stores had opened, two run by Portuguese, one by a Spaniard, and three by Senegalese. By 1912, the Mayor noted several others that had opened in response to a growing demand among the African population for foreign manufactured goods.[56] In 1927, Monseigneur Guichard reported that among his Brazzaville parishioners, many 'are poor and living conditions are difficult', yet for those with some education or some artisanal skills, 'although their situation is always precarious, they live in a certain degree of comfort'.[57] In 1932, a Swedish missionary found 'quite a lot of cozy home comfort' in the house of a Bacongo carpenter.[58]

Most of the factories at the Pool had a large selection of goods. In 1920, the Compagnie Française du Bas-Congo, for example, had laden shelves that stretched from the floor to the ceiling, with items such as lamps, tools, matches, cheap wine and rolls of tobacco, varieties of cloth, head-scarves, helmets, hats, shoes, shirts, sandals and second-hand clothes. The company employed three tailors with treadle Singer sewing-machines who sat on the veranda and took orders from those who bought cloth inside. Ready-made *boubous*, shorts and shirts hung along the wall behind them waiting for customers. Clients who wanted to choose their own styles could select one from a pile of catalogues that lay on the floor beside the tailors.[59]

Among individual European entrepreneurs who responded to the growing African market, the most prominent were the Portuguese who operated at a lower profit margin than the large British, French and Dutch companies, from whom they bought goods on credit. Along the Avenue Félix Faure, Portuguese stores opened to take advantage of

European and African customers who worked in the business district or disembarked from boats on the Congo river. In spite of a 1934 municipal decree that prohibited Europeans from owning business in the African sections of town, some Portuguese merchants also had outlets in Bacongo and Poto-Poto which were managed by African employees.[60]

The most famous store frequented by the African elites was owned by a leading figure in the Portuguese community, Mario de Figueiredo, who had arrived in Brazzaville in 1911 to trade and operate river transport. Four years later, he opened his first store on the Plaine and, in 1922, he moved it to an attractive building on the Avenue de Commerce.[61] Targeting African consumers, he called it 'Kitoko', meaning 'beautiful' or 'elegant' in Lingala and Kikongo. Kitoko was well stocked with everything from basins to bicycles, sugar to soap, and clocks to cloth, as well as shoes, hats, umbrellas and sunglasses, altogether a 'delirium of new images' for inexperienced African consumers.[62] Suppliers were generally British, French and Belgian, but in the 1930s Japan moved into the AEF market in spite of high tariffs levied by the colonial government. In 1938, Japan accounted for 40 per cent of the ready-made clothes imported into AEF. Before the Second World War, white canvas shoes from Japan called 'tennis' and shiny black shoes manufactured entirely from rubber made footwear more accessible for the population.[63]

Most people, however, wore second-hand clothes or outfits which they had commissioned from tailors and seamstresses. By the 1920s, Poto-Poto and Bacongo markets were described as a 'mass of cloths'.[64] Although a great deal of cloth was marketed by the Senegalese, Dahomean traders also established an important community in Brazzaville between the wars. Customers looking for good prices also crossed the Pool to Kinshasa markets, where cloth prices were often cheaper. A variety of cottons such as drill, calico, percale and holland were popular for men's trousers, jackets, shirts and suits. For women, wax and fancy prints sold by West Africans were most valued.[65]

By the 1920s, also, there was a large trade in second-hand clothes, which were dispatched to Africa through European and American suppliers who specialized in the business. After the First World War, a consignment of American army supplies abandoned in Europe arrived in Brazzaville.[66] The impact of the second-hand market was seen in the combinations of clothes that people wore. Descriptions from a favourite dance-hall in Kinshasa where a Brazzaville band played and which Brazzavillois visited with their friends shows the element of creativity in popular dress. All the men wore trousers and shirts, but there the similarity ended. 'The clothes of men were of every imaginable variety,' wrote one observer. There were trousers of all kinds, also football or cyclist's shorts and riding jodhpurs. Some dancers wore 'impeccable white tropical suits', smoking jackets, waist coats with brass buttons, and dress coats. Most wore shoes, but some were barefooted. Women wore both African cloth and European-style dresses. Some wore silk gowns with low-cut necklines; others, short skirts with blouses, and see-through jackets. Wealthy women wore cotton stockings in different shades and high-heeled leather shoes bought at Kinshasa's ABC store. Head-scarves, hair-dos decorated with ribbon, lace and flowers, sign-of-the-zodiac charm bracelets, pearl necklaces, or ivory and elephant-hair bracelets rounded out individual outfits.[67]

European dress was more and more adopted as the preferred attire of townsmen. A few wearing waist-cloths were still to be seen in the 1930s, especially in the streets of Poto-Poto where newly arrived workers from upper Congo were most likely to find lodgings, but they were looked down on, as European styles, refashioned in line with local tastes, became the norm. In Bacongo, where the largest number of office workers lived, most men wore trousers, shirts and jackets by this period. Possession of European-style clothes and correct attire was essential to social status. A joke about an illiterate man who dressed in pyjamas to attend church circulated among the elite.[68]

In many ways, consumption patterns signalled membership of a social group and drew people who had a common interest in clothes together.[69] As Balandier has noted in his preface to a book on the modern 'cult of elegance' among young men in Bacongo, fashion 'is a language in which one can distance oneself from others' and even 'express conflict'.[70] By the 1930s, the young men of Bacongo had much higher aspirations in matters of dress than the second-hand market would allow, their tastes running to the most expensive cloth and goods sold in the Portuguese stores. A letter from a young man, Camille Diata, a clerk–interpreter in the Treasury Office, shows a very conscious awareness of appropriate dress for membership of his social group. Writing to an out-of-town acquaintance who worked for the Post and Telegraph Service in Mossaka, Diata starts by complaining that his friend is not answering letters and conveys the news that a mutual friend has been imprisoned. He goes on:

I will also tell you of all that is happening in the village of Bacongo: it is forbidden to go out after nine at night; palavers over women; beer-drinking, dancing, the fashion Popo, etc. etc. ... [sic]. Do you know that in Brazzaville and Kinshasa all the gentlemen or young men are dressing in Popo? That is to say, owning a helmet from Ollivant's worth 150 francs; a shirt entirely made from silk; a suit of poplin, or other fabric that is worth 250 to 300 francs at least; and trousers which must reach down to touch the heels of one's shoes.

Well-dressed women are wearing silk head-scarves that cost 50 francs each and their cloths, costing 150 francs, must be well cut by a skilled tailor.

I do not want to tell you everything all at once since you don't write to me. There is a great deal to tell you, but I don't have the time. The town of Brazzaville is developing and so are its inhabitants. Everything is beginning to change. You must come for a little and find out for yourself; you will see thousands of people, some cars and bicycles; two-storeyed houses and a great many single-storey houses. Many young people, who left, have returned and they no longer want to go back to the bush.

There is only one thing to regret, that life is becoming more and more expensive.

p.s. your girl friend is married to another man called Kounka.[71]

By way of assessing the cost of fashion, it might be noted that clerk–interpreter–typists working for the government were paid 12 francs a day at the time.[72]

Between the wars Bacongo and Poto-Poto night-spots rivalled each other in elegance and prestige. When a big dance was organized not everyone could enter. A chief of protocol, called the 'president of the court', was charged with selecting the best-dressed couples and those who could best perform the European dances in vogue.[73] In a confidential report to the Governor-General's office on the activities of Matswa's supporters, the Lieutenant-Governor of Moyen-Congo ventured his opinion that 'the Brazzaville elites dress richly and even with elegance'.[74]

After the Second World War, the return of veterans, increased travel abroad and the growth of an international popular culture through music and the cinema helped to spread new fashion ideas. At the same time, the variety of consumer goods continued to improve. The opening of a textile factory in Léopoldville helped to bring down prices. In 1950, a report on the clothing market in AEF noted that the sale of ready-made clothes was still restricted, since most consumers bought cloth and had it made up by specialized tailors. The sale of woollen cloth had risen, not among Europeans who found it too hot in the tropics, but among elite African men who thought it elegant for suits. Some bought such cloth locally while others ordered it directly through French houses which specialized in sending samples and remnants by post. In 1950, 129 tons of clothing such as jackets, trousers and shirts, and 40 tons of accessories such as scarves, collars and ties had been imported: 80 per cent was kept in AEF and the rest re-exported to British and Belgian territories. Colonial helmets, previously worn by Europeans, were now worn by African elites while whites preferred felt hats. In 1950 also, 379 tons of shoes were imported from French, Belgian and East European suppliers, especially Czechoslovakia. Of these, 200 tons were made of rubber. Since 1949, a Brazzaville factory had produced leather shoes from hides imported from Chad and northern Ubangi, which had brought down prices.[75]

Informants, looking back on the 1940s and 1950s, remember their wardrobes with pride and in detail. The arrival of new synthetic fabrics in polyester was a landmark event, for it meant that clothes lasted longer and were easier to care for. 'I took very good care of my clothes,' said one man who claimed that he still had some of his clothes from the 1950s; 'they were made from polyester.' Another stated: 'I dressed very correctly. I wore a smoking jacket, a tie, and polyester trousers.'[76] A favourite style which lives on in popular memory involved very loose garments made from a light material which 'shimmered'. Called 'tra-la-la', it may have been inspired by a visit from a Latin American band whose members wore loose clothing. Other inspiration came from the cinema and from magazine photographs. Especially popular was the romantic singer and actor Tino Rossi, who gave his name to a style of dress.[77]

While men were firmly oriented to European dress, most women continued to prefer African cloth. In the 1950s, short dresses were worn by some young women when they went dancing, or by young wives of elite men, or young professional women, but they were not common in the general population, and were associated with age and schooling. Once married, it was less common for even an educated woman to wear European-style dress. Informants gave several reasons for the persistence of African cloth, some quite utilitarian and others relating to values and aesthetics. Some said that cloth was easier to wear and more comfortable, especially after a woman had had children. Others said that it was only in the 1950s that women had sufficient schooling to allow them to take up positions such as secretaries, teachers and nurses, where they might wear short dresses at work. So women, unlike men, did not become accustomed to wearing European dress. However, the look of cloth and its value was also extremely important in influencing styles. Values such as modesty influenced the wearing of African cloth. Cloth also had a great deal to do with 'worth' for the intrinsic importance of cloth as a store of value for women had not been lost. In the marriage of two Lari in 1959, the settlement included three *pagnes* and three head-scarves.[78] Cloth communicated worth and well-being, which European dress could not. People could 'read' the value of a *pagne*, which they could not do with short dresses.[79] Special occasions were marked by buying new cloth. For example, traders saw a big increase in sales just before the Fourteenth of July holiday, and female dance groups often bought matching cloth to display their friendship and identity.

A woman came to know her seamstress well and might bring in ideas from observation of fashionable styles at dances and parties. Ideas on fashion thus travelled by word of mouth, and the seamstress would do her best to replicate the fashion, such as the cut of the sleeves, neckline and bodice. Having fittings for a new outfit was a sociable time, and the customer might make several visits to the seamstress. The chief competitors for seamstresses were the tailors who sat with their treadle machines near the cloth sellers, for if a woman was in a hurry she could have her dress made up while she finished the rest of her shopping.[80]

However, it was the cloth that made the dress, even more than the style. Informants talked about prints and quality of cloth more than specific fashion. According to one man, people noticed when a woman wore a top-quality wax print bought from a Senegalese trader. 'If your wife wore that cloth, people would say "excellent". There goes a well-dressed woman.'[81] Although some classic patterns remained popular for years, manufacturers constantly introduced new prints to reflect current events and to maintain their sales, for women liked to keep up with the latest designs. Patterns reflected trends, events and personalities. Heroes such as Charles de Gaulle and Winston Churchill were popular after the war. The craze for things English which had started in the 1930s was taken up in the popular designs 'King George' and 'Queen Elizabeth'. Modern devices such as typewriters and pieces of machinery also appeared printed on cloth, as did the words of popular songs such as *'alinga yo alingi ngai'* (Lingala, 'what loves you loves me'). As new designs appeared, women gave them names, for example *'nzete ya bongo'* ('money tree') or *'miso ya pitain'* ('eyes of a whore'), so that cloth developed a 'hierarchy of value', according to its popularity.[82] Women also spent money on head-scarves which varied in style from a soft silk to a stiffer material worn in a peaked fashion similar to that of Antillean women.[83] And as footwear became cheaper, canvas shoes or sandals were part of dressing well in public. Professional women and the wives of elite men favoured sandals made by Hausa shoemakers or canvas shoes with cork soles sold by the Portuguese.[84] To go barefooted became synonymous with worthlessness. A popular ballad called 'Marie Thérèse', recorded by Jhimmy about 1950, referred to such a poor woman:

> Oh, soni te, oh tala ye,
> Siata, siata pata, fioloko,
> Eloko te, kitoko ndambo, makolo ngulu,
> Eloko ya pamba.

> Oh, what a pity, oh look at her,

What trash!
Worthless, unattractive, barefooted,
A thing of little worth.[85]

Controversial fashions

In the last two decades of colonial rule, controversy over fashion became quite strident, and it is probably not going too far to say that clothes not only symbolized change, but that they were also 'instruments of innovation' which 'created and constituted change'.[86] As fashion became a statement of aspirations relating to class, gender and age, so conflicting views were expressed in criticism of how people dressed. This was happening in the context of the last fifteen years of colonial rule when the capital was experiencing rapid population growth and the arrival of young migrants who wanted to be free of familial controls. In the uncertainties of the times, discussion of fashion embodied swirling controversies such as styles and sexuality, the costs of dressing well, and the relationship of outward appearance and inner person. Older issues of status and clothing also remained in the forefront of the discussion.

As access to clothing became more widespread, social leaders watched and commented, using the newly established African press as their forum. Writing in the newspaper of the *Union Educative et Mutuelle de la Jeunesse de Brazzaville*, Jean-Remy Ayouné warned of the dangers of giving too much attention to outward form rather than inner character. His words echoed those of early Catholic missionaries: 'To be truly judged an *évolué* is not only to be judged by our clothes, our houses, our language and our manners, but especially to be judged by our education, intelligence and good will. Clothes do not make a man; and ties and shoes do not make an *évolué*'.[87] A few years later in a Catholic magazine, Ayouné again criticized those leaders of the African community who 'wasted money which they have laboriously earned' in the consumption of luxury goods and the giving of elaborate champagne parties.[88] Yet, as had been the case earlier in the century, attempts to influence dress, whether motivated by attempts to protect positions of privilege or perceived moral standards, were doomed to failure or very limited success. Choice in dress was only part of a much larger dream which linked wealth and status with comfort and consumption.[89] Material goods were firmly tied to the enjoyment of leisure, whether in the form of bicycles to speed up transportation, household possessions such as furniture and lamps, or luxury items such as gramophones and radios. Peer pressure was also important. One informant in Poto-Poto explained the pressures of finding the means to buy materials for housing construction. Corrugated iron was expensive and a thatched roof disintegrated after a year and needed repair. 'Then, too, the Bacongo people would poke fun at you and say, "that boy came to town to earn a living, but look at him wasting money on a thatched roof".'[90]

Men also wrote articles in newspapers and journals, mostly read by other elite men, which focused on women's dress, both that of educated women and the young women who formed the associations that danced in elite bars such as 'Chez Faignond'. One account claimed that these women were like mannequins since they 'launched' new cloths and their success could boost sales throughout the colony.[91] In several publications, including the literary magazine *Liaison* and the Catholic newspaper *La Semaine*, men debated their views, with educated women occasionally writing a reply. Articles bore titles such as: 'A great social problem of contemporary Africa: the corruption of the customs of women called *Evoluées*', 'The evolution of African women', 'The zig-zag of African youth', 'The black woman as victim', 'Women's fashion: do clothes make the monk?', 'Young girls and fashion', and 'The voice of a courageous woman'.[92] Under the heading 'Modern clothing: a scourge', one writer who echoed Ayouné's view complained that women saw clothes as 'the ship of evolution' and added that 'cloth does not do much without morality'.[93]

The ambiguities of the times were well illustrated when the African organizer of a 'Miss AEF' beauty pageant arrived in Brazzaville in 1957. The competition for a 'Miss Brazzaville' sparked off a discussion about whether participants should wear African cloths or short skirts which would show their legs. At the 'Miss Bacongo' round of the contest, some of the audience, many of them off-duty soldiers, had booed when contestants appeared in cloth. According to the report, the two finalists representing Bacongo and Poto-Poto wore skimpy outfits, much to the satisfaction of the largely male audience.[94]

The fashion of wearing *djiguida*, strings of beads which women wore around their hips under their cloths for their erotic qualities, also came under attack.[95] Yet, while some men were critical of such open displays of sexuality, others encouraged it and used the beads as a sex symbol. A Paul Kamba song which celebrated the powerful music of his band, 'Victoria', ended with the verse:

Amba, mwana ya mama,
Ayei kobondela Polo,
Polo abondela, Polo asomba *djiguida*,
Somba e somba *djiguida*,
Ayoki Victoria akei kosomba *djiguida*.

Amba, my dear sister,
She came to beg Paul,
Begged Paul, so that he could buy her *djiguida*.
Buy them, buy the *djiguida*,
She heard Victoria's beat and went to buy *djiguida*.[96]

Fashion was thus important in the ongoing debate over fundamental issues such as male-female relations, bride-wealth, marriage, family and the role of women in society.[97] Similar discussions were taking place about the same time in the English-language press of East and Central Africa.[98]

In the last decade of colonial rule, young men of Bacongo established clubs that focused exclusively on fashion. These were the forerunners of the celebrated present-day *sapeurs*.[99] Not yet a counter-culture, as it was in the 1960s and 1970s, when fashion became a statement against economic deprivation and attempts at political dominance by the party youth organization, the young men of the colonial period blended their fascination for clothes with the formation of mutual-aid associations. Like grassroots football teams and music groups that joined the unemployed, the employed, the educated and those with no formal schooling, the proto-*sapeurs* clubs of the 1950s expressed the burgeoning interests of urban youth. Through their 'cult of elegance' young men sought to define their social distinctiveness, while at the same time deriving a great deal of personal pleasure from wearing stylish clothes, admiring each others' dress and, hopefully, attracting girls.[100] Among those remembered from the 1950s were the *Existentialistes* or *Existos* (so called because of students returned from Paris who were admirers of Sartre), *Cabaret* and *Simple et bien*. The idea of clubs based on clothing also spread to Poto-Poto where a student who had returned from Paris started the first association, called *Club des Six*. Groups of well-dressed young men from both sides of town would visit popular bars such as 'Chez Faignond' and 'Congo-Zoba' in Poto-Poto, and 'Mouani-Bar', 'Muendo-Koko' and 'Lumi-Congo' in Bacongo, competing with each other in their stylishness, as they danced to the latest pop music. Jackets with large shoulder-pads, trousers with wide legs tapered at the ankles, and moccasins with thick soles were in style. According to a former member who was a tailor and created styles for the *Existos*: 'We had to change our outfits at least twice a week.' In contrast to Western practice where mass-produced ready-to-wear clothes have less value than custom-made clothing from tailors and seamstresses, the *sapeurs* of the past and present set high store on bought clothes which set them apart from the masses. The average age of the *Existos* was about eighteen and, unlike the present-day *sapeurs*, most of them had jobs.[101]

The extravagance of such clubs was fiercely criticized in *Liaison* by those who held conflicting social values. An article on the theme 'Clothes do not make the man' castigated a young man who earned 7,000–8,000 francs per month, yet ordered a suit for 7,000 francs and two pairs of leather shoes for 6,000 francs. The writer pointed out the number of simple, good clothes that might have been bought for the same price, with enough left over to support the individual and his family. He went on to claim that such excesses drove young men into debt and fraudulent activities. Altogether, they were insidious role models for schoolboys who dreamed of dressing well like their older brothers.[102] Another claimed that it was only a 'stage' which young people must pass through. Critics should not overdramatize youthful excesses. This writer saw links to a world-wide youth culture, for he wrote that 'youth the world over adore the James Dean cult, are eccentric in their attitudes and ways of dressing and are contaminated by the "Rock and Roll" virus'.[103]

Conclusion

In an interview with a French radio station, a modern-day *sapeur* was asked why he and his friends had such a fascination with fashion, to which he replied: 'We are born like that. My father was like that, my grandfather also. We can only be like them.' He went on to compare his love of clothes to the acquisition of language, explaining: 'If I am dressed in this manner it is because my father was like that.'[104] The *sapeur* was, of course, accurate in his historical perspective, although the significance of dress goes much further back in Congolese history than he realized. Perhaps more than any other aspect of leisure, the shared perception that people should dress well cut across all other social divisions. In their appreciation of the powerful symbolism of clothes and the significance of dress in mediating social relations, modern-day Brazzavillois are celebrating a tradition that stretches back into the pre-colonial past but which town life has only strengthened.

Europeans liked to be photographed beside the Congo rapids. An illustration in her memoirs shows Gabrielle Vassal sitting on top of a boulder laughing at the camera, while apparently surrounded by the turbulent waters.[1] A group photograph of the Government House set in the mid-1920s shows elegantly dressed women standing beside white-uniformed men, all wearing helmets. They are smiling and apparently enjoying their outing to the favourite tourist spot, while the Congo cataracts, which had barred Europeans from the Pool for centuries, rush by in the background.[2] The whole image is of white power.

Recent research has shown, however, that the people we call 'Europeans' or 'colonizers' were neither as monolithic as those terms suggest, nor as invulnerable as their photographs make them seem. Even in settler colonies with substantial investment from private capital or colonial ministries, Europeans were often weak, impermanent and divided.[3] How much more so in French Equatorial Africa? Appearances were, therefore, highly important in colonial relationships, for they could mask uncertainty, project authority and create social and psychological distance between the 'colonizer' and the 'colonized'.

Leisure activities, significant in drawing imaginary lines, were also highly problematic, for they were more fluid and open to personal interpretation than activities at work where the relationship of boss and worker was clear. The question in the colonial relationship was how to create the social distance necessary for the security and well-being of the dominant group, both in the early period when white men were struggling to survive in the face of high mortality rates and poor resources, and at a later period when women and children also had to be protected and ensured a comfortable existence. In Brazzaville, three principal strategies were invoked to try and ensure sufficient social and psychological space between Europeans and Africans. These were racism which pervaded colonial relations, physical segregation put in place between 1910 and 1925, and elaborate social rituals which reminded Europeans of their position as a ruling class. As these strategies took root, those who broke ranks and fraternized with Africans were frowned upon, as they seemed to threaten the very basis of the colonial order.

Frontier leisure

Accounts by young European men during the first thirty years of the frontier settlement convey the malaise of life in a colonial backwater. Some were posted as administrators, soldiers or trading-company agents, while others were in transit, awaiting transport upriver or to the coast. Some adventurers worked sporadically for a factory or the administration, or profited from hunting big game. Those who recorded their Brazzaville experiences were attracted to Africa by a sense of adventure, by patriotism, by disillusionment with life in France, or by the need to escape unfavourable personal circumstances such as debt or scandal. Many, like Henri Bobichon, joined expeditions to the upper Ubangi and Chad in the last two decades of the nineteenth century, when colonialism was *à la mode*. Following the return of Brazza from his second African expedition, young men lined up to catch the eye of the great man and be recruited into his service.[4] The popular newspaper *Le Petit Journal* claimed to have received 2,000 letters of inquiry about how to contact the famous explorer.[5] Although early governments of the Third French Republic did not embrace imperialism enthusiastically, an active colonial lobby kept France's colonial 'mission' before the public eye through newspaper articles, illustrated magazines, exhibitions, speeches and social events. The Central African pavilion at the 1900 Paris Exhibition featured a panorama of the Marchand expedition, plans of Brazzaville, photographs of European pioneers, and a 'Congolese hut with some Africans brought from Loango' to lend a touch of authenticity.[6] African expansion was equated with national prestige, economic profit and the spread of 'civilization'.[7]

Much more of an unknown quantity to the French in the late nineteenth century than North and West Africa, Equatorial Africa held a special challenge. The artist Charles Castellani, living a placid existence, leapt at the chance to report and illustrate the Marchand expedition for the journal *L'Illustration*. Before leaving home, he recalled comparing in his imagination the woods around the French capital with the virgin Central African rain forests; the river Seine, polluted by factories along its banks with the mighty Congo; and the robbers and tramps of Paris with the 'famous cannibals' of the upper Ubangi.[8]

The reality of Brazzaville was profoundly disillusioning for such romantics. Almost universally, new arrivals found boredom and frustration where they had expected adventure and challenge. Brunache hurried over the last stretch of the arduous caravan route from the coast, hoping to find an important settlement where he could buy supplies, but he found that 'the large town of our dreams was hardly the size of a modest French village'.[9] Even after the arrival of concessionary companies in 1900 and the growth of the white population to about 250, living conditions remained at their most basic.[10] With no boarding-houses, new arrivals had to be billeted at the military post, or given hospitality at the Catholic mission, or taken in by a friendly trader.

Since the most basic infrastructure was lacking, it followed that institutions of leisure were almost non-existent. The general cry among Europeans was that there was 'nothing to do', a situation which has benefited historians who at least can read the journals and letters that were written by frustrated travellers in their 'spare time'. The Duc d'Uzès, seeing his career path blocked by political obstacles, persuaded his mother to fit out an expedition to the upper Congo. In 1892, he found himself stranded at the Pool for seven months. For him, Brazzaville combined the worst of two worlds. It had neither the adventures and challenges of the bush, nor the advantages of life in France. He some-times joined administrators on the Plateau for a leisurely lunch, after which he whiled away the afternoon hours with games of chess, whist, or the 'craze' of backgammon.[11] Castellani, stranded at the French post for four months, wrote after ten days, 'My God, how bored I am in Brazzaville', and claimed that 'everyone thinks like me'. He added mosquitoes, fevers and sickness to his list of ills.[12] Challaye noted: 'There is not much entertainment for whites in Brazzaville.' He played whist and chess and spent evenings eating, drinking and talking to friends. The most intriguing pastime was 'to study Africans, their language and culture', but most whites were 'insufficiently cultivated' to do this.[13] Colonel Moll, who was billeted at the military post while awaiting a boat to carry his expedition northwards, was fortunate enough to have access to a horse. In the early morning, he rode with a fellow officer along the river banks to the Congo and Djoué rapids. He also wrote of the monotony of life: 'nothing new is happening here' and 'the officers stationed here have a dull existence'.[14]

Within individual households, Africans and Europeans cohabited. With only seven white women in the population, and most of them nuns, many of the approximately 250 European men who made up Brazzavil-le's white population in 1900 lived with African women. Such 'temporary marriages' by officers and non-commissioned officers were an 'expected' part of life in the French African army.[15] The African concubine of a European man might play an important role in his household, organizing his servants and supervising the cooking and laundry arrangements. In other arrangements, such matters were left to the male domestic staff, and women were only expected to provide female companionship and sex.[16] African women had to keep their 'place' in the household, however. In one instance when a man had his 'housekeeper' eat with him at the table, other Europeans were appalled that he should stoop so low.[17]

Living in inescapable proximity to their African subjects and employees and with minimal means apart from arbitrary violence to control local populations, Europeans were able to gain some local prestige through certain leisure activities. Among these was hunting, which had the triple advantage of taking the hunter away from the mundanity of the Plateau or Plaine, supplying food to the white community and their dependants, and impressing African men in a 'language of power'.[18] In the late nineteenth century, elephants, hippos, crocodiles and antelopes were plentiful on the colonial frontier around Brazzaville. For the station chief, Charles de Chavannes, an overworked administrator who toiled over reports into the night for lack of daylight hours to spare, hunting on Sundays was hardly a recreational activity of choice. Food shortages and high prices forced him onto the river and into the forests in search of meat for his soldiers and workers. It was also a useful way of bolstering alliances with Tio chiefs. His skills made him known locally as *tata ya niama* (Lingala, 'father of the meat'). On a single day in 1885, he shot four elephants and seven hippos. Five of the hippos he gave to local chiefs.[19] Monseigneur Augouard earned a reputation as a fearless hunter while providing food for the Catholic mission. According to his biographer he shot 120 hippos during his years in Central Africa.[20] Malamine, the Senegalese sergeant left in charge of the French post when Brazza returned to France in 1880, would not have survived without his skills as a hunter, according to his contemporary, Léon Guiral. He distributed meat to influential Tio chiefs when his position was tenuous or exchanged his kill in the market-place for vegetables and other local produce.[21] Albert Veistroffer, head of the Brazzaville garrison in 1885, also went hunting once a week in the creeks around Stanley Pool in search of hippo meat to augment his men's diet.[22] Others such as Colonel Moll went hunting for entertainment to relieve the otherwise long monotonous days awaiting river transport.

Only a decade after the founding of the French post, however, the slaughter of big game for food, ivory and skins had pushed back the hunting frontier beyond the confines of Brazzaville. The Duc d'Uzès, as a member of the French aristocracy, was an experienced hunter and went out in the early mornings for sport. But he wrote to his mother that the large numbers of African and European hunters had killed off the game or forced them to withdraw, so that he either had to go a long way to find bigger animals or content himself with monkeys, antelopes, ducks and partridges.[23] A year later, in 1893, Jean Dybowski, *en route* to Chad, noted that it was exceptional to see elephants near the French settlement, although crocodiles, hippos and antelope were still common.[24] By the early twentieth century, hunting in Congo had passed into the 'second phase' outlined by John Mackenzie for British East, Central and Southern Africa. That is, for Europeans big game had ceased to be a 'vital expansionist resource'.[25] As in colonial Kenya, it had become the target of sportsmen and adventurers, but to participate in such a hunt it was necessary to travel well beyond the confines of the capital. Elephants were already so rare due to ivory hunters that the French Congo government introduced a conservationist measure, taxing and fixing the level of elephant hunting in decrees of 1904 and 1909.[26] By 1920 Vassal, who had shot tigers in Indochina, wrote of her disappointment on arriving in Brazzaville where she had assumed that big-game hunting would be a common sport. She found that wildlife was almost completely shot out around the Congo capital; even rabbits or large birds, the targets of African hunters, were rare.[27]

The many reunions and gatherings of Brazzaville's white population were occasions for cementing social bonds and creating buffers against the demands of daily life in a colonial outpost. While the ritualized social events of the later period only developed slowly, patterned conversations and activities reminiscent of social gatherings in Europe created bonds among white men and shut out their African environment. Among the administrators and military officers who lived on the Plateau and at the military camp, hunting-stories mingled with tales of high adventure, heroic deeds and friends 'martyred' for the cause of empire. News of France, recently arrived with comrades, by post or in newspapers, evoked nostalgia for things European. The opening of imported wines, liquor and preserves enhanced the ethnocentricity of social occasions. Pseudoscientific views of racial superiority were selectively reinforced as stories of 'primitive' Africans were exchanged. Such conversations went some way towards reassuring the white community that their frustrations, their physical deprivations and their high mortality rates were worthwhile.

The arrival of visitors was an occasion to socialize. Veistroffer, in the early days of the settlement, noted that 'the evenings were long', so visitors from the Catholic mission at Linzolo or from across the river at Léopoldville were a cause for celebration. On such occasions, 'we drank wine, diluted with water, for in principle it was kept for those who were ill. We also ate preserves called "food of the sick" since they were usually kept for those who were ill.'[28] The factory agent, Bouteillier, remembered in detail his achievement in producing a meal for surprise guests who arrived by boat from upriver. The menu included soup, olives, herring, sausage in pea sauce, aubergines, veal and tomato sauce, biscuits, red wine, white wine, champagne, coffee and cigars.[29] Describing a meeting with Brazza, Dolisie and Decazes, newly arrived from months in the interior, Chavannes noted: 'Never had Brazzaville seen such a reunion.' After dinner, Decazes produced whist and chess, which were 'indispensable parts of his baggage'. A short time before, Chavannes had noted with pleasure the arrival of a china dinner service from France to replace the old metal plates on such special occasions.[30] Father Zimmermann of the Linzolo mission was always sure of a welcome at the factory of the *Messagerie Fluviale Congolaise* where he could exchange news of home with the engineer, accountant and four other employees, who like him were from the Channel port of Dieppe.[31]

Social interaction with the larger and more prosperous European community in Léopoldville was also essential for the maintenance of the white community in Brazzaville. Between the wars, the Belgian Congo capital was valued for the variety of goods in its stores, and for its leisure facilities such as hotels and clubs. In the early colonial period, however, being in the company of a large group of Europeans in itself was important for Brazzaville's white population, and they visited Léopoldville frequently.[32] In 1898, when there were only a handful of white men in Brazzaville, Mandat-Grancey crossed to Léopoldville to spend the evening with thirty to forty military officers and river-boat captains.[33] As an international crossroads, Léopoldville exemplified the excitement of the imperial mission. In a few months, Veistroffer met the German explorer Wissmann, the Belgian explorer Coquilhat, Sims, an American missionary doctor, and the only physician on either side of the Pool at the time, the German Baron von Niptol, who commanded the Léopoldville station for the International African Association and the Italian Massari, who had travelled down the Nile from Egypt.[34] In 1909, Georges Bruel, who had returned to Brazzaville after a cartographical investigation in the interior, wrote to his mother of the many 'parties and receptions' that he had attended. Visitors from Léopoldville included the Count of Turin who was in the midst of a trans-Africa journey from Zanzibar; Prince Albert of Belgium; and the Belgian Minister of Colonies and his wife.[35]

Within thirty years of the establishment of the colonial settlement, Brazzaville's white population had developed into a diverse group of administrators, soldiers, missionaries and traders, with varied interests and perspectives influenced by their backgrounds in France, their reasons for being in Congo, and their adaptation to local conditions. The geography of the sprawling settlement accentuated differences between the administrators, soldiers, missionaries and traders. Those who lived on the Plateau and ran the administration, together with the officers at Chad who guaranteed its security, took on a superior attitude to the rest of the European community, although only a few came from upper-class backgrounds in France. In the face of so many coming and going, longevity, as in the case of Monseigneur Augouard and the traders Greshoff and Tréchot also conferred some status. But Greshoff, head of the Nieuwe Afrikaansche Handelsvereeniging, was Dutch and he together with Swedish missionaries, who were also Protestant, were looked on with suspicion and disdain by many of the French. Petty individual rivalries fuelled by gossip also created divisions among the European population.

Leisure to some extent solidified these divisions, since people tended to mix with those with whom they were most at ease. Among the senior administrators and high-ranking military officers on the Plateau and at Chad, there was an effort to perpetuate the gentility of upper-class France. Graduates of the military college at Saint Cyr, the *Ecole Polytechnique* and the *Ecole Coloniale* renewed old friendships. Some had shared previous assignments in West and North Africa, or had met on the long voyage from Bordeaux to Matadi. Dinner parties, especially with foreign dignitaries or when women were present, were formal occasions. For colonial administrators, white uniforms were obligatory. The presence of military officers, who were known to be 'fastidious in the extreme' in matters of dress, added an air of formality to the evening.[36]

In 1909, Colonel Moll was invited to dinner at the residence of Governor Cureau of Moyen-Congo and one of the few white men who had his wife with him. The conversation ranged over travels by balloon, articles in *La Rencontre*, the English school of painting and sea-bathing, the latest craze in France. The evening before his departure for Chad, Moll was invited to a party at the Governor-General's house, where after dinner and speeches, tables were set up for bridge. By 1909, a tennis court at the military camp was a favourite spot for entertaining female relatives and friends on Sunday afternoons or in the evening. Matches took place between 5 p.m. and 6 p.m. and afterwards the group gathered for drinks on a terrace overlooking the Congo rapids and watched the sun set over the river.[37] A tennis court at the Governor-General's residence was the scene of large parties, since the house was too modest to accommodate more than a few visitors. Georges Bruel, writing to his mother, described a New Year's Eve party in 1906 with paper lanterns strung around the court which served as a dance-floor for waltzes and

5   The first European club, *c.* 1908 (reproduced from Fernand Rouget, *L'Afrique Equatoriale Française illustrée*, Paris: Emile Larose, 1913)

quadrilles. The presence of only three women meant that men had to take turns dancing the women's parts. There was 'a good deal of laughter'.[38] Administrators also established their own club on the Plateau in 1904, a place where they could have meetings, with a library and a place to entertain friends.[39]

The gentility and cordiality of top administrators and their visitors at such social gatherings is well represented in accounts of their time in Brazzaville, but there are also glimpses of the roughness, brutality and crudeness of life on the frontier. Challaye blamed local conditions such as boredom, fevers and a 'sick liver' for the 'irritability of many whites', which they relieved with heavy drinking and abusive treatment of Africans.[40] The Duc d'Uzès decried the drunken and violent debauchery of traders, whom he described as 'just as savage as the Africans'.[41] Augouard blamed administrative agents, traders and soldiers alike for their 'violent and crude' behaviour. Such 'wretched Europeans' were responsible for a decline in 'moral and civilized' standards, and leading African Christians astray through bad example.[42] Mandat-Grancey described Europeans as being 'undisciplined and rebellious' and 'needing a firm hand'.[43] Bouteillier was particularly scathing about those he worked with in 1903. 'Frenchmen who say they are in Congo for glory are there to make money,' he noted. Conditions were so bad that only those attracted by free lodgings and food, and a percentage of ivory and rubber receipts, would work there. 'Death is so common', he noted, 'that one does not even ask what someone has died of.' He had wanted to raise chickens in his spare time but had been prohibited by the company director. 'Would it not be better to do this in my free time rather than visit the other factories to drink absinthe or exchange scandals that create discord, even hatred among Europeans?', he asked.[44]

In fact, racism was a key element in uniting Europeans in Brazzaville in the early period; not that it ever disappeared, but at a later stage there were other means of creating distance between the white and African populations and racism was less crude. Drawing on the notion of 'imagined community', Anne Stoler has suggested in her study of the Dutch in Java that racism was a useful way of drawing whites together and overcoming differences that might otherwise have undermined their ability to maintain their distinctiveness from subject populations.[45] In Brazzaville, in the early frontier stage of colonial rule, racism was accompanied by a great deal of violence towards Africans. Contemporaries tried to explain what they saw around them in various ways. The administrator Bonchamps blamed inexperienced young men. They 'treat the Africans like slaves', he noted in his 1900 report, and they 'even beat the Senegalese'.[46] Bouteillier agreed that 'the quality of whites who come here is very poor' and 'the Company is deluding itself if it thinks that it can get results with these individuals'.[47] Nor were administrators that much better in their treatment of their workers. William Cohen has noted in his account of the French colonial service that before the First World War, AEF was the 'least desirable assignment'. While a few high-level administrators were well trained and had a sense of service, positions were generally filled with less desirable appointees who, 'no matter how inefficient and brutal', were 'considered good enough for service in the Congo'.[48] On the spot, hard-pressed administrators and factory managers might recruit any white men into their service, whatever their backgrounds, experience or morality.

Among black administrators from the Antilles, Brazzaville had a reputation for its racism. Such was the experience of Félix Eboué, when he arrived en route to his first posting in Ubangi-Shari in 1909. According to his biographers, Eboué stayed in the capital only twenty-four hours before taking the opportunity to leave for the north. He found the 'small administrative capital, full of petty bureaucratic intrigue and rough adventurers, businessmen and officials who had left most of their scruples back in France' little to his liking. 'Aperitif conversation consisted of boasting about cheating Africans out of ivory or rubber or recounting how an administrator had tortured an African to collect taxes.'[49] While the calibre of the European men who found themselves in Brazzaville at the beginning of the century may have been low and they may have been inexperienced, life on a colonial frontier and the need to reassure themselves of their mission also seem to have been a powerful force, shaping their treatment of African populations.

Distant leisure

Between the wars white society in Brazzaville developed the trappings of a 'convincing ruling class', with public and conspicuous leisure figuring large in the process.[50] At the same time, Europeans became more self-absorbed, withdrawing into their own sub-communities and avoiding contact with Africans outside the workplace. Between 1910 and 1925, the residential segregation of European and African populations was imposed, and various edicts were introduced making it illegal for Europeans to live in Bacongo and Poto-Poto or to own businesses there. Although there were always some exceptions, the segregation of the town was all but complete.[51]

The public leisure facilities such as restaurants, cafes, parks and sports facilities, which were so much part of life in urban Europe, had hardly come into existence in Brazzaville by 1920. Puytorac, who arrived in that year at the age of twenty to work for the Compagnie Française du Bas-Congo, found, like his predecessors earlier in the century, that the monotony of the passing days was debilitating. He wrote: 'I was in Africa and my life was as dull as in a French province.' Entertainment was mostly self-made. He read 'a great deal', laid out a tennis court at his company's concession, and occasionally went on his bicycle to pass time at a restaurant on the Plateau. Like most single men, he took an African 'housekeeper' who lived with him for the duration of his stay in Brazzaville.[52]

Logistical problems meant that it was difficult to leave the town overland and so Léopoldville, with a regular ferry service, continued to be a major attraction. The difference between the economic development of the two towns was even more striking in the 1920s than it had previously been. Although under Antonetti Brazzaville started to develop more purposefully as the future terminus of the CFCO, the Belgian Congo capital, which had benefited from investment during and after the war, dwarfed the French town. To cross from the Belgian to the French side of the Pool was to leave 'the thousand and one lights of Léopoldville' for the 'flickering candles hiding the discreet poverty of the right bank of the Pool'.[53] For André Gide, who crossed the Pool in 1925 on his famous journey to Ubangi-Shari, 'Kinshasa is intensely alive and Brazzaville seems asleep – too big for its small activities. Its charm consists in its indolence.'[54]

The European population of the Belgian colonial capital was 1,515 in 1926, or almost four times that of Brazzaville.[55] It had about eighty trading companies, and two hundred cars compared to the six in Brazzaville. There were three hotels: the most favoured by the Vassals, who usually stayed overnight, was the two-storeyed 'ABC', with forty rooms, owned by one of the large commercial companies, the Société d'Alimentation du Bas Congo. Of the three clubs, the Vassals preferred the newly opened Portuguese establishment, the 'Grémio', which had a tea-room and billiard-tables on the ground level. Upstairs there was a large hall with a dance floor, open to a veranda on three sides and with a platform at one end. 'The music is enlivening, the electric light good, the women's dresses are pretty, the men are spick and span in their white suits,' recalled Madame Vassal.[56]

Mingling with white, cosmopolitan society in Léopoldville was not only good entertainment and a chance to admire the latest fashions, it also confirmed the excitement and sense of mission that had inspired early Europeans, but was easily lost in town life once the frontier had moved further into the interior. Vassal writes: 'A dance in Kinshasa means not only harmonious movement and pleasure to the senses, but opens visions of Africa.' She tried to convey her excitement to her reader, describing one evening:

My first dance is with an English ex-aviator, at present agent for a company dealing in ivory. My second is with an Italian doctor of Léopoldville, for the Belgian Congo is international and there are almost as many foreign doctors in government service as Belgians. My third partner is a Belgian lawyer, who has already two brothers and a sister in the Congo and who therefore knows the country well.

Later, a Portuguese merchant is telling us stories of elephant hunts up-country, an American engineer of adventures among primitive tribes, a Belgian administrator passing through on his way home relates his journeys of explorations from his post on the edge of the Sahara. Other partners might be a Portuguese dentist and a French doctor, who, by their conversation, give glimpses of the struggle it must be to set up in a foreign community independently of official help in a primitive country. There is certainly none of the tediousness of similar circumstances in Europe, but unexpected drawbacks and pitfalls await the pioneer. He places his world's possessions, his health, and his career on the edge of a precipice, and all his vigilance is needed to keep them safe and secure.[57]

In Kinshasa also, just about all the items necessary for the conspicuous consumption that was mandatory at parties on both sides of the river were available; from *foie gras* to lobsters, caviar, *patisserie* and wines.[58] Advertisements, placed by Kinshasa stores and companies in *L'Etoile* and the *Courrier d'Afrique*, kept Brazzaville's white community informed of newly arrived items. 'I'm going to Kin' was still a frequently heard phrase among Brazzaville whites on the eve of the Second World War.[59]

By the mid-1930s, however, especially after the completion of the railway, Brazzaville's white population was less dependent on crossing the Pool for recreation. If they did so, it was by choice rather than necessity. The social columns of *L'Etoile* show how far the French colonial capital had developed from its days as a frontier town. An enticing array of activities was announced and reported in the newspaper's *Chronique Locale*. There were three main establishments where white society could enjoy an evening out. Of these the principal competitors were the one major hotel, the 'Congo-Océan' on the Plateau, and a restaurant run by Greek proprietors, the Assanaki brothers on the Plaine. The completion of the railway and the arrival of Governor-General Reste and his entourage had given a shot in the arm to Brazzaville's 'high society'.

Describing the upbeat mood in the capital, the *L'Etoile* reporter noted that 'the establishments in Brazzaville are doing all they can to attract a clientele'. The report went on:

The Congo-Océan Hotel has already greatly improved the appearance of its establishment due to the decorations of Jean Réal. The ballroom is now one of the prettiest in Central Africa. Also, Madame McCourt is preparing such gourmet meals that the establishment on the Plateau is continually attracting a crowd. Twice a week they show talking films; the dancing and good cheer have all contributed to the reputation of the hotel.

At the Hotel des Messageries, Madame Hélène Petit has followed the optimistic mood that has reigned in the capital since the arrival of Governor Reste. She is opening up a new and extended restaurant on Sunday, 31 May.

The Assanakis Brothers are following in these infectious developments, and a veritable upheaval is taking place there with a great deal of painting. The charming design of the place, the marvellous cinema, a dance floor with a state-of-the art gramophone, will give to the Plaine what the Plateau already possesses, and that will be perfect.[60]

The 'Congo-Océan' and the Assanakis' establishment vied with each other to attract European customers. The 'Oasis' restaurant of Madame McCourt was especially famous for its cuisine, offering ten-course gourmet meals. Assanakis' had the best cinema, showing silent films in 1934 and talking films by 1936. Programmes included Pathé News, Mickey Mouse and Felix the Cat cartoons, and films featuring stars such as Charlie Chaplin, Maurice Chevalier, Jim Gerald and Florelle. The 'Palace-Parlant' company distributed to a circuit of cinemas in Brazzaville, Pointe-Noire, Léopoldville, Matadi and Stanleyville. Both establishments featured live bands on Sundays, sometimes with touring French singers and dancers, and light classical music or jazz at the cocktail hour from 5 p.m. to 6 p.m. After dinner the dancing began with popular foxtrots, tangos such as 'Marie-Lou', and the favourite one-step, 'King Kong'. The partying went on well into the night.[61]

The 'beautification' of the town also improved the social amenities for white society. The late afternoon was the time for Brazzaville's white population to venture out, to enjoy the cooler hours, to display their finery to each other, and to check up on who was promenading with whom. On Sundays, a military band gave outdoor concerts at a bandstand in one of the parks on the Plateau. The favourite spot for an outing, however, remained the Corniche along the river front. 'All of Brazzaville' could be found there in the early evening.[62] For 'beautiful women' it was a chance to 'show off the latest gowns received from Paris as their rickshaw boys move along at a slow pace'.[63] Important men drove by in cars, smiling and waving, including Adolphe Sicé, who could be seen taking his wife and four sons for a ride in his Citroën convertible.[64]

Between the wars, therefore, Europeans and Africans became increasingly segregated from each other in their leisure time. It was only at work that there was close contact. Outside the workplace, it increasingly became the social convention that Europeans and Africans did not mix. Portuguese and Greeks who lived with African women and maintained stores and residences in Poto-Poto and Bacongo illegally were considered derelicts by most whites, even traitors to their race, for they blurred the lines of colonial prestige and order. Stories, allegedly deriving from Africans, were exchanged among whites that derided the Portuguese as not being 'white men' but some lesser type of mortal.[65] European men still went to Poto-Poto and Bacongo in their off-duty hours in search of entertainment. Sex with African women was still tolerated, especially if the men involved were bachelors or from the military post, but it had gone more underground than in the earlier period and was considered 'scandalous' by some, and letting the side down. The editor of L'Etoile, who considered himself a guardian of white interests, ran an article in 1930 entitled 'Scandal in Poto-Poto' which complained of a 'completely drunken' white officer who had beaten up an African and broken into his house with a group of friends. The editor called on the administration to forbid access by whites to bars and cafes in Bacongo and Poto-Poto by 'day and night'.[66] Through separate organizations, segregation was taught at an early age both at the Catholic youth club and in Scout troops. The question of integrated Scouting was raised in the French organization's magazine and the decision left to local leaders, but one writer advised that 'there exists between these children too many profound differences in mentality, character, customs, from the point of view of families and of culture, to envisage a common programme'.[67]

Through residential segregation, segregated public amenities and segregated social gatherings, a curtain had been drawn between Brazzaville's African and European populations. For André Gide, it was as if 'civilization interposes its film', so that 'everything is veiled', making it 'impossible to get into contact with anything real'.[68] For the young Comtesse de Renéville, it was as if she was 'looking at a landscape from behind plate glass'. As the wife of the Governor-General's Aide-de-Camp, she found it impossible to break out of the constricting social group in which she found herself. Referring to her 'frustration' and 'uselessness', she wrote of 'this European community, oblivious or indifferent to everything beyond its own orbit, was not Africa. I was conscious of something vital and important, that lay beyond my reach, out there, in the blue distance.'[69]

As whites turned in on themselves, their conversations and social conventions reflected and reinforced the insularity of their society. This was particularly clear to those who were 'outsiders', either because they were passing through or because they were stationed in the interior. Pierre Pellerin, who lived as a boy in the Ubangi region where his father managed a plantation, was taken on a visit to Brazzaville by his mother. He noted that 'people entertained a great deal'. The conversation quickly turned to gossip, news from Paris, or complaints about servants. Concerning Africans, he noted that 'the lack of interest or ignorance was flagrant in many of these gatherings'.[70] After-dinner entertainment might include music, dancing and improvised skits, which acted out and caricatured colonial relationships, with Africans and colleagues alike becoming the butt of humour.[71] Some European visitors remarked on the pettiness of Brazzaville's white society. 'A mixture of unending, mundane obligation, protocol and indolence', wrote one report in the French magazine Le Monde Colonial Illustré; 'it made one wish for one thing: to take the first steamer as quickly as possible into the bush'.[72] The high proportion of administrators and military officers contributed to the excessive formalities. 'A society of white buttons, gold buttons, decorations,

6 High society at a ceremony to mark Armistice Day, 11 November 1925. In the centre is interim Governor-General Alfassa, and on the extreme left is the future Governor-General Reste talking to Madame Alfassa (reproduced from Etienne Crémieu-Alcan, *L'AEF et l'AOF de grand-papa*. Paris: Editions Ophrys, 1970)

braid and officers' stripes' was one description.[73] In the mid-1920s about two-thirds of the European population of the capital were administrators, military officers and their families.[74] In official estimates of 1931 and 1932, a third of the white population worked for the army or administration.[75] Other estimates from the 1930s refer to the high number of administrators, 'more than half' of Europeans in Brazzaville in one account, and about two-thirds in two other accounts.[76] In the period between the wars, the type and qualifications of administrators improved, but the system became more rigid, and individuals, especially in capital cities, were less in touch with local populations. According to Cohen, the French colonial administration 'did little to encourage the administrators to study the societies in which they were serving'. Most French administrators had 'remarkably little interest in indigenous societies' which shocked their British counterparts.[77]

Between the wars European leisure became not only more conspicuous and segregated, but also more 'clannish'.[78] Only on the Fourteenth of July, on New Year's Day and on the annual celebration for war veterans did white society forget its divisions and gather together in celebration at the Governor-General's residence.[79] As the European population increased and diversified, social divisions were expressed through clubs with limited membership. Some were based on common work experiences and interests (administrators, traders, war veterans); some on cultural interests (Society for Research in Congo, a literary and artistic club, French club); some on European origins (Bretons, Corsicans, Portuguese); some on religious and philosophical affiliation (Catholic club, Freemasons); and some on sporting interests (athletics, football, bowling, swimming, tennis, flying). To some extent, these clubs cut across class and occupation divisions within white society, allowing those from a lower social standing to mingle with others higher up the scale and to acquire useful patrons. For a young colonial officer, high-ranking companions were important.[80]

The most prestigious of the white social clubs were the Corsican club and the CAB, where senior administrators and military officers took leadership roles. Men from Corsica were an important element in the French colonial service, both in general and among those posted in Brazzaville. This has been explained by the poverty of the island, causing men to look elsewhere for careers and to a tradition of colonial service in certain Corsican families. In 1934, 20 per cent of Frenchmen in the colonial service and 22 per cent of the colonial army were Corsican.[81] In Brazzaville, Corsicans served at all levels of the colonial administration, but their status in the community was enhanced while Antonetti, a Corsican, was Governor-General for ten years. He established the Brazzaville Corsican club in 1931.[82] In 1936, its members included the Mayor of Brazzaville, the French Consul in Léopoldville, the President of the Courts of Justice, the chief adviser to the Governor-General, the Director of Medical Supplies and the Commander of the newly formed Air Force. Although Governor-General Reste was not a Corsican, but was from the eastern Pyrenees, he was the honorary club president. While the status of these already powerful men was reinforced through their official roles within this club, club membership also allowed low-level administrators who happened to be Corsican to make important social contacts. An invitation to the club ball, which was attended by the top people in white society, was much sought after. In 1936, like most important social events it was held at the Congo-Océan Hotel, whose ballroom had been transformed into a Corsican village.[83]

Exclusive sports clubs were also an important part of the white social scene, with the most prestigious being the oldest, the CAB.[84] Club members had to be French, although good Euro-African players and colonial officers from Martinique and Guadeloupe were allowed on teams.[85] Altogether, the club represented 'the elite young men of the colony'.[86] As with the Corsican club, the annual fund-raiser was an important social event on the Brazzaville European calendar. The programme for 1931 was given a full-page announcement in *L'Etoile*. Starting at 8.45 p.m. in the presence of the Governor-General, the Commander-in-Chief of the army, the Head of the Medical Service, the Chief Justice, and the President of the Bureau of Commerce, the programme featured a play with scenes from the history of sport, followed by a ball with a dance band, and a raffle. The 1936 event included a competition for 'the most elegant automobile'.[87]

Finally, the existence of a group of Freemasons did nothing to help smooth church and state antagonisms. In the 1930s, the lodge met every Sunday morning in a house built with money donated by Louis Tréchot, a long-surviving member of an old Brazzaville trading family. The secrecy of such meetings means that little is known about the organization. One can only assume that it was an influential body since its members included at least three Governor-Generals: Augagneur (1920–4), Reste (1935–9) and Eboué (1940–4).[88]

Apart from the formal structure of clubs, the social hierarchy of European society was preserved and emphasized by social conventions and etiquette that became extreme in the highest circles. The Comtesse de Renéville (or 'Mary Motley') had been introduced to her social set when she and her husband sailed with others in the Governor-General's entourage from Bordeaux to Pointe-Noire. During the two-week journey, they had visited points *en route*, been 'initiated' in crossing-of-the-Equator celebrations and socialized every evening. Most of the other administrators and their wives already knew each other, since they had served with Reste when he was Governor of the Ivory Coast, and were sharing in his promotion. The Countess's husband was a newcomer to the group and she was nervous of her position among the women. Fortunately, the somewhat eccentric Madame Reste took a liking to her and she was quickly integrated into the Governor's closest social circle, a position that she did not aspire to but felt locked into on account of her husband's career.[89]

As the wife of a high-ranking military officer, the Countess found herself part of a 'leisured class' with a very specific role to play in the upper echelon of colonial society. She found a white society that 'was divided into watertight compartments', with the civil and military authorities at the top, followed by those attached to the health service, the trading companies and the large banks. Officials working for the colonial administration were distinguished by their rank and function, and 'all were split into little cliques which hated each other'.[90]

Women through their leisure affirmed rank and order within white society. The young Countess had scarcely unpacked when 'the business of "calling" began'. Comparing her experiences in Paris to those 'under the Equator', she noted that calling cards were 'indispensable' and that 'the social life of Brazzaville was a survival from an earlier age':

All visits followed the same pattern. They were expected to last precisely a quarter of an hour; time to sip *porto blanc* and nibble delicately at a *foie gras* sandwich without taking off one's gloves. The only safe topics of conversation were the hostess's health and the shortcomings of your respective houseboys. There would be a discreet attempt to glean some inside information regarding the Restes or the Government House set, which it was wise to parry with general remarks about the climate.[91]

Probably unknown to the women of the Plateau were those further down the European social scale. A Swedish missionary, who arrived in Brazzaville with her husband in 1938, felt that she and her colleagues were doubly disadvantaged since they were neither French nor Catholic. From the point of view of the Government House set, their position on the social ladder was only slightly higher than that of Portuguese and Greek traders who lived on the Plaine. Unlike the women of the Plateau, missionary wives had little 'time to spare', however, and the Swedish Protestants kept to their own community, in which language and culture played a significant role.[92]

The description of 'Mary Motley' raises broader questions about the position and influence of colonial women. Clearly, they had an important role to play in allowing a transition from life on the frontier where there were few white women to an established, inward-turned colonial society. It was also a society where relationships among Europeans and between Europeans and Africans were bounded by rigid social conventions and rules which women had a part in enforcing. Generally, however, colonial women have been blamed by contemporaries and in more recent descriptions for their pettiness and prejudice, without much concern for the context of their behaviour and the gender relations of their times.[93]

The vast majority of white women in Brazzaville were not engaged in wage employment and did not keep regular work hours, like colonial men. Between the wars, only a few worked in professions and occupations such as teachers, midwives, nurses, missionaries and beauticians.[94] Most women who arrived in the French colonies were already married or, if single, were married soon after, since the shortage of white women presented them with many eligible bachelors. Most European women, whether the wives of army officers and administrators, or the wives of Portuguese and Greek traders, were expected to be just that, wives who did not pursue employment outside the home, where they supervised the servants. In the case of the Portuguese and Greek traders, wives might help out occasionally in the 'front shop'.[95] Some women who brought young children to Brazzaville spent a great deal of time looking after their welfare, rather than delegating it to servants, especially when health care was still minimal.[96] Women who worked outside the home were subject to a great deal of criticism. An article in the newspaper *La France de Brazzaville* in 1936 presented several reasons why colonial women should not seek employment. These included the 'problem' of leaving servants unsupervised; the erratic attendance of women at work; the 'problems' that women with independent incomes could present for men; and the fact that women provided cheap labour, undercutting men's chances of finding employment.[97] Even volunteer work could meet with derisive comments about 'bountiful ladies' and was discouraged by some men and women. It was more socially acceptable if the wife of a high-ranking administrator was involved, when there was the triple advantage of engaging in useful activities such as instructing African women in nutrition and child-care, displaying the largess of French colonialism, and being in the prestigious company of an important woman who might pass on a good word to her husband.[98]

While European women in the colonies had more 'free time' on their hands, given the availability of servants, this did not mean that it was unproductive time. Women's activities, even those that seemed most frivolous, were significant in perpetuating colonial relationships. Even the 'pettiness' with which they are charged may be seen as a contribution to the rank that they enjoyed through their marriages in colonial society. In Equatorial Africa, where postings were normally for a maximum of two years, such tight social etiquette allowed a newcomer to understand her place in society quickly and be integrated into it. In Nigeria, newly arrived wives had little choice but to join in a 'game' where the 'rules' were already in place, and this appears to have been the situation in Brazzaville as well.[99] Most significant was their adjunct status in relation to their husbands' careers and well-being, the activities of 'incorporated wives'.[100] Or, as 'Mary Motley' wrote, 'the ladies of Brazzaville took an active part in their husband's business'.[101] Whether it involved entertaining, having friends in high places, dressing well, being current with the gossip, managing a household, or being companions and sex partners, colonial women's success was largely measured in relation to the men they knew.

By the late 1920s, a debate was under way in French colonial circles about the position of women overseas and their appropriate role in society, although it was still measured in relation to men. For Georges Hardy, the director of the *Ecole Coloniale* from 1926 to 1933, 'a great many stupid things' had been written about European women in the colonies, with reference to scandals, poor judgement and 'their bad influence on colonial men' whom they lead 'into temptation'. While Hardy agreed that 'some of these arguments are not without foundation', he argued that French women could be a good influence on their husbands and help to stabilize colonial society. Women helped to 'maintain an intellectual and moral equilibrium', he wrote, and created a 'civilized' atmosphere for men.[102] Developing this thought, Hardy noted that 'there are no colonial scandals in regions where there are European women, whereas there are almost always one or two native women behind these sombre events'. While European women might be 'excessively stimulating' for men, Hardy concluded that the presence of white women in the colonies did more good than harm.[103] Maurice Delafosse, the highly respected colonial administrator and teacher, in an article in the widely read *Dépêche Coloniale*, also supported French women in the colonies as a stabilizing influence. However, he emphasized the importance of their 'occupying their leisure time usefully' and suggested that they engage in volunteer work.[104] Clothilde Chivas-Baron, who herself had lived abroad and published several works on French women overseas, was openly critical of the *Ecole Coloniale* for not training colonial women, and suggested that a programme be introduced. In her handbook for colonial women published in 1929, she suggested tips on how to occupy leisure time positively. She urged them to take along their musical instruments, to write letters, to keep 'alert' and to get out of the house at least once a day. They had a particular obligation to be 'graceful' and 'elegant' since they 'represented the newly imposed civilization' to the indigenous populations.[105]

In Brazzaville, European women clearly played a distinctive role in shaping colonial society, contributing to a more self-contained white society and to racial exclusiveness. The arrival of women meant that Europeans kept more to their own company in their leisure hours. Although the 'scandals' that involved African woman may have declined, those that involved white society certainly increased. According to one colonial couple, spouses changed their partners 'as often as they changed their shirts', but this was more acceptable than a married man having an affair with a woman of Bacongo or Poto-Poto, as the 'problem' was thus contained within white society.[106]

Yet, although the arrival of women increased social distance between the European and African populations, women did not create a segregated society in Brazzaville. Rather, they were part of a process that was already in motion long before they arrived in substantial numbers and justified by many reasons that had little to do with the presence of women. In fact, the segregation of urban time and space had begun in the early twentieth century through official decrees, and the first white segregated recreational club dated from 1904. Margaret Strobel's discussion of the relation between the arrival of white women and the growth of segregated colonial societies is particularly relevant.[107] While not disputing that European wives 'in substantial numbers made possible the creation of an exclusive group, socially distanced from indigenous peoples', she criticizes the stereotypes that white women 'destroyed' close relationships between white men and local societies. Although European men lived close to their African 'wives' in the earlier period, there is no evidence that these relationships had a positive influence on attitudes to indigenous people, and this is confirmed by the Brazzaville situation. To suggest otherwise is to negate the element of subordination in the relationship. White women have also been seen as contributing to the deterioration of relationships between European men and African men, because of an alleged fear of sexual attack on white women by African men. Perhaps this is true, although the 'threat' seems to have been more in the minds of white men than the white women who lived close to their servants all day. Strobel notes that 'colonial women's memoirs often do not mention fear of indigenous men', nor does this fear appear in the lives of 'Motley' and Vassal, the two European women whose accounts of daily life in colonial Brazzaville survive. Vassal, in describing the modest villa she and her husband were allotted on the Plateau, compared it to her house in Saigon, where there had been an upper storey. This she said was preferable, since it allowed the European woman, who was at home most of the day, some 'peace and privacy'. But there is no hint in her account that she in any way feared her servants, whom she actually wrote about in the most scathing terms, only saying that living in a house with a veranda all around with people peering in and watching her movements was annoying.[108] Such perceived threats of African servants to white women may, however, have been in the minds of colonial men, who saw their women as in need of protection or at least needing to be distanced from possible rivals. An incident from Brazzaville lends credence to this view. In 1924, a rickshaw driver was brought before the Native Tribunal charged with stealing a pair of silk stockings from a French woman. Found guilty of the offence, he was sentenced to three years in jail. The seriousness of the crime in the eyes of the French judge is shown by the fact that of the seventy-two cases that appear in the court register for that year, mostly involving robbery or assault or both, only five received harsher sentences.[109] The severity of the punishment was, however, commensurate with the crime, that is the theft of an intimate garment belonging to a white woman. As clothing could symbolically help to create distance, so could it also close the gap. In this case, the unfortunate rickshaw driver had crossed a social barrier impermissible to an African man, and he had to bear the consequences.

Parallel leisure

The legal situation of Africans in AEF improved considerably after the Second World War, especially when compared to the position in Belgian Congo where segregation was still part of official policy. Belgian visitors made comparisons with Léopoldville which put Brazzaville in a good light. One who went for a day's outing in 1958 'could find no racism' and found that 'the blacks are customers as well as servants'.[110] Another, one of many white men who crossed the Pool to enjoy the nightclubs of Poto-Poto at a time when it was still illegal for whites to enter the African sections of Léopoldville after dark, noted that 'the crowds are friendly' and 'one would never find such familiarity between whites and blacks in Léopoldville'.[111] Certainly, African life under French rule was very different from living in the Belgian Congo. Equatorial Africa had been integrated into the French Union with some representation in Paris since 1944, the *indigénat* had been abolished in 1945, Brazzaville had an elected African Mayor from 1956, a decree of 1947 prohibited segregation of social amenities, and 157 *petits blancs* (lower-class whites) lived in Poto-Poto in 1950. The distance between Europeans and Africans seemed to have shrunk a great deal.[112] A closer inspection of social relations from the African perspective reveals a different story, however, for it transpires that although whites could move freely in Poto-Poto or Bacongo, the reverse was not true. The once firmly closed door of segregation had opened, but passage through it was mostly in one direction. Or as a writer in *AEF Nouvelle* put it more succinctly: 'If laws and decrees create rights, they do not create realities.'[113]

After the Second World War, the European population of Brazzaville, like the African population, grew dramatically, drawn to the colonial city by the work opportunities created by the post-war Economic and Social Plan, and propelled to Africa by the poor state of the French economy. In Central Africa, Europeans were assured of better material rewards than in France through subsidized housing and higher wages which offset distance from home and risks of ill-health. Between 1945 and 1960, the white population more than tripled and its composition changed, since many were lower-class whites, who arrived with their families and planned to stay for extended periods. Social amenities improved and, given the low wages of servants, most wives worked outside the house in jobs such as secretaries, further improving their families' standards of living. It was also the *petits blancs*, who in some instances could not find affordable housing in the white part of the town, who lived in Poto-Poto. Thus the white population was much less homogeneous than it had previously been, not only through stronger class distinctions but also through distinctions between those who had lived in the colonies for some time and the newcomers.[114]

Whatever the composition of white society, however, social interaction with Africans outside the workplace had not changed much from previous decades. The status and prestige built up throughout the colonial period and bolstered by the huge material and technological advantages of whites contributed to their ability to keep Africans at a distance. And the *petits blancs* who lived in Poto-Poto did little to smooth race relations since Africans blamed them, especially European women, for taking scarce jobs. They also exhibited racist attitudes, were seen as 'bad whites' by local populations and were at the centre of several skirmishes in the mid-1950s.[115]

Observations by sociologists in the 1950s confirm the continued distancing of European and African populations outside the workplace. Balandier wrote in 1957 that whites were 'enclosed' within the narrow range of their social contacts. 'Withdrawn' and 'on their guard', they were 'unwilling to be contaminated by their African surroundings'.[116] Althabe, in his study of the unemployed on the eve of independence, confirmed Balandier's findings. Contacts between Africans and Europeans are 'extremely limited', he wrote. Living in different parts of the city, 'Africans only have contacts with Europeans in the work place, and it is in this context that each forms the impression of the other'.[117] Although there was no legal segregation of amenities, Brazzaville's colonial rulers kept Africans at a distance through the continuing power structure. 'There is no regulation that prevents an African from sitting on a cafe terrace,' wrote the sociologist Jean Dresch, 'but no African would do so without risking an incident.'[118] Personal experience confirms the situation. Even the Gabonese Jean-Hilaire Aubame, one of the first *notables évolués*, whom Eboué had appointed as the President of the Poto-Poto Municipal Council, still had trouble getting admission to the cinema in the white part of the town in the 1940s.[119]

Contacts between some Africans and Europeans, especially the elites who were taking important positions in the administration, were greater than before, but almost always within clearly defined contexts. For Joseph Loukou, the large receptions for the Fourteenth of July or New Year's Day were seen by many leaders as 'false appearances of brotherhood' because 'everyone knows that they are just for show'.[120] Such gestures were part of what Sylvain Bemba has referred to as 'giving some "signals" of goodwill without ever giving up on the essentials'.[121] The cultural centres, where whites gave advice, classes and lectures, were in part started by colonial officials to bring a *rapprochement* in relations between the different communities, 'not much emphasized up until now due to the indifference of whites in the social domain'.[122] As we have already noted, some individual whites also gave invaluable assistance to African sports teams, both financial and coaching. In the mid-1950s, the first mixed football team to represent Brazzaville played in a match against a Belgian Congo club, and the CAB started fielding integrated teams. But sports that were less 'popular' and those involving special facilities such as tennis and swimming remained for whites only. They were part of the 'struggle for African sport' written about with some vehemence by Jean-Claude Ganga. It was eight years after independence before the segregation barrier at the exclusive 'Caïmans' swimming club was broken.[123] Ordinary people watched from a distance. Some shared the resentment of continuing white dominance symbolized in such matters as 'the Grandstand to protect them in the rain and sun' and 'their swimming pool and numerous sports fields reserved for them'; not to mention the fact that 'they also had their special wing at the hospital and they almost never died'.[124] But most townspeople never came into contact with whites. Poto-Poto and Bacongo grew in size, Africans took over commune administration, and the popular culture of the African sections of town absorbed leisure time.[125]

One article in the magazine *Liaison* in 1958 summed up the problem of 'blacks and whites' as a situation in which 'two peoples, bound by the same laws and living side by side daily, lead parallel lives where mutual understanding is too often lacking'. Having noted that only a small number of Europeans came to Africa by choice or out of interest, the writer found that they 'leave having learned nothing about Africans ... of whom their only memory is in some office, some workshop or construction site'; thus 'dialogue is not possible'.[126] However, this article is one of the very few on the subject of race relations that appeared in *Liaison* over the years, and certainly fewer than appeared on gender relations. It might be argued, rather obviously, that male-female relations were a great deal more important for the young elite men who wrote in the magazine than any other issue. It might also be said that the authors still felt the weight of European sponsorship behind their journal. To write about race relations was considered 'courageous'.[127] It is also possible, however, that the African elite had too much to lose to launch a critical attack on European colonial society at that stage. Such an explanation for lack of resistance has been given by Elikia M'Bokolo, for example, who has argued that in AEF the elite did not see problems in racial terms but rather tended to blame 'bad whites' when they were the victims of discrimination. Having been long delayed in enjoying the privileges of a *petite bourgeoisie* through the lateness of adequate education in AEF, the numbers of those with post-primary schooling and good jobs had seen a 'spectacular development' after the Second World War both in the public and private sector. But this class did not have the 'capability' or even the 'desire' to develop an anti-colonial political ideology. At the same time, workers were too dispersed in terms of organization to play an autonomous role in politics.[128] Thus Europeans and Africans were faced with a stand-off, and when independence came it was won more because of events outside Equatorial Africa than to political developments within the colony.

Conclusion

Ideology, status and prestige were essential in bolstering the European presence in colonial Africa.[129] The Mayor of Brazzaville shared this view on the importance of distance in defining relationships when he wrote that 'in order to preserve European prestige, Europeans should not live in the native villages'.[130] On the other side of the Pool the same sentiment was echoed by a Belgian who noted: 'Towns are precarious in terms of black-white relations. The whole question of the prestige of the white is in jeopardy and on this prestige the security of whites and the future of the colony depends.'[131]

In the frontier period, the physical proximity of populations could hardly be avoided, and it was only gradually that white power reached the point where Europeans could create segregated living space. Having distanced themselves physically and socially from the rest of the town's population, Europeans then tried consciously to protect their image, defend their prestige and affirm their status through conspicuous consumption and social ritual. Distance was a key tool in this strategy, as can be seen in the criticism of those who crossed imaginary lines and threatened the imperial image: hence, the condemnation of the Portuguese who mingled with Africans in daily life and of European men who were involved in drunken brawls in Bacongo and Poto-Poto; the creation of the isolated village of Saint Firmin on the outskirts of the town for Euro-Africans, whose presence in the urban population was a constant reminder of boundaries blurred; the debate concerning the position of white women; and the concern that the wrong type of film might reach the screens of Bacongo and Poto-Poto. In the long run, such discussions may have been more reassuring to whites than influential in Bacongo and Poto-Poto. The creation of distance also meant creating space that Africans filled with their own activities, images and symbols.

Conclusion

Leisure turns out to be a very broad category of human activity, experienced by townspeople in many different ways. As a means of structuring time and space, it was imposed and taught by Europeans for a variety of reasons, whether the need to order the workforce, train Christians, or simply affirm the rightness of the *mission civilatrice*. As a means of understanding time and space, concepts of work and leisure touched urban populations only partially and were most fully appropriated by the educated elite and wage-earners. On the other hand, for just about everyone, living in the town did mean experiencing in some measure new temporal schedules, for they were all around, imposed by the law, taught in schools and church, and lived by friends. Yet the tyranny of the clock never fully replaced older notions of task-oriented time, as Westerners trying to keep appointments in Brazzaville soon discover. Furthermore, the battle over work-discipline is still being waged. In 1986–7, banners on government offices and signs painted on walls at major crossroads carried such slogans as: 'Stop absenteeism and lateness to work' (*Halte à l'absentéisme et au retard au travail*); 'Put a halt to laziness' (*Halte à la paresse*); 'Everyone has to earn their wage, their daily bread' (*Chacun doit mériter son salaire, son pain quotidien*); 'Those who don't work don't have a right to a wage' (*Qui n'a pas travaillé, n'a pas le droit de salaire*); and 'The success of the plan means devotion to work by all' (*Le succès du plan dépend au ardeur de travail de tous*).

Integrated into the everyday life of the colonial town were the recreational activities introduced by foreigners, not only Europeans but also foreign Africans and West Indians, who were conduits of new cultural forms. Sport, fashion, dancing, clubs and associations, festivals and the sociability of bars, beer-gardens and stadiums were at the heart of the urban experience and a major force in attracting migrants to Brazzaville. Yet people from remote or nearby villages did not show up empty-handed or empty-headed, but rather brought with them pre-existing traditions which were re-formed to suit their individual needs and shape communities. Thus, retired football players became elders to be consulted in important decisions, and those who came from the Pool region thought of their team, *Diables Noirs*, as 'the team of our ancestors'. Musicians combined their training in military, church or cultural-centre bands with musical traditions deeply rooted in rural society. And dancers from the middle Alima used their puppets as a form of social commentary in the town as they did in village life, while incorporating representations of remarkable Europeans in their repertoire.

Whereas relations in the workplace tended to be clearly drawn, the limits of leisure were often more fluid. Symbols could be used in striking and visible ways to create distance, mark boundaries or bridge gaps and, here again, the old and new mediated social transformations. Thus, hats were fun and stylish in an urban way but they also evoked success in more traditional terms, and shoes, a novel form of dress taken over from Europeans, could become a vehicle for contesting colonial hegemony. Uniforms could convey white power but, worn by Scouts or dance groups, they also indicated place in Bacongo and Poto-Poto society.

Perhaps most of all, leisure was the human face of town life, making the unfamiliar familiar, bringing laughter out of sadness, helping the vulnerable feel more secure, and restoring dignity in the face of ridicule and coercion. In spite of constraints resulting from income or gender, people had a degree of choice, some more than others. Individual tastes could come into play in choosing recreational activities, whether dancing in the Grande Place of Poto-Poto, watching a football game, crossing the Pool to visit friends, going to a *maringa* dance-hall, playing cards, or observing the Lord's Day.

Far from being trivial, entertainment was essential not only for individual re-creation but for the forging of sub-communities which provided networks of friends. As has been shown in this study, the emergence of a large, settled urban population was long delayed in Brazzaville. Rather, there was a small nucleus of townspeople and a majority who came and went; and this continued for much of the colonial period. Such a situation did not allow the paramountcy of any particular identity – class versus ethnicity, for example – but rather a multiplicity of loyalties that coexisted, with some bursting forth into significance in times of crisis. In the broad view, the most important division in Brazzaville was between the community of interests that made up Bacongo, specifically identified over time with people from the Pool and the lower Congo, who also spoke Kilari, Kikongo or Kituba, sent their children to school and espoused Matswaism as a political and religious force; and those who lived in Poto-Poto, markedly heterogeneous in their origins but using the new lingua franca of Lingala, and widely varying in their class orientation and level of integration into urban society. While these divisions were played out and even reinforced through leisure activities, they took on a new meaning with the emergence of a politicized ethnicity in the last decade of colonial rule. In political terms, the Lari gave their support to the *Union Démocratique pour la Défense des Interêts Africains* led by the priest Fulbert Youlou, who was thought by some to have inherited the messianic qualities of André Matswa. The main opposition party, the *Mouvement Socialiste Africain* was led by the Mbochi politician Jacques Opangault, whose supporters mainly came from 'upriver' and in Brazzaville lived in Poto-Poto. In 1959 when fighting broke out in Poto-Poto over personalities, power, resources and the future direction of national politics, rival factions coalesced around the 'northerners' and 'southerners', and the Lari had to flee to Bacongo on the other side of the town. This was hardly the result of the 'traditional rivalries of the South and North', or 'the old tribal quarrels of the M'Bochis and the Bakongo', as some writers have suggested.[1] It was much more based on a twentieth-century ethnicity that had developed in the specific context of the colonial town where populations had formed their communities, often giving visible expression to them in their leisure time.[2]

Perhaps this study has shown most of all the creative genius of townspeople as they sought to deal with European authorities, take advantage of opportunities for advancement in daily life, and create structures that shaped the urban environment and society. While the coming and going from rural areas provided support and inspiration, it can well be argued that in colonial Congo, a great deal of the force to resist colonial oppression had to be found in the town. The brutal and violent experience of forced labour and taxation in rural areas, and the draining of human and natural resources from the countryside, undermined pre-existing structures, what Georges Dupré has called the 'destruction of an order', or Jan Vansina the 'end of a tradition'.[3] However, as has been emphasized here, townspeople actively sought to reconstitute societies through the knowledge and experience brought from rural areas. To these were added the new technical skills, values and beliefs gained through exchanging ideas and negotiating relations in urban surroundings. At the end of the colonial period, as the numbers of people living in the capital mushroomed, the structures were fragile, contested and incomplete, but the creative enterprise was well under way.

Notes

INTRODUCTION

1 This incident is more fully elaborated in chapter 4. See also Phyllis M. Martin, 'Colonialism, youth and football in French Equatorial Africa', *The International Journal of the History of Sport*, 8, 1 (May 1991), 56–71.

2 ANB, GG363(2); for precise citations of documents see notes in chapter 4.

3 Philip Mayer, *Townsmen and tribesmen: conservation and the process of urbanization in a South African city* (Cape Town: Oxford University Press, 1951), 14–17; David Coplan, *In township tonight! South Africa's black city music and theatre* (London: Longman, 1985), 232; Chris Waterman, *Juju: a social history and ethnography of an African popular music* (Chicago: University of Chicago Press, 1990), 6–7.

4 This phrase was used by J. H. Nketia, 'The gramophone and contemporary African music in the Gold Coast', *Proceedings of the fourth annual conference of the West African Institute of Economic and social Research* (Ibadan, 1955), 189–200.

5 Frederick Cooper (ed.), *Struggle for the city: migrant labor, capital and the state in urban Africa* (Beverly Hills, Calif.: Sage Publications, 1983), 34.

6 *Livre d'or du centenaire de Brazzaville* (Brazzaville: Publi-Congo, 1980) is an official account of the town's history which was sponsored by the administration in honour of the centenary.

7 'Le Congo: banlieue de Brazzaville', special issue of *Politique Africaine*, 31 (October 1988).

8 In 1965, five years after independence, Congo was 35 per cent urbanized, a figure only exceeded in Africa by South Africa, three North African countries, and Mauritius. In 1985, 40 per cent of Congo's population of some two million lived in towns. Today, half the country's population lives in Brazzaville or the Atlantic port of Pointe-Noire. See Bahjat Achikbache and Francis Anglade, 'Les villes prises d'assaut: les migrations internes', *Politique Africaine*, 31 (October 1988), 7–14; and World Bank, 'Urban population as a percentage of total population', *World development report* (Washington, D.C.: World Bank, 1985).

9 E. E. Evans-Pritchard, 'Nuer time-reckoning'', *Africa*, 12, 2 (1939), 207–9.

10 For example, for the Tio, see Jan Vansina, *The Tio kingdom of the middle Congo 1880–1892* (London: Oxford University Press, 1973), 159, 163–8.

11 For example, "time for amusement/games" in Lingala, *ntango ya masano* and in Kikongo, *ntangu ya nsaka*.

12 Abraham Ndinga-Mbo, *Introduction à l'histoire des migrations au Congo* (Brazzaville and Heidelberg: P. Kivouvou Verlag, 1984), 30.

13 Le laboratoire d'anthropologie, 'Structure spatio-temporelle chez les négro-africains: l'exemple des Kongo', *CCAH*, 4 (1979), 7.

14 Jacques Le Goff, *Time, work and culture in the Middle Ages* (Chicago: University of Chicago Press, 1980), 35–6, 45–7.

15 Eviatar Zerubavel, *Hidden rhythms: schedules and calendars in social life* (Chicago: University of Chicago, 1981), 45–6.

16 David S. Landes, 'Clocks: revolution in time', *History Today*, 34 (January 1984), 23–4; also his *Revolution in time: clocks and the making of the modern world* (Cambridge, Mass.: Harvard University Press, 1983), 73–5.

17 E. P. Thompson, 'Time, work-discipline and industrial capitalism', *Past and Present* 38 (December 1967), 56–97; and Herbert G. Gutman, 'Work, culture and society in industrializing America, 1815–1919', *American Historical Review* 78 (June 1973), 531–88.

18 See Witold Rybczynski, *Waiting for the weekend* (New York: Viking, 1991), 8, 50–1; and John Lowerson and John Myerscough, *Time to spare in Victorian England* (Hassocks: Harvester Press, 1977), 12.

19 Rybczynski, *Waiting for the weekend*, 51.

20 Keletso E. Atkins, '"Kafir time": preindustrial temporal concepts and labour discipline in nineteenth century colonial Natal', *JAH*, 29, 2 (1988), 229–44; also her *The moon is dead! Give us our money!* (Portsmouth, N.H.: Heinemann, 1993).

21 See chapter 3.

22 Le Goff, *Time, work and culture in the Middle Ages*, 48; Atkins, '"Kafir time"', 238.

23 Robert Rotenberg, *Time and order in metropolitan Vienna* (Washington, D.C.: Smithsonian Institution Press, 1992), 1–7, 149.

24 Zerubavel, *Hidden rhythms*, 19–21.

25 Maurice Halbwachs, 'La mémoire collective et le temps', *Cahiers internationaux de sociologie*, 2 (1947), 3–31; and Rotenberg, *Time and order in metropolitan Vienna*, 194.

26 Le Goff, *Time, work and culture in the Middle Ages*, 49; Thompson, 'Time, work-discipline and industrial capitalism', 70–3.

27 Atkins, '"Kafir time"', 237–8; and Atkins, *The moon is dead!*, 86 ff.

28 Frederick Cooper, 'Colonizing time: work rhythms and labor conflict in colonial Mombasa', in Dirks (ed.), *Colonialism and culture*, 209–11.

29 Philip Bonner et al. (eds.), *Holding their ground: class, locality and culture in 19th and 20th Century South Africa* (Johannesburg: Witwatersrand University Press, 1989).

30 See chapters 1, 2 and 7.

31 Eugen Weber, 'Work suspended: strenuous leisure and the invention of the weekend', *Times Literary Supplement*, 20 December 1991, 3.

32 Nicholas B. Dirks, 'Introduction', in *Colonialism and culture*, 3.

33 Weber, 'Work suspended', 4.

34 Belinda Bozzoli, 'History, experience and culture', commenting on a chapter

on African football by Tim Couzens in Bozzoli (ed.), *Town and countryside in the Transvaal*, 21–2.

35 T. O. Ranger, *Dance and society in eastern and central Africa, 1890–1970: the Beni Ngoma* (London: Heinemann, 1975), 2 (emphasis in the original).

36 Anthony Giddens, 'Notes on the concepts of play and leisure', *Sociological Review*, n.s., 12, 1 (March 1964), 73–89.

37 Johan Huizinga, *Homo ludens: a study of the play element in culture* (Boston: Beacon Press, 1962), 1–15.

38 For a discussion of work and leisure in pre-colonial Tio society, see Vansina, *The Tio kingdom*, 159, 163–8.

39 The modern Republic of Congo corresponds to the former territory of Moyen-Congo.

40 Catherine Coquery-Vidrovitch, 'Investissements privés, investissements publiques en AEF, 1900–1940', *AEH*, 12 (1983), 13–16.

41 Ralph A. Austen and Rita Headrick, 'Equatorial Africa under colonial rule', in Birmingham and Martin (eds.), *History of Central Africa*, vol. II, 27–94; also Catherine Coquery-Vidrovitch, 'Mutation de l'impérialisme colonial français dans les années 30', *AEH*, 4 (1977), 103–152; and her 'Investissements privés, investissements publiques', *AEH*, 12 (1983), 13–31.

42 Henri Brunschwig, *Brazza explorateur: l'Ogooué, 1875–1879* (Paris: Mouton, 1966); and his *Brazza explorateur: les traités Makoko, 1880–1882* (Paris: Mouton, 1972); Catherine Coquery-Vidrovitch, *Brazza et la prise de possession du Congo: la mission de l'Ouest Africain, 1883–1885* (Paris: Mouton, 1969); and Elisabeth Rabut, *Brazza Commissaire Général: le Congo Français, 1886–1897* (Paris: Editions de l'EHESS, 1989).

43 Catherine Coquery-Vidrovitch, *Le Congo au temps des grandes compagnies concessionaires 1898–1930* (Paris: Mouton, 1972).

44 For example the work of Pierre-Philippe Rey, *Colonialisme, neo-colonialisme et transition au capitalisme: example de la 'Comilogue' au Congo-Brazzaville* (Paris: Maspéro, 1971); also Georges Dupré, *Un ordre et sa destruction* (Paris: ORSTOM, 1982).

45 For example, Antoine-Marie Aïssi, 'La "justice indigène" et la vie congolaise (1886–1936)', thèse de 3è cycle, University of Toulouse-Le Marail, 1978; Raymond Bafouetela, 'La "politique indigène" de la France au Moyen-Congo, 1886–1930', thèse de 3è cycle, University of Paris, VII, 1974; Rita Headrick, 'The impact of colonialism on health in French Equatorial Africa, 1880–1934', Ph.D. thesis, University of Chicago, 1987; Joseph Gamandzori, 'Chemin de fer, villes et travail au Congo (1921–1955)', thèse de doctorat, University of Paris VII, 1987; Gilles Sautter, 'Notes sur la construction du chemin de fer Congo-Océan, 1921–34', *CEA*, 7 (1967), 219–300.

46 For example, Georges Balandier, *Sociologie des Brazzavilles noires* (Paris: Presses de la Fondation Nationale des Sciences Politiques, 1985, 2nd edn); and his *The Sociology of black Africa* (London: Andre Deutsch, 1970); Marcel Soret, *Démographie et problèmes urbains en AEF: Poto-Poto–Bacongo–Dolisie* (Brazzaville: IECA, 1954); Pierre Vennetier, 'Un Quartier suburbain de Brazzaville: Moukondji-Ngouaka', *Bulletin de l'IECA* 20 (1960), 91–124, and his *Pointe-Noire et la façade maritime du Congo-Brazzaville* (Paris: ORSTOM, 1968); Jeanne-Françoise Vincent, *Femmes*

africaines en milieu urbain (Paris: ORSTOM, 1966). The most up-to-date bibliography is Carlo Carozzi and Maurizio Tiepolo, (eds.), *Congo Brazzaville: bibliografia generale/bibliographie générale* (Turin: Edizioni Libreria Cortina, 1991).

47 For example, Catherine Coquery-Vidrovitch (ed.), *Processus d'urbanization en Afrique* (Paris: L'Harmattan, 1988), 2 vols.; also see the extensive bibliography in her paper 'The process of urbanization in Africa (from the origins to the beginning of independence)', *African Studies Review*, 34, 1 (April 1991), 1–98. A recent thesis at the University of Paris VII points to a new interest in cultural and social history as opposed to the process of urbanization. See Charles Didier Gondola, 'Migrations et villes Congolaises au XXe siècle: processus et implications des mouvements campagnes/villes à Léopoldville et Brazzaville (c.1930–1970)', thèse de doctorat, University of Paris VII, 1993.

48 Publications that include the work of the faculty at the University Marien Ngouabi are *Cahiers congolais de l'Imaginaire*, 1 (1988) and *Cahiers congolais d'Anthropolgie et d'Histoire*, 1 (1978). Particularly noteworthy among monographs are the history of music by the Congolese intellectual Sylvain Bemba, *50 ans de musique du Congo-Zaïre* (Paris: Présence Africaine, 1984); and two books on the fashion of young men of Bacongo by the sociologist Justin-Daniel Gandoulou, *Entre Paris et Bacongo* (Paris: Centre Georges Pompidou, 1984); and his *Dandies à Bacongo: le culte de l'élégance dans la société Congolaise contemporaine* (Paris: L'Harmattan, 1989). Other items, mostly articles scattered through French publications by Congolese authors appear in the notes and bibliography.

1 AN AFRICAN CROSSROADS, A FRONTIER POST AND A COLONIAL TOWN, *c.* 1880–1915

1   Léon Guiral, *Le Congo Français du Gabon à Brazzaville* (Paris: Plon, 1889), 224. Ntamo or Kintamo was also the name of the Tio village on the south bank of the Pool near where Leopold II's Congo Free State established its post. See *ibid.*, 234; W. Holman Bentley, *Pioneering on the Congo* (London: The Religious Tract Society, 1900), vol. I, 342–53; François Bontinck, 'Quand Brazzaville se trouvait à Kinshasa', *Zaïre-Afrique*, 148 (October 1980), 487–99.

2   During the colonial period the Pool was generally called Stanley Pool and on present-day atlases its official name is Malebo Pool. But in Brazzaville, it is simply referred to as 'the Pool', which is the name used here. For a fuller description of the geography, see Paul Briart, 'Le Stanley Pool hier, aujourd'hui, demain', *Le mouvement géographique*, 28 (1911), cols. 199–203, and 'Le Stanley Pool Commercial', *Le mouvement géographique*, 28 (1911), cols. 439–43; Gilles Sautter, *De l'Atlantique au fleuve Congo: une géographie du sous-peuplement* (Paris: Mouton, 1966), vol. I, 331–56.

3   The best discussion of the middle Congo river trade is in Robert Harms, *River of wealth, river of sorrow: the central Zaire basin in the era of the slave and ivory trade, 1500–1891* (New Haven: Yale University Press, 1981).

4   Charles de Chavannes, *Avec Brazza: souvenirs de la Mission de l'Ouest-*

Africain. Mars 1883–janvier 1886 (Paris: Librairie Plon, 1935), 327; also Colonel Baratier, *Au Congo: souvenirs de la Mission Marchand* (Paris: Arthème Fayard & Co., 1914), 118–19; Albert Veistroffer, *Vingt ans dans la brousse africaine: souvenirs d'un ancien membre de la Mission Savorgnan de Brazza dans l'Ouest africain (1883–1903)* (Lille: Mercure de Flande, 1931), 64; Paul Brunache, *Le centre de l'Afrique: autour du Tchad* (Paris: F. Alcan, 1894), 32.

5   The history of the Central African slave trade and the role of the Pool traders is now quite well known. See, for example, Joseph C. Miller, *The Way of death: merchant capitalism and the Angolan slave trade 1730–1830* (Madison: University of Wisconsin Press, 1988), 3–207; Harms, *River of wealth*; Phyllis M. Martin, *The external trade of the Loango coast 1576–1870: the effects of changing commercial relations on the Vili kingdom of Loango* (Oxford: The Clarendon Press, 1972), 33–135; Jan Vansina, *Paths in the rainforests: towards a history of political tradition in equatorial Africa* (Madison: University of Wisconsin Press, 1990), 197–237; Anne Hilton, *The kingdom of Kongo* (Oxford: The Clarendon Press, 1985), 50–121; John K. Thornton, *The kingdom of Kongo: civil war and transition 1641–1718* (Madison: University of Wisconsin Press, 1983), 25–6, 53–5, 97–103.

6   Bentley, *Pioneering*, vol. I, 460; Vansina, *The Tio kingdom*, 250; Harms, *River of wealth*, 39–40.

7   R. P. Augouard, 'Voyage à Stanley Pool', *MC*, 14 (1882), 141. Vansina finds this an overestimate: see *The Tio kingdom*, 250, 274–7, 298; also Sautter, *De l'Atlantique au fleuve Congo*, vol. I, 369.

8   A comprehensive account of items that might have been on sale can be found in Vansina, *The Tio kingdom*, 265–81.

9   The Tio of the Mbe plateau and those who lived on both sides of the Pool when the Europeans arrived are linguistically and culturally part of the larger group commonly referred to in present-day Brazzaville as the Teke, which is the Kikongo word for them. See Vansina, *The Tio kingdom*, 8–13, 471–3; Gilles Sautter, 'Le plateau congolais de Mbé', *CEA*, 1, 2 (May 1960), 11–12.

10 An account of Brazza's negotiations with the Makoko Iloo and with the Tio chiefs at the Pool can be found in Brunschwig, *Brazza explorateur: les traités Makoko*, 52–83, 267–79; and Coquery-Vidrovitch, *Brazza*, 114.

11 See Sautter, *De l'Atlantique au fleuve Congo*, vol. I, 367, and 'Le plateau congolais de Mbé', 34–5.

12 Baratier, *Au Congo*, 94; Marc Michel, *La Mission Marchand 1895–1899* (Paris: Mouton, 1972), 109; Coquery-Vidrovitch, *Brazza*, 117.

13 Vansina, *The Tio kingdom*, 256, suggests a population on both banks of the Pool of some 10,000. For a more detailed description of the villages at Brazzaville based on contemporary sources, see Roger Frey, 'Brazzaville, capitale de l'Afrique Equatoriale Française', *Encyclopédie Mensuelle d'Outre-Mer*, 48–9 (August-September 1954), 23–37.

14 Vansina, *The Tio kingdom*, 257–8, 310–11.

15 Miller, *Way of death*, 58; see Harms, *River of wealth*, 143–236, on other settlements upstream from the Pool.

16 Sautter, *De l'Atlantique au fleuve Congo*, vol. I, 321, 377; Vansina, *The Tio kingdom*, 8, 257–60.

17   The modern town hall of Brazzaville is located in the centre of the city on the Pool front, adjacent to the site of the old village of Mfoa.

18   Guiral, *Le Congo Français*, 226–9.

19   Chavannes, *Avec Brazza*, 227–9; 'Communauté de Saint-Hippolyte, à Brazzaville', *BCPSE*, 17 (1893–6), 546. From here on, references to reports from Brazzaville in this mission periodical will simply be referred to as 'Brazzaville'. Also Jean Dybowski, *La route du Tchad: du Loango au Chari* (Paris: Librairie de Firmin-Didot et Co., 1893), 72, 216; Guiral, *Le Congo Français*, 228–9; Bentley, *Pioneering*, vol. I, 460, vol. II, 17–18, 152; Harms, *River of wealth*, 140, 224; Vansina, *The Tio kingdom*, 8, 256.

20   Bentley, *Pioneering*, vol. II, 19; also Dybowski, *La route du Tchad*, 70; Baratier, *Au Congo*, 94.

21   Guiral, *Le Congo Français*, 228.

22   This process has been the subject of several studies, for example, Ndinga-Mbo, *Introduction à l'histoire des migrations au Congo*; and Dominique Ngoië-Ngalla, *Les Kongo de la vallée du Niari* (Brazzaville: Les Editions CELMAA, 1982); André Massengo, 'Connaissez-vous les Lari?', *Liaison*, 46 (1955), 33–4; Vansina, *The Tio kingdom*, 8–11, 303.

23   The verb *vula* means to become wealthy by illicit means or speculation. See Alphonse Sita, 'Les institutions sociales et politiques des Bakongo du Pool (Congo): chefferies traditionelles et administratives, 1905–1946', thèse de doctorat, University of Paris VII, 1988, 63, fn 43. I am also grateful to Marie-Thérèse Oumba for clarifying this point.

24   Dolisie to Minister of Colonies, Libreville, 6 July 1897, published in Rabut, *Brazza*, 109; Coquery-Vidrovitch, *Le Congo*, 25–46, 75.

25   'Brazzaville', *BCPSE*, 16 (1891–3), 535.

26   Administrator Bonchamps to the Commissioner-General of French Congo in Libreville, 'Rapport sur la région de Brazzaville', Brazzaville, 1 May 1900. I am grateful to Roger Frey for loaning me his copy of this document.

27   'Mission de l'Oubangui: aperçu général', *BCPSE*, 21 (1901–2), 663.

28   Michael Adams, 'From avoidance to confrontation: peasant protest in pre-colonial and colonial Southeast Asia', in Dirks (ed.), *Colonialism and culture*, 89.

29   Report of Commander Pradier, 1886, in Coquery-Vidrovitch, *Brazza*, 462; 'Brazzaville', *BCPSE*, 15 (1889–91), 578–91, and 21 (1901–2), 667; 'Informations diverses: Oubanghi', *MC*, 39 (1907); 412; Vansina, *The Tio kingdom*, 109–18, 303–4; Sautter, 'Le plateau congolais de Mbé', 44–5.

30   L. Girard, 'Brazzaville', *BCAF: renseignements coloniaux* (March 1916), 29; Félicien Challaye, *Le Congo Français: la question internationale du Congo* (Paris: Félix Alcan, 1909), 30; Louis Papy, 'Les populations Batéké (Afrique Equatoriale Française)', *Cahiers d'outre-mer*, 2, 6 (1949), 131.

31   Bentley, *Pioneering*, vol. II, 143; Dybowski, *La route du Tchad*, 72; E. de Mandat-Grancey, *Au Congo: impressions d'un touriste* (Paris: Librairie Plon, 1900), 220; Sautter, 'Le plateau congolais de Mbé', and his *De L'Atlantique au fleuve Congo*, vol. I, 383–5; Vansina, *The Tio kingdom*, 250, 303–4, 416–30, 470–84.

32   Raymond Colrat de Montrozier, *Deux ans chez les anthropophages* (Paris: Plon-Nourrit, 1902), 23.

33 Challaye, *Le Congo Français*, 30; Sautter, *De l'Atlantique au fleuve Congo*, vol. I, 384–5; Papy, 'Les populations Batéké (AEF)', 122, 127–8.

34 Chavannes, *Avec Brazza*, 233–4, 250, 271–4, 323 and his *Le Congo Français. Ma collaboration avec Brazza (1886–1894)* (Paris: Librairie Plon, 1937), 74.

35 Bonchamps, 'Rapport sur la région de Brazzaville'; AOM, 4(2)D1, Brazzaville Administrator to Commisioner-General of French Congo, Brazzaville, 13 July 1901.

36 'Communauté de St. Joseph de Linzolo', *BCPSE*, 24 (1906–8), 290; 'Brazzaville', *BCPSE*, 25 (1909–10), 513; 'Résidence de St. Philippe à Mbamou', *BCPSE*, 28 (1914–18), 171.

37 P. A. Westlind, *Société de la mission suédoise au Congo* (Stockholm: Librairie de la Société de la Mission Suédoise, 1922), 33.

38 Chavannes, *Avec Brazza*, 170 and *Le Congo Français*, 74; Dybowski, *La route du Tchad*, 70, 81; Bonchamps, 'Rapport sur la région de Brazzaville'.

39 Augouard to Brazza, Brazzaville, 10 January 1897, in Rabut, *Brazza*, 156; Thoiré to Chavannes, Brazzaville, 20 July 1892, in *ibid.* 343–4; Charles Castellani, *Les femmes au Congo* (Paris: Ernest Flammarion, 1898), 104; Girard, 'Brazzaville', 42.

40 *JO*, 26 November 1904.

41 'Mission de l'Oubangui: aperçu général' and 'Brazzaville', *BCPSE*, 21 (1901–2), 662–3, 666–7; Girard, 'Brazzaville', 29–30.

42 ASMF, E.10, Brev frän Kongo, Teofil Ceder to SMF Board, Brazzaville, 19 July 1911; E.14, Brev frän Kongo, H. Lindgren to SMF Board, 5 February 1914; Westlind, *Société de la mission suédoise au Congo*, 5–33.

43 Challaye, *Le Congo Français*, 30; Girard, 'Brazzaville', 30–1.

44 Duchesse D'Uzès, *Le voyage de mon fils au Congo* (Paris: Librairie Plon, 1894), 71; AOM, 4(2)D1, Brazzaville Administrator to Commissioner-General in Libreville, 14 December 1900; 'Stationen i Brazzaville', *MF* (1912), 249; Castellani, *Les femmes au Congo*, 133; Harms, *River of wealth*, 224.

45 'Brazzaville', *BCPSE*, 27 (1913–14), 55; AGPSE, B706, Brazzaville Mission Journal, 25 September 1910, 1 December 1913.

46 Fernand Rouget, *L'Afrique Equatoriale Illustrée* (Paris: Emile Larose, 1913), 104–5.

47 AOM, 4(2)D1, Brazzaville Administrator to Governor of French Congo in Libreville, 13 August 1901.

48 Veistroffer, *Vingt ans*, 86.

49 Brunache, *Le centre de l'Afrique*, 13.

50 Challaye, *Le Congo Français*, 30.

51 Brunache, *Le centre de l'Afrique*, 13; Gabrielle M. Vassal, *Life in French Congo* (London: T. Fisher Unwin, 1925), 37–8, 41–5; interview with Père Schaub, Brazzaville, 15 October 1986.

52 Brunache, *Le centre de l'Afrique*, 13–14; D'Uzès, *Le voyage de mon fils*, 93.

53 Jean de Puytorac, *Makambo: une vie au Congo (Brazzaville-M'Bondo)* (Paris: Zulma, 1992), 46.

54 Gaston Bouteillier, *Douze mois sous l'équateur* (Toulouse: Imprimerie Adolphe Trinchant, 1903), 38–9, 45, 86.

55 Capt. Deschamps, *De Bordeaux au Tchad par Brazzaville* (Paris: Société Française d'Imprimerie et de Librairie, 1911), 26.

56 'Communauté du Sacre-Coeur de Loango', *BCPSE*, 21 (1901–2), 624; Bonchamps, 'Rapport sur la région de Brazzaville'.

57 D'Uzès, *Le voyage de mon fils*, 93.

58 See chapter 7.

59 *JO*, 1 July 1912; Girard, 'Brazzaville', 44.

60 Guiral, *Le Congo Français*, 17; E. Froment, 'Trois affluents français du Congo: Alima, Likouala, Sanga', *Bulletin de la société de géographie de Lille*, 9 (1887), 458; 'Brazzaville', *BCPSE*, 15 (1889–91), 583. On comparative schooling in the colonies of AEF, see David E. Gardinier, 'Schooling in the states of Equatorial Africa', *Canadian Journal of African Studies*, 7, 3 (1974), 517–38.

61 See chapters 4 and 6.

62 Challaye, *Le Congo Français*, 41; Charles Castellani, *Vers le Nil français avec la Mission Marchand* (Paris: Ernest Flammarion, 1898), 41, 111–12; 'Communauté du Sacre-Coeur de Loango', *BCPSE*, 27 (1913–14), 21; J. Bonnefont, 'Brazzaville: la ville et la mission', *AA* (July-August, 1926), 108–9; Puytorac, *Makambo*, 54–7; interview with Mère Emilie, Brazzaville, 13 June 1989.

63 Letter of Sam Hede, Brazzaville, 12 October 1914, *MF* (1915), 8.

64 ANB, GG4, Report of Administrator Cureau to Lieutenant-Governor of Moyen-Congo, 1 June 1909; AOM, 4(2)D3, Annual report of Moyen-Congo, 1909.

65 AOM, 4(2)D11, Annual report of Moyen-Congo, 1912; Headrick, 'The impact of colonialism on health', 135, 804.

66 Chavannes, *Le Congo Français*, 120, and *Avec Brazza*, 46, 53–5; Brazza to Manas, Leketi, 8 October 1887, in Rabut, *Brazza*, 365; Charles Mangin, *Souvenirs d'Afrique (lettres et carnets de route)* (Paris: editions Denoël et Steele, 1936), 31; Coquery-Vidrovitch, *Brazza*, 35–8, 238, 252. For the often low social origins of the Senegalese *tirailleurs*, see Myron Echenberg, *Colonial conscripts: the 'tirailleurs sénégalais'* (Portsmouth, N.H.: Heinemann, 1991), 5–18.

67 *Ibid.*, 18.

68 Brunache, *Le centre de l'Afrique*, 9–10.

69 Mangin, *Souvenirs*, 8–20; also Casimir Maistre, *A travers l'Afrique Centrale du Congo au Niger 1892–1893* (Paris: Librairie Hachette & Co., 1895), 3–4.

70 Veistroffer, *Vingt ans*, 102; Coquery-Vidrovitch, *Brazza*, 36–8, 238.

71 AOM, 4(2)D2, Annual report of Moyen-Congo, 1908; Léon Bemba, 'L'AEF dans la première guerre mondiale,' thèse de 3è cycle, University of Paris VII, 1984, 20, 40–1; Henri Brunschwig, *Noirs et blancs dans l'Afrique noire française ou comment le colonisé devient colonisateur (1870–1974)* (Paris: Flammarion, 1983), 137.

72 Bouteillier, *Douze mois sous l'équateur*, 35–40.

73 AOM, 1st series, TP152, Mission Fillon, report on the Brazzaville workforce by M. Henri, 2 June 1913.

74 Baratier, *Au Congo*, 76; Colrat de Montrozier, *Deux ans*, 18.

75 Guiral, *Le Congo Français*, 17.

76 AOM, 4(2)D1, Brazzaville Administrator to Commissioner-General in Libreville, 2 February 1901; Girard, 'Brazzaville', 33.
77 *JO*, 11 March 1905.
78 Veistroffer, *Vingt ans*, 193; Challaye, *Le Congo Français*,30–1; interview with Habibou Soumbre, Brazzaville, 11 November 1986.
79 Interviews with Mère Emilie, 12 June 1989; Bernard Mambeke-Boucher, 10 December 1986; Bonchamps report, 'Rapport sur la région de Brazzaville'; ASMF, Brev frän Kongo, E.10, Ceder to SMF, Brazzaville, 6 June 1912. According to Gilbert Amagatcher (personal communication, 25 June 1992) in Ada in eastern Ghana, a large house called 'Congo House', built by a local man who made money in Brazzaville, still stands and is used for receptions and festivals.
80 ASMF, E.10, Brev frän Kongo, T.Ceder to SMF Director, Brazzaville, 6 June 1912.
81 The history of Antilleans serving in AEF is little known and seems to have been very much overshadowed by the extraordinary career of Eboué, who rose to be Governor-General during the Second World War. There are several biographies: see for example, the account of Brian Weinstein, *Eboué* (New York: Oxford University Press, 1972).
82 See chapter 5.
83 AOM, 1st series, TP 152, Mission Fillon, Report of M. Henri on the Brazzaville workforce, 5 May and 13 May 1913; reply of M. Russon, Head of Public Works Department, 15 May 1913.
84 Girard, 'Brazzaville', 30–3.
85 James Vandrunen, *Heures africaines: l'Atlantique-le Congo* (Brussels: Ch. Bulens, 1899), 165.
86 Bemba, 'L'AEF dans la première guerre mondiale', 36.
87 Chavannes, *Le Congo Français*, 72–3; Veistroffer, *Vingt ans*, 139–40; Dybowski, *La route du Tchad*, 71–2; Alfred Fourneau, *Au vieux Congo: notes de route (1884–1891)* (Paris: Edition du Comité de l'Afrique Française, 1932), 260–1.
88 'Brazzaville', *BCPSE*, 17 (1893–6), 541–51, 579–87, and 18 (1897–8), 598–607, and 19 (1898–9), 418; 'Brazzaville', *BCSSJC*, 43 (1896), 658; *Les Soeurs de Saint-Joseph de Cluny en Afrique Centrale, 1886–1986* (Brazzaville: Imprimerie Saint-Paul, 1986), 34–55; Veistroffer, *Vingt ans*, 191; Baratier, *Au Congo*, 119; Mandat-Grancey, *Au Congo*, 182, 198–204.
89 Bonchamps, 'Rapport sur la région de Brazzaville'.
90 'Oubangui', *MC* (1902), 615.
91 AOM, 4(2)D11, Annual report of the Administrator of Moyen-Congo, 1912.
92 Challaye, *Le Congo Français*, 27.
93 Chavannes, *Avec Brazza*, 250, 269–74, and *Le Congo Français*, 263; Dybowski, *La route du Tchad*, 68–9; Mandat-Grancey, *Au Congo*, 131–2; Bonchamps, 'Rapport sur la région de Brazzaville'; 'Chronique des missions: Brazzaville', *AA* (June 1899), 258; Challaye, *Le Congo Français*, 25–7.
94 Challaye, *Le Congo Français*, 34; Bonchamps, 'Rapport sur la région de Brazzaville'; AOM, 4(2)D1, Brazzaville Administrator to Libreville, 12 January 1901.
95 Castellani, *Vers le Nil français*, 132.

96 AOM, AP648, Decree for the creation of a Commune at Brazzaville, 5 October 1911; speech of Governor-General Merlin, *BCAF*, 10 (1910), 331; AOM, 4(2)D7, Annual report of Moyen-Congo, Brazzaville, 1911.

97 Girard, 'Brazzaville', 36.

98 Mandat-Grancey, *Au Congo*, 182.

99 Veistroffer, *Vingt ans*, 103; Baratier, *Au Congo*, 121.

100 Colonel Moll, *Une âme de colonial: lettres du Lieutenant-Colonel Moll* (Paris, Emile-Paul, 1912), 10; Deschamps, *De Bordeaux au Tchad*, 22–5; Frey, 'Brazzaville', 44–6; Girard, 'Brazzaville', 32–3, 38–40.

101 For urban architecture in colonial Africa, see, Philip D. Curtin, 'Medical knowledge and urban planning in tropical Africa', *AHR*, 90, 3 (June 1985), 594–613; Raymond F. Betts, *Uncertain dimensions: western overseas empires in the twentieth century* (Minneapolis: University of Minnesota Press, 1985), 114–46; Odile Goerg, 'Réflexion sur l'architecture européenne le long de la côte africaine à partir de l'exemple de la Guinée', in Almeida-Topor and Riesz (eds.), *Rencontres franco-allemandes sur l'Afrique*, 81–92; and Gwendolyn Wright, 'Tradition in the service of modernity: architecture and urbanism in French colonial policy, 1900–1930', *Journal of Modern History*, 59 (June 1987), 291–316.

102 Girard, 'Brazzaville', 34.

103 For the history and significance of the Fourteenth of July in Brazzaville, see Phyllis M. Martin, 'National holidays transformed: the fourteenth of July in Brazzaville', paper presented at the thirty-seventh annual meeting of the African Studies Association, Toronto, November 1994.

104 Bonchamps, 'Rapport sur la région de Brazzaville'.

105 Girard, 'Brazzaville', 36.

106 Speech of Governor-General Merlin, *BCAF*, 10 (1910), 337.

107 Gabrielle and Joseph Vassal, *Français, Belge et Portugais en Afrique Equatoriale* (Paris: Pierre Roger, 1926), 42.

108 Headrick, 'The impact of colonialism on health', 221.

109 Curtin, 'Medical knowledge and urban planning', 594–7.

110 Ibid., 598–609; also Headrick, 'The impact of colonialism on health', 143–4, 801–2.

111 Bonchamps, 'Rapport sur la région de Brazzaville'.

112 Frey, 'Brazzaville', 44; Sautter, *De l'Atlantique au fleuve Congo*, vol. I, 398.

113 Challaye, *Le Congo Français*, 219.

114 *JO*, 19 November 1904.

115 Bonchamps, 'Rapport sur la région de Brazzaville'; also AOM, 4(2)D1, Brazzaville Administrator to Commissioner-General in Libreville, 13 July 1901.

116 Quoted in Headrick, 'The impact of colonialism on health', 383.

117 *JO*, 20 May 1905.

118 AGPSE, 510BVI, Annual reports 'Oeuvres de la Sainte-Enfance', 24 October 1901, 1 January 1903, 10 November 1912.

119 Girard, 'Brazzaville', 42. *Chikouangue* is a reference to manioc bread.

120 AOM, TP152, 1st series, Mission Fillon, Report of M. Henri on the Brazzaville workforce, 1913.

121 Girard, 'Brazzaville', 38–9.

122 AGPSE, B706, Brazzaville Mission Journal, 29 May 1908; R. P. C. Grillot,
      'Dans le Haut-Congo Français', *MC* (1914), 140–1.
123 Girard, 'Brazzaville', 38–9.
124 See, for example, J.-P. Chrétien and G. Prunier (eds.), *Les ethnies ont une
      histoire* (Paris: Karthala, 1989); Leroy Vail (ed.), *The creation of tribalism in
      southern Africa* (London: James Currey, 1989; Chris Gray, *Modernization
      and cultural identity: the creation of national space in rural France and colonial
      space in rural Gabon* (Bloomington: Indiana University Center on Global
      Change and World Peace, 1994); Terence Ranger, 'The invention of tradition
      in colonial Africa', in Hobsbawm and Ranger (eds.), *The invention of
      tradition*, 211–62, which he has revised as 'The invention of tradition
      revisited: the case of colonial Africa', in Terence Ranger and Olufemi
      Vaughan (eds.), *Legitimacy and the state in 20th century Africa* (London:
      Macmillan, 1993), 62–111. In the revision of his essay, Ranger has been
      influenced, among others, by Benedict Anderson, *Imagined communities:
      reflections on the origins and spread of nationalism* (London: Verso, 1983).
125 Harold W. Fehderau, *The origin and development of Kituba (Lingua Franca
      Kikongo)* (Kisangani: Université Libre du Congo, 1966) suggests that
      Kituba was a language associated with the slave trade; William J. Samarin,
      'The origins of Kituba and Lingala', *Journal of African Languages and
      Linguistics*, 12, 1 (September 1991), 47–77, suggests that its diffusion was
      more related to foreign railway workers in the lower Congo.
126 ASMF, E11. Brev från Kongo, Lindgren to SMF, 18 October 1911; B and
      E. no. 1, Korr., Lindgren to SMF, 11 November 1911; F. no. 1, Dagbok, 22
      February 1914; Brev från Kongo, G. A. Hult to SMF, 11 January 1918.
127 Speech of Governor-General Merlin, *BCAF*, 10 (1910), 337.
128 Girard, 'Brazzaville', 38–9; AOM, 4(2)D13, Report from the Pool district,
      Brazzaville, May 1913.
129 Mumbansa mwa Bawele, 'Y a-t-il des Bangalas?' *Zaïre-Afrique*, 78 (October
      1973), 471–84; Samarin, 'The origins of Kituba and Lingala', 47, 57–69, and
      'Bondjo ethnicity and colonial imagination', *Canadian Journal of African
      Studies*, 18 (1984), 345–65.
130 'Brazzaville', *BPSE*, 25 (1909–10), 511; AGPSE, B706, Brazzaville Mission
      Journal, 29 May 1908, 25 September 1910, 1 December 1913.
131 See chapters 3 and 4.
132 Grillot, 'Dans le Haut-Congo Français', 139; 'Brazzaville', *BCPSE*, 27
      (1913–14), 55; P. Augouard, *Quarante-quatre années au Congo* (Evreux:
      Poussin, 1934), 50, 72–3, 105.
133 Girard, 'Brazzaville', 29, 30.
134 AOM, 4(2)D5, Administrative report, Moyen-Congo, September–November
      1910.
135 Frederick Cooper, 'Urban space, industrial time, and wage labor in Africa',
      in his *Struggle for the city*, 23.

2 TAKING HOLD OF THE TOWN, *c.* 1915–1960

1   Soret, *Démographie et problèmes urbains*, 24; interview with Maya Alden, 7
      November 1986; Martial Sinda, *Le messianisme congolais et ses incidences*

politiques (Paris: Payot, 1972), 181 ff. See later in this chapter, pp. 68–69, for more on Matswa.

2 Soret, *Démographie et problèmes urbains*, 26–8; Vincent, *Femmes africaines*, 23–4.

3 See chapter 7.

4 Coquery-Vidrovitch, 'Investissements privés, investissements publiques', 13–16.

5 Most accounts of the First World War deal with campaigns and generals. There is little research on the social impact of the war, as has been carried out for East and British Central Africa, and for West Africa. The best account is in Léon Bemba, 'L'AEF dans la première guerre mondiale': see 107–11. Also AGPSE, 183BII, Report of Mgr Augouard, 1 December 1915 and 1 December 1916.

6 AGPSE, 510BVI, Report of Mgr Augouard, 'Oeuvres de la Sainte-Enfance', 1 October 1918; Augouard, *Quarante-quatre années au Congo*, 167, 177–8, 190, 197, 290–2; ASMF, E.14, Sam Hede to SMF, 21 September and 21 October 1914.

7 'Brazzaville', *BPSE* (1914–18), 452–3; Augouard, *Quarante-quatre années au Congo*, 167, 171, 300–2; ASMF, E.14, Hede to SMF, 21 September 1914, 12 and 21 October 1914, 27 May 1915; E.18, Ceder to SMF, 18 December 1918, and G. A. Hult to SMF, 7 December 1918; Bemba, 'L'AEF dans la première guerre mondiale', 140–2, 170, 197, 231–7; Coquery-Vidrovitch, *Le Congo*, 526.

8 Bemba, 'L'AEF dans la première guerre mondiale', 179–83; AGPSE, 183BI, Five-year report of the Brazzaville Mission, 1 January 1920. Also, see the intriguing novel about war veterans by Sylvain Bemba, *Le soleil est parti à M'Pemba* (Paris: Présence Africaine, 1982).

9 Coquery-Vidrovitch, 'Investissements privés, investissements publiques', 17–21.

10 Albert Sarraut, *La mise en valeur des colonies françaises* (Paris: Payot, 1923), 414–19, 432–4; William B. Cohen, *Rulers of empire: the French colonial service in Africa* (Stanford: Hoover Institute Press, 1971), 108–11.

11 The best account is in Sautter, 'Notes sur la construction du chemin de fer Congo-Océan, 1921–34'.

12 ANB, GG444(1), Report on CFCO workers in Brazzaville, 3 September 1929; GG104, Report of the Mayor of Brazzaville, 12 September 1929; AOM, TP779(2), 'CFCO expenses', Brazzaville, 2 August 1933; TP155/14, Report of Inspector Huet, 25 January 1933. There are many contemporary accounts of the CFCO construction which both support and condemn the operation. On the Brazzaville camps, see Henri Auric, *L'avenir du Congo et le 'Congo-Océan'* (Paris: Librairie Picart, 1934), 92; Marcel Gousset, *En brousse AEF* (Paris: Editions Fernand Sorlot, 1943), 101–2; Albert Londres, *Terre d'ébène: la traite des noirs* (Paris: A. Michel, 1929), 231–2.

13 AGPSE, 277AVII, Annual reports, 'Oeuvres de la Sainte-Enfance', Brazzaville, 15 September 1929; 277AVI, Annual report of the Brazzaville mission, 25 September 1932; AOM, 4(2)D55, Report for the third trimester, Autonomous Subdivision of Brazzaville, 4 February 1933; Marcel Homet, *Congo: terre de souffrances* (Paris: Editions Montaigne, 1934), 133; Catherine

Coquery-Vidrovitch, 'Mutation de l'impérialisme colonial français dans les années 30', 103–52.

14 AOM, 4(2)D55, Report for the first trimester, Administrator Lotte, 1932; AGPSE, 377AVII, Report of P. Le Duc, Brazzaville Catholic mission, 25 September 1932; Coquery-Vidrovitch, 'Mutation de l'impérialisme colonial français dans les années 30', 129–31.

15 AOM, 4(2)D65, Report for the third trimester, Autonomous Subdivision of Brazzaville, 1934.

16 *L'Etoile de l'AEF*, 24 January 1930; ANB, GG104, Report of Commissioner of Police, Brazzaville, 2 October 1930.

17 See chapter 4.

18 See, for example, the account of Adolphe Sicé, *L'Afrique Equatoriale au service de la France* (Paris: Presse Universitaire, 1946). Sicé was the chief doctor of AEF and director of the Pasteur Institute when war broke out. He was a major figure in rallying AEF to de Gaulle. Some newer approaches are suggested in *Brazzaville, janvier-février 1944: aux sources de la décolonisation* (Paris: Plon, l'Institut Charles-de-Gaulle, 1988).

19 Interview with Julien Nkounkou, 24 July 1974, reported in Jérôme Ollandet, 'L'AEF dans la deuxième guerre mondiale', mémoire de maîtrise, University Marien Ngouabi, 1974, 16.

20 Interview with Bernard Mambeke-Boucher, 1 December 1986.

21 Interview with Hilaire Nkoukou, 22 November 1986.

22 Interview with Madame Walymeya and Madame Adèle, 14 June 1989.

23 Ollandet, 'L'AEF dans la deuxième guerre mondiale', 50–1 and his *Brazzaville, capitale de la France Libre: histoire de la résistance française en Afrique (1940–1941)* (Brazzaville: Editions de la Savane, n.d.), 10, 70–4.

24 See *AEF Nouvelle* (August 1948).

25 Interview with Hilaire Nkoukou, 22 November 1986.

26 Ollandet, *Brazzaville*, 12–50, 90–1 and 'L'AEF dans la deuxième guerre mondiale', 10, 50, 67.

27 Ollandet, *Brazzaville*, 124–7.

28 Interviews with Soeur Clothilde, 10 November 1986; Soeur Scholastique, 13 November 1986.

29 Interview with Madame Walymeya and Madame Adèle, 14 June 1989.

30 Interviews with Antoine Boudzoumou, 16 November 1986; Clement Massengo, 27 October 1986; Ollandet, 'L'AEF dans la deuxième guerre mondiale', 9, and *Brazzaville*, 117–18.

31 Interviews with Clement Massengo, 27 October 1986; Antoine Boudzoumou, 16 November 1986; Hilaire Nkoukou, 22 November 1986.

32 Austen and Headrick, 'Equatorial Africa under colonial rule', 82–6.

33 Frey, 'Brazzaville', 54.

34 *Ibid.*, 52; Waterman, *Juju*, 93.

35 AGPSE, 355BVI, Five-year report of the work of the Catholic mission, Brazzaville, 1950–5.

36 M. Connillière, 'Les problèmes de la main d'oeuvre africaine dans les agglomerations urbaines', *BDAEF*, 169 (1952), 4.

37 Balandier, *Sociologie des Brazzavilles noires*, 40–3.

38 Soret, *Démographie et problèmes urbains*, 27–31; also Vincent, *Femmes*

africaines, 24; Roland Devauges, *Le Chômage à Brazzaville en 1957* (Paris: ORSTOM, 1958), 14.

39 Soret, *Démographie et problèmes urbains*, 42; Vincent, *Femmes africaines*, 24–5; Pierre Vennetier, *Géographie du Congo-Brazzaville* (Paris: Gauthier-Villars, 1966), 69.

40 Joseph-François Reste, *Action économique et sociale en AEF, 1936–1938* (Brazzaville: Imprimerie Officielle, 1938), 57, 167–71; AOM, 63/B41, Commission Guernier, 'AEF: Note sur les reformes politiques et sociales', Brazzaville, 12 July 1936.

41 AGPSE, 277VIA, Annual report of Mgr Guichard, Brazzaville Catholic mission, 1928.

42 Elikia M'Bokolo, 'Forces sociales et idéologies dans la décolonisation de l'AEF', *JAH*, 22, 3 (1981), 397–9; David E. Gardinier, 'The French impact on education in Africa, 1817–1960', in Johnson (ed.), *Double impact*, 333–62.

43 Jean-Michel Wagret, *Histoire et sociologie politiques de la République du Congo (Brazzaville)* (Paris: R. Pichon et R. Durand-Auzias, 1963), 140–1.

44 'Bulletins des communautés: district du Congo', *BCSSJC*, 230 (1948–53), 740–8; and 247 (1953–8), 810–20.

45 Frey, 'Brazzaville', 53.

46 M'Bokolo, 'Forces sociales et idéologies', 398–9.

47 Raymond F. Betts, 'Imperial designs: French colonial architecture and urban planning in sub-Saharan Africa', in Johnson (ed.), *Double impact*, 198.

48 Chalux, (pseud.), *Un an au Congo Belge* (Brussels: Librairie Albert Dewit, 1925), 159; Madelaine Poulaine, *Une blanche chez les noirs* (Paris: J. Tallandier, 1931), 13; Vassal, *Français, Belges et Portugais*, 39–50.

49 Maurice Rondet-Saint, *Sur les routes du Cameroun et de l'AEF* (Paris: Société d'Editions Géographiques, Maritimes et Coloniales, 1933), 147–8; also, speech by Governor-General Antonetti quoted in Frey, 'Brazzaville', 48; Betts, 'Imperial designs', 202.

50 'Brazzaville', *ASSJC*, 9 (1929), 29.

51 Andrée Blouin, *My country, Africa: autobiography of the black pasionaria*, in collaboration with Jean Mackellar (New York: Praeger, 1983), 58–60.

52 Robert Poulaine, *Etapes africaines (voyage autour du Congo)* (Paris: Nouvelle Revue Critique, 1930), 20.

53 Julien Maigret, 'Le rail qui joindra l'Afrique Centrale à la mer: le Brazzaville-Océan', *MCI*, 67 (March 1929), 69; and 'Brazzaville d'hier - Brazzaville d'aujourd'hui', *MCI*, 75 (November 1929), 274–9.

54 ANB, GG104, Report of engineer responsible for development of Brazzaville Gardens, 2 April 1931; Report of Parks and Gardens supervisor, 30 September 1932; AOM, 4(2)D54, Annual report of the Subdivision of Brazzaville, 25 January 1933; *L'Etoile de l'AEF*, 19 December 1936; *Paris-Congo*, 28 August 1936.

55 Scholastique Dianzinga, 'Evolution d'une ville coloniale: Brazzaville de 1884 à 1945', *CCAH*, 12 (1991), 91.

56 ANB, GG105, correspondence of President of *Le Souvenir Colonial Français* with the Governor-General of AEF, 6 December 1921, 11 March 1922, 17 April 1937, 9 December 1938; 'Brazzaville', *BCSSJC*, 215 (August 1948), 938.

57   Emmanuel Dadet, 'Petite histoire du football congolais', *La Semaine Afri-caine*, 22 March 1970; AOM, 5D18, Decree authorizing the establishment of the CAB, 15 March 1926; Reste, *Action économique et sociale*, 199–200; *Paris-Congo*, 24 April 1936.
58   See chapter 7.
59   *L'Etoile de l'AEF*, 31 January 1931; *Paris-Congo*, 28 August 1936; Reste, *Action économique et sociale*, 199–200.
60   Puytorac, *Makambo*, 58–9.
61   Vassal, *Life in French Congo*, 96–7.
62   ANB, GG348, Inspector of Administrative Affairs to the Governor-General, 20 April 1926.
63   AOM, 4(2)D15, Annual report of Moyen-Congo, 1914; 4(2)D59, Report for the second trimester, Autonomous Subdivision of Brazzaville, 30 June 1933; 4(2)D59, Report for the second trimester, Autonomous Subdivision of Brazzaville, 30 June 1934.
64   ANB, GG113, Governor-General to Mayor, 4 February 1928. The reference was to manioc bread.
65   AOM, 4(2)D54, Annual report of the Autonomous Subdivision of Brazza-ville, 25 January 1933; and 4(2)D57, Annual report of the Autonomous Subdivision of Brazzaville, 31 December 1933.
66   AOM, 4(2)D57, Annual report of the Autonomous Subdivision of Brazza-ville, 31 December 1933.
67   ANB, GG104, Commissioner of Police report, Brazzaville, 2 October 1930.
68   ANB, GG104, Police report, Autonomous Subdivision of Brazzaville, 26–27 December 1932.
69   ANB, GG104, Lieutenant-Governor of Moyen-Congo to Mayor of Brazza-ville, 7 January 1933.
70   ANB, GG104, Mayor of Brazzaville to Lieutenant-Governor of Moyen-Congo, 3 and 9 January 1933.
71   See chapter 3.
72   Girard, 'Brazzaville', 38–9.
73   ANB, GG104, Decree of Lieutenant-Governor of Moyen-Congo, 11 July 1931, modifying that of 12 December 1922.
74   AOM, 4(2)D65, Report for the third trimester, 30 September 1934.
75   ANB, GG104, Lieutenant-Governor of Moyen-Congo to Chief Adminis-trator of the Circumscription of the Pool, 16 July 1931.
76   Jean-Pierre Banzouzi, 'La représentation de l'histoire du Congo à travers les noms des rues de Brazzaville', in *Journées d'étude sur Brazzaville: actes du colloque, Brazzaville, 25–28 avril 1986* (Brazzaville: Mission Française de Coopération et d'Action Culturelle, 1987), 83–4; also Balandier *Sociologie des Brazzavilles noires*, 255.
77   Bouteillier, *Douze mois sous l'équateur*, 29–33, 53, 78.
78   Puytorac, *Makambo*, 71–3. The 'market of dogs', so called because of the number of animals roaming around it, was a Poto-Poto landmark until recently, when it was destroyed to make way for new constructions.
79   *CARA de Brazzaville: album souvenir, 1951–1982* (Brazzaville: Gamma/ Athène, 1982), 6. The acronym stands for *Club Athlètique Renaissance*

Aiglons, or, 'the Athletic Club of the Rising Eagles'. See more about football beginnings in chapter 4.

80 Interview with Bernard Mambeke-Boucher, 1 December 1986; ASMF, Privata Dagböcker, no. 4, Diary of Petrus Petterson-Temdahls, 14 August 1932.

81 Dadet, 'La petite histoire du football Congolais', 29 March 1970.

82 ANB, GG363(2), letter from team captains to the Governor-General, 13 May 1936; Dadet, 'La petite histoire du football congolais', 29 March 1970.

83 'Rapport du térritoire de Moyen-Congo', first semester 1933, quoted in Balandier, *Sociologie des Brazzavilles noires*, 24.

84 AGPSE, 355BVI, Five-year report of the Brazzaville mission, 1950–5; 278AIII, Report on parish activities, Brazzaville Mission, 1953; 516AVIII, Mission of Sainte-Marie d'Ouenze, 1953; Vennetier, 'Un quartier suburbain de Brazzaville', 91–3; *Brazzaville: coeur de la nation congolais*, 13, 1969; Maurice Jeannin, 'Un quartier récent de Brazzaville: Makélékélé, ses activités économiques traditionnelles', thèse de 3e cycle, University of Bordeaux, 1969–70, 27–30.

85 Vincent, *Femmes africaines*, 13.

86 AOM, AP2150/3, Minutes of Cabinet of the High Commissioner of AEF, March 1950; ANB, GG121, Notes on the housing situation in AEF, Office of Political Affairs, AEF, March 1950; GG22, Report on social services, Brazzaville, November 1949; Gallin-Douathe, 'Nouveau Bacongo donne libre cours à un malaise', *Liaison*, 10 (April 1951), 14.

87 AP2302/1, Inspection Ruffel, Report of M. Zoccolat on the urbanization of Brazzaville, 2 June 1948.

88 *Service de l'Information*, Office of the Governor-General, Brazzaville, 26 November 1949.

89 SDAM, Report of the Mayor, n.d., *c*. 1954.

90 'Les habitants de la Corniche de Bacongo protestent', *La Semaine*, 20 November 1954.

91 *AEF Nouvelle* (November 1948).

92 Frey, 'Brazzaville', 54.

93 Interview with Papa Moustapha, 15 June 1989.

94 Interview with Madame Walymeya and Madame Adèle, 14 June 1989.

95 AOM, AP2150/3, Reply of the High Commissioner for AEF to report by the Ruffel Mission of Inspection, 1 December 1948.

96 Soret, *Démographie et problèmes urbains*, 46.

97 For example, Girard, 'Brazzaville', 38–9; AOM, AE96, Governor-General Reste to Mayor of Brazzaville, 13 March 1937.

98 'Afrique Equatoriale Française: pour le sport à Brazzaville,' *Le Courrier d'Afrique*, 21 May 1937.

99 AOM, AE96, Governor-General to Mayor of Brazzaville, 13 March 1937.

100 A. Kranitz, 'Brazzaville: les missions du Bas-Congo', *APSE* (February 1931), 53.

101 ANB, GG458(2), Chief of Civil Affairs, Moyen-Congo, to Governor-General, 9 February 1934.

102 AOM, 4(2)D59, Report for the second trimester, 1933; and 4(2)D54, Annual report of Autonomous Subdivision of Brazzaville, 25 January 1933.

103 ANB, GG104, Commissioner of Police to Mayor of Brazzaville, 11 February 1932.

104 Sinda, *Le messianisme congolais*, 160ff.
105 Antoine Marie Aïssi, 'Le tournant des années 30: les blancs du Congo face à l'éveil politique congolais', *CCAH*, 7 (1982), 39–50. Also AOM, 5D88, Statement of Mayor of Brazzaville on incidents in Brazzaville, 2 and 3 April 1930.
106 AOM, 5D88, Commissioner of Police report, April 1930.
107 For a discussion of rural-to-urban migration and the effects of the Depression on urban populations around the Pool, see Gondola, 'Migrations et villes congolaises'.
108 Massengo, 'Connaissez-vous les Lari?', 33–4; Sautter, *De l'Atlantique au fleuve Congo* vol. I, 384; Vansina, *The Tio kingdom*, 10–11, 303, 304 fn 42; Bertil Söderberg, *Les instruments de musique au Bas-Congo et dans les régions avoisinantes* (Uppsala: L'Institut Scandinave d'Etudes africaines, 1978), 21–2. The "r" and the "l" are interchangeable in Bantu languages.
109 Placide N'zala-Backa, *Le tipoye doré* (Brazzaville: Imprimerie Nationale, 1968), 90.
110 Balandier, *Sociologie des Brazzavilles noires*, 22.
111 AOM, 4(2)D54, Annual report of the Autonomous Subdivision of Brazzaville, 1932; AGPSE, 516AII, 'Journées d'études', 17 April 1951.
112 Balandier, *Sociologie des Brazzaville noires*, 22; AGPSE, 516AVIII, 'Petite histoire de la mission Sainte-Marie d'Ouenze', 1952.
113 *Plan Havas de Brazzaville* (Brazzaville: L'Imprimerie Centrale d'Afrique, 1953).

3   THE EMERGENCE OF LEISURE

1   Jean and John Comaroff, *Of revelation and revolution: Christianity, colonialism and consciousness in South Africa*, (Chicago: Chicago University Press, 1991), 12; also T. O. Beidelman, *Colonial evangelism: a socio-historical study of an East African mission at the grassroots* (Bloomington: Indiana University Press, 1982), 3–6.
2   AOM, 4(2)D13, Annual report of Moyen-Congo, 1913.
3   Théophile Obenga, 'Temps et astronomie chez les Mbochi de l'Alima', *CCAH*, 7 (1982), 11–15; Dominique Ngoïe-Ngalla, 'Temporalité et vision de l'histoire chez les Négro-Africains: le cas des Kongo', *La Semaine Africaine*, 15–21 November 1979, and 22–28 November 1979; Ndinga-Mbo, *Introduction à l'histoire des migrations au Congo*, 26–9; Mpey-Nka Ngub'usim and Bidum Kuyunsa, 'Gestion du temps et organisation traditionnelle du travail: la semaine traditionnelle chez les Yansi et quelques autres tribus du Zaïre', *Zaïre-Afrique*, 231–2 (January-February 1989), 16, 18; Karl Laman, *The Kongo*, (Uppsala: Studia Ethnographica Upsaliensa, no. 16, 1962), vol. IV, 2–8.
4   Obenga, 'Temps et astronomie', 15–18; Ndinga-Mbo, *Introduction à l'histoire des migrations au Congo*, 29–30; Maurice Briault, *Dans la forêt du Gabon* (Paris: Bernard Grasset, 1930), 112–13; John H. Weeks, *Among the primitive Bakongo* (New York: Negro Universities Press, repr. 1969), 198–9; interviews with Antoine Kébadio, 4 October 1986; Bernard Mambeke-Boucher, 20 November 1986.

5   Laman, *The Kongo*, vol. IV, 8.

6   See sources in n 3.

7   Weber, 'Work suspended', 3–4.

8   Interviews with Veronique Mbemba, 15 January 1987; Marie-Paula Samba, 13 January 1987; Bernard Mambeke-Boucher, 20 November 1986.

9   Ngub'usim and Kuyunsa, 'Gestion du temps', 15–16; Vansina, *The Tio kingdom*, 162, 167.

10   Vansina, *The Tio kingdom*, 160, 162.

11   Interviews with Marie-Paula Samba, 13 January 1987; Veronique Mbemba, 15 January 1987.

12   Wrist-watches which were mass produced in the 1860s were considered effeminate in Europe and the United States in the early part of the century, and were only widely worn by men after the First World War, when soldiers found it more convenient to carry time on their wrists. See John Boslough, 'The enigma of time', *National Geographic*, 177, 3 (March 1990), 115. On catalogue ordering, see Raymond Vacquier, *Au temps des factories, 1900–1950* (Paris: Karthala, 1986), 101–3.

13   Dolisie to Minister of Colonies, Libreville, 17 February 1895, published in Rabut, *Brazza*, 394.

14   William Samarin, *The black man's burden: African colonial labor on the Congo and Ubangi rivers, 1880–1900* (Boulder: Westview Press, 1989), 25–7.

15   Weeks, *Among the primitive Bakongo*, 308–9.

16   Brazza to Manas, Lékéti, 8 October 1887, in Rabut, *Brazza*, 364; also Coquery-Vidrovitch, *Le Congo*, 91, 94.

17   Bouteillier, *Douze mois sous l'équateur*, 35–41; Coquery-Vidrovitch, *Le Congo*, 91.

18   Dolisie to Minister of Colonies, Libreville, 17 February 1895, published in Rabut, *Brazza*, 394; Chavannes, *Avec Brazza*, 192, 221, 233–4; Uzès, *Le voyage de mon fils*, 85; Bouteillier, *Douze mois sous l'équateur*, 39–41, 49; Mandat-Grancey, *Au Congo*, 216–17; Challaye, *Le Congo Français*, 25.

19   Veistroffer, *Vingt ans*, 39, 161.

20   AOM, 1st series, TP152, Mission Fillon, Report of M. Henri on the Brazzaville workforce, 5 May 1913.

21   'Communauté de Saint-Joseph de Linzolo', *BCPSE*, 13 (1883–6), 934.

22   'Saint-Hippolyte de Brazzaville: Congo Français', *AA*, 38 (April 1895), 47; Père Zimmermann, *Mémoire d'un congolais, 1896–1941* (Madingou: Imprimerie de la Mission, 1941), 9; Baron Jehan De Witte, *Monseigneur Augouard: sa vie, ses notes de voyage et sa correspondance* (Paris: Emile-Paul Frères, 1924), 4; Frey, 'Brazzaville', 62; personal communication Père Bernard Noël, 10 June 1986.

23   Grillot, 'Dans le Haut-Congo Français', 141.

24   AGPSE, 6/B/1V, 'Mémoire sur les missions des noirs en général et sur celle de la Guinée en particulier, présentée par l'Abbé Libermann Supérieur des Missionaires du Saint Coeur de Marie', 1846, 11.

25   Père Carrie, *Coutumier de l'oeuvre des enfants dans le vicariat apostolique du Congo Français* (Loango: Imprimerie de la Mission, 1890), 4; Carrie to Brazza, Loango, 25 January 1888, published in Rabut, *Brazza*, 149–50.

26 P. Carrie, 'Règlements des écoles primaires dans les missions', in his *Coutumier de l'oeuvre des enfants*, 74–5.

27 Josef Pieper, *Leisure: the basis of culture* (New York: Pantheon Books, 1957), quoted in Rybczynski, *Waiting for the weekend*, 75.

28 Carrie, 'Règlements des écoles primaires', 30–5.

29 The Catholic missionary journals and the Brazzaville mission reports describe these events in detail.

30 Bouteillier, *Douze mois sous l'équateur*, 29–30.

31 ANB, GG258, Decisions by the Moyen-Congo administration on African employees, 4 December 1933, 15 May, 1 and 24 September 1934.

32 Girard, 'Brazzaville', 38.

33 AOM, 5D118, Monseigneur Biéchy to Governor-General, 17 November 1941.

34 Efraim Andersson, *Churches at the grass-roots: a study in Congo-Brazzaville* (London: Lutterworth Press, 1968), 72–3, 177–9; interviews with Veronique Mbemba, 15 January 1987; Maya Alden, 10 December 1986.

35 AOM, AE96, Governor-General to Mayor of Brazzaville, 13 March 1937.

36 ANB, GG479(1), Attendance lists, adult education classes, Urban School, March 1913; Director of Political Affairs to Director of Health Services, 5 June 1913; Mayor of Brazzaville to Lieutenant-Governor, 6 June 1913; Lieutenant-Governor to Governor-General, 14 March 1913; Military Commander to Governor-General, 14 March 1913; Principal's report, Urban School, 31 March 1914.

37 Atkins, '"Kafir Time"', 229–44.

38 Andersson, *Churches at the grass-roots*, 72.

39 SMF, F.1, Dagbök, Brazzaville, 6 April and 3 May 1913; AOM, 1st series, TP152, Report of M. Henri on the Brazzaville workforce to Inspector Fillon, 7 May 1913.

40 ANB, GG481, Principal of the Urban School to Lieutenant-Governor of Moyen-Congo, 31 December 1913; interview with Soeur Clothilde, 10 November 1986.

41 ANB, GG481, Principal of Urban School to Lieutenant-Governor of Moyen-Congo, 31 December 1913.

42 ASMF, E.14, Anvill to SMF, 28 June 1914.

43 ANB, GG481, 'Situation des écoles,' Lieutenant-Governor of Moyen-Congo to Governor-General, Report for the third trimester, 1915; Report on the Urban School, 1917.

44 ANB, GG479(3), Governor-General to Lieutenant-Governor of Gabon, 19 December 1921; Lieutenant-Governor of Chad to Governor-General, 2 February 1922; Lieutenant-Governor of Ubangi-Shari to Governor-General, 16 April 1922; and GG484(1), Lieutenant-Governor of Chad to Director of Political Affairs, AEF, 31 March 1933.

45 ANB, GG481, Report of the Urban School, 31 March 1914.

46 'Brazzaville', *BCSSJC*, 128 (December 1917), 481.

47 *Le Bon Message*, second year, 1 January 1934.

48 Interviews with Bernard Mambeke-Boucher, 20 November 1986; Father Schaub, 15 October 1986. See chapter 5 on Sunday afternoon dancing.

49 Pierre Vennetier, 'Banlieue noire de Brazzaville: la vie rurale et les rapports

entre la ville et la campagne à Bacongo', *Les Cahiers d'Outre-Mer*, 38 (April–June 1957), 146.

50 AOM, 4(2)65, Report for the third trimester, Autonomous Subdivision of Brazzaville, 1934; also see Gondola, 'Migrations et villes congolaises', 93.

51 N'Zala-Backa, *Le tipoye doré*, 90; Vassal, *Life in French Congo*, 42–3.

52 Vassal, *Life in French Congo*, 44.

53 Eugène Guernier, *Afrique Equatoriale Française* (Paris: Encyclopédie Coloniale et Maritime, 1950), 184; *La Semaine*, 13 February 1954.

54 ANB, GG121, Daily report, Mayor's office, Brazzaville, 13 November 1950.

55 ANB, GG282, Union of printing workers of AEF to Governor-General, 23 October 1947; Inspector of Labour for AEF to Governor-General, 18 November 1947.

56 ANB, GG282, 'Note on the single period work day', Director of Personnel for AEF to Governor-General, 21 August 1947.

57 Martin, 'National holidays transformed'.

58 Sinda, *Le messianisme congolais*, 188–9; AOM, 4(2)D55, Report for the second trimester, Autonomous Subdivision of Brazzaville, 1932 and 1936.

59 Hugh Cunningham, *Leisure in the industrial revolution* (London: Croom Helm, 1980), 13.

60 William B. Cohen, *The French encounter with Africans: white response to blacks, 1530–1880* (Bloomington: Indiana University Press, 1980), xviii–xix, 210–82.

61 See chapter 7.

62 Félix Eboué, *La nouvelle politique indigène en l'Afrique Equatoriale Française* (Brazzaville: Afrique Française Libre, 1941), 32.

63 AOM, AP3123, Report of Inspector Frézouls to the Minister of Colonies, 14 April 1911.

64 *JO*, 1926, 423, quoted in Aïssi, 'La "justice indigène"', 182.

65 P. L. Tchibamba, 'Pour mettre fin au règne des "Mboulou-Mboulou"', *Liaison*, 38 (August 1953), 3–5.

66 AOM, 4(2)D2, Annual report of Moyen-Congo, 1908.

67 AOM, 4(2)D3, Reports for the first and second trimesters, Moyen-Congo, 1909.

68 The most comprehensive discussion of the *indigénat* and other legislation on issues such as 'vagrancy' and labour regulations is that of Aïssi, 'La "Justice Indigène"'.

69 Attempts to obtain a consistent picture of what people read were unsuccessful. Informants said that they simply read whatever came their way, which confirms Georges Balandier's discussion in *Ambiguous Africa: cultures in collision* (New York: Pantheon Books, 1966), 188–9. Both missions had printing presses, and religious literature was the reading most readily available to literate Africans perhaps as late as the Second World War. See Andersson, *Churches at the grass-roots*, 79–80; Westlind, *Société de la mission suédoise au Congo*, 50–1.

70 Augouard, *Quarante-quatre années au Congo*, 187.

71 R. Piacentini, *Maboni: le Père J. Bonnefont de la Congrégation du Saint-Esprit* (Issy-les-Moulineaux: Presses Missionaires, 1951), 55.

72 ANB, GG484, Annual Report on the Urban School, 1931–2.

73 ANB, GG675, Administrator of Ouaka Conscription to Lieutenant-Governor of Ubangi-Shari, 24 May 1932.

74 ANB, GG675, Minister of Colonies to President of the Republic, Paris, 1932; Minister of Colonies to Governor-General of AEF, 17 March 1934.

75 ANB, GG675, Minister of Colonies to Governor-General, March 1934.

76 *Ibid.*

77 ANB, GG675, Minutes of the Film Board, November 1934.

78 ANB, GG675, Governor-General to Mayor of Brazzaville, Brazzaville, 20 May, 10 September 1938 and 28 April 1939; Minister of Colonies to Governor-General of AEF, Paris, 24 March 1939.

79 ANB, GG675, Director of Intercolonial Service of Information and Documentation to Governor-General of AEF, Paris, 30 May 1940.

80 ANB, IGE123, Various correspondence on films, 1945–56; GG681(1) and GG681(2), Various files on films received and equipment purchased for Bacongo and Poto-Poto cultural centres and for schools; GG22, Director of Film Agency of Overseas France to Cinematographic Service of AEF, 18 December 1950.

81 'Réalisation de films éducatifs pour les Africains', *Courrier d'Afrique*, 12 October 1951.

82 Pierre Eticault, 'La danse et le cinéma, poisons de notre jeunesse', *La Semaine*, 13 December 1959; also Jacques Okoko, 'L'enfant noir et le cinéma', *La Semaine*, 19 October 1958 and 2 November 1958; interview with Maya Alden, 7 November 1986.

83 'Les missions et le cinéma', *La Semaine*, 19 April 1953.

84 AGPSE, 527AIII, Monseigneur Biéchy to Governor-General, Brazzaville, 12 December 1947.

85 AGPSE, 527AIII, Governor-General to Monseigneur Biéchy, 22 December 1947 and 29 January 1948.

86 Okoko, 'L'enfant noir et le cinéma'.

87 Frey, 'Brazzaville', 53.

88 Max Turmann, *Au sortir de l'école: les patronages* (Paris: V. Lecoffre, 1909, 5th edn), 187–218.

89 J. Remy, 'Congo Français: une procession à Brazzaville', *AA*, (September 1912), 229; 'Mission de l'Oubangui: aperçu générale', *BCPSE*, 21 (1901–2), 658–60, 666; 'Brazzaville', *BCPSE*, 28 (1914–18), 157.

90 The club was named after a patron saint, as was the custom in France. Activities are mentioned in the Brazzaville mission journal and more fully reported in the *Bulletin* of the Holy Ghost Fathers. See AGPSE, B706, Brazzaville Mission Journal, 27 October 1907, 19 November 1913, 25 December 1913, 27 December 1914, and elsewhere. Also AGPSE 183BIII, Reports of Mgr Augouard to Propagation de la Foi, 25 October, 25 December 1913, 1 January 1920; 'Brazzaville', *BCPSE*, 28 (1914–18), 157–8; Augouard, *Quarante-quatre années au Congo*, 54–5.

91 'Brazzaville', *BCPSE*, 27 (1913–14), 58–60; Augouard, *Quarante-quatre années au Congo*, 54–5, 122–3.

92 'Inauguration d'un patronage,' *Le Petit Courrier Colonial*, 17 February 1913, also 10 February 1913.

93 'Brazzaville', *BCPSE*, 28 (1914–18), 157–8.

94 AGPSE, 516AVIII, Extract from a report by an Inspector of Administrative Affairs, Brazzaville, 1925.

95 John R. Gillis, *Youth and history: tradition and change in European age relations, 1779–present* (New York: Academic Press, 1974), 95–184; Ted W. Margadant, 'Primary schools and youth groups in pre-war Paris: les "Petites A's"', *Journal of Contemporary History*, 13, 2 (1978), 323–36.

96 Aline Coutrot, 'Youth movements in France in the 1930s', *Journal of Contemporary History*, 5, 1 (1970), 23–36.

97 AOM, AE96, Governor-General to Mayor of Brazzaville, 13 March 1937.

98 ANB, GG141, Speech of Governor-General Reste, May 1939.

99 AOM, AP662, Minister of Colonies to Governor-General Reste, January 1936.

100 For more on African football, see chapter 4. The article cited was 'Afrique Equatoriale Française: pour le sport à Brazzaville', *Courrier d'Afrique*, 21 May 1937. The writer is identified as 'L.T.'

101 AGPSE, 527AV, Report of Mgr Biéchy, 29 June 1942; 227AVII, Report from the Brazzaville mission, July 1944.

102 See chapter 4.

103 AOM, 5D159, 'La 1ère Brazzaville des Scouts de France' by Father le Bail, Brazzaville, 1 May 1936.

104 AGPSE, 277VIIA, Annual report of Brazzaville mission, Father le Duc, 25 September 1932.

105 AGPSE, 527AIV, 'Le Scoutisme en AEF'; and, AOM, 5D159, 'La 1ère Brazzaville des Scouts de France'.

106 AOM, 5D159, 'La 1ère Brazzaville Scouts de France'.

107 AOM, 5D159, 'Note sur le Scoutisme en Afrique Equatoriale Française', by J. Benilan, Brazzaville, 1 May 1936; J. Benilan to the Director of Political Affairs, 31 July 1936.

108 AGPSE, 277AVII, Report on the work with children, Brazzaville, 1 November 1941; 'Bulletins des Communautés: District du Congo Français', *BCSSJC*, 215 (August 1948), 935.

109 Interviews with Clement Massengo, 24 November 1986; Bernard Mambeke-Boucher, 20 November 1986. For the significance of clothing see, Phyllis M. Martin, 'Contesting clothes in colonial Brazzaville,' *JAH*, 35, 3 (1994), 401–26; also chapter 6.

110 Maurice Briault, 'Quelques jours à Brazzaville', *APSE* (June 1933), 192.

111 ANB, IGE144(1), Report from the Department of Youth, Sport and School Hygiene, 1952–3.

112 AGPSE, 516AII, 'Extraits de la journée d'études, 17 avril 1951: le nouveau vicariat de Brazzaville'.

113 AGPSE, 527AIV, Report on Scouting, 28 May 1945, and 'Le Scoutisme en AEF'; 'Les évolués et nous', *La Semaine*, 18 July 1953.

114 AOM, 4(2)D55, Report for the first and second trimesters, Autonomous Subdivision of Brazzaville, 1932.

115 AGPSE, 277AVII, Annual report, Brazzaville mission, 8 September 1935; Five-year report, Brazzaville mission, 11 April 1940; AOM, 5D159, 'Associations diverses', Director of Political and Social Affairs of AEF.

116 Cohen, *Rulers of Empire*, 138; David E. Gardinier, *Historical dictionary of*

Gabon (Metuchen, N.J.: The Scarecrow Press, 1981), 31–5, 183–4; Weinstein, *Eboué*, 275–8.

117 René-Paul Sousatte, 'Le programme d'action de l'Union Educative et Mutuelle de la Jeunesse de Brazzaville', 'Comptes-rendus divers', and 'Rapport annuel', *L'Education de la Jeunesse Africaine*, various numbers for 1942–4.

118 *Service d'Information*, Brazzaville, 19 November 1949.

119 See chapters 4–7.

120 ANB, GG22, decree no. 655, 19 November 1943; Governor-General to Governor of Moyen-Congo, 2 December 1946; IGE, 151, 'Enseignement, AEF, 1950'.

121 ANB, GG682, Governor-General to governors of AEF territories, 10 September 1949; GG121, G. Eckomband, Vice-President of Poto-Poto cultural centre to Governor of Moyen-Congo, 1951.

122 ANB, GG121, Budget for Bacongo cultural centre, 10 August 1950.

123 AOM, AP2150/3, Governor-General to Director of Political Affairs, 1 December 1948; 'Programme of social and cultural action', May 1949; ANB, IGE151, 'Enseignement, AEF, 1950'.

124 AOM, 5D159, membership application form.

125 AOM, 5D159, 'Elite Africaine de Brazzaville votre Cercle est né', 13 November 1948; 'Liste des membres du Cercle Culturel et d'Action sociale de Brazzaville (Section de Bacongo)'.

126 See the comments of Balandier, *Sociologie des Brazzavilles noires*, 166–7.

127 See chapter 5.

128 AOM, 5D159, Captain Fall to President of Poto-Poto cultural centre.

129 See Jean-Marie Mignon, *Afrique: jeunesses uniques, jeunesse encadrée* (Paris: L'Harmattan, 1984); and Hélène d'Almeida-Topor and Odile Goerg (eds.), *Le mouvement associatif des jeunes en Afrique noire francophone au XXè siècle* (Paris: L'Harmattan, 1989). For Congo, in the latter book, see Joseph Gamandzori, 'Le mouvement associatif des jeunes dans la dynamique sociale au Congo, 1945–1973', 69–90. Also, see articles on Congo in the collection of essays from a 1990 conference on African youth at the University of Paris, Hélène d'Almeida-Topor et al. (eds.), *Les jeunes en Afrique* (Paris: L'Harmattan, 1992, 2 vols).

130 AGPSE, 227VIIA, 'Oeuvres de Saint-Enfance', Mgr Guichard, 20 September 1931.

131 AGPSE, 277VIIA, 'Oeuvres de Saint-Enfance', Report of Mgr Biéchy, 1 September 1937.

132 M. Briault, 'Quelques jours à Brazzaville', *APSE* (June 1933), 192.

4 FOOTBALL IS KING

1 Interview with Fulbert Kimina-Makumbu, Brazzaville, 10 October 1986.

2 Jean-Claude Ganga, *Combats pour un sport africain* (Paris: L'Harmattan, 1979), 81.

3 Interview with Clement Massengo, 27 October 1986.

4 *CARA de Brazzaville*, 6.

5 *Ibid.*, 7.

6 On the role of British missionaries in spreading Western sport, see, James A. Mangan, 'Ethics and ethnocentricity: imperial education in British tropical Africa', in Baker and Mangan (eds.), *Sport in Africa*, 138–171.

7 Richard Holt, *Sport and society in modern France* (London: Macmillan, 1981), 11, 48–9, 62, 190–1; Eugen Weber, 'Gymnastics and sport in *fin-de-siècle* France: opium of the classes?', *AHR*, 76, 1 (February 1971), 70–98.

8 ANB, GG479(1), Ecole Urbaine, Année Scolaire, 1913–14, timetable.

9 W. Sjöholm and J. E. Lundahl (eds.), *Dagbräckning i Kongo* (Stockholm: Svenska Missionsförbundets Kongomissions, 1911), 237; interview with Hilaire Nkoukou, 22 November 1986.

10 'L'oeuvre des enfants de Brazzaville,' letter from F. Hervé Gaonach, *APSE*, (June 1928), 171; Augouard, *Quarante-quatre années au Congo*, 97; Maurice Rondet-Saint, *Dans notre empire noir* (Paris: Société d'Editions Géographiques, Maritimes et Coloniales, 1929), 105; Dadet, 'La petite histoire du football congolais', *La Semaine Africaine*, 22 March 1970. This account of Brazzaville football by a pioneer of African sport in the 1920s was serialized in *La Semaine* in five issues. The name of the newspaper will not be included in future citations, only the publication date.

11 Tim Couzens, 'Introduction to the history of football in South Africa', in Bozzoli (ed.), *Town and countryside in the Transvaal*, 198–214; Janet Lever, *Soccer madness* (Chicago: University of Chicago Press, 1983), 39–41.

12 Dadet, 'La petite histoire du football congolais,' 22 March 1970. *Gobi* was the name that Africans gave to French NCOs in the colonial army. See Anthony Clayton, *France, soldiers and Africa* (London: Brassey's, 1988), 351.

13 ASMF, F.1, Dagböck, Brazzaville, 12 December 1915; AGPSE, B706, Brazzaville Mission Journal, 12 February 1914; *JO*, 15 June 1914.

14 Dadet, 'Petite histoire du football congolais', 22 March 1970; interview with Fulbert Kimina-Makumbu, 10 October 1986; AOM, 5D18, Decree authorizing the establishment of the CAB, 15 March 1926.

15 Théophile Muka, *Evolution du sport au Congo* (Kinshasa: Editions Okapi, 1970), 19–27; Eugène Luboya, *Sports, loisirs en RDC et dans le monde* (Kinshasa: Editions Okapi, 1970), 3.

16 ANB, GG363(2), Ex-team captains to Governor-General, 13 May 1936; also interview with Bernard Mambeke-Boucher, Brazzaville, 1 December 1986.

17 An excellent survey of the history of sport is William J. Baker, *Sports in the western world* (Totowa, N.J.: Rowman & Littlefield, 1982).

18 John Blacking, 'Games and sport in pre-colonial African societies', in Baker and Mangan (eds.), *Sport in Africa*, 3–21.

19 Félix Eboué, 'Le sport en Afrique Equatoriale', *MCI*, 103 (March 1932), 60–1; Weinstein, *Eboué*, 47–8.

20 Emmanuel Dadet, 'Une lutte traditionnelle congolaise,' *La Semaine*, 2 April 1955.

21 Achôt Melik-Chakhnazarov, *Le sport en Afrique* (Paris: Présence Africaine, 1970), 11.

22 Laman, *The Kongo*, vol. I, 67–8; vol. II, 20. On wrestling throughout this area, see Muka, *Evolution du sport au Congo*, 17–18; Bentley, *Pioneering*, vol.

II, 289–92; E. Darré, 'La tribu Bondjo', *BSRC*, 3 (1923), 69–70; Sigrid Paul, 'The wrestling tradition and its social function', in Baker and Mangan (eds.), *Sport in Africa*, 31–2, 36–42.

23 Vansina, *The Tio kingdom*, 164; Weeks, *Among the primitive Bakongo*, 121; W. Holman Bentley, *Dictionary and grammar of the Kongo language* (London: Baptist Missionary Society, 1887), 492–3.

24 Laman, *The Kongo*, vol. I, 11.

25 Vansina, *The Tio kingdom*, 164; Darré, 'La tribu Bondjo', 70; Weeks, *Among the primitive Bakongo*, 127–8; Blacking, 'Games and sport in pre-colonial African societies', 7–8, 15–16.

26 Sylvère Tsamas, 'Le kyébé-kyébé', *Liaison*, 59 (September–October 1957), 63–4.

27 See discussion later in this chapter.

28 Interview with Bernard Mambeke-Boucher, 1 December 1986; Rondet-Saint, *Sur les routes*, 148; ASMF, Privata Dagböcker, no. 4, Diary of Petrus Petterson-Temdahls, 14 August 1932.

29 Ganga, *Combats pour un sport africain*, 32–54.

30 ANB, GG363(2), Ex-team captains to the Governor-General, Brazzaville, 13 May 1936; Dadet, 'La petite histoire du football congolais', 22 and 29 March 1970; interview with Fulbert Kimina–Makumbu, 10 and 16 October 1986.

31 ANB, GG363(2), Ex-team captains to Governor-General, 13 May 1936.

32 *L'Etoile*, 24 January 1931; AGPSE, 516AIII, Report on Vicariat Apostolique of Brazzaville, Mgr Biéchy, 1934.

33 AOM, 5D88, Procureur-Général Sanner to the Governor-General, 8 April 1930; Aïssi, 'Le tournant des années 30', 39–50.

34 *L'Etoile de l'AEF*, 24 January 1930.

35 AOM, 5D18, Lieutenant-Governor of Moyen-Congo to Governor-General, 23 March 1932.

36 AOM, 5D18, Governor-General to Lieutenant-Governor of Moyen-Congo, 7 June 1932.

37 Holt, *Sport and society in Modern France*, 190–211; Coutrot, 'Youth movements in France in the 1930s', 23–36.

38 ANB, GG484(1), AEF, Report on schools, 1931–2.

39 Cohen, *Rulers of empire*, 105–7; Holt, *Sport and society in modern France*, 193–4.

40 ANB, GG363(2), Ex-team captains to Governor-General, 13 May 1936; Dadet, 'La petite histoire du football congolais', 29 March 1970; AOM, 5D18, Jean Mouly to Lieutenant-Governor of Moyen-Congo, 17 February 1932; *JO*, 1 August 1931, Report on request for a Federation des Sociétés Indigènes de Sports.

41 *JO*, 1 August 1931.

42 AGPSE, 277IVA, 'Oeuvres de la Sainte-Enfance', Mgr Guichard report, 20 September 1931.

43 *Le Bon Message*, 1 and 2 (1933).

44 *JO*, 25 November 1931, Decree of the Lieutenant-Governor of Moyen-Congo.

45 AOM, 5D18, Lieutenant-Governor of Moyen-Congo to Jean Mouly, 26

January 1932; Mouly to Lieutenant-Governor, 17 February 1932; Lieutenant-Governor to Governor-General, 23 March 1932; Governor-General to Lieutenant-Governor, 7 June 1932.

46 Interviews with Bernard Mambeke-Boucher, Brazzaville, 1 December 1986; Fulbert Kimina-Mukumbu, Brazzaville, 10 October 1986; Dadet, 'La petite histoire du football congolais', 29 March 1970.

47 ANB, GG363(2), Minutes of the Executive Committee of the Native Sports Federation, 21 March 1936; Dadet, 'La petite histoire du football congolais', 29 March 1970.

48 Joseph Gabio, *La fabuleuse histoire des Diables Rouges* (Brazzaville: Editions BDT, 1983), 2; Dadet, 'La petite histoire du football congolais', 12 April and 31 May 1970.

49 *Paris-Congo*, 13 March 1936 and 6 May 1937; ANB, GG363(2), Minutes of the Executive Committee of the Native Sports Federation, 21 March 1936; Dadet, 'La petite histoire du football congolais', 19 April 1970.

50 AOM, 5D18, Lieutenant-Governor of Moyen-Congo, Department of Civil Affairs, to Governor-General, 26 May 1934; Dadet, 'La petite histoire du football congolais', 31 May 1970.

51 Dadet, 'La petite histoire du football congolais,' 31 May 1970.

52 AOM, 5D18, Report to the Governor-General on the Native Sports Federation, April 1934; *L'Etoile de l'AEF*, 25 January 1935; ANB, GG363(2), Ex-team captains to Governor-General, 13 May 1936; Dadet, 'La petite histoire du football congolais', 31 May 1970.

53 *Le Bon Message*, 5 (May 1934). See also 10 (October 1935); 12 (December 1938).

54 Interview with Soeur Scholastique, Brazzaville, 13 November 1986; AOM, 5D18, Capt. Daudet to Governor-General, 11 April 1934.

55 AOM, 5D18, Report for the Governor-General on the Native Sports Federation, Capt. Daudet, April 1934.

56 AOM, 5D18, Dr G. Saleun, President of the CAB, to Governor-General, 23 June 1938; Governor-General to Dr Saleun, 12 August 1938.

57 Rita Headrick has argued that the health of those who lived under French rule in Equatorial Africa actually deteriorated under colonialism: see Headrick, 'The impact of colonialism on health'.

58 ANB, GG363(2), Minutes of the Executive Committee of the Native Sports Federation, 21 March 1936.

59 See chapter 6.

60 ANB, GG363(2), Ex-team captains to Governor-General, Brazzaville, 13 May 1936. The letter is signed by Louis Ebene, captain of *L'Etoile*, a mechanic, living in Poto-Poto; Henri Kabessa, captain of *Renaissance*, unemployed, living in Poto-Poto; Maurice M'Bouyou, captain of the *Coqs d'AEF*, employed by the Finance Department, living in Bacongo; and Antoine Mombilou, captain of *Nomades*, employed by the Army Supplies Depot, living in Poto-Poto. According to Bernard Mambeke-Boucher, who was seventeen at the time and playing for the *Ecole Edouard Rénard*, Ebene and Kabessa were from the Belgian Congo, and Kabessa was also famous as a middle-weight boxing champion. M'Bouyou was from the Loango region. Mombilou was a clerk whose father had come from Belgian Congo to settle

in Brazzaville at the end of the nineteenth century (interview with Bernard Mambeke-Boucher, 1 December 1986).

61 ANB, GG363(2), Ex-team captains to Governor-General, 13 May 1936.

62 ANB, GG363(2), 'Elements of a reply by President Benilan of the Native Sports Federation', sent to Director of the Cabinet and Director of Political Affairs, Brazzaville, 19 June 1936.

63 ANB, GG363(2), Governor-General to Mayor of Brazzaville, July 1936.

64 AOM, 5D18, President of CAB to Governor-General, 18 January 1938; Decree of Governor-General, 12 August 1938.

65 Interview with Bernard Mambeke-Boucher, Brazzaville, 1 December 1986. This point has been confirmed by other African football players.

66 A. Boizieau, 'Les fêtes en l'honneur de l'arrivée de Mgr Biéchy', *APSE* (June 1937), 173.

67 AGPSE, 277AVII, Annual Report of Mgr Biéchy, 5 September 1937.

68 Interview with Clement Massengo, 27 October 1986. The significance of clothing in general and shoes in particular in relation to status is discussed in chapter 6.

69 ANB, JS6, 'Rapport à Monsieur l'Administrateur-Maire de Brazzaville à l'occasion d'un incident de Fédération des Sports de l'AEF et la Fédération Athlètique Congolaise', Le Médecin Lt Dr Lieutenant-Colonel Bellocq, n.d., *c.* 1948.

70 The phrase is used by Fulbert Kimina-Makumbu, 'Le sport école d'humanité', special issue, *La Semaine Africaine*, 28 August 1983, to mark the centennial celebrations of the work in Congo of the Holy Ghost Fathers.

71 AGPSE, 277IVA, 'Oeuvres de la Sainte-Enfance, 1945–46'; Kiminu-Makumbu, 'Le sport école d'humanité'.

72 The stadium had been built under joint state and mission sponsorship negotiated under Eboué. Although the Governor-General was a Freemason, he was also a pragmatist who realized that in the midst of the Second World War, the best means of promoting African sport was through the Catholic mission.

73 Interview with Bernard Mambeke-Boucher, 1 December 1986; ANB, IGE144(1), Captain of *Lorraine* to Governor-General, 9 February 1950.

74 ANB, IGE144(1), President of *Renaissance* to Director of Social Services, 15 June 1951; Minutes of the Executive Committee of *Renaissance*, 3 August 1951.

75 ANB, IGE44(1), President of *Renaissance* 'A' to Director of Social Services of AEF, 15 June 1951; Director of Social Services of AEF to Director of Social Services for Brazzaville, 25 June 1951; Director of Brazzaville Social Services to Director of Social Services for AEF, 19 July 1951; Captain of *Renaissance* "A" to President of *Jeunesco*, 18 September 1951; Minutes of the Executive Committee of *Jeunesco*, 22 September 1951.

76 Interview with Bernard Mambeke-Boucher, 1 December 1986.

77 The story of this schism is told in *CARA de Brazzaville*, 5–7. According to this official account, the name CARA came into use in 1963, the inspiration coming from a rumba of that name made famous by the 'OK Jazz'.

78 Interview with Clement Massengo, 27 October 1986.

79 'Un grand champion: Diables Noirs', *La Semaine*, 17 January 1965.

80 *Ibid.*; also *La Semaine*, 29 June 1957.

81 Other tops teams in this period were *Racing*, *Lorraine* (another breakaway team from the FAC organization), *Police*, *Gendarmerie*, *CAB Africain*, *CGTA* and *Daring*.

82 Interviews with Fulbert Kimina-Makumbu, 16 October 1986; Clement Massengo, 27 October 1976; reports in *La Semaine*, 3 March 1953, 4 and 10 March 1954, 19 January 1958.

83 '24e homme' (Sylvain Bemba), 'Un scandale qui doit prendre fin: l'exploitation des joueurs', *La Semaine*, 31 January 1960.

84 *La Semaine*, 7 October 1957; Dr Heraud, 'Le développement sportif en AEF', *Tropiques*, 56th year, 402 (January 1958), 22; Gabio, *La fabuleuse histoire des Diables Rouges*, 4.

85 AOM, 5D18, Captain Daudet to Governor-General, 11 April 1934.

86 ANB, JS7, Minutes of a meeting of the Federal Committee on Sport (AEF), 9 November 1954.

87 ANB, JS6, 'Rapport à Monsieur l'Administration-Maire de Brazzaville'.

88 Dadet,'La petite histoire du football congolais', 19 April 1970.

89 AOM, 5D18, Capt. Daudet to Governor-General, 11 April 1934; Statutes of Native Sports Federation, 11 April 1934; Dr Capt. Foubert to Governor-General, 8 May 1937; *L'Etoile*, 7 March 1931.

90 *La France de Brazzaville*, 7 November 1935.

91 *CARA de Brazzaville*, 7.

92 Ganga, *Combats pour un sport Africain*, 87.

93 Talk by M. Bertrand, Director of Municipal Social Services, to students at the Urban School, reported in *Liaison*, May 1951.

94 Collected from newspaper reports and Gabio, *La fabuleuse histoire des Diables Rouges*.

95 Bernard Mambeke-Boucher was first introduced to me as a football star and someone who could help me with the history of the sport in Brazzaville. It was only later that I learned that he had been a cabinet minister.

96 *La Semaine*, 29 June 1959.

97 Interviews with Bernard Mambeke-Boucher, 1 December 1986; Fulbert Kimina-Makumbu, 10 October 1986; *La Semaine*, 26 February 1955; Virginia Thompson and Richard Adloff, *Historical dictionary of the People's Republic of the Congo* (Metuchen, N.J.: Scarecrow Press, 1984, 2nd edn), 65, 144. Mambeke-Boucher served as Georges Balandier's research assistant during his field research in Brazzaville in the late 1940s. Dadet was the author of the serialized articles on the history of Brazzaville football which appeared in *La Semaine Africaine*, and which have been referred to in the footnotes to this chapter. He also started the first modern African dance band in Brazzaville in the 1930s (see chapter 5), and published a novel in 1950.

98 See, for example, John Iliffe, *A modern history of Tanganyika* (Cambridge: Cambridge University Press, 1975), 267, 393; David Parkin, *The cultural definition of political response* (London: Academic Press, 1978), 169; Tony Mason, *Association football and English society, 1863–1915* (Brighton: Harvester, 1980), 21–58; Eric A. Wagner (ed.), *Sport in Asia and Africa: a comparative handbook* (New York: Greenwood Press, 1989), 32–3, 198–9; Lever, *Soccer madness*, 5–6.

99 AGPSE, 527VA, Sports Club Records, 12 June 1945. These are records submitted to Père le Comte when he was Secretary of the ASAEF.

100 Interview with Antoine Kébadia, 4 October 1986.

101 Interview with Clement Massengo, 27 October 1986.

102 Interview with Fulbert Kimina-Makumbu, 16 October 1986.

103 *La Semaine*, 26 February 1955.

104 Interview with Fulbert Kimina-Makumbu, 16 October 1986. I am also grateful to Marie-Thérèse Oumba for clarifying this point.

105 Interview with Bernard Mambeke-Boucher, 1 December 1986.

106 *CARA de Brazzaville*, 7, 16.

107 Tsamas, 'Le kyébé-kyébé', 61; Darré, 'La tribu Bondjo', 69.

108 Terence Ranger, 'Pugilism and pathology: African boxing and the black urban experience in Southern Rhodesia', in Baker and Mangan (eds.), *Sport in Africa*, 196–211; also Ian Phimister and Charles van Onselen, 'The political economy of tribal animosity: a case study of the 1929 Bulawayo location "faction fight"', *Journal of Southern African Studies*, 6 (1979), 31–4.

109 N. A. Scotch, 'Magic, sorcery and football among the urban Zulu', *Journal of Conflict Resolution*, 5 (1961), 70–4.

110 Remi Clignet and Maureen Stark, 'Modernisation and football in Cameroun', *Journal of Modern African Studies* 12, 3 (1974), 416–17; personal communication from Augustine Konneh, 14 April 1992.

111 Parkin, *The cultural definition of political response*, 169.

112 Harms, *River of wealth*, 199.

113 Luboya, *Sports, loisirs*, 102.

114 Interview with Clement Massengo, 27 October 1986.

115 Interview with Bernard Mambeke-Boucher, 1 December 1986.

116 Dadet, 'Petite histoire du football congolais', 12 April 1970; 'Un grand champion: Diables Noirs', *La Semaine*, 17 January 1965.

117 Dadet, 'Petite histoire du football congolais', 12 April 1970.

118 Interviews with Antoine Kébadia, 4 October 1986; Fulbert Kimina-Makumbu, 16 October 1986; Clement Massengo, 27 October 1986; Bernard Mambeke-Boucher, 1 December 1986; Dadet, 'Petite histoire du football congolais', 19 April 1970; article by '24e homme' (Sylvain Bemba), *La Semaine*, 7 June 1959.

119 Interview with Antoine Boundzoumou, 16 November 1986.

120 AOM, 5D233; the file on this subject contains catalogues and newsletters from dealers and letters from African customers which were acquired by the AEF and French security police. There is also correspondence between the High Commissioner's office and the police.

121 Based on reports of games in newspapers and official reports from the 1930s–1950s by both European and African commentators.

122 The notorious British variant is not a modern phenomenon, but has existed since the beginnings of football in the late nineteenth century. See Eric Dunning et al. (eds.), *The roots of football hooliganism: an historical and sociological study* (London: Routledge & Kegan Paul, 1988); for Brazil see Lever, *Soccer madness*, 84–5.

123 These are all reasons that were suggested by informants or in written accounts.

124 Dadet, 'La petite histoire du football congolais', 29 March 1970; interview with Fulbert Kimina-Makumbu, 10 October 1986.
125 AOM, 5D159, 'Note on Scouting' by J. Benilan, Inspector of Education, 1 May 1936.
126 ANB, JS6, Report on African football in Brazzaville by Bellocq, 1948.
127 Dadet, 'La petite histoire du football congolais', 22 March and 31 May 1970; interview with Fulbert Kimina-Makumbu, 10 and 16 October 1986.
128 AOM, 5D18, Capt. Daudet to Governor-General, 11 April 1934.
129 AGPSE, 527VA, Letter from Mgr Biéchy, 29 June 1942.
130 ANB, JS6, Report on African football in Brazzaville by Bellocq.
131 Emmanuel J. Dadet, 'Le rôle du supporteur sportif', La Semaine, 26 February 1955.
132 AOM, 4(2)D57, Annual report, Autonomous Subdivision of Brazzaville, 1933.
133 For example, reports in France-Equateur, 26 April, 11 September and 22 November 1954; La Semaine, 26 February 1955, 18 January 1959.
134 Report by '24e homme' (Sylvain Bemba), La Semaine, 7 June 1959.
135 La Semaine, 7 June 1959. For political events, see Wagret, Histoire et sociologie politiques, 64–194.

5   ABOUT THE TOWN

1   'Congo music' is the term generally used to describe the music of Congo-Zaire, used today as a shorthand for music from this region on programmes such as 'Afropop' on contemporary radio. The significance of trans-Pool contacts has been so great that it is virtually impossible to consider Brazzaville music without referring to that of Kinshasa as well, especially with the development of a 'music industry' since the 1950s. The work of Sylvain Bemba, 50 ans de musique du Congo-Zäire, is the starting-point for any study of the topic and, unlike most studies, it gives adequate consideration to the contribution of musicians from the north side of the river. With the commercialization of music in the huge Kinshasa market, the hub of the 'industry' moved to that side of the river and the contribution of Congolese (that is from the Republic of Congo) musicians has often been overlooked. On the Zaire side, see the articles by Kazadi wa Mukuna, for example, 'The origins of Zairean modern music: a socio-economic aspect', African Urban Studies, 6 (1979–80), 31–9, and other items by him listed in the bibliography. See also Gondola, 'Migrations et villes congolaises', and his 'Ata ndele...et l'independance vint. Musique, jeunes et contestation politique dans les capitales congolaises', in Almeida-Topor et al. (eds.), Les jeunes en Afrique, 463–87.
2   Bouteillier, Douze mois sous l'équateur, 30, 53; Coquery-Vidrovitch, Le Congo, 99.
3   Interviews with Mère Emilie, 12 June 1989; Papa Moustapha, 15 June 1989.
4   Coquery-Vidrovitch, Brazza, 209–10; Rabut, Brazza, 364–6.
5   Baratier, Au Congo, 14. In fact, alcohol had been an essential part of any trading transaction since the beginnings of the slave trade. See, Martin, The external trade of the Loango coast, 50–127; Norm Schrag, 'Mboma and the

lower Zaire: a socioeconomic study of a Kongo trading community, *c.* 1785–1885', Ph.D. dissertation, Indiana University, 1985, 50–256.

6   Bouteillier, *Douze mois sous l'équateur*, 29, 32, 33; Hilaire Babassana, *Travail forcé, expropriation et formation du salariat en Afrique noire* (Grenoble: Presses Universitaires de Grenoble, 1978), 28–30; Challaye, *Le Congo Français*, 218.

7   Interviews with Mère Emilie, 13 June 1989; Madame Walymeya and Madame Adèle, 14 June 1989; Papa Moustapha, 15 June 1989; Papa Albert, 17 June 1989; *France-Equateur*, 23 October 1954.

8   Babassana, *Travail forcé*, 31; Vacquier, *Au temps des factories*, 165; Coquery-Vidrovitch, *Le Congo*, 99, 144–6; *JO*, 1927, 552.

9   ANB, GG357, Chief of Judicial Service to Governor-General, 15 March 1939; GG22, Report of Social Services of AEF, November 1949.

10   Blouin, *My country, Africa*, 68–9; interviews with Bernard Mambeke-Boucher, 12 December 1986; Papa Moustapha, 15 June 1989.

11   Blouin, *My country, Africa*, 68.

12   Dybowski, *La route du Tchad*, 84–9; see also Martin, 'National holidays transformed'.

13   Tsamas, 'Le kyébé-kyébé', 61–4; André Ossoungou, 'Connaissez-vous le "kyébé-kyébé"?', *La Semaine*, 19 September 1955; Blouin, *My country, Africa*, 69.

14   P. Decapmaker, 'Danses des Bakongo', *La mission et les joies populaires: compte-rendu de la XVè semaine de missiologie de Louvain, 1938* (Brussels: Edition universelle, 1938), 47; Kazadi wa Mukuna, 'Congolese music', in *The new Grove dictionary of music and musicians*, IV (1980), 659; Kanza Matondo ne Mansangaza, *Musique Zaïroise moderne* (Kinshasa: Publications du CNMA, 1972), 36–7; Sylvain Bemba, 'L'évolution de la musique congolaise', *Liaison*, 37 (March–April, 1957), 37, and his *50 ans de musique du Congo-Zaïre*, 32.

15   Anne Stamm, 'La société créole à Saint-Paul de Loanda dans les années, 1836–1848', *Revue Française d'Histoire d'Outre-Mer*, 59, 217 (June 1977), 578–610; João de Mattos e Silva, *Contribução para o estudo da região de Cabinda* (Lisbon: Typographia Universal, 1904), 320; E. Pechuël-Loesche, *Volkskunde von Loango* (Stuttgart: Strecker & Schröder, 1907), 122.

16   Bouteillier, *Douze mois sous l'équateur*, 78.

17   Andersson, *Churches at the grass-roots*, 178; Decapmaker, 'Danses des Bakongo', 44–7.

18   Pierre de Vaucleroy, 'Promenade à Brazzaville', *Expansion Belge*, 8 (1929), 15–18. The dance described here seems to correspond very closely to that described by Kazadi wa Mukuna, 'The genesis of urban music in Zaïre', *African Music*, 7, 2 (1992), 76, although in an earlier article he also suggested that both the partnered and unpartnered dancing may have generically been known as *maringa*. See Kazadi wa Muzuna, 'The origins of Zairean modern music', 37.

19   Interviews with Mère Emilie, 12 June 1989; Anne Ngondjo, 15 June 1989; Papa Moustapha, 15 June 1989; interview with Papa Albert, 17 June 1989. See also, Kazadi wa Mukuna, 'Congolese music', 659; Kanza Matondo ne Mansangaza, *Musique Zaïroise moderne*, 38; Chris Stapleton and Chris May,

African all-stars: the pop music of a continent (London: Quartet Books, 1987), 14–15, 135–6.

20   Andersson, *Churches at the grass-roots*, 260, fn 6. Bemba, 'L'évolution de la musique congolaise', 37, suggests that *maringa* came to signify modern dance in general in the period before the *rumba*. Bernard Mambeke-Boucher agreed, and noted that *kolinga* means 'to dance' in Lingala: interview 12 December 1986.

21   J. Van Wing, 'Les danses Bakongo', *Congo*, 2, 2 (July 1937), 128; Jean Cuvelier, 'Les missions catholiques en face des danses des Bakongo', *Africanae Fraternae Ephemerides Romanae* (1939), 153.

22   Van Wing, 'Les danses Bakongo', 128.

23   AOM, 4(2)D65, Report for the third trimester, Autonomous Subdivision of Brazzaville, 1934.

24   Chalux, *Un an au Congo Belge*, 111–12, 122–3; Rondet-Saint, *Sur les routes du Cameroun*, 158; Gondola, 'Migration et villes congolaises au XXe siècle,' 112, 118; but estimates vary widely, as they do for Brazzaville due to problems of census-taking.

25   The point is the integrating thesis of Gondola, 'Migration et villes congolaises au XXe siècle', and 'Kinshasa et Brazzaville: brève histoire d'un mariage séculaire', *Zaïre-Afrique*, 249–50 (November–December 1990), 494–60.

26   Sylvain Danse, *Carnet de route: d'Elisabeth à Boma* (Elisabethville: Imprimerie l'Etoile du Congo, 1923), 474; Vassal, *Life in French Congo*, 49–50; interview with Clement Massengo, 27 October 1986.

27   See chapter 6.

28   Chalux, *Un an au Congo Belge*, 157–8; Hermann Norden, *Auf neuen Pfaden im Kongo: quer durch das dunkelste Afrika* (Leipzig: F. A. Brockhaus, 1926), 261–3.

29   Norden, *Auf neuen Pfaden*, 262.

30   Chavannes, *Avec Brazza*, 24.

31   Augouard, *Quarante-quatre années au Congo*, 12, 131; de Witte, *Monseigneur Augouard*, 443. African servants were also familiar with European instruments through amateur enthusiasts who imported instruments. For example, Eboué transported his wife's piano to the Ubangi-Shari region, and the point of dispute between the Frenchman Grégoire and his servant, Bima, in 1931 which resulted in the death of the former was the transportation of a piano on the Congo ferry. See Weinstein, *Eboué*, 86, 89; and Aïssi, 'Le tournant des années 30', 40.

32   Augouard, *Quarante-quatre années au Congo*, 50, 54; 'Brazzaville', BCPSE, 27 (1913–14), 59; AGPSE, 277AVII, Report of Père le Duc, 25 September 1934; *La France de Brazzaville*, 7 November 1935.

33   Andersson, *Churches at the grass-roots*, 73, 74, 234 fn 10; Söderberg, *Les instruments de musique*, 133. Interviews with Antoine Boudzoumou, 16 November 1986; Gabriel Ngonga-Nzonzi, 10 December 1986.

34   Henri L. Becquet, 'Our first Christmas in Belgian Congo', *The Bandsman and Songster* (21 December 1935), 410; ASA Zaïre(2), Becquet to Blowers, 5 October 1937 and 29 November 1937; Zaïre(1), Report by Becquet, 1939.

35   Veistroffer, *Vingt ans*, 181, 183, 188.

36   Interview with Bernard Mambeke-Boucher, 17 November and 10 December

1986. The influence of West Indian soldiers is noted for West Africa in the nineteenth century: see John Collins, *African pop roots: the inside rhythms of Africa* (London: Foulsham, 1985), 13.

37 Dadet, 'La petite histoire du football congolais', 12 April 1970; interview with Bernard Mambeke-Boucher, 10 December 1986.

38 AOM, 5D18, Daudet to Lieutenant-Governor of Moyen-Congo, 15 March 1934; Daudet to Governor-General, 11 April 1934; Lieutenant-Governor of Moyen-Congo to Governor-General, 27 June 1934.

39 Bouteillier, *Douze mois sous l'équateur*, 125; Vassal, *Life in French Congo*, 176; Mary Motley, *Devils in waiting* (London: Longman, 1960), 36.

40 Blouin, *My country, Africa*, 67.

41 Interviews with Clement Massengo, 24 November and 10 December 1986; Sylvain Bemba, 2 January 1987; Bernard Mambeke-Boucher, 10 December 1986. This liking for items made in England was linked by informants to the fascination among the Brazzaville elite for the events surrounding the abdication of Edward VIII and his subsequent marriage to Wallis Simpson who then became the Duchess of Windsor. Bemba says that the famous Zairois singer Antoine Wendo's name was derived from an Africanization of 'Windsor'. See Bemba, *50 ans de musique du Congo-Zaïre*, 72.

42 Kranitz, 'Brazzaville: les missions du Bas-Congo', 53. See chapter 2.

43 ANB, GG675, Governor-General to Minister of Colonies, May 1934; *JO*, Letter from Minister of Colonies to Governor-General, 5 August 1934. See chapter 3.

44 Collins, *African pop roots*, 115.

45 Stapleton and May, *African all-stars*, 14–15, 265.

46 Interview with Sylvain Bemba, 2 January 1987; Bemba, 'L'évolution de la musique congolaise', 37; interview with Bernard Mambeke-Boucher, 10 December 1986. See also Waterman, *Juju*, 46–7.

47 ASMF, Privata Dagböcker, no. 4, Diary of Petrus Petterson-Temdahls, 14 August 1932.

48 Marcel Sauvage, *Sous le feu de l'équateur: les secrets de l'Afrique noire* (Paris: Editions Denöel, 1937), 70.

49 Kazadi wa Mukuna, 'Congolese music', 25; and also Stapleton and May, *African all-stars*, 136.

50 Janheinz Jahn, *Muntu: an outline of the new African culture* (New York: Grove Press, Inc., 1961), 84. For a general discussion of the rumba, its possible antecedents, and its many forms in Cuba, see 62–95.

51 Interviews with Mandayela Mpea, 22 December 1986; Phillippe Mokwami, 10 January 1987; Bernard Mambeke-Boucher, 10 December 1986. Also, *L'Etoile*, 28 May, 29 August, 17 October 1936; and Bemba, *50 ans de musique du Congo-Zaïre*, 49.

52 *L'Education Africaine*, 41 (1942); interview with Bernard Mambeke-Boucher, 10 December 1986.

53 *La Semaine*, 20, 27 March 1954.

54 *France-Equateur*, 8, 14, 29 January 1955; Alain Gheerbrant, *Congo noir et blanc* (Paris: Gallimard, 1955), 19.

55 These are the bars most frequently mentioned by informants and advertised in newspapers.

56   Ganga, *Combats pour un sport africain*, 46; interview with Bernard Mambeke-Boucher, 10 December 1986.

57   From various issues of *France-Equateur* for January 1955; also advertisements in *Liaison*.

58   Patrice Joseph Lhoni, 'Brazzaville: art, littérature, folklore', *Brazzaville: revue de l'action municipale*, 2 (March–April 1967), n.p.

59   Interview with Mandayela Mpea, 22 December 1986; *France-Equateur*, 8 January 1955.

60   *France-Equateur*, 4 October 1954; *Liaison* (September-October, 1952), 20; Bemba, *50 ans de musique du Congo-Zaïre*, 50–1; interview with Roger Frey, 9 July 1987. Many informants referred to 'Chez Faignond', either as an important nightspot in Brazzaville by repute or because they had visited it.

61   Gheerbrant, *Congo noir et blanc*, 16–17.

62   *Ibid.*, 22–4; Balandier, *Sociologie des Brazzavilles noires*, 145–8; Balandier, *Ambiguous Africa*, 192–3; interview with Mère Emilie, 12 June 1989.

63   Balandier, *Sociologie des Brazzavilles noires*, 145.

64   Interviews with Marie-Paula Samba, 13 January 1987; Mère Emilie, 13 June 1989; also, Emilienne Raoul-Matingou, 'Activités des femmes en milieu urbain: le cas de Brazzaville', thèse de 3è cycle, University of Science and Technology of Lille, 1982, 227–8; Bemba, *50 ans de musique du Congo-Zaïre*, 68.

65   Suzanne Comhaire-Sylvain, *Femmes de Kinshasa, hier et aujourd'hui* (Paris: Mouton, 1968), 48; *France-Equateur*, 1 and 13 September 1954.

66   See chapter 1.

67   AOM, 4(2)D51, Annual report of the Autonomous Subdivision of Brazzaville, 1932; Homet, *Congo: terre de souffrances*, 189; also see chapter 1.

68   ANB, GG4, Report of Inspector-General of Health Services, 12 July 1940.

69   ANB, GG4, R. Mandell to Governor-General, 15 August 1940; Report of Director of Political and Social Affairs, AEF, 19 October 1940.

70   Interviews with Papa Moustapha, 15 June 1989; Martin Balossa, 17 June 1989; Maya Alden, 7 November 1986.

71   Interview with Madame Walymeya and Madame Adèle, 14 June 1989.

72   ANB, GG456, Report of the Director of Political and Social Affairs for AEF, 1946.

73   See Introduction.

74   Henri Gallard, 'Le "kitemo"', *BCAF: renseignements coloniaux*, 5 (1919), 199–201.

75   J. Bernard, 'La mutualité chez les Bacongos: le kitemo', *BSRC*, 2 (1922), 9–14. The report was written in 1915. See also Gallard, 'Le "kitemo"'.

76   AOM, 4(2)D59, Report for the second trimester, Autonomous Subdivision of Brazzaville, 1933.

77   Interviews with Adèle Nsongolo, 16 June 1989; Madame Walymeya and Madame Adèle, 14 June 1989; Anne Ngondjo, 15 June 1989; Hilaire Nkoukou, 22 November 1986; Raoul-Matingou, 'Activités des femmes en milieu urbain', 304.

78   Balandier, *Sociologie des Brazzavilles noires*, 145.

79   Interview with Bernard Mambeke-Boucher, 17 November 1986.

80   Interviews with Adèle Nsongolo, 16 June 1989; Anne Ngondjo, 15 June

1989; Madame Walymeya and Madame Adèle, 14 June 1989; Louis Lingouala, 22 December 1986.

81 See Muff Anderson, *Music in the mix: the story of South African popular music* (Johannesburg: Ravan Press, 1981).

82 Bemba, *50 ans de musique du Congo-Zaïre*, 72; Balandier, *Sociologie des Brazzavilles noires*, 143–4.

83 *France-Equateur*, 13 September 1954.

84 On associations in general and administration policy, see Gamandzori, 'Le mouvement associatif des jeunes', 69–90.

85 AOM, 5D159, AEF, Office of Political and Social Affairs: Report on associations; Paul Kamba to the Director of Political and Social Affairs, 23 November 1948; Association Presidents to Massamba 'Lebel'; Circular note to presidents of associations, 24 November 1948. Elaine Pepper was a graduate of the Paris Conservatory who went to Brazzaville with her husband, an ethnomusicologist, during the Second World War. She also wrote the well-known 'Messe des Piroguiers' which was premiered in the Sainte-Anne cathedral in Poto-Poto in the 1950s.

86 Stapleton and May, *African all-stars*, 142–5; Söderberg, *Les instruments de musique*, 177–8; Antoine Moundanda and André Nkouka, *Biakongo: chansons congolaises* (Brazzaville: mimeographed, n.d.), 1–5, 16–24.

87 Interview with Sylvain Bemba, 2 January 1987; Bemba, *50 ans de musique du Congo-Zaïre*, 18, 44; ASA, Zaïre(1), Report for 1942, Léopoldville; Kanza Matondo ne Mansangaza, *Musique zaïroise moderne*, 40. For developments since the 1960s, see Pierre Kazadi, 'Congo music: Africa's favorite beat', *Africa Report* (April 1971), 25–7; and René Balbaud, 'Profile: "Seigneur" Rochereau's swinging sounds', *Africa Report* (April 1971), 28–9, and several of the books cited in the bibliography and in the notes, especially Stapleton and May, *African all-stars* and Gary Stewart, *Breakout: profiles in African rhythm* (Chicago: University of Chicago Press, 1992), which contain interviews with Zairois musicians.

88 Interviews with Phillippe Mokwami, 10 January 1987; Mandayela Mpea, 22 December 1986; Bernard Mambeke-Boucher, 10 December 1986; AOM, 5D159, Report of Director of cultural centre, Poto-Poto, 6 December 1948; Bemba, *50 ans de musique du Congo-Zaïre*, 72; Jérôme Bandila, 'A la mémoire de Paul Kamba', *Liaison*, 9 (March 1951), 14.

89 Interviews with Mandayela Mpea, 22 December 1986; Bernard Mambeke-Boucher, 12 December 1986.

90 *Voix de la Révolution* Discothèque, Ngoma Records, no. 271.

91 Stewart, *Breakout*, 19, also, 16–17; Bemba, *50 ans de musique du Congo-Zaïre*, 36–7.

92 Stewart, *Breakout*, 19.

93 Ganga, *Combats pour un sport africain*, 46.

94 Interviews with Antoine Boudzoumou, 16 November 1986; Bernard Mambeke-Boucher, 10 December 1986; AOM, 5D159, Committee list, cultural centre, Bacongo; *La Semaine*, 12 March 1955; Bemba, *50 ans de musique du Congo-Zaïre*, 71–3.

95 Bemba, *50 ans de musique du Congo-Zaïre*, 81, 95–7; interview with Bernard Mambeke-Boucher, 10 December 1986; Stewart, *Breakout*, 16–17.

96 Voix de la Révolution Discothèque, La voix de son maître, K1P23.
97 According to Sylvain Bemba, who interviewed Jhimmy in the 1980s, the musician has never explained why he gave up his career so suddenly.
98 This period in the history of Congo-Zaire music is quite well-documented. Bemba, *50 ans de musique du Congo-Zaïre*, 18, 36–7, 106, 110–11; Kazadi wa Mukunda, 'The genesis of urban music', 71–9; Gondola, 'Migration et villes congolaises'; and 'Kinshasa et Brazzaville', 495–6; *La Semaine*, 23 May 1965 and 20 September 1979.
99 Gheerbrant, *Congo noir et blanc*, 20–2; Stewart, *Breakout*, 19, quoting an interview with Doctor Nico in March 1985; Bemba, *50 Ans de musique du Congo-Zaïre*, 33; Gondola, 'Kinshasa et Brazzaville', 495.
100 Gheerbrant, *Congo noir et blanc*, 20.
101 Bemba, 'L'évolution de la musique congolaise', 38.
102 Michel Kongo, 'Petits métiers et commerce de l'artisanat à Brazzaville', thèse de 3è cycle, University of Bordeaux III, 1975, 120, 147–8; interview with Bernard Mambeke-Boucher, 10 December 1986.
103 Taken from programme listings in the three main newspapers that were read by Brazzaville's European community as well as African elites: *La France de Brazzaville*, *Paris-Congo*, *L'Etoile*.
104 ANB, GG672, Report on Radio Brazzaville, Governor-General to Secretary of State Council for Information, Paris, 26 August 1949; Frey, 'Brazzaville', 50–3; Direction des Postes et Télécommunications de l'AEF, 'Postes et télécommunications', in Guernier, *Afrique Equatoriale Française*, 497–8; Francis Bebey, *La radiodiffusion en Afrique noire* (Paris: Éditions Saint-Paul, 1963), 47–9.
105 *Courrier d'Afrique*, 2 May 1951; *France-Equateur*, 27 April 1951 and 23 August 1951; interviews with Phillippe Mokwami, 10 January 1987; Louis Lingouala, 22 December 1986; Antoine Mangoyo, 29 December 1986; Bernard Mambeke-Boucher, 10 December 1986.
106 *France-Equateur*, 23 August 1951.
107 *France-Equateur*, 27 April and 23 August 1951; *Courrier d'Afrique*, 2 May 1951.
108 Daily programmes appeared in newspapers such as *La Semaine, Courrier d'Afrique*, and *France-Equateur*.
109 Programme listings consulted were in *La Semaine, France-Equateur* and *Courrier d'Afrique*.
110 For the 'craze' for Congo music in Lagos, see Waterman, *Juju*, 93; also Billy Bergman, *African pop: goodtime kings* (Poole, Dorset: Bladford Press, 1985), 44–8.
111 There are many articles that discuss the content of Congo songs and their relation to reality and the world of the imagination. Most of these deal with a more recent period and, therefore, more recent songs than are under consideration here. See, for example in the *Cahiers Congolais de l'Imaginaire*, Abel Kouvouama, 'Le role de l'imaginaire dans la chanson "Loufoulakari" de Youlou Mabiala', 1 (January 1988), 29–37; Matondo Kubu Ture, 'Amour et permutation ludique des rôles sociaux entre l'homme et la femme dans la chanson contemporaine d' orchestres Congolo-Zaïroise', 2 (July 1988), 20–4; and, Honoré Mobonda, 'De la poetique de la chanson Congolo-

Zaïroise', 3 (January 1989), 34–45. Also, see the three articles in *La Semaine* by Honoré Mobonda, 'La rôle de l'enfant dans la société Congolo-Zaïroise', 4–10 October 1984; 'Les allusions à l'homme blanc dans la musique Congolo-Zaïroise', 25–31 October 1984; 'L'unité africaine, préoccupation du musicien Congolo-Zaïrois', 8–14 November 1984. Also Honoré Mobonda, 'Petite histoire chantée de cent ans de présence européenne en Afrique', in *Centenaire de la conference de Berlin (1884–1885): actes du colloque international, Brazzaville, April 1985* (Paris: Présence Africaine, 1987), 403–28. There are also several articles by scholars from the Kinshasa side of the Pool that have been published in *Zaïre-Afrique*. See, for example, Tshonga-Onyumbe, 'Nkisi, nganga et ngangankisi dans la musique Zaïroise moderne de 1960 à 1981', 169, November 1982, 555–66.

112 Bemba, *50 ans de musique du Congo-Zaïre*, 92.
113 Moundanda and Nkouka, *Biakongo: chansons congolaises*, 31.
114 Bemba, *50 ans de musique du Congo-Zaïre*, 46–7, 83; Balandier, *Sociologie des Brazzavilles noires*, 255–7; and his *Ambiguous Africa*, 192.
115 Bemba, *50 ans de musique du Congo-Zaïre*, 83.
116 Sung by Mandayela Mpea at an interview, 22 December 1986.
117 Interviews with Jean-Pierre Ngole, 13 October 1988; Mère Emilie, 12 June 1989; Papa Albert, 17 June 1989.
118 Frey, 'Brazzaville', 97.
119 Interviews with Papa Moustapha, 15 June 1989; Louis Lingouala, 22 December 1986.
120 Austen and Headrick, 'Equatorial Africa under colonial rule', 75.
121 *France-Equateur*, 10 and 15 June 1953.
122 Luise White, *The comforts of home: prostitution in colonial Nairobi* (Chicago: University of Chicago Press, 1990).
123 Vincent, *Femmes africaines*, 124, 195–6.
124 Interview with Marie-Paula Samba, 13 January 1987.

6 DRESSING WELL

1 Bouteillier, *Douze mois sous l'équateur*, 73–4, 78.
2 Susan Orlean, *Saturday night* (New York: Knopf, 1990), interviewed on PBS radio, 27 September 1990; also, Zerubavel, *Hidden rhythms*, 122–3.
3 N'Zala-Backa, *Le tipoye doré*, 1968, 93; ASMF, F.1, Brazzaville Mission Journal, 4 April 1915; interviews with Bernard Mambeke-Boucher, 20 November 1986; Roger Frey, 9 July 1987.
4 ANB, GG258, Report on 'clerk Massengo', Native Personnel files. 22 September 1934.
5 Interviews with Bernard Mambeke-Boucher, 20 November 1986; Papa Albert, 17 June 1989; Homet, *Congo: terre de souffrances*, 218; Peggy Sabatier, 'Did Africans really learn to be French? The francophone elite of the Ecole William Ponty', in Johnson (ed.), *Double impact*, 181–2.
6 Mary Douglas and Baron Isherwood, *The world of goods: towards an anthropology of consumption* (New York: Basic Books, 1979), 10; Balandier, *Sociologie des Brazzavilles noires*, 93.
7 Brunschwig, *Brazza explorateur: les traités Makoko*, 52.

8   *Ibid.*, 53.

9   See, for example, E. Froment, 'Un voyage dans l'Oubangui', *Bulletin de la Société de Géographie de Lille*, 11 (1889), 196, 199; Dybowski, *La route du Tchad*, 152–5; Vassal, *Life in French Congo*, 115–24; Gide, *Travels in the Congo* (Berkeley: University of California Press, 1962), 51–2; Maurice Briault, *Dans la forêt du Gabon*, 153–6; Raymond Bafouetela, 'Etude morphologique et vestimentaire sur le groupe Bondjo de la Likouala', *CCAH*, 5 (1980), 69–72; Vansina, *The Tio kingdom*, 151–2.

10 Willy Bal (ed.), *Description du royaume de Congo et des contrées environmentes, par Filippo Pigafetta et Duarte Lopes (1591)* (Louvain: Nauwelaerts, 1963), 36–7; E. G. Ravenstein, *The strange adventures of Andrew Battell in Angola and adjoining regions* (London: The Hakluyt Society, 1901), 69; also Théophile Obenga, 'Habillement, cosmétique et parure au royaume de Kongo, XVè-XVIIIè', *CCAH*, 4 (1979), 21–38.

11 See Phyllis M. Martin, 'Power, cloth and currency on the Loango coast', *AEH*, 15 (1986), 1–12.

12 Vansina, *The Tio kingdom*, 152, 159.

13 Martin, 'Power, cloth and currency'.

14 Vansina, *The Tio kingdom*, 151–4, 274, 283–4, 307–9; Harms, *River of wealth*, 47, 63–4, 89.

15 Mary Ellen Roach and Joanne Bubolz Eicher, 'The language of personal adornment', in Cordwell and Schwarz (eds.), *The fabrics of culture* (The Hague: Mouton, 1979), 9–10; also Hilda Kuper, 'Costume and identity', *Comparative Studies in Society and History*, 15 (1973), 355.

16 Coquery-Vidrovitch, *Brazza*, 401–2.

17 Sketches of these tusks can be found in E.Pechuël-Loesche, *Volkskunde*, 76–7; also Jan Vansina, *Art history in Africa* (New York: Longman, 1984), 131.

18 Gordon D. Gibson and Cecilia R. McGurk, 'High-status caps of the Kongo and Mbundu peoples', *Textile Museum Journal*, 4, 4 (1977), 73.

19 Vansina, *The Tio kingdom*, 154, 453.

20 J. Picton and J. Mack, *African textiles: looms, weaving and design* (London: British Museum Publications, 1979), 175.

21 Uzès, *Le voyage de mon fils*, 15.

22 Jean Dybowski, *Le Congo méconnu* (Paris: Librarie Hachette, 1912), 161; Castellani, *Vers le Nil français*, 33; ASOM, Fonds Bruel, B-213–50, 'Gabonnaises à Libreville, 1908'; Yvonne Knibiehler and Régine Goutalier, *La femme au temps des colonies* (Paris: Editions Stock, 1985), photographs.

23 'Brazzaville', *BCPSE*, 21 (1901–02), 668.

24 Bouteillier, *Douze mois sous l'équateur*, 73–4; Augouard, *Quarante-quatre années au Congo*, 83, 191; Louis Augouard, *Guirlande enchevêtrée d'anecdotes congolais* (Evreux: M.Poussin, 1934), 51; J.Remy, 'Une procession à Brazzaville', 229; letter from Sam Hede, *MF*, 1914, 86–7; Challaye, *Le Congo Français*, 30.

25 Interviews with Papa Albert, 17 June 1989; Papa Moustapha, 15 June 1989; Maurice Briault, 'La mode chez les noirs', *APSE* (March 1929), 89–96; (April 1929), 124–8.

26 Interview with Mère Emilie, 12 June 1989; Dybowski, *Le Congo Méconnu*, 161; ASOM, Fonds Bruel, B-212–50, photos from the Bruel collection;

postcards from the Roger Frey collection; report from the *Union Congolais*, 1904, quoted in Vacquier, *Au temps des factories*, 177; Bonnefont, 'Brazzaville: la ville et la mission', 109.

27   Interviews with Sylvain Bemba, 2 January 1987; Bernard Mambeke-Boucher, 1 December 1986; see also Gandoulou, *Dandies à Bacongo*, 6.

28   Puytorac, *Makambo*, 46; Vassal, *Life in French Congo*, 27, 115; Gandoulou, *Dandies à Bacongo*, 11.

29   Rouget, *L'Afrique Equatoriale illustreé*, 70, 73, 77.

30   Docteur Fougerat de David de Lastours, 'Hygiène, nudité, soleil aux Colonies', communication to the Société de Médicine et d'Hygiène tropicale, 1927; R. Frey, 'Soleil et colonies', *L'Etoile de l'AEF*, 6 August 1938; Vacquier, *Au temps des factories*, 179–180; and Pellerin, *Une enfance en brousse congolaise* (Paris: Editions Arthaud, 1990), 14–15.

31   Leland Barrows, 'The impact of the French armed forces, 1830–1920', in Johnson (ed.), *Double impact*, 78.

32   Hilary Callan, 'Introduction', in Callan and Ardener (eds.), *The incorporated wife*, 1–5. See also chapter 7.

33   Vassal, *Daily life in French Congo*, 27–9, 115.

34   Blouin, *My country, Africa*, 62; Vacquier, *Au temps des factories*, 101.

35   'Informations diverses: Oubangui', *Missions Catholiques* (1904), 184, 460; AGPSE, 510BVI, Letters of Augouard to the Central Committee of the Propagation de la Foi, 1 December 1891, 2 September 1897, 1 December 1915; de Witte, *Monseigneur Augouard*, 52, 62, 84, 347.

36   Carrie, *Coutumier de l'oeuvre des enfants*, 43–4.

37   Andersson, *Churches at the grass-roots*, 189.

38   See chapters 3 and 4.

39   ANB, GG481, Reports by the Principal of the Urban School to the Mayor of Brazzaville, 31 December 1913, 31 March and 25 June 1914.

40   AOM, 5D181, Governor of Moyen-Congo to Governor-General, 17 July 1948.

41   R. P. Jaffre, 'De Plougastch au Congo', *ASSJC*, 23 (1930), 2; 'La mission essentielle de Saint-Joseph de Cluny', *ASSJC*, 69 (1938), 71; AGPSE, photograph collection.

42   Quoted in J. Marthey, 'L'oeuvre missionaire pour la population féminine au Congo', *Revue d'Histoire des Colonies*, 5, 154, (1957), 81, (underlined in the original). Also, on the training of girls, see *Les Soeurs de Saint-Joseph de Cluny*, 8.

43   Interviews with Mère Emilie, 13 June 1989; Papa Moustapha, 15 June 1989.

44   Carrie, *Coutumier de l'oeuvre des enfants*, 17, 37; and his *Oeuvres des Soeurs de Saint-Joseph de Cluny dans la mission du Congo Français* (Loango: Imprimerie de la Mission, 1897), 6; Maurice Briault, 'Le cinquantenaire de la mission du Congo Français: Brazzaville, 1888–1938', *Revue d'Histoire des Missions*, 15 (December 1938), 509.

45   Ranger, *Dance and society in eastern Africa*, 166.

46   Pellerin, *Une enfance en brousse congolaise*, 125.

47   Bonnefont, 'Brazzaville: la ville et la mission', 108–9; 'Brazzaville', *BCPSE*, 27 (1910–13), 55; Briault, 'La mode', 124–6.

48   Vassal, *Français, Belges et Portugais*, 153.

49   AOM, 4(2)D55, Report for the third trimester, Autonomous Subdivision of Brazzaville, 1932; 5D55, Annual report of Moyen-Congo, 1932.

50   'Communauté du Sacre-Coeur à Brazzaville (Haut-Congo Français)', *BCSSJC*, 157 (1925), 467; 187 (1933), 539–40; and 202 (1938), 582–84; interview with Martin Balossa, 17 June 1989; personal communication, Marie-Thérèse Oumba, 15 August 1993; Blouin, *My country, Africa*, 14, 15, 34, 83–5, 113–14.

51   Georges Balandier, 'Evolution de la société et de l'homme', in Guernier (ed.), *Afrique Equatoriale Française*, 126.

52   Soret, *Démographie et problèmes urbains*, 91.

53   Balandier, *Sociologie des Brazzavilles noires*, 92.

54   Gérard Althabe, *Le chômage à Brazzaville en 1957: étude psychologique* (Paris: ORSTOM, 1958), 10, 12; Devauges, *Etude du chômage à Brazzaville*, 83.

55   Coquery-Vidrovitch, *Brazza*, 209–10; Rabut, *Brazza*, 364–6.

56   Girard, 'Brazzaville', 30–1.

57   AGPSE, 227AVII, Annual report of Mgr Guichard, 15 August 1927.

58   ASMF, Privata Dagböcker 4, Petterson-Tendahls, Brazzaville, 14 August 1932.

59   Puytorac, *Makambo*, 47–50, 56; see Vacquier, *Au temps des factories*, for a comprehensive account of the stock carried by stores of the *Compagnie Française Occidentale* which had an outlet in Brazzaville.

60   Girard, 'Brazzaville', 30, 33; Scholastique Dianzinga, 'Histoire de Brazzaville de 1910 à 1940', Mémoire de maîtrise, University of Paris VII, 1979, 43; interviews with Habibou Soumbre, 11 November 1986; Papa Moustapha, 15 June 1989.

61   *L'Etoile*, 9 November 1930; Roger Frey, 'La colonie portugaise', *Perspectives d'Outre-Mer: Afrique Equatoriale Française*, 18 (May 1956), 51, 61.

62   Blouin, *My country, Africa*, 66.

63   'Le marché de l'habillement en AEF', *Courrier d'Afrique*, 8 November 1951; 'L'expansion japonaise en Afrique', *BCAF* (1934), 496–7.

64   Vaucleroy, 'Promenade à Brazzzaville,' 17.

65   Interviews with Mère Emilie, 12 June, 1989; Papa Moustapha, 15 June, 1989; Soeur Scholastique, 13 November 1986; Pellerin, *Une enfance en brousse congolaise*, 125; Vassal, *Français, Belges et Portugais*, 153; Vacquier, *Au temps des factories*, 169–72.

66   Puytorac, *Makambo*, 50; Pellerin, *Une enfance en brousse congolaise*, 125.

67   Chalux, *Un an au Congo Belge*, 157–8; Norden, *Auf neuen Pfaden im Kongo*, 262.

68   Interviews with Bernard Mambeke-Boucher, 20 November 1986; Mère Emilie, 12 June 1989; Soeur Clothilde, 10 November 1986; Maya Alden, 7 November 1986; Sauvage, *Les secrets de l'Afrique noire*, 70–1; Rondet-Saint, *Sur les routes*, 139; Roger Frey, 'Modes africaines', *Paris-Congo*, 24 July 1938; Bemba, *50 ans de musique du Congo-Zaïre*, 81; AOM, 5D88, Confidential report of Lieutenant-Governor of Moyen-Congo to Governor-General of AEF, 12 April 1930.

69   This point is well developed in Elizabeth A. Perkins, 'The consumer frontier: household consumption in early Kentucky', *Journal of American History* 78, 2 (September 1991), 486–510.

70 Georges Balandier in the preface of Gandoulou, *Dandies à Bacongo*, 6.
71 AOM, 5D88, Camille Diata to Paul Mayoukou, 19 March 1930. Africans who spoke French also distinguished between the European 'town' and the African 'villages'. The style 'Popo' was inspired by loose shirts worn by men from Dahomey (where Grand Popo is located), according to informants. Camille Diata, who was persecuted by the French as a Matswa leader, was nineteen when he wrote this letter; see Sinda, *Le messianisme congolais*, 1972, 254, fn 1. The letter was confiscated with other papers when his house was raided by the police. It is preserved in the files of the Colonial Ministry.
72 ANB, GG444(2), Report of the Government Hospital, Brazzaville, 1930.
73 Bonnefont, 'Brazzaville: la ville et la mission,' 108–9; Bemba, *50 ans de musique du Congo-Zaïre*, 73.
74 AOM, 5D88, Lieutenant-Governor of Moyen-Congo to Governor-General, 12 April 1930.
75 'Le marché de l'habillement en AEF', *Courrier d'Afrique*, 8 November 1951.
76 Interviews with Antoine Mangoyo, 29 December 1986; Honoré Monabeka, 27 December 1986.
77 Interviews with Phillippe Mokwami, 10 January 1987; Antoine Mangoyo, 29 December 1986; Louis Lingouala, 22 December 1986; Gandoulou, *Dandies à Bacongo*, 30; Bemba, *50 ans de musique du Congo-Zaïre*, 76, 82–3.
78 Vincent, *Femmes africaines*, 209.
79 This discussion is based on interviews with Mère Emilie, 12 June 1989; Anne Ngondjo, 15 June 1989; Papa Mustapha, 15 June 1989; Sidone Ngole, 12 May 1988; photographs from the family album of Bernard Mambeke-Boucher; Bonnefont, 'Brazzaville: la ville et la mission', 108; Blouin, *My country, Africa* 113–14; letter from J. F. N'Kounka, *La Semaine*, 14 February 1953.
80 Blouin, *My country, Africa*, 113–14; interviews with Sidone Ngole, 12 May 1988; Marie-Thérèse Oumba, 15 August 1993.
81 Interviews with Papa Moustapha, 15 June 1989; Mère Emilie, 12 June 1989; Anne Ngondjo, 15 June 1989; Sidone Ngole, 12 May 1988.
82 Interviews with Mère Emilie, 12 June 1989; Augustine Massalo, 23 December 1986; Sidone Ngole, 12 May 1988; Blouin, *My country, Africa*, 90; François Mosingue, 'La corruption des moeurs des femmes dites évoluées', *Liaison*, 58 (March–April, 1957), 33; Jacques Audibert, 'Une compagnie commerciale en République Populaire du Congo: le CFAO', travail d'études et de recherches, University of Bordeaux III, 1973, 38–9; Emilienne Raoul-Matingou, 'Activités des femmes en milieu urbain', 238.
83 Interview with Albertine Mowango, 26 December 1986; 'L'élégance au village', *France-Equateur*, 1 September 1954.
84 Interviews with Mère Emilie, 13 June 1989; Papa Moustapha, 15 June 1989; Blouin, *My country, Africa*, 29–30.
85 Discothèque, Voix de la Revolution, His Master's Voice, no. 5.
86 Grant McCracken, *Culture and consumption: new approaches to the symbolic character of consumer goods and activities* (Bloomington: Indiana University Press, 1988), 60–1.
87 J.-R. Ayouné, 'Notre but', *L'Education Africaine*, 2 (1942).

88 *Brazzaville*, 2nd year, 17 (April 1951).

89 See articles on consumerism, its definition and implications, in a special issue of *Culture and History*, 7 (1990).

90 Interviews with Papa Moustapha, 15 June 1989; Sylvain Bemba, 2 January 1987; Bernard Mambeke-Boucher, 10 December 1986.

91 Gheerbrant, *Congo noir et blanc*, 23.

92 Mosingue, 'La corruption des moeurs des femmes', 30–4; Joseph Pouabou, 'L'évolution de la femme africaine', *Liaison*, 15 (December 1951), 13–14; Jérôme Bandila, 'Le zig-zag de la jeunesse', *Liaison*, 35 (May 1953), 18–19; Paul Kaya, 'La fille noire, cette "victime"', *Tam-Tam*, 5 (March 1956), 10–13; Pika, 'La mode féminine: l'habit fait-il le moine?', *La Semaine*, 31 January 1953; Raphaël Bouabala, 'Les jeunes filles et la mode', *Liaison*, 21–2 (February-March 1952), 11–12; Madelaine M'Bombo, 'La voix d'une femme courageuse', *Liaison*, 39 (September 1953), 16–17.

93 Mosingue, 'La corruption des moeurs des femmes', 33.

94 'L'élection de Miss Poto-Poto', *France-Equateur*, 4 May 1957; 'L'élection de Miss Africaine', *France-Equateur*, 6 May 1957.

95 Interviews with Mandayela Mpea, 22 December 1986; Adèle Nsongolo, 16 June 1989; Pika, 'La mode feminine'; Bemba, *50 ans de musique du Congo-Zaïre*, 65–6.

96 Voix de la Révolution Discothéque, 'Djiguida', Ngoma no. 275.

97 In its history from 1950 to 1959, the journal *Liaison* published many articles and letters on these topics.

98 Audrey Wipper, 'African women, fashion, and scapegoating', *Canadian Journal of African Studies*, 6, 2 (1972), 329–49.

99 *La sape* is a French slang word meaning clothing, with the added connotation of elegance and high fashion. For present-day *sapeurs* of Bacongo, and the *aventuriers* of Paris (that is, young Bacongo men who have found their way to Paris, an essential part of the experience of being a *sapeur*), the word *sape* also stands for their *La société des ambianceurs et des personnes elégantes*. See Gandoulou, *Dandies à Bacongo*, 12–13, and his *Entre Paris et Bacongo*, 13, 18.

100 Gandoulou, *Dandies à Bacongo*, 34, based on his interview with old men who were members of these clubs in the 1950s. Also Mireille Duteil, 'Congo: travail de "sape"', *Le Monde*, no. 860, 13 March 1989, 106.

101 Gandoulou, *Dandies à Bacongo*, 34–5. Showing off the brand name on the tag of an article of clothing is very much part of modern 'sapeur' display. See, for example, the photograph in Bergman, *African pop*, 54. For a similar phenomenon on the Kinshasa side of the Pool, see Stewart, *Breakout*, 8. Gandoulou makes other points of comparison between the clubs of the 1950s, and present-day *sapeurs*: see *Dandies à Bacongo*, 36–43.

102 Jean Etho, 'L'habit ne fait pas le moine', *Liaison*, 38 (August 1953), 26.

103 Sylvain Bemba, 'Face à son destin, la jeunesse du Moyen-Congo, est-elle prête à assurer la relève?', *Liaison*, 59 (September–October 1957), 13–15.

104 Quoted in Gandoulou, *Dandies à Bacongo*, 11.

7 HIGH SOCIETY

1 Vassal, *Life in French Congo*, 49–52, opp. 58.

2 Etienne Crémieu-Alcan, *L'AEF et l'AOF de grand-papa* (Paris: Éditions Ophrys, 1970), plate IV.

3 See special issue of the *JAH*, 20, 4 (1979), entitled 'White presence and power in Africa'. Also Dane Kennedy, *Islands of white: settler society and culture in Kenya and Southern Rhodesia, 1890–1939* (Durham, N.C.: Duke University Press, 1987).

4 Henri Bobichon, *Le vieux Congo Français et l'AEF* (Paris: Éditions Héraklès, 1939), 62–3.

5 William H. Schneider, *An empire for the masses: the French popular image of Africa, 1870–1900* (Westport, Conn.: Greenwood Press, 1982), 66–7.

6 Augouard, *Anecdotes*, 76.

7 Stuart M. Persell, *The French colonial lobby, 1889–1938* (Stanford: Hoover Institution Press, 1983), 4–5, 15–16; Schneider, *The French Popular Image of Africa*.

8 Castellani, *Vers le Nil français*, 2.

9 Brunache, *Le centre de l'Afrique*, 29, 32.

10 See Table 2.

11 Uzès, *Le voyage de mon fils*, 66–86.

12 Castellani, *Vers le Nil français*, 147–8.

13 Challaye, *Le Congo Français*, 42–3.

14 Moll, *Une âme de colonial*, 15.

15 Clayton, *France, soldiers and Africa*, 14, 351.

16 Challaye, *Le Congo Français*, 41; Castellani, *Vers le Nil français*, 32–3; Richard West, *Brazza of the Congo: European exploration and exploitation in French Equatorial Africa* (London: Jonathan Cape, 1972), 133; Puytorac, *Makambo*, 54–7.

17 Puytorac, *Makambo*, 146.

18 William Storey, 'Big cats and imperialism: lion and tiger hunting in Kenya and northern India, 1898–1930', *Journal of World History*, 2, 2 (Fall 1991), 135–74.

19 Chavannes, *Avec Brazza*, 194–6, 205–8, 242–4.

20 P.Augouard, 'Note sur la fondation de Brazzaville en 1884', *BSRC* 20 (1935), 16–20; de Witte, *Monseigneur Augouard*, 39–40.

21 Guiral, *Le Congo Français*, 230–1.

22 Veistroffer, *Vingt ans*, 93.

23 Uzès, *Le Voyage de mon fils*, 86.

24 Dybowski, *La route du Tchad*, 75–6.

25 John M. Mackenzie, *The empire of nature: hunting, conservation and British imperialism* (Manchester: Manchester University Press, 1988), 86.

26 Rouget, *L'Afrique Equatoriale illustreé*, 150.

27 Vassal, *Life in French Congo*, 150.

28 Veistroffer, *Vingt ans*, 94.

29 Bouteillier, *Douze mois sous l'équateur*, 78.

30 Chavannes, *Avec Brazza*, 278, 325.

31 Zimmermann, *Mémoire d'un congolais*, 27.

32 Veistroffer, *Vingt ans*, 103; Guiral, *Le Congo français*, 234; Chavannes, *Avec Brazza*, 221.
33 Mandat-Grancey, *Au Congo*, 259.
34 Veistroffer, *Vingt ans*, 94.
35 ASOM, B-6–15, Fonds Bruel, Bruel to Maman, Brazzaville, 17 August 1909.
36 Barrows, 'The impact of empire', 78.
37 Moll, *Une âme de colonial*, 11, 18, 21–2.
38 ASOM, B-5–31, Fonds Bruel, Bruel to his mother, Brazzaville, 9 January 1907.
39 Challaye, *Le Congo Français*, 26, 42.
40 *Ibid.*, 43.
41 Uzès, *Le voyage de mon fils*, 68.
42 AGPSE, 510BVI, 'Oeuvres de la Sainte-Enfance', 14 October 1903.
43 Mandat-Grancey, *Au Congo*, 23.
44 Bouteillier, *Douze mois sous l'équateur*, 51, 60–1, 65, 72, 114–15.
45 Anne Stoler, 'Rethinking colonial categories: European communities and the boundaries of rule', *Comparative Studies in Society and History* 31, 1 (1989), 134–81.
46 Bonchamps, 'Rapport sur la région de Brazzaville'.
47 Bouteillier, *Douze mois sous l'équateur*, 57.
48 Cohen, *Rulers of empire*, 46, 81.
49 Weinstein, *Eboué*, 29, 33–4, 262. See also, the similar account of Elie Castor and Raymond Tarcy, *Félix Eboué* (Paris: L'Harmattan, 1984), 18.
50 A phrase used by Terence Ranger in his essay, 'The invention of tradition in colonial Africa', in Hobsbawm and Ranger, *The invention of tradition*, 215.
51 AOM, 5D182, R. Chabert to Mayor of Brazzaville, 28 November 1950.
52 Puytorac, *Makambo*, 92, 150, 158, 162.
53 Poulaine, *Etapes*, 16.
54 Gide, *Travels in the Congo*, 16.
55 *L'Etoile*, 21 February 1935.
56 Vassal, *Life in French Congo*, 50–2; Chalux, *Un an au Congo Belge*, 111, 120–2; Crémieu-Alcan, *L'AEF et L'AOF de grand-papa*, 30, 51.
57 Vassal, *Life in French Congo*, 51–2.
58 Chalux, *Un an au Congo Belge*, 112; Vassal, *Life in French Congo*, 173–6.
59 Interviews with Roger Frey, 9 July 1987; Geneviève and François Pierret, 31 July 1987; Soeur Scholastique, 13 November 1986.
60 *L'Etoile*, 28 May 1936.
61 Based on accounts in *L'Etoile*, *Paris-Congo* and *La France de Brazzaville* for 1934–1937. Also, Rondet-Saint, *Sur les routes*, 151; Frey, 'Brazzaville', 51; and Roger Frey, personal communication, 25 July 1987 and 27 June 1988.
62 Motley, *Devils in waiting*, 26–7. Mary Motley was the pen-name of an Englishwoman married to a French army officer, Guy de Renéville. She had the title of the Comtesse de Renéville.
63 Julien Maigret, 'Nos grandes cités coloniales: Brazzaville', *MCI*, 32 (April 1926), 83.
64 Crémieu-Alcan, *L'AEF et l'AOF de grand-papa*, 58–9.
65 For example, in Sauvage, *Les secrets de l'Afrique noire*, 313–4; also inter-

views with Geneviève and François Pierret, 31 July 1987; Maya Alden, 10 December 1986.

66 *L'Etoile*, 29 November 1930.

67 M. Lefèvre, 'Le scoutisme colonial', *Le Chef* (March 1936), 100; AGPSE, 183B1, Five-year report of the Brazzaville Mission, 1 January 1920; Gamandzori, 'Le mouvement associatif des jeunes', 77.

68 Gide, *Travels in the Congo*, 16.

69 Motley, *Devils in waiting*, 42.

70 Pellerin, *Une enfance en la brousse congolaise*, 17.

71 Crémieu-Alcan, *L'AEF et l'AOF de grand-papa*, 49–52.

72 Lieutenant Runner, 'De Brazzaville au Caire', *MCI*, 47 (July 1927), 148.

73 Maigret, 'Nos grandes cités coloniales', 83.

74 *Ibid.*, and his 'Brazzaville d'hier – Brazzaville d'aujourd'hui', 274–9; Bonnefont, 'Brazzaville: la ville et la mission', 108.

75 AOM, 4(2)D51 Annual report of Moyen-Congo, Autonomous Subdivision of Brazzaville, 31 December 1931 and 31 December 1932.

76 AGPSE, 227BVI, Letter of P. le Comte, May 1938; Homet, *Congo: terre de souffrances*, 215; Sauvage, *Les secrets de l'Afrique noire*, 68.

77 Cohen, *Rulers of empire*, 108, 121–8, 141.

78 A word used in Pellerin, *Une enfance en la brousse congolaise*, 126; and *L'Etoile*, 18 October 1930.

79 Interviews with Geneviève and François Pierret, 31 July 1987; Maya Alden, 10 December 1986.

80 Interview with Geneviève and François Pierret, 31 July 1987.

81 Cohen, *Rulers of empire*, appendix 4 and 5; Marien Martini, *Les corses dans l'expansion française* (Ajaccio: Editions 'les Myrtes', 1953), 9–13.

82 *L'Etoile*, 10 January, 21 February, 14 March and 25 April 1931.

83 AOM, 5D133, President of Corsican Club to Governor-General Reste, 21 April and 30 August 1936; *L'Etoile*, 3 and 10 October 1935 and 19 September 1936; *La France de Brazzaville*, October 1935 and September 1936.

84 See chapter 4.

85 Dadet, 'La petite histoire du football congolais', 29 March 1970.

86 J. M. Pichat, *Brazzaville-Paris* (Paris: Editions Larose, 1933), 18.

87 *L'Etoile*, 24 January 1931; 'Bulletin sportif', *BSRC*, 16 (1932), 163, 167.

88 Crémieu-Alcan, *L'AEF et l'AOF de grand-papa*, 64; Weinstein, *Eboué*, 64, 75; interview with François Pierret, 31 July 1987.

89 Motley, *Devils in waiting*, 18–19.

90 *Ibid.*, 35.

91 *Ibid.*, 35. For the ritual of 'calling' in Northern Rhodesia, see Karen Tranberg Hansen, 'White women in a changing world: employment, voluntary work and sex in post-World War II Northern Rhodesia', in Chaudhuri and Strobel (eds.), *Western women and imperialism: complicity and resistance*, 247–68.

92 Interview with Maya Alden, 7 November 1986.

93 For contemporaries, see, Pellerin, *Une enfance en la brousse congolaise*, 127; Augouard, *Quarante-quatre années au Congo*, 174. See also, Margaret Strobel, *European women and the second British empire* (Bloomington:

Indiana University Press, 1991) 1–15; Beverly Gartrell, 'Colonial wives: villains or victims?' in Callan and Ardener (eds.), *The incorporated wife*, 165–8; Helen Callaway, *Gender, culture and empire: European women in colonial Nigeria* (Urbana: University of Illinois Press, 1987), 228–9.

94 Names of colonial teachers and nurses appear in administrative reports; missionaries worked with the Swedish Evangelical Mission or were nuns at the convent of the Sisters of Saint Joseph of Cluny. Some beauticians and other professionals who supported the white community advertised their services in *L'Etoile*.

95 Vacquier, *Au temps des factories*, 123–4.

96 According to Madame Pierret, interview 31 July 1987, she and other mothers in the 1930s preferred to look after their children themselves, making sure that they had an adequate diet, medical care and schooling.

97 *La France de Brazzaville*, 31 October and 7 November 1936.

98 Vassal, *Life in French Congo*, 93–4; Motley, *Devils in waiting*, 69–77; Headrick, 'The impact of colonialism on health', 695–8.

99 Callaway, *Gender, culture and empire*, 229.

100 Hilary Callan, 'Introduction', in Callan and Ardener, (eds.), *The incorporated wife*, 1–19.

101 Motley, *Devils in waiting*, 35.

102 Georges Hardy, *Histoire sociale de la colonisation française* (Paris: Larose, 1953) 134–6.

103 *Ibid.*, 136–7.

104 *Dépêche Coloniale*, 13 March 1922

105 Clothilde Chivas-Baron, *La femme française aux colonies* (Paris: Larose, 1929), 108, 121, 140.

106 Interview with Geneviève and François Pierret, 31 July 1987.

107 Strobel, *European women and the second British empire*, 2–7.

108 Vassal, *Life in French Congo*, 27, 39–40.

109 Archives de la Justice, Le Tribunal de Première Instance de l'AEF, Minutes des Judgements Correctionels, 1924.

110 Robert Haffmans, 'Klein-Parijs in de Evenaarsteppe: Brazzaville,' *Africa Christo*, 5 (1958), 21–7.

111 Gheerbrant, *Congo noir et blanc*, 15.

112 *AEF Nouvelle*, August 1948; Jean Dresch, 'Villes congolaises: étude de géographie urbaine et sociale', *La Revue de Géographie Humaine et d'Ethnologie* 3 (July-September, 1948), 3–24. Florence Bernault-Boswell, 'Le rôle des milieux coloniaux dans la décolonisation du Gabon et du Congo-Brazzaville (1945–1964)', in Ageron and Michel (eds.), *L'Afrique noire française*, 285–96.

113 *AEF Nouvelle*, August 1948.

114 AOM, AP2302/1, Inspector Ruffel to Governor-General, Brazzaville, 29 June 1948; Wagret, *Histoire et sociologie politiques*, 138; Balandier, *Sociologie des Brazzavilles Noires*, 83; Bernault-Boswell, 'Le rôle des milieux coloniaux dans la décolonisation'. A similar transformation took place in the white population of Gabon and Senegal: see Guy Lasserre, *Libreville: la ville et sa région* (Paris: Armand Colin, 1958), 266–7, and Rita Cruise O'Brien, *White society in Black Africa: the French of Senegal*, (Evanston, Ill.: Northwestern University Press, 1972), 48–99.

115 Bernault-Boswell, 'Le rôle des milieux coloniaux dans la décolonisation'.
116 Balandier, *Ambiguous Africa*, 169–70; also his *Sociologie des Brazzavilles noires*, 203–8.
117 Althabe, *Le chômage à Brazzaville*, 16.
118 Dresch, 'Villes congolaises', 10.
119 Weinstein, *Eboué*, 277.
120 Joseph Loukou, 'Blancs et noirs...', *Liaison*, 65 (September-October 1958), 18.
121 Bemba, *50 ans de musique du Congo-Zaïre*, 81, 87.
122 AOM, AP2150/3, Governor-General to Director of Political Affairs, 1 December 1948.
123 Ganga, *Combats pour un sport africain*, 18–19.
124 N'Zala-Backa, *Le tipoye doré*, 96.
125 Interview with Mère Emilie, 12 June 1989.
126 Loukou, 'Blancs et noirs...', 17–18. See a similar comment concerning Libreville in Lasserre, *Libreville*, 273.
127 Loukou, 'Blancs et noirs', 17.
128 M'Bokolo, 'Forces sociales et idéologies', 393–407.
129 See Terence Ranger, 'Making Northern Rhodesia imperial: variations on a royal theme, 1924–1938', *African Affairs*, 79, 314 (1980), 349–72; also, Jean-Luc Vellut, 'Matériaux pour une image du blanc dans la société coloniale du Congo Belge', in Jean Pirotte (ed.), *Stéréotypes nationaux et préjugés raciaux aux XIXe et XXe siècles* (Louvain: Editions Nauwelaerts, 1982), 91–116.
130 ANB, GG104, Mayor of Brazzaville to Lieutenant-Governor of Moyen-Congo, 9 September 1930, quoted in Dianzinga, 'Evolution d'une ville coloniale', 100.
131 Chalux, *Un an au Congo Belge*, 128.

CONCLUSION

1 For example, Wagret, *Histoire et sociologie politiques*, 61, and for a full account of the parties and politicians, 54ff.; also Sinda, *Le messianisme congolais*, 281.
2 See chapter 1, n25 for citations.
3 Dupré, *Un ordre et sa destruction*; Vansina, *Paths in the rainforests*, especially 239–48.

Bibliography

INTERVIEWS

The following interviews were mostly carried out in Congo. A few were conducted in France, Sweden and the United States. The inquiry sought out a range of informants in terms of education, gender, region of origin and occupation. Interviews started with open-ended questions about the individual's life and reasons for arrival and stay in Brazzaville. They were followed by more specific questions relating to recreational interests. In some cases, for example when the question of fashion arose, informants were asked for their comments on photographs, and they sometimes produced their own. Interviews in French were conducted by the author, also interviews in Lingala with some help from a research assistant. Given the size of the town and the possible range of informants, research assistants were used when the informants did not speak French or Lingala. In this case, the interviews followed the procedure outlined above, with some open-ended questions and followed by others that picked up on the informant's interests. I am especially grateful to Léa Ngole and Honoré Ngonza for their assistance with interviews. Several others have offered advice with translations of particular points in the sources. These have included Jean Dzong, Kisanga Salamu Gray, Marie-Cécile Groelsma, Yeno Matuka, Jean-Pierre Ngole and Jean-Pierre Nkara. Copies of tapes are deposited with the Archives of Traditional Music, Indiana University, Bloomington.

The names given for informants are those by which they identified themselves.

IN CONGO

Alden, Maya, 7 November and 10 December 1986. Retired missionary of the SMF. Arrived in Brazzaville with her husband in 1937. Worked in Bacongo, especially with women and children.

Balossa, Martin, 17 June 1989. From the Pool region. Lived in Brazzville since he was a boy. Veteran of the Second World War. Member of a dance association.

Bemba, Sylvain, 2 and 13 January 1987. One of Congo's leading intellectuals, has published plays, novels, and articles in *Liaison* and *La Semaine*. Author of important book on music. Lives in Bacongo.

Boudzoumou, Antoine, 16 November 1986. Born about 1927 and arrived in Brazzaville from the lower Congo in 1940s. Primary education at Protestant school, clerk.

Ebale, Marie, 3 January 1987. From the Likuala region but has lived in Brazzaville since early 1930s. Never attended school. Farmer. Lives in Poto-Poto. Member of dance group.

Kébadia, Antoine, 4 October 1986. Born in the Pool region in 1948. Gardener and domestic servant. Football fan. Supports *Diables Noirs*.

Kimina-Makumbu, Fulbert, 10 and 16 October 1986. Born in 1939. Leading sports journalist, writes for *La Semaine*; supports *Diables-Noirs*.

Lingouala, Louis, 22 December 1986. About sixty-eight years old. Arrived in Brazzaville from Bolobo in the late 1940s. Attended school for about two years. Fisherman and trader. Has lived in Poto-Poto and Ouenze.

Madame Adèle, 14 June 1989. Farmer, petty trader. Lives at Mpila. Remembers the Second World War. Association member.

Madame Walymeya, 14 June 1989. About seventy years old. Has lived in Brazzaville most of her life. Remembers Second World War. Association member.

Mambeke-Boucher, Bernard, 17 and 20 November, 1, 10, 12 December 1986. Born in 1919 in Poto-Poto; died in 1990. Teacher, research assistant at ORSTOM in late 1940s; played for *L'Etoile de Congo* and earned the nickname *Roi de la Plaine* ('King of the Playing-field); elected member of regional assembly and cabinet minister in first Opangault government.

Mangoyo, Antoine, 29 December 1986. About seventy years old. Arrived in Brazzaville from Bobangi region about 1947. Fisherman, hunter and fish-seller. Attended a Protestant school for a short time.

Massalo, Augustine, 23 December 1986. About sixty-five years old. Arrived in Brazzaville with her husband from Plateau region about 1940. Manioc bread preparation and trader; fish trader. Lives in Poto-Poto. Never attended school. Member of a dance association.

Massengo, Clement, 27 October and 24 November 1986. Born in 1933; star of *Diables Noirs* in the 1950s, when he was known as 'Dr Fu-Mancho' on account of his football wizardry. Radio sports broadcaster; worked for Air France. Lives in Bacongo.

Mbemba, Veronique, 15 December 1986 and 15 January 1987. From the Pool region. Leader of Protestant women's organization. Farmer and trader.

Mère Emilie, 12 and 13 June 1989. About seventy years old. Lived in Brazzaville all her life. Father from the Gold Coast and mother from Kinshasa. Attended the convent school. Member of women's group which danced in bars.

Miayedimina, Yvonne, 25 November 1986. Educated at the secondary school of the Sisters of Saint Joseph of Cluny. Leader of women's association in the Catholic church.

Mokwami, Phillippe, 10 January 1987. About seventy years old. Born in Brazzaville. Attended Catholic school. Nurse and clerk in government office. Played the accordion and was a member of Paul Kamba's 'Victoria Brazza' music group and band. Lives in Mpila.

Monabeka, Honoré, 27 December 1986. About seventy years old. Arrived in

Brazzaville as a child about 1920. Never attended school. Fisherman, mason and policeman. Lives in Poto-Poto.

Mowango, Albertine, 26 December 1986. About sixty years old. Arrived in Brazzaville in 1948 from the Plateau region. Manioc bread preparation and trader; also fish trader. Lives in Poto-Poto.

Mpea, Mandayela, 22 December 1986. About sixty-five years old. Born in Bolobo, Belgian Congo, and arrived in Brazzaville about 1937 to go to school. Fisherman, also clerk with trading company. Lives in Poto-Poto.

Néoneka, Gabrielle, 8 January 1987. About eighty years old. Arrived in Brazzaville with her husband who was a fisherman on Mbamu Island about 1945. Manioc-bread preparation and trader; also fish-trader. Lives in Poto-Poto.

Ngondjo, Anne, 15 June 1989. About sixty years old. Has lived in Brazzaville since childhood; trader.

Ngonga-Nzonzi, Gabriel, 10 December 1986. From the Niari region. Educated in Protestant schools; teacher in a teacher-training college.

Nkoukou, Hilaire, 22 November 1986. Born in 1923; educated in Protestant schools and became a monitor. From the lower Congo region. Lives in Bacongo.

Nsongolo, Adèle, 16 June 1989. About seventy years old. Has lived in Brazzaville most of her life. Never attended school; manioc-bread preparation and trader. Member of women's association.

Papa Albert, 17 June 1989. Arrived Brazzaville about 1930. About seventy-five years old. Mason by trade; football referee.

Papa Moustapha, 15 June 1989. About sixty-five years old. Second World War veteran; has lived in Brazzaville since then.

Peka, Stephanie Josephine, 15 June 1989. About sixty years old. Born in Brazzaville; farmer and trader.

Père Schaub, 14 and 15 October 1986. Eighty-eight years old and retired missionary of the Holy Ghost Fathers. Arrived in Brazzaville in 1926.

Samba, Marie-Paula, 13 January 1987. A social worker and project director for the World Health Organization.

Soeur Clothilde, 10 November 1986. About eighty-five years old. Retired missionary of the Sisters of Saint Joseph of Cluny. Arrived in Brazzaville in 1923.

Soeur Scholastique, 13 November 1986. Seventy-four years old and missionary of the Sisters of Saint Joseph of Cluny. Arrived in Brazzaville in 1930s.

Soumbre, Habibou, 11 November 1986. Member of a Senegalese family which has lived in Brazzaville for decades. An important businessman and leader of the Muslim community. Lives in Poto-Poto.

IN FRANCE

Frey, Roger, 9 July 1987, Saint-Raphael. Arrived in Brazzaville in 1937 as a colonial administrator, and remained until after independence to advise the government on tourism; amateur historian of Brazzaville from French perspective (see bibliography).

Pierret, François and Geneviève, 31 July 1987, Meyreuil. Arrived in Brazzaville in

1936, and remained in AEF until 1960, mostly in Ubangi-Shari and Chad. She raised several children in Africa.
He died in 1987.

IN SWEDEN

Söderberg, Bertil, 25 May 1986. Missionary in Congo for SMF, 1930s-1950s; ethnomusicologist and ethnographer.
Widman, Ragmar, 27 May 1986. Missionary in Congo for SMF, 1930s-1950s. Published a book on funeral practices in the lower Congo.

IN THE UNITED STATES

Ngole, Jean-Pierre, 13 October 1988. Born and raised in Brazzaville from the 1940s. Now professor of modern languages at Marien Ngouabi University; secretary of CARA football club.
Ngole, Sidone, 12 May 1988. Born and raised in Brazzaville. Attended the secondary school established by the Sisters of Saint-Joseph of Cluny; housewife and accountant-secretary in a leading bank.
Oumba, Marie-Thérèse, 15 August 1993. Born and raised in Bacongo. Parents from the Linzolo area where her family were active in the congregation at the Catholic mission of the Holy Ghost Fathers. Graduate of Marien Ngouabi University.

ARCHIVES

Archives de la Justice, Palais de Justice, Brazzaville
Archives Générales des Pères du Saint-Esprit, Chevilly-Larue
Archives Nationales du Congo, Brazzaville
Archives Nationales, Centre des Archives d'Outre-Mer, Aix-en-Provence
Archives of the Salvation Army, London
Arkivet, Svenska Missionsförbundet, Riksarkivet, Stockholm
Archives de l'Académie des Sciences d'Outre-Mer, Paris
Archief, Nieuwe Afrikaansche Handelsvereeniging, Algemeen Rijksarchief, The Hague
Service de la Documentation et des Archives Municipal, Brazzaville

CONTEMPORARY NEWSPAPERS AND JOURNALS

AEF Nouvelle, 1948–9
Annales Apostoliques, 1886–1927; became, Annales des Pères du Saint-Esprit, 1927–46
Annales des Soeurs de Saint-Joseph de Cluny, 1892–1960
Brazzaville: Revue de l'Action Municipale, 1967–9
Brazzaville: Supplement à la Vie Catholique Illustrée, 1950–2
Bulletin de la Comité de l'Afrique Française, 1892–1939
Bulletin de la Congregation des Soeurs de Saint-Joseph de Cluny, 1892–1960

Bulletin de la Société des Recherches Congolaises, 1922–39; became *Bulletin de l'Institut d'Etudes Centrafricaines*, 1945–60
Bulletin d'Information d'A.E.F., 1931–6
Bulletin d'Information et de Documentation du Gouvernement-Général, 1949–53; became *Bulletin de Documentation d'AEF*, 1953–60
Bulletin Général de la Congrégation des Pères du Saint-Esprit, 1883–1939
Courrier d'Afrique, 1943–59
France-Equateur, 1952–5; became *France-Equateur l'Avenir*, 1956–60
Journal Officiel du Congo Français, 1904–10; became *Journal Officiel de l'Afrique Équatoriale Française*, 1910–59.
La France de Brazzaville, 1935–6
La Semaine de l'AEF, 1952–60; became *La Semaine Africaine*, 1960–present
Le Bon Message, 1933–8
L'Education Africaine: Bulletin Trimestriel d'Information, 1942; became *L'Education de la Jeunesse de Brazzaville*, 1942–5.
Le Monde Colonial Illustré, 1923–39
Le Petit Courrier Colonial, 1913–14
L'Etoile de l'AEF, 1930–9
Liaison, Brazzaville, 1950–9
Missions Catholiques, 1881–1938
Missionsförbundet, 1909–38
Paris-Congo, 1936–9
Svenska Missionsförbundets Arsberättelse, 1909–20
Tam-Tam, 1954–8

OTHER SOURCES

Adams, Michael. 'From avoidance to confrontation: peasant protest in pre-colonial and colonial Southeast Asia', in Dirks (ed.), *Colonialism and culture*, 89–126.
Ageron, Charles-Robert, and Michel, Marc (eds.) *L'Afrique noire française: l'heure des indépendances*. Paris: CNRS Editions, 1992.
Aïssi, Antoine-Marie. 'La "justice indigène" et la vie congolaise (1886–1936)'. Thèse de 3è cycle, Université de Toulouse-le Mirail, 1978.
    'Sociologie politique de la condemnation d'un chef indigène: le Ma-Loango Moe Poati II (1926– 27)', *CCAH*, 5 (1980), 47–64.
    'Le tournant des années 30: les blancs du Congo face à l'éveil politique congolais', *CCAH*, 7 (1982), 39–50.
    ' "Les peuples de l'AEF face au système juridictionnel colonial', *Actes du colloque international (Brazzaville, avril 1985)*, 363–88.
Allégret, Marc. *Carnets du Congo: voyage avec Gide*. Paris: Presses du CNRS, 1987.
Almeida-Topor, Hélène d' and Goerg, Odile (eds.) *Le mouvement associatif des jeunes en Afrique noire francophone au XXè siècle*. Paris: L'Harmattan, 1989.
Almeida-Topor, Hélène d' and Riesz, Janos (eds.) *Rencontres franco-allemandes sur l'Afrique*. Paris: L'Harmattan, 1992.
Almeida-Topor, Hélène d', Coquery-Vidrovitch, Catherine, Goerg, Odile and Guitart, Françoise (eds.) *Les jeunes en Afrique*. 2 volumes. Paris: L'Harmattan, 1992.

Althabe, Gérard. *Le chômage à Brazzaville en 1957: étude psychologique.* Paris: ORSTOM, 1958.

Anderson, Benedict. *Imagined communities: reflections on the origins and spread of nationalism.* London: Verso, 1983.

Anderson, Muff. *Music in the mix: the story of South African popular music.* Johannesburg: Ravan Press, 1981.

Andersson, Efraim. *Messianic popular movements in the lower Congo.* Uppsala: Studia Ethnographica Upsaliensia, 1958.

 Churches at the grass-roots: a study in Congo-Brazzaville. London: Lutterworth Press, 1968.

Anthony, David H. 'Culture and society in a town in transition: a people's history of Dar es Salaam, 1865–1939'. Ph.D. thesis, University of Wisconsin, 1983.

Atkins, Keletso E. '"Kafir time": preindustrial temporal concepts and labour discipline in nineteenth century colonial Natal', *JAH*, 29, 2 (1988), 229–44.

 The moon is dead! give us our money! the cultural origins of an African work ethic, Natal, South Africa, 1843–1900. Heinemann: Portsmouth, N.H., 1993.

Audibert, Jacques. 'Une compagnie commerciale en République Populaire du Congo: le CFAO'. Travail d'études et de recherches, University of Bordeaux III, 1973.

Augouard, Louis. *Guirlande enchevêtrée d'anecdotes congolais.* Evreux: Poussin, 1934.

Augouard, Mgr. 'Voyage à Stanley Pool', *MC*, 13 (1881), 517–18; 14 (1882), 113–16, 125–8, 140–1.

 28 années au Congo: lettres de Mgr. Augouard. Poitiers: Société française d'Imprimerie et de Librairie, 1905.

 36 années au Congo. Poitiers: Société française d'Imprimerie et de Librairie, 1914.

 'A propos de Brazzaville', *BCAF* (1917), 95–102.

 44 années au Congo. Evreux: Poussin, 1934.

Auric, Henri. *L'avenir du Congo et le 'Congo-Océan'.* Paris: Librairie Picart, 2nd edn, 1934.

Austen, Ralph A. and Headrick, Rita. 'Equatorial Africa under colonial rule', in Birmingham and Martin (eds.) *History of Central Africa*, vol. II, 27–94.

Babassana, Hilaire. *Travail forcé, expropriation et formation du salariat en Afrique noire.* Grenoble: Presses Universitaires de Grenoble, 1978.

Bafouetela, Raymond. 'Etude morphologique et vestimentaire sur le groupe Bondjo de la Likouala', *CCAH*, 5 (1980), 65–73.

 'Le travail sous la période coloniale au Congo (1897–1945)', *CCAH*, 6 (1981), 77–94.

Baker, William J. and Mangan, James A. (eds.) *Sport in Africa: essays in social history.* New York: Africana Publishing House, 1987.

Balandier, Georges. 'Evolution de la société et de l'homme', in Guernier (ed.) *Afrique Equatoriale Française*, 125–32.

 Ambiguous Africa: culture in collision. Translated by Helen Weaver. New York: Pantheon Books, 1966.

'The colonial situation: a theoretical approach (1951)', in Immanuel Wallerstein (ed.) *Change and the colonial situation*. New York: Wiley, 1966, 34–61.

The sociology of black Africa. Translated by Douglas Garman. London: Andre Deutsch, 1970.

Sociologie des Brazzavilles noires. Paris: Presses de la Fondation Nationale des Sciences Politiques, 2nd edn, 1985.

Balesi, Charles. *From adversaries to comrades-in-arms: West Africans and the French military, 1885–1918*. Waltham, Mass.: Crossroads Press, 1979.

Banzouzi, Jean-Pierre. 'La représentation de l'histoire du Congo à travers les noms des rues de Brazzaville', in *Journées d'études sur Brazzaville*. 75–84.

Baratier, Albert Ernest Augustin. *Epopées africaines*. Paris: Fayard, 1912.

Au Congo: souvenirs de la Mission Marchand. Paris: Arthème Fayard & Co., 1914.

A travers l'Afrique. Paris: Arthème Fayard & Co., 1942.

Barber, Karen. 'Popular arts in Africa', *African Studies Review*, 30, 3 (September 1989), 1–78.

Bebey, Francis. *La radiodiffusion en Afrique noire*. Paris: Editions Saint-Paul, 1963.

Beidelman, T. O. *Colonial evangelism: a socio-historical study of an East African mission at the grassroots*. Bloomington: Indiana University Press, 1982.

Bemba, Léon. 'L'AEF dans la première guerre mondiale'. Thèse de 3è cycle, University of Paris VII, 1984.

Bemba, Sylvain. 'L'évolution de la musique congolaise', *Liaison*, 37 (March-April, 1957) 37–41.

'Face à son destin, la jeunesse du Moyen-Congo, est-elle prête à assurer la relève?', *Liaison*, 59 (September-Ocotober 1957), 13–15.

Rêves portatifs. Dakar: les Nouvelles Editions Africaines, 1979.

Le soleil est parti à M'Pemba. Paris: Présence Africaine, 1982.

50 ans de musique du Congo-Zaïre. Paris: Présence Africaine, 1984.

Bender, Wolfgang. *Sweet mother: modern African music*. Chicago: University of Chicago Press, 1991.

Bentley, W. Holman. *Dictionary and grammar of the Kongo language*. London: Baptist Missionary Society, 1887.

Pioneering on the Congo. 2 volumes. London: The Religious Tract Society, 1900.

Bergman, Billy. *African pop: goodtime kings*. Poole, Dorset: Bladford Press, 1985.

Bernard, J. 'La mutualité chex les Bacongos: le Kitemo', *BSRC*, 2 (1922), 9–14.

Bernault, Florence. 'La semaine de l'AEF, 1952–1960: un hébdomadaire chrétien d'information et d'action sociale'. 2 volumes. Mémoire de Maîtrise d'Histoire, University of Paris I, 1985.

Bernault-Boswell, Florence. 'Le rôle des milieux coloniaux dans la décolonisation du Gabon et du Congo-Brazzaville, 1945–1964', in Ageron and Michel (eds.) *L'Afrique noire française: l'heure des indépendances*, 285–96.

Bertrand, Hugues. *Le Congo: formation sociale et mode de développement economique*. Paris: Maspéro, 1975.

Betts, Raymond F. *Assimilation and association in French colonial theory, 1890–1914*. New York: ASM Press, 1961.

'Dakar: ville impériale (1857–1960)', in Ross and Telkamp (eds.) *Colonial cities*, 192–206.

'Imperial designs: French colonial architecture and urban planning in sub-Saharan Africa', in Johnson (ed.) *Double impact*, 191–207.

Bibliographie ethnographique de l'Afrique Equatoriale Française 1914–1948. Afrique Equatoriale Française Service de Statistique. Paris: Imprimerie Nationale, 1948.

Birmingham, David and Martin, Phyllis M. (eds.) *History of Central Africa*, 2 volumes. London: Longman, 1983.

Birmingham, David. 'Carnival at Luanda', *JAH*, 29, 1 (1988), 93–113.

Blacking, John. 'Games and sport in pre-colonial African societies', in Baker and Mangan (eds.) *Sport in Africa*, 3–21.

Blouin, Andrée. *My country, Africa: autobiography of the black pasionaria*. New York: Praeger, 1983.

Boahen, A. Adu (ed.) *Africa under colonial domination, 1880–1935*. volume VII, UNESCO *General history of Africa*. London: Heinemann, 1985.

African perspectives on colonialism. Johns Hopkins University Press, 1987.

Bobichon, Henri. *Le vieux Congo Français et l'AEF*. Paris: Héraklès, 1939.

Bonner, Philip, Hofmeyr, Isabel, James, Deborah, and Lodge, Tom (eds.) *Holding their ground: class, locality and culture in 19th and 20th century South Africa*. Johannesburg: Witwatersrand University Press, 1989.

Bontinck, François. 'Quand Brazzaville se trouvait à Kinshasa', *Zaïre-Afrique*, 148 (October 1980), 487–99.

'La dernière décennie de Nshasa (1881– 1891)', *Zaïre-Afrique*, 169 (November 1982), 535–52; 170 (December 1982), 619–33.

Boslough, John. 'The enigma of time', *National Geographic*, 177, 3 (March 1990), 109–32.

Bouchaud, J.S. 'Les missions catholiques', in Guernier (ed.) *Afrique Équatoriale Française*, 578–87.

Bouteillier, Gaston. *Douze mois sous l'équateur*. Toulouse: Imprimerie Adolphe Trinchant, 1903.

Bozzoli, Belinda (ed.) *Town and countryside in the Transvaal*. Johannesburg: Witwatersrand University Press, 1983.

Class, community and conflict: South African perspectives. Johannesburg: Ravan Press, 1987.

Braudel, Fernand. *On history*. Translated by Sarah Matthews. Chicago: Chicago University Press, 1980.

Brazzaville, coeur de la nation congolaise. Archives Municipales, Mairie de Brazzaville (Service Culturel), Brazzaville: Imprimerie Nationale, 1973.

Brazzaville, janvier-février 1944: aux sources de la décolonisation. Colloque organisé par l'institut Charles-de-Gaulle et l'institut d'histoire du temps présent, les 22 et 23 mai 1987. Paris: Plon, l'Institute Charles-de-Gaulle, 1988.

Brazzaville: ville sportive. Ministère de la Culture, des Arts et des Sports: Brazzaville, 1980.

Briart, P. 'Le Stanley Pool commercial', *Le Mouvement Géographique*, 28 (1911), cols. 439–43.

Briart, P. 'Le Stanley Pool hier, aujourd'hui, demain', *Le Mouvement Géographique*, 28 (1911), cols. 199–203.

Briault, Maurice. *Sous le zéro équatorial: études et scènes Africaines*. Paris: Blond & Gay, 1926.

   'La mode chez les noirs', *APSE* (March 1929), 89–96; (April 1929), 124–8.

   Dans la forêt du Gabon. Paris: Bernard Grasset, 1930.

   'Le Congo-Océan et les missions catholiques', *Revue d'Histoire des Missions*, 12 (1935), 71–6.

   'Le cinquantenaire de la mission du Congo Français: Brazzaville 1888–1938', *Revue d'Histoire des Missions*, 15 (December 1938), 504–22; 16 (March, 1939), 37–58.

Bruel, Georges. *Bibliographie de l'Afrique Equatoriale Française*. Paris: Larose, 1914.

   La France Equatoriale Africaine. Paris: Larose, 1935.

Brunache, Paul. *Le centre de l'Afrique: autour du Tchad*. Paris: F. Alcan, 1894.

Brunschwig, Henri. *Brazza explorateur: L'Ogooué, 1875–1879*. Paris: Mouton, 1966.

   Brazza explorateur: les traités Makoko, 1880– 1882. Paris: Mouton, 1972.

   Noirs et blancs dans l'Afrique noire française ou comment le colonisé devient colonisateur (1870–1974). Paris: Flammarion, 1983.

Brustier, Louis. *Cendrillon africaine*. Paris: Les Editions du Scorpion, 1962.

Burke, Peter. *Popular culture in early modern Europe*. New York: Harper, 1978.

Brisset-Guibert, Hervé. 'L'architecture coloniale française à Brazzaville (1860–1960): évolution, caractères, classification', *Ultramarines: Bulletin des Amis des Archives d'Outre-Mer*, 2 (January, 1991), 3–11.

Callan, Hilary and Ardener, Shirley (eds.) *The incorporated wife*. London: Croom Helm, 1984.

Callaway, Helen, *Gender, culture and empire: European women in colonial Nigeria*. Urbana: University of Illinois Press, 1987.

Capelle, E. M. *La cité indigène de Léopoldville*. Brussels: Centre d'Études Sociales Africaines, 1947.

CARA de Brazzaville: album souvenir 1951–1982. Brazzaville: Gamma/Athène, 1982.

Carozzi, Carlo and Tiepolo, Maurizio (eds.) *Congo Brazzaville: Bibliografia generale/bibliographie générale*. Turin: Edizione Libreria Cortina, 1991.

Carrie, P. *Coutumier de l'oeuvre des enfants dans le vicariat apostolique du Congo Français*. Loango: Imprimerie de la Mission, 1890.

   Oeuvre des soeurs de Saint-Joseph de Cluny dans la mission du Congo Français. Loango: Imprimerie de la Mission, 1897.

   Organisation de la mission du Congo Français. Loango: Imprimerie de la Mission, 1898.

   Règlements du petit séminaire du Congo Français. Loango: Imprimerie de la Mission, 1898.

Castellani, Charles. *Les femmes au Congo*. Paris: Ernest Flammarion, 1898.

   Vers le Nil français avec la Mission Marchand. Paris: Ernest Flammarion, 1898.

Castor, Elie and Tarcy, Raymond. *Félix Éboué*. Paris: L'Harmattan, 1984.

Céline, Louis-Ferdinand. *Voyage au bout de la nuit*. Paris: Denoël & Steele,1932; Gallimard, 1962.

Centenaire de la conférence de Berlin 1884–1885. Actes du colloque international (Brazzaville, Avril 1985). Paris: Présence Africaine, 1987.

Challaye, Félicien. *Le Congo Français: la question internationale du Congo*. Paris: Félix Alcan, 1909.

   Souvenirs sur la colonisation. Paris: Librairie Picard, 1935.

Chalux (pseud.) *Un an au Congo Belge*. Brussels: Librairie Albert Dewit, 1925.

Chanock, Martin. *Law, culture and social order: the colonial experience in Malawi and Zambia*. Cambridge: Cambridge University Press, 1985.

Chaudhuri, Nupur and Strobel, Margaret (eds.) *Western women and imperialism: complicity and resistance*. Bloomington: Indiana University Press, 1992.

Chaumel, Alfred. 'Une mission de propagande par le film en AEF', *BSRC*, 5 (1924), 11–15.

Chavannes, Charles de. 'Note sur la fondation de Brazzaville en 1884', *BSRC*, 20 (1935), 1–22.

   Avec Brazza: souvenirs de la mission de l'Ouest-Africain. Mars 1883–janvier 1886. Paris: Librairie Plon, 1935.

   Le Congo Français. Ma collaboration avec Brazza (1886–1894). Nos relations jusqu'à sa mort (1905). Paris: Librairie Plon, 1937.

Chivas-Baron, Clothilde. *La femme française aux colonies*. Paris: Larose, 1929.

Chrétien, J.-P. and Prunier, G. (eds.) *Les ethnies ont une histoire*. Paris: Karthala, 1989.

Clayton, Anthony. 'Sport and African soldiers: the military diffusion of western sports throughout sub-Sahara Africa', Baker and Mangan (eds.) *Sport in Africa*, 114–37.

   France, soldiers and Africa. London: Brassey's, 1988.

Clignet, Remi and Stark, Maureen. 'Modernisation and football in Cameroun', *Journal of Modern African Studies*, 12, 3 (1974), 409–21.

Cohen, Abner. *Custom and government in urban Africa*. Berkeley: University of California Press, 1969.

Cohen, David William and Atieno Odhiambo, E. S. *Siaya: the historical anthropology of an African landscape*. London: James Currey, 1989.

Cohen, William B. *Rulers of empire: the French colonial service in Africa*. Stanford: Hoover Institute, 1971.

   The French encounter with Africans: white response to blacks, 1530–1880. Bloomington: Indiana University Press, 1980.

   'Malaria and French imperialism', *JAH*, 24, 1 (1983), 23–36.

Collins, John. *African pop roots. The inside rhythms of Africa*. London: Foulsham, 1985.

Colrat de Montrozier, Raymond. *Deux ans chez les anthropophages*. Paris: Plon-Nourrit, 1902.

Comaroff, Jean, and Comaroff, John. *Of revelation and revolution: Christianity, colonialism and consciousness in South Africa*. Chicago: Chicago University Press, 1991.

Comhaire-Sylvain, Suzanne. 'Jeux congolais', *Zaire*, 6, 4 (April 1952), 351–62.

   Femmes de Kinshasa hier et aujourd'hui. Paris: Mouton, 1968.

Connillière, M. 'Les problèmes de la main d'oeuvre africaine dans les agglomérations urbaines', *BDAEF*, 169 (1952), 3–7.

Cooper, Frederick (ed.) *Struggle for the city: migrant labor, capital and the state in urban Africa*. Beverly Hills, Ca.: Sage Publications, 1983.

'Urban space, industial time and wage labor in Africa', in Cooper (ed.) *Struggle for the city*, 7–50.

On the waterfront: urban disorder and the transformation of work in colonial Mombasa. New Haven: Yale University Press, 1987.

'Colonizing time: work rhythms and labor conflict in colonial Mombasa', in Dirks (ed.) *Colonialism and culture*, 209–45.

Cooper, Frederick and Stoler, Anne. 'Tensions of empire: colonial control and vision of rule', *American Ethnologist*, 16 (1989), 609–21.

Coplan, David. 'Go to my town, Cape Coast! The social history of Ghanaian Highlife', in Bruno Nettl (ed.) *Eight urban musical cultures: tradition and change*. Urbana: University of Illinois Press, 1978, 96–114.

In township tonight! South Africa's black city music and theatre. London: Longman, 1985.

Coquery-Vidrovitch, Catherine. *Brazza et la prise de possession du Congo: la mission de l'Ouest Africain 1883–1885*. Paris: Mouton, 1969.

Le Congo au temps des grandes compagnies concessionnaires 1898–1930. Paris: Mouton, 1972.

'Mutation de l'impérialisme colonial français dans les années 30', *AEH*, 4 (1977), 103–52.

'Investissements privés, investissements publique en AEF, 1900–1940', *AEH*, 12 (1983), 13–31.

Coquer-Vidrovitch, Catherine (ed.). *Processus d'urbanisation en Afrique*. 2 volumes. Paris: L'Harmattan, 1988.

'The process of urbanization in Africa (from the origins to the beginning of independence)', *African Studies Review*, 34, 1 (April, 1991), 1–98.

Cordwell, Justine M. and Schwarz, Ronald A. (eds.) *The fabrics of culture: the anthropology of clothing and adornment*. The Hague: Mouton, 1979.

Coutrot, Aline. 'Youth movements in France in the 1930s', *Journal of Contemporary History*, 5, 1 (1970), 23–36.

Couzens, Tim. '"Moralizing leisure time": the transatlantic connection and black Johannesburg, 1918–1936', in Shula Marks and Richard Rathbone (eds.) *Industrialisation and social change in South Africa*. Harlow, Essex: Longman, 1982, 314–37.

'Introduction to the history of football in South Africa', in Bozzoli (ed.) *Town and countryside*, 198–214.

Crémieu-Alcan, Etienne. *L'AEF et l'AOF de grand-papa*. Paris: Editions Ophrys, 1970.

Croce-Spinelli, Michel. *Les enfants de Poto-Poto*. Paris: L'Harmattan, 1967.

Cunningham, Hugh. *Leisure in the industrial revolution, c.1780– 1880*. London: Croom Helm, 1980.

Curtin, Philip D. 'Medical knowledge and urban planning in tropical Africa', *AHR*, 90, 3 (June 1985), 594–613.

Cuvelier, Jean. 'Les missions catholiques en face des danses des Bakongo', *Africanae Fraternae Ephemerides Romanae*, (1939), 143–76.

Dadet, Emmanuel J. 'La petite histoire du football congolais', *La Semaine Africaine*, 22 and 29 March, 12 and 19 April, 31 May 1970.

Danse, Sylvain. *Carnet de route: d'Elisabethville à Boma par le Lomami, le Kasaï et le Bas-Congo (avril-juin 1920)*. Elisabethville: Imprimerie L'Etoile du Congo, 1923.

Davesne, André. *Croquis de brousse*. Marseilles: Editions du Sagittaire, 1943.

Decapmaker, P. 'Danses des Bakongo', in *La mission et les joies populaires: compte-rendu de la XVIè semaine de missiologie de Louvain, 1938* (Brussels: Edition universelle, 1938), 41–50.

Delcommune, Alexandre. *Vingt années de la vie africaine, 1874– 93*. 2 volumes. Brussels: Larcier, 1922.

Delobeau, Jean-Michel and Ngoulou, Sylvain. 'Le tissage du raphia en pays Kukua: de l'industrie à l'art', *CCAH*, 10 (1985), 45–51.

Deschamps, Capt. *De Bordeaux au Tchad par Brazzaville*. Paris: Société Française d'Imprimerie et de Librairie, 1911.

Devaud, L. 'Les conditions du travail et la condition du travailleur en AEF'. Mémoire ENROM. Paris, 1948.

Devauges, Roland. *Le chômage à Brazzaville en 1957. Etude sociologique*. Paris: ORSTOM, 1958.

Deville-Danthu, Bernadette. 'L'AOF pépinière d'athlètes: révélations, illusions et désillusions', *Histoire Moderne et Contemporaine*, 1 (1991), 255–70.

Dianzinga, Scholastique. 'Histoire de Brazzaville de 1910 à 1940'. Mémoire de Maîtrise, University of Paris VII, 1979.

    'Evolution d'une ville coloniale: Brazzaville de 1884 à 1945', *CCAH*, 12 (1991), 89–102.

Dirks, Nicholas B. (ed.) *Colonialism and culture*. Ann Arbor: University of Michigan Press, 1992.

Douglas, Mary and Isherwood, Baron. *The world of goods: towards an anthropology of consumption*. New York: Basic Books, 1979.

Dresch, Jean. 'Villes congolaises. Etude de géographie urbaine et sociale', *La Revue de Géographie Humaine et d'Ethnologie*, 3 (July-September 1948), 3–24.

Dupré, Georges. *Un ordre et sa destruction*. Paris: ORSTOM, 1982.

Dupré, Marie-Claude. 'Comment être femme. Un aspect du rituel mukisi chez les Teké de la République Populaire du Congo', *Archives de Sciences Sociales des Religions*, 461 (1978), 57–84.

Duteil, Mireille. 'Congo: travail de "sape"', *Le Monde*, 860 (13 March 1989).

Dybowski, Jean. *La route du Tchad: du Loango au Chari*. Paris: Librairie de Firmin-Didot & Co., 1893.

    Le Congo méconnu. Paris: Librairie Hachette, 1912.

Eboué, Félix. 'Le sport en Afrique Equatoriale', *MCI*, 103 (March 1932), 60–1.

    La nouvelle politique indigène en l'Afrique Equatoriale Française. Brazzaville: Afrique Française Libre, 1941.

Echenberg, Myron. *Colonial conscripts: the 'tirailleurs sénégalais' in French West Africa*. Portsmouth, N.H.: Heinemann, 1991.

Esme, Jean d'. *Les maîtres de la brousse*. Paris: Les Editions de France, 1933.

Etudes africaines offertes à Henri Brunschwig. Paris: ORSTOM, 1982.

Evans-Pritchard, E. E. 'Nuer time-reckoning', *Africa*, 12, 2 (1939), 189–216.

Fabian, Johannes. 'Popular culture in Africa: findings and conjectures', *Africa*, 48, 4 (1978), 315–34.

　　Language and colonial power: the appropriation of Swahili in the former Belgian Congo, 1880–1938. Cambridge: Cambridge University Press, 1986.

Fanon, Frantz. *Black skin, white masks: the experiences of a black man in a white world*. Translated by Charles Lam Markmann. New York: Grove Press, 1967.

Faure, J. L. *La vie aux colonies: préparation de la femme à la vie coloniale*. Paris: Larose, 1938.

Fehderau, Harold Werner. *The origin and development of Kituba (lingua franca Kikongo)*. Kisangani: Université Libre du Congo, 1966.

Feierman, Steven. *Peasant intellectuals: anthropology and history in Tanganyika*. Madison: University of Wisconsin Press, 1990.

Fetter, Bruce. *The creation of Elisabethville, 1910–40*. Stanford: Stanford University Press, 1976.

Foucault, Michel. *The archaeology of knowledge*. Translated by A. M. Sheridan Smith. New York: Pantheon Books, 1972.

　　Discipline and punish: the birth of the prison. Translated by Alan Sheridon. New York: Vintage Books, 1989.

Fourneau, Alfred. *Au vieux Congo: notes de route 1884–1891*. Paris: Edition du Comité de l'Afrique Française, 1932.

Frey, Roger. 'Brazzaville, capitale de l'Afrique Equatoriale Française', *Encyclopédie Mensuelle d'Outre-Mer*, 48–9 (August-September 1954), special issue.

　　'La colonie portugaise', *Perspectives d'Outre-Mer*, 18 (May 1956), 53–64. Special issue on AEF.

Friedman, Jonathan. 'The political economy of elegance: an African cult of beauty', *Culture and History*, 7 (1990), 101–25.

Froment, E. 'Trois affluents français du Congo à Alima, Likouala, Sanga', *Bulletin de la Société de Géographie de Lille*, 9 (1887), 458–74.

　　'Un voyage dans l'Oubangui', *Bulletin de la Société de Géographie de Lille*, 11 (1889), 180–216.

Gabio, Joseph. *La fabuleuse histoire des Diables Rouges*. Brazzaville: Editions BDT, 1983.

Gallard, Henri. 'Le "Kitemo"', *BCAF: Renseignements Coloniaux*, 5 (1919), 199–201.

Gamandzori, Joseph. 'Chemin de fer, villes et travail au Congo (1921–1953)'. Thèse de doctorat, University of Paris VII, 1987.

　　'Le mouvement associatif des jeunes dans la dynamique sociale au Congo, 1945–1973', in Almeida-Topor and Goerg (eds.) *Le mouvement associatif des jeunes en Afrique noire francophone au XXè siècle*, 69–90.

Gandoulou, Justin-Daniel. *Entre Paris et Bacongo*. Paris: Centre Georges Pompidou, 1984.

　　Dandies à Bacongo: le culte de l'élégance dans la société congolaise contemporaine. Paris: L'Harmattan, 1989.

Ganga, Jean-Claude. *Combats pour un sport african*. Paris: L'Harmattan, 1979.

Gardinier, David E. 'Education in the states of Equatorial Africa: a bibliographical essay', *Africana Journal*, 3, 3 (1972), 7–20.

　　'Schooling in the states of equatorial Africa', *Canadian Journal of African Studies*, 7, 3 (1974), 517–38.

Historical dictionary of Gabon. African Historical Dictionaries, no.30. Metuchen, N.J.: The Scarecrow Press, 1981; 2nd ed, 1994.

Gartrell, Beverly. 'Colonial wives: villains or victims?', in Callan and Ardener (eds.), *The incorporated wife*, 165– 85.

Gauze, René. *The politics of Congo-Brazzaville.* Stanford, Ca: Hoover Institute Press, 1973.

Geary, Christraud M. 'Photographs as materials for African history: some methodological considerations', *History in Africa*, 13 (1986), 89–116.

Geertz, Clifford. *The interpretation of cultures.* New York: Basic Books, 1973.

Gheerbrant, Alain. *Congo noir et blanc.* Paris: Gallimard, 1955.

Gibson, Gordon .D. and McGurk, C. R. 'High status caps of the Kongo and Mbundu peoples', *Textile Museum Journal*, 4, 4 (1977), 71–96.

Giddens, Anthony. 'Notes on the concepts of play and leisure', *The Sociological Review*, n.s., 12, 1 (March 1964), 73–89.

Gide, André. *Travels in the Congo.* Translated by Dorothy Bussy. Berkeley and Los Angeles: University of California Press, 1962.

Gillis, John R. *Youth and history: tradition and change in European age relations 1770–present.* New York: Academic Press, 1974.

Girard, L. 'Brazzaville', *BCAF: Renseignements Coloniaux*, (March 1916), 26–44.

Goerg, Odile. 'Chefs de quartier et "tribal headmen"', in Chrétien and Prunier (eds.), *Les ethnies ont une histoire*, 267–82.

'Réflexion sur l'architecture européenne le long de la côte africaine à partir de l'exemple de la Guinée', Almeida-Topor and Riesz (eds.) *Rencontres franco-allemandes sur l'Afrique*, 81–92.

Goma-Foutou, Célestin. 'Le centenaire de Brazzaville', *Spécial Etumba*, 563, 4 October 1980.

Gondola, Ebonga Charles Didier. 'Kinshasa et Brazzaville: brève histoire d'un mariage séculaire', *Zaïre-Afrique*, 249–250 (November-December, 1990), 493–500.

'*Ata ndele* ... et l'indépendance vint. Musique, jeunes et contestation politique dans les capitales congolaises', in Almeida-Topor et al. (eds.) *Les jeunes en Afrique*, 463–87.

'Migration et villes congolaises au XXe siècle: processus et implications de mouvements campagnes/villes à Léopoldville et Brazzaville (*c.* 1930–1970)'. Thèse de doctorat, University of Paris VII, 1993.

Gousset, Marcel. *En brousse AEF.* Paris: Editions Fernand Sorlot, 1943.

Goyi, Dominique. 'Les missions catholiques et l'évolution sociale au Congo Brazzaville de 1880 à 1930'. Thèse de 3è cycle, University of Bordeaux, 1969.

Gray, Christopher. *Modernization and cultural identity: the creation of national space in rural France and colonial space in rural Gabon.* (MacArthur Scholar Series, Occasional Papers, no. 21). Bloomington: Indiana University Center on Global Change and World Peace, 1994.

Guernier, Eugène (ed.) *Afrique Equatoriale Française.* Paris: Encyclopédie Coloniale et Maritime, 1950.

Guillemot, Marcel. *Notice sur le Congo Français.* Paris: J.André, 1901.

Guiral, Léon. *Le Congo Français du Gabon à Brazzaville.* Paris: Plon, 1889.

Gutman, Herbert G. 'Work, culture and society in industrializing America, 1815–1919', *AHR*, 78 (June 1973), 531–88.

Haffmans, Robert. 'Klein-Parijs in de Evenaarsteppe: Brazzaville', *Africa Christo*, 5 (1958), 21–70.

Halbwachs, Maurice. 'La mémoire collective et le temps', *Cahiers internationaux de Sociologie*, 2 (1947), 3–31.

Hall, Stuart. 'Notes on deconstructing the popular', in R. Samuel (ed.) *People's history and socialist theory*. London: Routledge and Kegan Paul, 1981, 227–40.

Hansen, Karen Tranberg. *Distant companions: servants and employers in Zambia 1900–1985*. Ithaca, NY: Cornell University Press, 1989.

   'White women in a changing world: employment, voluntary work and sex in post-World War II Northern Rhodesia', in Chaudhuri and Strobel (eds.) *Western women and imperialism: complicity and resistance*, 247–68.

Hardy, Georges. *Eléments de l'histoire coloniale*. Paris: La Renaissance du Livre, 1921.

   Histoire sociale de la colonisation française. Paris: Larose, 1953.

Harms, Robert W. *River of wealth, river of sorrow: the central Zaire basin in the era of the slave and ivory trade, 1500–1891*. New Haven: Yale University Press, 1981.

Haut Commissariat de l'Afrique Equatoriale Française. *Annuaire statistique de l'Afrique Equatoriale Française: I. 1936–1950*. Brazzaville: Service de la Statistique, 1950.

   Annuaire statistique de l'Afrique Equatorial Française: II. 1951–1955. Brazzaville: Service de la Statistique, 1955).

Hay, Margaret Jean and Sticher, Sharon (eds.) *African women south of the Sahara*. Harlow, Essex: Longman, 1984.

Headrick, Rita. 'Archival research in the People's Republic of the Congo', *History in Africa*, 7 (1980), 351–4.

   'The impact of colonialism on health in French Equatorial Africa, 1880–1934'. Ph.D. thesis, University of Chicago, 1987.

   Colonialism, health and illness in French Equatorial Africa, 1885–1935. Edited by Daniel R. Headrick. Atlanta: African Studies Association Press, 1994.

Heraud, Dr. 'Le développement sportif en AEF', *Tropiques*. 56th year, 402 (January 1958), 19–25.

Higginson, John. *A working class in the making: Belgian colonial labor policy, private enterprise and the African mineworker, 1907–1951*. Madison: University of Wisconsin Press, 1991.

Hilton, Anne. *The kingdom of Kongo*. Oxford: The Clarendon Press, 1985.

Hobsbawm, Eric and Ranger, Terence (eds.) *The invention of tradition*. Cambridge: Cambridge University Press, 1983.

Holt, Richard. *Sport and society in modern France*. London: Macmillan, 1981.

Homet, Marcel. *Congo: terre de souffrances*. Paris: Editions Montaigne, 1934.

Huizinga, Johan. *Homo ludens: a study of the play element in culture*. Boston: Beacon Press, 1962.

Hunt, Nancy Rose. 'Domesticity and colonialism in Belgian Africa: Usumbura's foyer social, 1946–1960', *Signs*, 15, 3 (Spring 1990), 447–74.

'Negotiated colonialism: domesticity, hygiene and birth work in the Belgian Congo'. Ph.D. thesis, University of Wisconsin, Madison, 1992.

Iliffe, John. *A modern history of Tanganyika*. Cambridge: Cambridge University Press, 1975.

The African poor: a history. Cambridge: Cambridge University Press, 1987.

Isaacman, Allen, 'Peasants and rural social protest in Africa', *African Studies Review*, 33, 2 (1990), 1–120.

Jahn, Janheinz. *Muntu: an outline of the new African culture*. Translated by Marjorie Grene. New York: Grove Press, 1961.

Jeannin, Maurice. 'Un quartier récent de Brazzaville: Makélékélé, ses activités économiques traditionnelles'. Thèse de 3è cycle, University of Bordeaux, 1969–70.

Jewsiewicki, Bogumil. 'La contestation sociale et la naissance du prolétariat au cours de la première moitié du XXè siècle', *Canadian Journal of African Studies*, 10, 1 (1976), 47–70.

'The great depression and the making of the colonial economic system in the Belgian Congo', *AEH*, 4 (Fall 1977), 153–76.

Johnson, G. Wesley (ed.) *Double impact: France and Africa in the age of imperialism*. Westport, Conn.: Greenwood Press, 1985.

Journées d'étude sur Brazzaville: actes du colloque ORSTOM - programme santé et urbanisation. Association des géographes du Congo, 25–28 April 1986. Brazzaville: Mission Française de Coopération et d'Action Culturelle, 1987.

July, Robert W. *An African voice: the role of the humanities in African independence*. Durham, N.C.: Duke University Press, 1987.

Kanza Matondo ne Mansangaza. *Musique Zaïroise moderne*. Kinshasa: Publications du CNMA, 1972.

Kazadi, Pierre Cary. 'Congo music: Africa's favorite beat', *Africa Report*, (April, 1971), 25–7.

'Trends of 19th and 20th century music in the Congo-Zaire', in Robert Günther (ed.) *Musikkulturen asiens, afrikas und ozeaniens im 19. jahrhundert*. Regensburg: Gustav Bosse Verlag, 1973, 267–84.

Kazadi wa Mukuna. 'The origin of Zairean modern music: a socio- economic aspect', *African Urban Studies*, 6 (1979–1980), 31–9.

'Congolese music', *The new Grove dictionary of music and musicians*. London: Macmillan, 1980, vol. IV, 659–61.

'The genesis of urban music in Zaire', *African Music*, 7, 2 (1992), 72–84.

Kennedy, Dane. *Islands of white: settler society and culture in Kenya and Southern Rhodesia, 1890–1939*. Durham, N.C.: Duke University Press, 1987.

Kimina-Makumbu, Fulbert. 'Le sport école d'humanité', *La Semaine Africaine*, special issue, 28 August 1983.

Knibiehler, Yvonne and Goutalier, Régine. *La femme au temps des colonies*. Paris: Stock, 1985.

Kongo, Michel. 'Petits métiers et commerce de l'artisanat à Brazzaville'. Thèse de 3è cycle, University of Bordeaux III, 1975.

Kranitz, A. 'Brazzaville: les missions du Bas-Congo', *APSE* (February 1931), 51–5; (January 1931), 12–15; (March 1931), 80–3.

Kuper, Hilda. 'Costume and identity', *Comparative Studies in Society and History*, 15 (1973), 348–67.

La Hausse, Paul. 'The struggle for the city: alcohol, the *ematsheni* and popular culture in Durban, 1902–1936'. MA thesis, University of Cape Town, 1984.

Laman, Karl. *The Kongo.* 4 volumes. Uppsala: Studia Ethnographica Upsaliensia, 1953–68.

Landes, David S. *Revolution in time: clocks and the making of the modern world.* Cambridge, Ma.: Harvard University Press, 1983.

　　'Clocks: revolution in time', *History today,* 34 (January 1984), 19–26.

Lasserre, Guy. *Libreville: la ville et sa région.* Paris: Armand Colin, 1958.

Lears, J.Jackson. 'The concept of cultural hegemony: problems and possibilities', *AHR,* 90 3 (June 1985), 567–593.

'Le Congo: banlieue de Brazzaville', *Politique Africaine,* 31 (October 1988), special issue.

Le Goff, Jacques. *Time, work and culture in the Middle Ages.* Translated by Arthur Goldhammer. Chicago: University of Chicago Press, 1980.

Le laboratoire d'anthropologie. 'Structure spatio-temporelle chez les négro-africains: l'exemple des Kongo', *CCAH,* 4 (1979), 7–10.

Les guides bleus illustrés: Brazzaville, Léopoldville, Pointe- Noire. Paris: Hachette, 1958.

Les Soeurs de Saint-Joseph de Cluny en Afrique Centrale, 1886– 1986. Brazzaville: Imprimerie Saint-Paul, 1986.

Lever, Janet. *Soccer madness.* Chicago: University of Chicago Press, 1983.

Lhoni, Patrice Joseph. 'Brazzaville: acte, littérature, folklore', *Brazzaville: Revue de l'Action Municipale,* 2 (March-April 1967), n.p.

Linden, Ian and Linden, Jane. *Catholics, peasants, and Chewa resistance in Nyasaland, 1889–1939.* London: Heinmann, 1974.

Little, Kenneth. *West African urbanization: a study of voluntary associations in social change.* Cambridge: Cambridge University Press, 1965.

Livre d'or du centenaire de Brazzaville. Brazzaville: Publi- Congo, s.d.

Londres, Albert. *Terre d'ébène. La traite des noirs.* Paris: A. Michel, 1929.

Lonoh, Michel. *Essai de commentaire de la musique congolaise moderne.* Kinshasa: SEI/ANC, 1972.

Lopes, Henri. *Tribaliks: contemporary Congolese stories.* London: Heinemann, 1971.

　　La nouvelle romance. Yaounde: Editions CLE, 1980.

Luboya, Eugène. *Sports, loisirs en RDC et dans le monde.* Kinshasa: Éditions Okapi, 1970.

MacGaffey, Wyatt. *Religion and society in Central Africa.* Chicago: University of Chicago Press, 1986.

Mackenzie, John M. *The empire of nature: hunting, conservation, and British imperialism.* Manchester: Manchester University Press, 1988.

Maigret, Julien. 'Nos grandes cités coloniales: Brazzaville', *MCI,* 32 (April 1926), 83.

　　'Le rail qui joindra l'Afrique Centrale à la mer: le Brazzaville-Océan', *MCI,* 67 (March 1929), 69.

　　'Brazzaville d'hier-Brazzaville d'aujourd'hui', *MCI,* 75 (November 1929), 274–9.

　　Afrique Equatoriale Française. Paris: Société d'Editions Géographiques, Maritimes et Coloniales, 1931.

Maistre, Casimir. *A travers l'Afrique Centrale du Congo au Niger 1892–1893*. Paris: Librairie Hachette & Co., 1895.

Mandat-Grancey, E. de. *Au Congo: impressions d'un touriste*. Paris: Librairie Plon, 1900.

Mangin, Charles. *Souvenirs d'Afrique (lettres et carnets de route)*. Paris: Editions Denoël et Steele, 1936.

Manuel, Peter. *Popular music of the non-western world: an introductory survey*. New York: Oxford University Press, 1988.

Maran, René. *Batouala*. Paris: Albin Michel, 1921.

Marie, Eugene Armand. *Le Congo à six jours de Paris*. Paris: Les Etincelles, 1931.

Margadant, Ted W. 'Primary schools and youth groups in pre-war Paris: les "Petites A's"', *Journal of Contemporary History*, 13, 2 (April 1978), 323–36.

Marthey, J. 'L'oeuvre missionnaire pour la population féminine au Congo', *Revue d'Histoire des Colonies*, 5, 154 (1957), 79–101.

Martin, Phyllis M. *The external trade of the Loango Coast 1576– 1870: the effects of changing commercial relations on the Vili kingdom of Loango*. Oxford: Clarendon Press, 1972.

  'Power, cloth and currency on the Loango coast', *AEH*, 15 (1986), 1–12.

  'Colonialism, youth and football in French Equatorial Africa', *The International Journal of the History of Sport*, 8, 1 (May 1991), 56–71.

  'Organizing youth in colonial Brazzaville: the search for order and identity, 1900–1940', in Almeida-Topor et al. (eds.) *Les jeunes en Afrique*, 271–85.

  'Leisure and the making of a ruling class in colonial Brazzaville', in Patricia Galloway (ed.) *Proceedings of the seventeeth meeting of the French Colonial Historical Society, Chicago, May 1991*. Lantham, Md.: University Press of America, 1993, 99– 114.

  'National holidays transformed: the fourteenth of July in Brazzaville', paper presented at the thirty-seventh annual meeting of the African Studies Association, Toronto, November 1994.

  'Contesting clothes in colonial Brazzaville', *JAH*, 35, 3 (1994), 401–26.

Martini, Marien. *Les corses dans l'expansion française*. Ajaccio: Editions 'Les Myrtes', 1953.

Massengo, Clément. 'Les grands courants de la musique africaine contemporaine". Unpublished paper.

Massengo, Prosper. *Brazzaville: la terre des ancêtres*. Montrouge, France: E. G. Editeur, 1991.

Maximy, René de. *Kinshasa: ville en suspens*. Paris: ORSTOM, 1984.

M'Bokolo, Elikia. 'Forces sociales et idéologies dans la décolonisation de l'AEF', *JAH*, 22, 3 (1981), 393–407.

  'French colonial policy in Equatorial Africa in the 1940s and 1950s', in Prosser Gifford and W. R. Louis (eds.) *The transfer of power in Africa*. New Haven, Conn.: Yale University Press, 1982, 173–210.

McCracken, Grant. *Culture and consumption: new approaches to the symbolic character of consumer goods and activities*. Bloomington: Indiana University Press, 1988.

Melik-Chakhnazarov, Achôt. *Le sport en Afrique*. Paris: Présence Africaine, 1970.

Michel, Marc. *La Mission Marchand 1895–1899*. Paris: Mouton, 1972.

Mignon, Jean-Marie. *Afrique: jeunesses uniques, jeunesse encadrée*. Paris: L'Harmattan, 1984.

Miller, Christopher L. *Blank darkness: Africanist discourse in French*. Chicago: University of Chicago Press, 1985.

Miller, Joseph C. *Way of death: merchant capitalism and the Angolan slave trade 1730–1830*. Madison: University of Wisconsin Press, 1988.

Mitchell, J. Clyde. *The Kalela dance*. Manchester: Manchester University Press, 1956.

Mobonda, Honoré. 'Les allusions à l'homme blanc dans la musique Congolo-Zaïroise', *La Semaine Africaine*, 25–31 October 1984.

'De la poétique de la chanson Congolo-Zaïroise', *CCAH* 3 (January, 1989), 34–45.

'Petite histoire chantée de cent ans de présence européenne en Afrique', *Actes du colloque international (Brazzaville, avril 1985)*, 403–28.

Moll, (Colonel). *Une âme de colonial: lettres du Lieutenant-Colonel Moll*. Paris: Emile-Paul, 1912.

Motley, Mary. *Devils in waiting*. London: Longman, 1960.

Moundanda, Antoine and Nkouka, André 'Courant'. *Biakongo: chansons congolaises*. Brazzaville: mimeographed, n.d.

Mudimbe, V. Y. *The invention of Africa: gnosis, philosophy and the order of knowledge*. Bloomington: Indiana University Press, 1988.

Muka, Théophile. *Evolution du sport au Congo*. Kinshasa: Editions Okapi, 1970.

Le sport scolaire et universitaire en R.D.C. Kinshasa: Editions Okapi, 1971.

Mumbanza mwa Bawele. 'Y a-t-il des Bangala?' *Zaïre-Afrique*, 78 (1973), 471–83.

Ndinga-Mbo, Abraham. *Introduction à l'histoire des migrations au Congo: hommes et cuivre dans le 'Pool' et la Bounza avant le XXè siècle*. Brazzaville and Heidelberg: P. Kivouvou Verlag, 1984.

Ngoïe-Ngalla, Dominique. 'Temporalité et vision de l'histoire chez les négro-africains: le cas des Kongo', *La Semaine Africaine*, 15–21 November 1979; 22–28 November 1979.

Les Kongo de la vallée du Niari: origines et migrations XIII-XIXè siècle: Bakamba, Badondo, Bakunyi, Basundi, Babeembe. Brazzaville: Les Editions CELMAA, 1982.

Ngub'Usim, Mpey-Nka and Kuyunsa, Bidum. 'Gestion du temps et organisation traditionnelle du travail: la semaine traditionnelle chez les Yansi et quelques autres tribus du Zaïre', *Zaïre-Afrique* 231–2 (January–February 1989), 11–22.

Nketia, J.H. 'The gramophone and contemporary African music in the Gold Coast', *Proceedings of the fourth annual conference of the West African Institute of Economic Social Research* (Ibadan, 1955), 189–200.

Nord, Pierre. *L'Eurafrique: notre dernière chance*. Paris: Librairie Arthème Fayard, 1955.

Norden, Hermann. *Auf neuen Pfaden im Kongo: quer durch das dunkelste Afrika*. Leipzig: F. A. Brockhaus, 1926.

N'Zala-Backa, Placide. *Le tipoye doré*. Brazzaville: Imprimerie Nationale, 1968.

Obenga, Théophile. 'Habillement, cosmétique et parure au royaume de Kongo', *CCAH*, 4 (1979), 21–38.

'Temps et astronomie chez les Mbochi de l'Alima', *CCAH*, 7 (1982), 7–24.

Les Bantu: langues, peuples et civilisations. Paris: Présence Africaine, 1985.

O'Brien, Rita Cruise. *White society in black Africa: the French of Senegal*. Evanston, Ill.: Northwestern University Press, 1972.

O'Deyé, Michèle. *Les associations en ville africaine: Dakar-Brazzaville*. Paris: L'Harmattan, 1985.

Ollandet, Jérôme. 'L'AEF dans la deuxième guerre mondiale'. Mémoire de Maîtrise, Marien Ngouabi University, 1974.

   Brazzaville: capitale de la France Libre: histoire de la résistance française en Afrique (1940–1941). Brazzaville: Editions de la Savane. n.d.

Orlean, Susan. *Saturday night*. New York: Knopf, 1990.

Ossebi, Henri. 'Un quotidien en trompe l'oeil: bars et "nganda" à Brazzaville', *Politique Africaine*, 31 (October 1988), 67–72.

Palmer, G. (ed.) *Mästaren pa Kongos stigar: fran Svenska Missionsförbundets arbete i Kongo aren 1881–1941*. Stockholm: Svenska Missionsförbundet, 1941.

Parkin, David. *The cultural definition of political response* London: Academic Press, 1978.

Pellerin, Pierre. *Une enfance en brousse congolaise*. Paris: Editions Arthaud, 1990.

Penvenne, Jeanne M. *African workers and colonial racism: Mozambican strategies and struggles in Lourenço Marques, 1877–1962* (Portsmouth, N.H.: Heinemann, 1994.

Phimister, Ian and van Onselen, Charles. 'The political economy of tribal animosities: a case study of the 1929 Bulawayo location "faction fight"', *Journal of Southern African Studies*, 6 (1979), 1–43.

Pichat, J. M. *Brazzaville-Paris*. Paris: Editions Larose, 1933.

Picton, J. and Mack, J. *African textiles: looms, weaving and design*. London: British Museum Publications, 1979.

Pieper, Josef. *Leisure: the basis of culture*. Translated by Alexander Dru. New York: Pantheon Books, 1952.

Plan Havas de Brazzaville. Brazzaville: L'Imprimerie Centrale d'Afrique, 1953.

Poulaine, Madelaine. *Une blanche chez les noirs*. Paris, 1931.

Poulaine, Robert. *Etapes africaines (voyage autour du Congo)*. Paris: Nouvelle Revue Critique, 1930.

Prochaska, David. *Making Algeria French: colonialism in Bône, 1870–1920*. Cambridge: Cambridge University Press, 1990.

Puytorac, Jean de. *Makambo: une vie au Congo (Brazzaville-M'Bondo)*. Paris: Zulma, 1992.

Rabut, Elisabeth. *Brazza Commissaire Général: le Congo Français, 1886–1897*. Paris: Editions de l'EHESS, 1989.

Ramphele, Mamphela. *A bed called home: Life in the migrant labour hostels of Cape Town*. Cape Town: David Philip, 1993.

Ranger, Terence. *Dance and society in eastern Africa, 1890–1970: the Beni Ngoma*. London: Heinemann, 1975.

   'Making Northern Rhodesia imperial: variations on a royal theme, 1924–1938', *African Affairs*, 79, 314 (1980), 349–72.

   'The invention of tradition in colonial Africa', in Hobsbawm and Ranger (eds.) *The invention of tradition*, 211–62.

'Taking hold of the land: holy places and pilgrimages in 20th century Zimbabwe', *Past and Present*, 117 (November 1987), 158–94.

'Pugilism and pathology: African boxing in the black urban experience in Southern Rhodesia', in Baker and Mangan (eds.), *Sport in Africa*, 196–211.

'The invention of tradition revisited: the case of colonial Africa', in Terence Ranger and Olufemi Vaughan (eds.) *Legitimacy and the state in 20th century Africa: essays in honour of A. H. M. Kirk-Greene*. London: Macmillan, 1993, 62–111.

Raoul-Matingou, Emilienne. 'Activités des femmes en milieu urbain: le cas de Brazzaville'. Thèse de 3e cycle. University of Science and Technology of Lille, 1982.

Remy, J. 'Congo Français: une procession à Brazzaville', *AA* (September 1912), 229–32.

Répertoire des archives du gouvernement-général de l'Afrique Equatoriale Française. Brazzaville: Service des Archives Nationales, 1972.

Répertoire des archives de l'inspection-générale de l'enseignement de l'Afrique Equatoriale Française. Brazzaville: Service des Archives Nationales, 1976.

République du Congo, Service de Statistique. *Recensement de Brazzaville 1961*. Paris: INSEE, Service de Coopération, 1965.

Reste, Joseph-François. *Action économique et sociale en AEF, 1936–1938*. Brazzaville: Imprimerie Officielle, 1938.

'Grands corps et grands commis de la France d'outre-mer', *Revue des Deux Mondes* (March 1959), 321–36.

Rey, Philippe. *Colonialisme, néo-colonialisme et transition au capitalisme*. Paris: Maspéro, 1971.

Roach, Mary Ellen and Eicher, Joanne Bubolz. 'The language of personal adornment', in Cordwell and Schwarz (eds.) *The fabrics of culture*, 7–21.

Roberts, Andrew (ed.) *Cambridge History of Africa*, vol. VII: *1905–1960*. Cambridge: Cambridge University Press, 1986.

'African cross-currents', in A. Roberts (ed.) *Cambridge history of Africa*, vol. VII, 223–66.

Robertson, Claire and Berger, Iris (eds.) *Women and class in Africa*. New York: Holmes & Meier, 1986.

Roden, Donald. 'Baseball and the quest for national dignity in Meiji Japan', *AHR*, 85, 3 (June 1980), 511–34.

Rondet-Saint, Maurice. *L'Afrique Equatoriale Française*. Paris: Plon-Nourrit, 1911.

Dans notre empire noir. Paris: Société d'Editions Géographiques, Maritimes et Coloniales, 1929.

Sur les routes du Cameroun et de l'AEF. Paris: Société d'Editions Géographiques, Maritimes et Coloniales, 1933.

Ross, Robert J. and Telkamp, Gerald J. (eds.) *Colonial cities: essays on urbanism in a colonial context*. The Hague: Martinus Nijhoff, 1984.

Rotenberg, Robert. *Time and order in metropolitan Vienna*. Washington, D.C.: Smithsonian Institution Press, 1992.

Rouget, Fernand. *L'expansion coloniale au Congo Français*. Paris: Emile Larose, 1906.

L'Afrique Equatoriale illustrée. Paris: Emile Larose, 1913.

Rummelt, Peter. *Sport in kolonialismus, kolonialismus in sport: zur genese und funktion des sports in kolonial-Afrika von 1870 bis 1918*. Cologne: Pahl-Rugenstein, 1986.

Rybczynski, Witold. *Waiting for the weekend*, New York: Viking, 1991.

Sabatier, Peggy. 'Did Africans really learn to be French? The francophone elite of the Ecole William Ponty', in Johnson (ed.), *Double Impact*, 179–87.

Saintoyant, Jules François. *L'affaire du Congo, 1905*. Paris: Epi, 1960.

Samarin, William. 'Bondjo ethnicity and colonial imagination', *Canadian Journal of African Studies*, 18 (1984), 345–65.

   The black man's burden: African colonial labor on the Congo and Ubangi Rivers, 1880–1900. Boulder: Westview Press, 1989.

   'The origins of Kituba and Lingala', *Journal of African Languages and Linguistics*, 12, 1 (September 1991), 47–77.

Sarraut, Albert. *La mise en valeur des colonies françaises*. Paris: Payot, 1923.

Sautter, Gilles. 'La population', in Guernier (ed.) *Afrique Equatoriale Française*, 95–104.

   'Aperçu sur les villes "africaines" du Moyen-Congo', *L'Afrique et l'Asie*, 14 (December 1951), 34–53.

   'Le plateau Congolais de Mbé', *CEA*, 1, 2 (May 1960), 5–48.

   De l'Atlantique au fleuve Congo. 2 volumes. Paris: Mouton, 1966.

   'Notes sur la construction du chemin de fer Congo-Océan, 1921–34', *CEA*, 7 (1967), 219–300.

Sauvage, Marcel. *Sous le feu de l'équateur: les secrets de l'Afrique noire*. Paris: Editions Denöel, 1937.

Schneider, William H. *An empire for the masses. The French popular image of Africa 1870–1900*. Westport, Conn.: Greenwood Press, 1982.

Scotch, N. A. 'Magic, sorcery and football among the urban Zulu', *Journal of Conflict Resolution*, 5 (1961), 70–4.

Scott, James C. *Weapons of the weak: everyday forms of peasant resistance*. New Haven: Yale University Press, 1985.

Sicé, Adolphe. *L'Afrique Equatoriale au service de la France*. Paris: Presses Universitaires de France, 1946.

Simenon, Georges. *African trio* (includes three Equatorial African stories, *Le coup de lune*, 1933, *45 dégres à l'ombre*, 1936, and *Le blanc à lunettes*, 1951). Translated by Stuart Gilbert, Paul Austen and Lydia Davis. London: Hamish Hamilton, 1979.

Sinda, Martial. *Le messianisme congolais et ses incidences politiques*. Paris: Payot, 1972.

Sita, Alphonse. 'Les institutions sociales et politiques des Bakongo du Pool (Congo): chefferies traditionnelles et administratives, 1905–1946'. Thèse de doctorat, University of Paris VII, 1988.

Sjöholm, W. and Lundahl, J. E. (eds.) *Dagbräckning i Kongo*. Stockholm: Svenska Missionsförbundets Kongomission, 1911.

Söderberg, Bertil. *Les instruments de musique au Bas-Congo et dans les régions avoisinantes*. Falköping: A.J. Lindgrens Boktrycken, 1952.

Söderberg, Bertil and Widman, Ragnar. *Publications en Kikongo: bibliographie relative aux contributions suédoises entre 1885 et 1970*. Uppsala: l'Institut Scandinave d'Etudes Africaines, 1978.

Soixante-quinzième anniversaire de la fondation de Madzia et de l'evangelisation du Congo par les missionnaires protestants. Växjo: Carl Svanberg Trycken AB, 1984.

Soret, Marcel. *Démographie et problèmes urbains en AEF: Poto-Poto-Bacongo-Dolisie.* Mémoire d'Institut d'Etudes Centrafricaines, Brazzaville (AEF). Montpellier: Imprimerie Chanté, 1954.

——— *Les Kongo nord-occidentaux.* Paris: Presses Universitaires de France, 1959.

Stapleton, Chris and May, Chris. *African all-stars: the pop music of a continent.* London: Quartet Books, 1987.

Steinhart, E. I. 'Hunters, poachers and gamekeepers: toward a social history of hunting in colonial Kenya', *JAH*, 30, 2 (1989), 247–64.

Stewart, Gary. *Breakout: profiles in African rhythm.* Chicago: University of Chicago Press, 1992.

Stoler, Anne. 'Rethinking colonial categories: European communities and the boundaries of rule', *Comparative Studies in Society and History*, 31, 1 (1989), 134–81.

Storey, William. 'Big cats and imperialism: lion and tiger hunting in Kenya and northern India, 1898–1930', *Journal of World History*, 2, 2 (Fall 1991), 135–74.

Strayer, Robert W. *The making of a mission community in East Africa: Anglicans and Africans in colonial Kenya, 1875– 1935.* London: Heinemann, 1978.

Strobel, Margaret. *European women and the second British empire.* Bloomington: Indiana University Press, 1991.

Suret-Canale, Jean. *French colonialism in tropical Africa, 1900–1945.* Translated by Jill Gotheiner. New York: Pica Press, 1968.

Tati-Loutard, Jean-Baptiste. 'L'intervention de son Excellence Monsieur J.B. Tati-Loutard, Ministre Congolais de la Culture et des Arts, Président de l'UNEAC'. Speech at the opening of an exhibition on Congo art at the thirty-second annual meeting of the African Studies Association, Atlanta, Ga., 1989.

Thomas, Keith. 'Work and leisure in pre-industrial society', *Past and Present*, 29 (December 1964), 50–62.

Thomas, Nicholas. *Entangled objects: exchange, material culture and colonialism in the Pacific.* Cambridge, Ma.: Harvard University Press, 1991.

Thompson, E. P. 'Time, work-discipline and industrial capitalism', *Past and Present*, 38 (December 1967), 56– 97.

Thompson, Virginia and Adloff, Richard. *The emerging states of French Equatorial Africa.* Stanford, Ca.: Stanford University Press, 1960.

Thornton, John K. *The kingdom of Kongo: civil war and transition 1641–1718.* Madison: University of Wisconsin Press, 1983.

Trautmann, René. *Au pays de 'Batouala'. Noirs et blancs en Afrique.* Paris: Payot & Co., 1922.

Trézenem, Edouard. *L'Afrique Equatoriale Française.* Paris: Editions Maritimes et Coloniales, 1955.

Tsamas, Sylvère. 'Le kyébé-kyébé', *Liaison*, 59 (September-October 1957), 61–5.

Turmann, Max. *Au sortir de l'école: les patronages.* Paris: V. Lecoffre, 5th edn, 1909.

Uzès, Duchesse d'. *Le voyage de mon fils au Congo.* Paris: Librairie Plon, 1894.

Vacquier, Raymond. *Au temps des factories, 1900–1950.* Paris: Karthala, 1986.

Vail, Leroy (ed.) *The creation of tribalism in southern Africa*. London: James Currey, 1989.

Vail, Leroy and White, Landeg. 'Plantation protest: the history of a Mozambican song', *Journal of Southern African Studies*, 55, 1 (October 1978), 1–25.

Valette, Jacques. 'L'AEF: le cas du Congo, 1958–1960', in Ageron and Michel (eds.) *L'Afrique noire française: l'heure des indépendances*, 315–26.

Vandrunen, James. *Heures africaines: l'Atlantique-le Congo*. Brussels: Ch. Bulens, 1899.

Van Onselen, Charles. *Studies in the social and economic history of the Witwatersrand, 1886–1914*. 2 volumes. London: Longman, 1982.

Vansina, Jan. *The Tio kingdom of the middle Congo 1880–1892*. London: Oxford University Press, 1973.

　　Art history in Africa. New York: Longman, 1984.

　　Oral tradition as history. Madison: University of Wisconsin Press, 1985.

　　Paths in the rainforests: towards a history of political tradition in equatorial Africa. Madison: University of Wisconsin Press, 1990.

Van Wing, J. 'Les danses Bakongo', *Congo: Revue Générale de la Colonie Belge*, 2, 2 (July, 1937), 121–8.

Vassal, Gabrielle M. *Life in French Congo*. London: T. Fisher Unwin, 1925.

Vassal, Gabrielle and Joseph. *Français, Belges et Portugais en Afrique Equatoriale: Pointe-Noire, Matadi, Lobito*. Paris: Editions Pierre Roger, 1926.

Vaucleroy, Pierre de. 'Promenade à Brazzaville', *Expansion Belge*, 8 (1929), 15–18.

Veistroffer, Albert. *Vingt ans dans la brousse africaine: souvenirs d'un ancien membre de la Mission Savorgnan de Brazza dans l'Ouest africain (1883–1903)*. Lille: Mercure de Flandre, 1931.

Vellut, Jean-Luc. 'Matériaux pour une image du blanc dans la société coloniale du Congo Belge', in Jean Pirotte (ed.) *Stéréotypes nationaux et préjugés raciaux aux 19è et 20è siècle*. Louvain: Editions Nauwelaerts, 1982, 91–116.

　　'Mining in the Belgian Congo', in Birmingham and Martin (eds.) *History of Central Africa*, vol. II, 126–63.

Vennetier, Pierre. 'Banlieue noire de Brazzaville, la vie rurale et les rapports entre la ville et la campagne à Bacongo', *Les Cahiers d'Outre-Mer*, 38 (April-June, 1957), 131–57.

　　'Un quartier suburbain de Brazzaville: Moukondji-Ngouaka', *Bulletin d'IECA*, 20 (1960), 91–124.

　　'L'urbanisation et ses conséquences au Congo (Brazzaville)', *Les Cahiers d'Outre-Mer*, (1963), 260–81.

　　Géographie du Congo-Brazzaville. Paris: Gauthier-Villars, 1966.

　　L'atlas du Congo. Paris: Jeune Afrique, 1977.

Vincent, Jeanne-Françoise. *Femmes africaines en milieu urbain*. Paris: ORSTOM, 1966.

Wagret, Jean-Michel. *Histoire et sociologie politiques de la République du Congo (Brazzaville)*. Paris: R. Pichon et R. Durand-Auzias, 1963.

Waterman, Christopher Alan. *Juju: a social history and ethnography of an African popular music*. Chicago: University of Chicago Press, 1990.

Weber, Eugen. 'Gymnastics and sport in *fin-de-siècle* France: opium of the classes?' *AHR*, 76, 1 (February 1971), 70–98.

　　France: fin-de-siècle. Cambridge, Ma.: Harvard University Press, 1986.

'Work suspended: strenuous leisure and the invention of the weekend', *Times Literary Supplement*, 20 December 1991, 3–4.

Weeks, John H. *Among the primitive Bakongo*. New York: Negro Universities Press, 1914; repr., 1969.

Weinstein, Brian. *Eboué*. New York: Oxford University Press, 1972.

West, Richard. *Brazza of the Congo: European exploration and exploitation in French Equatorial Africa*. London: Jonathan Cape, 1972.

Westfall, Gloria D. *French colonial Africa: a guide to official sources*. London: Hans Zell Publishers, 1992.

Westlind, P. A. *Société de la mission suédoise au Congo*. Stockholm: Librairie de la Société de la Mission Suédoise, 1922.

White, Luise. *The comforts of home: prostitution in colonial Nairobi*. Chicago: University of Chicago Press, 1990.

Wipper, Audrey. 'African women, fashion and scapegoating', *Canadian Journal of African Studies*, 6, 2 (1972), 329–49.

Witte, Jehan de. *Les deux Congo*. Paris: Plon, 1913.

   Monseigneur Augouard. Paris: Emile-Paul Frères, 1924.

Wright, Gwendolyn. 'Tradition in the service of modernity: architecture and urbanism in French colonial policy, 1900–1930', *Journal of Modern History*, 59 (June 1987), 291–316.

Zerubavel, Eviatar. *Hidden rhythms: schedules and calendars in social life*. Chicago: University of Chicago Press, 1981.

   The seven day cycle: the history and meaning of the week. New York: The Free Press, 1985.

Zieglé, Henri. *Afrique Equatoriale Française*. Paris: Berger- Levrault, 1952.

Zimmermann, P. *Mémoire d'un congolais 1896–1941*. Madingou: Imprimerie de la Mission, 1941.

Index

Other books in the series